ARTIFICIAL INTELLIGENCE AND MACHINE LEARNING FOR BUSINESS

AAP Advances in Artificial Intelligence & Robotics

ARTIFICIAL INTELLIGENCE AND MACHINE LEARNING FOR BUSINESS

Namita Mishra, PhD

A. V. Senthil Kumar, DSc

Editors

AAP | APPLE ACADEMIC PRESS

First edition published 2025

Apple Academic Press Inc.
1265 Goldenrod Circle, NE,
Palm Bay, FL 32905 USA

760 Laurentian Drive, Unit 19,
Burlington, ON L7N 0A4, CANADA

CRC Press
2385 NW Executive Center Drive,
Suite 320, Boca Raton FL 33431

4 Park Square, Milton Park,
Abingdon, Oxon, OX14 4RN UK

Library and Archives Canada Cataloguing in Publication

Title: Artificial intelligence and machine learning for business / Namita Mishra, PhD, A.V. Senthil Kumar, PhD, editors.
Names: Mishra, Namita, editor. | Kumar, A. V. Senthil, 1966- editor
Description: First edition. | Series statement: AAP advances in artificial intelligence & robotics book series | Includes bibliographical references and index.
Identifiers: Canadiana (print) 20240496027 | Canadiana (ebook) 20240494679 | ISBN 9781774917237 (hardcover) | ISBN 9781774917244 (softcover) | ISBN 9781003535850 (ebook)
Subjects: LCSH: Artificial intelligence—Industrial applications. | LCSH: Business enterprises—Data processing. | LCSH: Industrial management—Decision making. | LCSH: Machine learning.
Classification: LCC TA347.A78 A78 2025 | DDC 658/.0563—dc23

Library of Congress Cataloging-in-Publication Data

CIP data on file with US Library of Congress

ISBN: 978-1-77491-723-7 (hbk)
ISBN: 978-1-77491-724-4 (pbk)
ISBN: 978-1-00353-585-0 (ebk)

AAP Advances in Artificial Intelligence & Robotics

The new book series *AAP Advances in Artificial Intelligence & Robotics* provides detailed coverage of innovations in artificial life, computational intelligence, evolutionary computing, machine learning, robotics, and applications. The list of topics covers all the application areas of artificial intelligence and robotics such as: computational neuroscience, social intelligence, ambient intelligence, artificial life, virtual worlds and society, cognitive science and systems, computational intelligence, human-centered and human-centric computing, intelligent decision making and support, intelligent network security.

With this innovative era of simulated and artificial intelligence, much research is required in order to advance the field and also to estimate the societal and ethical concerns of the existence robotics and scientific computing. The books in this series are practically relevant, so that the results will be useful for managers in leadership roles related to AI and robotics, researchers, data analysts, project managers, and others. Therefore, both theoretical and managerial implications of the research need to be considered.

The book series broadly considers the contributions from the following fields:

- Artificial Intelligence Applications in Security
- Artificial Intelligence in Bioinformatics
- Robot Structure Design and Control
- Artificial Intelligence in Biomedical and Healthcare
- Multi-Robot Intelligent Aggregation Mechanisms and Operation Platforms
- Artificial Intelligence and Learning Environments
- Advances in AI-Driven Smart System Designs
- Robot Navigation, Positioning, and Autonomous Control
- Robot Perception and Data Fusion
- Advances in Artificial Intelligence research
- Advances in AI-Driven Data Analytics and Innovation
- Application of Intelligent Systems for Solving Real-World Problems
- Hybrid Systems Design and Applications Using AI

- Robot Grabbing and Operation
- Robot Behavior Decision and Control
- Robot Motion and Path Planning
- Applications of Intelligent Systems and Computer Vision

For additional information, contact:
Book Series Editor: Subhendu Kumar Pani
Professor & Research Co-ordinator
Dept. of Computer Science and Engineering
Orissa Engineering College, Bhubaneswar, India
Email: pani.subhendu@gmail.com

BOOKS IN THE SERIES

Advancements in Artificial Intelligence, Blockchain Technology, and IoT in Higher Education: Mitigating the Impact of COVID-19
Editors: Subhendu Kumar Pani, PhD, Kamalakanta Muduli, PhD, Sujoy Kumar Jana, PhD, Srikanth Bathula, PhD, and Golam Sarwar Khan, PhD

The Fusion of Artificial Intelligence and Soft Computing Techniques for Cybersecurity
Editors: M. Ajabbar, PhD, Sanju Tiwari, PhD, Subhendu Kumar Pani, PhD, and Stephen Huang, PhD

Incorporating AI Technology in the Service Sector: Innovations in Creating Knowledge, Improving Efficiency, and Elevating Quality of Life
Editors: Maria Jose Sousa, PhD, Subhendu Pani, PhD, Francesca dal Mas, PhD, and Sergio Sousa, PhD

Handbook of Research on Artificial Intelligence and Soft Computing Techniques in Personalized Healthcare Services
Editors: Uma N. Dulhare, PhD, A. V. Senthil Kumar, Amit Dutta, PhD, Seddik Bri, PhD, and Ibrahiem M. M. EI Emary, PhD

Fusion of Artificial Intelligence and Machine Learning for Advanced Image Processing, Data Analysis, and Cyber Security
Editors: Arun Rana, PhD, Rashmi Gupta, PhD, Sharad Sharma, PhD, Ahmad A. Elngar, PhD, and Sachin Dhawan, PhD

Artificial Intelligence and Machine Learning for Business
Editors: Namita Mishra, PhD, and A. V. Senthil Kumar, PhD, DSc

Advances in Autonomous Navigation through Intelligent Technologies
Editors: Niharika Singh, PhD, Thipendra P. Singh, PhD, and Brian Azzopardi, PhD

About the Editors

Namita Mishra, PhD
Professor, I.T.S School of Management, Mohan Nagar, India

Namita Mishra, PhD, is working as a Professor at the I.T.S. School of Management,is a distinguished professional with an in-depth association with education and research projects. Her teaching experience is in finance and accounting, with over 18 years of expertise. Academically she holds MCOM, MBA, and PhD degrees from reputed universities. She is a certified financial analyst from IIM Kashipur, India. She has authored three books and two edited volumes with national and international publishers. Professor Mishra has published more than 35 research papers in national and international conference proceedings of repute and has 17 patents to her credit. Her exceptional contributions have earned her accolades such as the Dr. S. Radhakrishnan Memorial Award (2009) from the Healthy Universe Foundation for her excellent contribution in education. She is associated as a life member of various academic bodies.

A. V. Senthil Kumar, PhD
Director and Professor, Department of Research and PG in Computer Applications, Hindusthan College of Arts and Science, Coimbatore, India

A. V. Senthil Kumar, DSc, is working as a Professor and Director of the PG and Research Department of Computer Applications at Hindusthan College of Arts and Science in Coimbatore, Tamilnadu, India. To his credit, he has five years of industrial experience and 27 years of teaching experience. He has published 46 book chapters, 223 papers in international and national journals, and 64 papers in international and national conferences, and he has edited 12 books and two textbooks. He is an Associate Editor of the journal IEEE Access. He is an editor-in-chief for many journals and a key member for India for the Machine Intelligence Research Lab (MIR Labs). He is an editorial board member and reviewer for various international journals. He is also a committee member for various international conferences. He has guided 16 PhD scholars and is currently guiding four PhD scholars. He received his Doctor of Science (DSc) in Computer Science.

Contents

Contributors

P. Saleem Akram
Department of ECE, Koneru Lakshmaiah Education Foundation (Deemed to be University), Guntur, Andhra Pradesh, India

S. Anitha
Assistant Professor, Department of Computer Applications, Faculty of Science and Humanities, SRM Institute of Science and Technology, Tiruchirappalli, Tamil Nadu, India

B. Sathish Babu
Professor and Head, Department of AI & ML, R. V. College of Engineering, Bangalore, Karnataka, India

P. Bhanumathi
Associate Professor, Ramaiah Institute of Management, Bangalore, Karnataka, India

Ajay Bhardwaj
Department of Electrical Engineering, Swami Keshvanand Institute of Technology, Management & Gramothan, Jaipur, Rajasthan, India

Andrew J. Brennan
Department of Accounting, Finance and Economics, Curtin University, Perth, Western Australia

Ankita Chaturvedi
Associate Professor, IIS (Deemed to be University), Jaipur, Rajasthan, India

Umrah Dar
Department of Advanced Computing, St. Joseph's University, Bangalore, Karnataka, India

Mahuya Deb
Assistant Professor, Department of Commerce, Gauhati University, Assam, India

Bharti Gawali
Department of Computer Science and Information Technology, Dr. Babasaheb Ambedkar Marathwada University, Aurangabad, Maharashtra, India

P. Gayathiri
Assistant Professor, Department of Information Technology, Nirmala College for Women, Coimbatore, Tamil Nadu, India

Ramdas Gore
Department of Computer Science and Information Technology, Dr. Babasaheb Ambedkar Marathwada University, Aurangabad, Maharashtra, India

Sunanda Vincent Jaiwant
CHRIST (Deemed to be University), Bangalore, Karnataka, India

R. Jeevitha
Assistant Professor, Ramaiah Institute of Management, Bangalore, Karnataka, India

Filbert H. Juwono
Computer Science Program, University of Southampton Malaysia, Johor, Malaysia

R. K. Kamat
Vice Chancellor, Dr. Homi Bhabha State University, Mumbai, Maharashtra, India

R. S. Kamath
Associate Professor, Chhatrapati Shahu Institute of Business Education and Research, Kolhapur, Maharashtra, India

K. Sampath Kini
Department of CSE, N.M.A.M. Institute of Technology, Nitte, Karkala, Karnataka, India

G. S. Sai Kruthi
CHRIST (Deemed to be University), Bangalore, Karnataka, India

A. V. Senthil Kumar
Director & Professor, Hindustan College of Arts and Science, Coimbatore, Tamil Nadu, India

M. Lakshmana Kumar
Department of ECE, Koneru Lakshmaiah Education Foundation (Deemed to be University), Guntur, Andhra Pradesh, India

S. Maheswari
Associate Professor, Department of Computer Science and Engineering, Faculty of Engineering and Technology, SRM Institute of Science and Technology, Tiruchirappalli, Tamil Nadu, India

Shaifali Mathur
Assistant Professor, IIS (Deemed to be University), Jaipur, Rajasthan, India

A. Muthusamy
Assistant Professor, Department of Computer Technology (UG), Kongu Engineering College, Perundurai, Erode, Tamil Nadu, India

Jobrun Nandong
Department of Chemical and Energy Engineering, Curtin University Malaysia, Sarawak, Malaysia

B. H. Karthik Pai
Department of ISE, N.M.A.M. Institute of Technology, Nitte, Karkala, Karnataka, India

Pramod Painuly
Professor, UPES, Dehradun, Uttarakhand, India

Ashish Porwal
Assistant Professor, Finance and Accounting, Institute of Law, Nirma University, Ahmedabad, Gujarat, India

R. P. Puneeth
Department of CSE, N.M.A.M. Institute of Technology, Nitte, Karkala, Karnataka, India

S. R. Reeja
Professor, School of Computer Science and Engineering (SCOPE), VIT-AP University, India

Dhanuskodi Rengasamy
Department of Accounting, Finance and Economics, Curtin University Malaysia, Sarawak, Malaysia

Hinika Shail
Student, BBA-Digital Marketing, UPES, Dehradun, Uttarakhand, India

Meenakshi Sharma
Assistant Professor-SS, UPES, Dehradun, Uttarakhand, India

Mukta Sharma
Associate Professor, Trinity Institute of Professional Studies, Delhi, India

Priyanka Sharma
Department of Computer Science and Engineering, SKIT, Jaipur, Rajasthan, India

Ksh. Krishna B. Singha
Associate Professor, Trinity Institute of Professional Studies, Delhi, India

Minakshi Sonawane
Department of Computer Science and Information Technology, Dr. Babasaheb Ambedkar Marathwada University, Aurangabad, Maharashtra, India

Desai Karanam Sreekantha
Professor, Department of Computer Science and Engineering, NMAM Institute of Technology, Nitte (Deemed to be) University, Mangalore, Karnataka, India

Stephanie Stephanie
Department of Economics and Finance, Curtin University Malaysia, Sarawak, Malaysia

S. Sumathy
Assistant Professor and Head, Department of Computer Science, Sir Theagaraya College, Shift II Chennai, Tamil Nadu, India

Preface

Artificial intelligence and machine learning are integral parts of business, used in areas ranging from finance, strategic decision-making, HR operations, sales and marketing, and manufacturing. There is a general perception that artificial intelligence and machine learning are only utilized in the IT sector by large companies with extensive research teams. The goal of this book is to demonstrate how artificial intelligence and machine learning can be applied in every aspect of business and can serve as a foundation for complex decision-making. These technologies are not only useful in business decision-making but also in financial services fraud detection, retail purchase predictions, and online customer support interactions.

This book provides a brief overview of artificial intelligence (AI) techniques used in business, covering the most popular and frequently used methods, procedures, and models to manage business activities. It aims to explain AI standards and concepts easily for management executives and students. The book introduces students to artificial intelligence and machine learning in different chapters, emphasizing the potential business opportunities and benefits derived from using AI and machine learning.

Introduction

Artificial intelligence and machine learning have transformed essential technologies in the modern business landscape. These powerful tools enable businesses to automate processes, gain valuable insights from data, and make informed decisions to facilitate growth and competitive advantage. In this introduction, we will explore the fundamentals of AI and ML and discuss their applications and benefits in a business context.

Artificial intelligence refers to the advancement of intellectual machines that can achieve tasks that normally require human intelligence. It encompasses an extensive range of techniques, including natural language processing, computer vision, robotics, and machine learning. Artificial intelligence aims to duplicate human intellectual abilities, such as knowing things through learning, reasoning, problem-solving, and managerial decision-making.

Machine learning, a subgroup of AI, emphasizes building algorithms and statistical models that permit computers to learn from and make forecasts or take actions based on data, without being unambiguously programmed. It involves the use of large datasets to train models that can generalize designs and make correct forecasts or decisions.

In the realm of business, AI and ML offer transformative capabilities that drive innovation, efficiency, and strategic decision-making. Below are selected significant areas where AI and ML can benefit businesses:

- *Automation:* AI and ML technologies can automate tedious and routine tasks and can release human capital for more value-added actions. This includes automating customer service interactions, data entry, inventory management, and production processes.
- *Data Analysis and Insights:* Businesses produce huge amounts of data, and AI and ML can help create valuable insights from this data. By analyzing patterns, trends, and correlations within data, businesses can make data-driven decisions, identify market opportunities, optimize operations, and personalize customer experiences.
- *Predictive Analytics:* ML systems can be trained to forecast future results based on historical data. This enables businesses to forecast demand, anticipate customer behavior, adjust pricing strategies, and reduce risks. Predictive analytics can also help in fraud detection, supply chain optimization, and predictive maintenance.

- *Enhanced Customer Experience:* AI-powered chatbots can provide tailored and prompt customer support, improving response times and overall customer satisfaction. Additionally, AI can facilitate targeted marketing campaigns by analyzing customer preferences and behavior, enabling businesses to deliver personalized recommendations and offers.
- *Risk Management:* AI and ML algorithms can help identify potential risks and anomalies in various business processes, such as fraud detection, cybersecurity, and compliance. By continuously monitoring data streams, businesses can proactively detect and mitigate risks, safeguarding their operations and reputation.
- *Decision Support:* AI and ML can provide decision support systems that assist executives in making informed and data-driven decisions. By analyzing complex datasets and generating insights, these systems can offer recommendations on pricing strategies, market segmentation, resource allocation, and strategic planning.

It is noteworthy that while AI and ML offer immense potential, their successful implementation requires a thoughtful approach. Factors such as data quality, privacy, ethics, and regulatory compliance should be considered to ensure responsible and beneficial use of these technologies.

To sum up, AI and ML are transforming the way businesses operate and make decisions. From automation to data analysis and predictive analytics, these technologies offer numerous opportunities for businesses to gain a competitive edge, enhance customer experiences, and optimize various aspects of their operations. Embracing AI and ML can empower businesses to unlock new possibilities and thrive in the increasingly digital and data-driven business landscape.

This book provides insights into how artificial intelligence has become an integral part of every business and performs decision-making and make it easier managers in policymaking or in enabling existing business processes to be more cost-effective. This book also focuses on the applications of AI and how it is poised to take the lead in any business operations or managerial decision-making. AI is widely used by companies that include Amazon, Walmart, Google, etc., for strategic decisions, identifying customer preferences, and allowing recommendations. Therefore, with various capacities, applications of AI are evident as a game-changer for each type of industry.

The chapters focus on novel ideas and research for providing a broader outlook of AI in business operations and then narrowing down into the identification of decision-making processes in managerial practices. The book covers current trends and future scope of management practices and business operations by encompassing artificial intelligence methodologies and applications.

CHAPTER 1

Generic Framework for AI-Based E-Learning for Employee Training and Quality Learning Experience

P. BHANUMATHI,[1] R. JEEVITHA,[2] and B. SATHISH BABU[3]

[1]*Associate Professor, M.S. Ramaiah Institute of Management, Bengaluru, Karnataka, India*

[2]*Assistant Professor, M.S. Ramaiah Institute of Management, Bengaluru, Karnataka, India*

[3]*Professor and Head, Department of AI & ML, R. V. College of Engineering, Bengaluru, Karnataka, India*

ABSTRACT

Employee training is a continuous process in organizational development and has become a strategic element in business administration. Having your employees trained on the latest technologies, standards, norms, etc., will make them more productive, research-oriented, and innovative in the workplace.

Industries are investing a significant chunk of their financial resources into training employees, especially knowledge industries like software development. The need for employee training entirely depends on the project on hand and projects in the future. Enterprises are transforming the model of training from in-person to online. It will minimize their cost of training, as well as provide convenience. The common challenges in these training platforms are lack of customized content, single-size-fits-all model, generic

Artificial Intelligence and Machine Learning for Business. Namita Mishra, A. V. Senthil Kumar (Eds.)

content with no personalization, difficulty in assessing the training effectiveness, and lesser scope for blended learning model to match heterogeneous crowds, etc.

Therefore, industries have started using artificial intelligence to create new learning experiences in employee training and promote active learning. AI-based e-learning platforms focus on collecting as many data points as possible in real-time about the learner and build a model that continuously assesses the learner based on the patterns and keeps classifying them into various classes. The adaptive learning system will use these classes to propose created learning paths that provide a quality experience.

1.1 INTRODUCTION

For a community, nation, or industry to survive and lead, the working-age group must be provided mass learning/education to be well-equipped with the newest essential skill sets for various economic, logical, and intellectual activities.

Education and training for the employee group on a gigantic scale, for economic survival and the ever-changing requirements, is impossible through the conventional education system. Technologies have occasioned a more effective and lucrative mode of learning over the traditional way of knowing in increasing business productivity and efficiency [1]. E-learning is the modern form of distance learning facilitated by the Internet and World-Wide Web. In our ever-changing world, employees must access up-to-date information and knowledge to succeed in upskilling and reskilling.

E-learning (Virtual) in the workplace facilitates continuous learning and makes employees more effective and efficient. The e-learning research combines technical know-how, pedagogical, and organizational concerns within socio-cultural factors. The major benefits of e-learning for employees in any company are increased scalability, saving the company money, reduced learning time, touching on the latest concepts and technologies, accessibility anywhere, accessibility to key resources, conducive environment for learning.

In the digital age, to increase business productivity and efficiency, companies are turning to e-learning. It is a known fact that the world is more and more mobile. Employees use laptops, tablets, and smartphones to a greater extent for their organization's day-to-day activities. It is imperative to deliberate how we can make learning materials reachable for all learners where they're at – regardless of whether they're in the office or not [2, 3]. These platforms offer course-based, group, one-on-one, and video-based learning. E-learning platforms are web-based facilities that share structured learning materials and courses for a larger group. Usually, e-learning platforms favor static content delivery to all the employees over collaborative features. Some of the popular e-learning platforms used by many companies are mentioned in Table 1.1 [8–10].

TABLE 1.1 E-Learning Platforms

LinkedIn Learning	Courses for Teams and Organizations Through Online Mode
Pluralsight	An E-learning platform helps in upskilling the team with design, development, security, and cloud.
Udemy	Corporate-based learning platform offers courses in technology, design, and business.
Coursera	Association with renowned universities and businesses to give quality training and courses to organizations.
Skillsoft	Education materials and most extensive knowledge offered to the employees of companies.
uQualio	It is video-based and comes with quizzes and gamification features.
Mind Tools	Management and leadership training that provides a list of learning resources.
Cornerstone	Tailor-made material best fits an organization's learning management system (LMS).
Open Sesame	It helps the organization to choose the specific content as per the requirement.
Grovo	Microlearning platform offers corporate customers bite-sized mixed-media lessons.
Udacity	Train technical employees on various topics like Artificial Intelligence, Machine learning, and data science.
NPTEL	Employees can acquire knowledge from experts. The platform provides flexibility for employees to learn at their own pace.
edX	Learning paths are based on the needs of the organization.

1.2 ISSUES AND LIMITATIONS IN NON-AI-BASED E-LEARNING PLATFORMS

Just like in-person learning, e-learning also has certain disadvantages. The understanding of various issues and challenges of e-learning is of utmost importance for future practices [3, 4]:

- E-learning leads to social isolation as it is not face-to-face learning and has minimal interaction scope.
- Sometimes e-learning is inaccessible due to instability and insufficient bandwidth internet connection. They do depend on Internet cafes or public Wi-Fi.
- Many of the e-learning platforms lack a proper monitoring mechanism.
- Learning through online platforms requires all employees' self-motivation and proper time management skills.
- There is a lack of hands-on experience for the organizational requirements.
- Creating fantastic e-learning experiences for employees is challenging since it involves creativity and innovation.
- Companies need to keep up with up-to-date modern technology to improve e-learning delivery to employees. It is hard to decide on the value proposition of new learning technology.
- Designing and developing e-learning courses for various generations like Gen Z, Gen X, Millennials, and Baby Boomers is challenging as each generation has unique needs and traits.
- Identifying and selecting the perfect authoring tool to create e-learning courses.
- LMSs in the market have a complex user interface (UI), which makes it difficult for employees to navigate, search, adapt, and find relevant learning content in the long run. This complex UI ultimately results in reduced User Experience.

1.3 NON-AI-BASED E-LEARNING TO AI-BASED E-LEARNING TRANSFORMATION CHALLENGE

The organization's challenges in integrating AI into e-learning platforms are as follows [12, 14]:

- Many organizations don't realize the need for AI in e-learning platforms as they often feel reluctant to bring significant changes in the way the organization functions. Adopting AI with the existing platform is a significant shift that involves higher risks and uncertainties.
- AI infusion in learning platforms requires high-quality data to train the employees as per the organizational requirements.

- Integration of AI in e-learning platforms requires the right skill sets and experience to design, develop, and make it work.
- Organizations can't find an appropriate use case on AI-based e-learning platforms for better understanding and institutionalizing the same. It calls for managers to understand AI technologies, possibilities, and limitations.
- Training challenges: It is easy for someone to mislead the AI model with wrong data. If managers or trainers don't do proper data validation before developing the AI model, it may negatively impact the business. For example, AI chatbots can be attacked by information poisoning, leading to incorrect learning and inappropriate business responses.
- Initial investments in infrastructure, and creative thinking.
- Lack of AI explainability in understanding how the e-learning platform works. Ensuring AI explainability is critical across various industries where smart systems are applied.
- Organizations often choose not to adopt AI in e-learning platforms, fearing initial investment and upgrading.
- Poor architecture choices: Deriving accurate predictions is not the only thing to be considered in any AI system. In multi-tenant applications serving thousands of users, performance, scalability, and effortless management should be well-thought-out or lead to poor AI architecture.
- Upscaling Artificial Intelligence: Most companies lack the technical talent, skill sets, and tools to implement large-scale intelligent systems. Continuous knowledge transfer might be a viable solution to this problem. This way, companies could upscale their in-house competencies and capabilities before developing AI prototypes.
- Companies will have to deal with AI ethical issues and moral implications.
- AI-based e-learning will reduce bias and have better AI Governance.
- Integration challenges are a major constraint for an organization.
- Myths that avoid AI adoption in the e-learning platform to provide training for employees of an organization.

In recent years, we have seen various applications of AI that make business processes effective, efficient, and more intelligent. So, AI is not new. Some myths that prevent AI adoption are listed below [17]:

- Artificial intelligence is new.
- Artificial intelligence and machine learning are the same.

- Artificial intelligence will provide results based on the implementation.
- Artificial intelligence involves advanced algorithms and complex mathematics.
- Artificial Intelligence lacks human-like empathy.
- Artificial Intelligence can analyze and interpret any unstructured data.
- Business requires expertise in data science and ML and a considerable budget for AI.
- The "Cognitive Artificial Intelligence" technologies can understand all problems like the human brain.
- Artificial Intelligence has human-like characteristics.
- Machine learning with the help of "neural nets" means that computers can learn how humans learn.
- Artificial Intelligence will take away jobs.
- Artificial Intelligence is more intelligent than people.

Some of the AI-based learning is discussed in Table 1.2 [4–7, 18].

TABLE 1.2 Some of the AI-based Learning Platform

	AI-Based Learning Platform
Woonoz-personalized learning	A learning retention platform caters to sectors like health, finance, energy, transport, etc. This AI platform uses neuroscience and adaptive learning to create and develop an e-learning solution for personalized learning content, maximizing the employee retention rate and enhancing the learning rate.
Duolingo	AI personalizes courses, adapting to trainees' strengths, weaknesses, and preferences. It uses natural language processing to create chatbot experiences that provide trainees an opportunity to practice conversation in real-time.
Querium	This virtual tutoring program analyzes the steps trainees take in finding a solution for STEM problems and provides feedback on whether the trainee/learner is doing right or wrong.
KEA	AI-based learning experience platform is used in industries to customize and personalize employee training programs and workplace learning. KEA converts any data or documents into 'trackable' content for training. It provides a smooth onboarding experience.
Uni career	It is an E-learning career development platform for working professionals. This platform provides counseling, mentorship, career guidance, and also on various topics which are subject-oriented.
Self-study	Professionals are provided with an AI-powered cloud platform to personalize the content. It assesses each professional and identifies the most relevant learning content using machine learning.

1.4 A GENERIC FRAMEWORK FOR AN EFFECTIVE AI-BASED E-LEARNING PLATFORM AND ITS FUNCTIONING

In this section, the discussion will be on how AI technology facilitates changes and functions [11, 19].

1.4.1 PERSONALIZED LEARNING EXPERIENCES

As we know, learners are alike and process information differently, which requires many adaptations of various learning theories and training approaches. Creating a personalized learning experience is more resource-based and yields better outcomes. Technologies like AI and ML can identify and recognize learners' or trainees' learning patterns. The machine learning component learns and teaches to recognize the learners' learning patterns. It uses A-B testing during the individual's learning experience.

Employees' learning profiles are refined over time with more and more data. Once sufficient data has been gathered, the AI selects learning objects and delivery methods to be included in the personalized learning recommendations. The implementation of cognitive insight AI utilizes the output of Robotic Process Automation.

1.4.2 INTEGRATED WORKFLOW TRAINING

The employees will usually focus on completing routine activities and less on learning. The training content can be divided into bite-sized chunks and integrated into the organization's workflow. This facilitates the teaching of trainees in less time. AI-based Robotic Process Automation (RPA) can explain the learning objects categorized into a group and tag them. Further, cognitive insight AI identifies time slots between day-to-day tasks and intelligently supports and encourages the learning process in breaks during the day [19].

These AIs are found within a good learning platform's Content Provisioning (RPA) and Invite Engine (CI). These platforms provide recommendations (Recommendations Engine AI) to ensure whether employees consume relevant learning objects or not.

1.4.3 REINFORCED LEARNING AND DEVELOPMENT

Employees might not complete or forget the learning because they are preoccupied with the day-to-day activities and tasks of the organization. AIs can help encourage employees or trainees to achieve their learning tasks and return to topics that need further reinforcement. This is possible by applying gamification principles, extracting questions from learning objects, generating quizzes, administering tests, and so forth. AIs can schedule learning events, send reminders, and use psychological and social incentives to engage trainees/learners further. This also invites groups of learners into a social 'Club,' where they would be able to exhibit their knowledge gained.

Many learning and development platforms offer a Content Creation AI and an Invites Engine AI. These would benefit from the results of Content Provisioning, User Provisioning, and Recommendations Engine AIs.

Usually, the problem persists in learning platforms that it is complex and challenging to identify the exact portion of training content at the point of necessity. Identifying the right training content can be reduced by integrating with AI. The solution would be automatic content provisioning AI which can be used to parse, tag, and categorize the content. Administrators are not required to tag the content with search or keywords conventionally. Learners can quest keywords to discover what they are looking for every time.

1.4.4 AI-BASED DIGITAL COACHES

AI-based digital coaching is one of the emerging trends in the e-learning space. The deployment of AI-based digital coaching in social skills training, nutrition coaching, psychotherapy coaching, leadership coaching, and others has enabled specialized skills training for executives and professionals.

1.4.5 IMPROVED COMPLETION RATES

The number of successful training completions is one of the major concerns in the training industry. Due to many reasons, including personal and professional, trainees fail to complete the offered training. AI-based solutions come in handy in these situations. They will provide personalized recommendations, create deadlines, reward and award mechanisms, motivate the learner, and simultaneously create a decent amount of pressure to meet the deadlines. These features will help in improving the completion rates of the training. AI-based mechanisms correctly identify the easy, moderate, and high commitments required from the trainees and make the complete learning cycle customized to the individual trainee's needs [19].

1.4.6 LEARNING AND TRAINING EFFECTIVENESS MEASUREMENT

ML-based performance measurement provides more accurate predictions of trainee performance. It is very effectively done by correctly mapping learning objectives and outcomes to the performance metrics. Proper interventions during learning will help the learner to make the learning cycle very adaptive to the individual learner. These interventions are created with AI and ML by analyzing the historical data; through this, it is possible to make informed decisions.

1.4.7 UNIVERSALITY

The primary aim of AI-based learning is to cater to heterogeneous learners' needs. The needs primarily revolve around the content delivered. The content modulation can be done by considering the trainee's background, level of education, spoken language, domicile, and, most importantly, personality traits. Today's platforms are better equipped with features for content translation, reformatting, republishing, and so on. This feature calls for thoroughly understanding your trainees, collecting enough data points, and training the suitable ML model.

1.5 IMPACT OF DYNAMIC LEARNING PATHS ON THE TRAINEE

In the previous section, the discussion was on how AI technology facilitates changes and functions. This section will discuss how AI-based eLearning platforms impact and improve trainees' learning [13, 15].

Artificial Intelligence-powered tools and solutions are being used extensively in workplaces. Artificial Intelligence adoption in companies in various capacities in the HR department during hiring, onboarding, induction process, employee skills training, and personality development programs. As technology does menial and everyday tasks, every employee is likely to focus on the value creation in the company. The employee must be expected to perform effectively and efficiently in an organization. This is precisely where AI technology can offer more excellent value to organizational requirements. In the era of technology disruption, which resulted in greater skills gaps, integrating Artificial Intelligence in e-learning platforms will give several advantages in upskilling and reskilling employees to meet organizational expectations [16]. Furthermore, this enhances employee capability and professional improvement and stays tuned and relevant in the way of functioning of the organization.

Integrating AI results in understanding an employee's behavior and knowledge, giving learning pathways to improve the learning process. Such predictive analytics can help create more innovative content to meet the learners' needs. AI-infused e-learning platforms allow companies to leverage e-learning solutions (LMSs, LXPs – learning experience platforms, LAPs – learning assessment pathways, etc.) to a more significant level. It will transform the way employees learn, unlocking new educational possibilities [21].

The way the AI will transform the e-learning process is discussed below:

1. **AI will Define the Learner's Path:** The critical aspects of AI are collecting and analyzing the learner's data whenever they interact with the technology platform. It helps define the learner's path through the learning progression more effectively and efficiently. Artificial Intelligence responds to end-users, can identify the learner's capability, direct the learner to the next level by providing the relevant content, and also based on the individual learner's learning style and pace with which they learn [20].
2. **Personalized Session:** Any learning process will not be a one-size-fits-all solution because each learner has their learning style, abilities, and pace. AI will help track the learner's past performance, identify the gaps in each learner's proficiency, and use data to alter learning materials, thus personalizing an enriching learning experience.
3. **Content Analytics:** There will be a great pool of unstructured materials like documents, texts, audio, media, and images, and it's a challenge for tutors and administrators to process them accurately. AI can process and analyze vast amounts of data sets quickly and efficiently so that users get more out of the course materials. It gives insights into the individual learning style, gaps, and the learner's pace; and highlights the content to the learner for further processing, deliberations, and interpretation of the data [13].
4. **Deeper Learner Engagement with Virtual Reality (VR) and Chatbots:** Virtual reality levels up the e-learning process. The technology platform provides online training simulations based on real-life scenarios. Thus, learners can study the subject more profoundly, get hands-on practice, and enrich the learning experience and engagement level.

5. **Round-the-Clock Counseling:** AI-based assistants understand fundamental human language and respond accordingly. They monitor the learner's behavior, offer additional learning materials, impart knowledge from an expert, and provide custom-tailored feedback and guidance to everyone. Technology assistants enhance the learner's productivity.
6. **Automatic Grading:** Artificial Intelligence facilitates grading for learners. Integration of AI in e-learning can speed up assessment, classify learners' understanding of various concepts, and provide feedback.
7. **Real-Time Questioning:** AI can respond to queries at a faster rate, accurately, and efficiently. Artificial technologies can process user questions and reply in real time with all the reasoning and clarifications. An AI-integrated platform discloses resources that suggest learning material and reduces the efforts and time needed to develop it manually.
8. **Gamification:** This technique is a robust approach to e-learning to engage and motivate learners to acquire knowledge. AI can be used to implement gamification in a personalized manner, and the courses can be created relevant to the learner's requirements or industry needs.
9. **Visualizing:** AI can drive employees with newer ways of experiencing information, such as visualization, simulation, and web-based studies, to be more effective and efficient in their learning activities [20].
10. **Virtual Facilitators:** Trending technology such as augmented reality is integrated with developing e-learning platforms that use gesture 3-D gaming and computer animation for realistic virtual characters and interactions that add to the experience.
11. **Intelligent Dashboards:** Dashboards are developed using AI-based prescriptive and predictive analytics. They cover the performance of employees based on historical and current data. Dashboards will process the historical data to identify and discover the employees' patterns, trainees' learning styles, and optimization of training. Dashboards classify and analyze data gathered by an LMS, which helps the organization understand how users interact with it and find improvement opportunities. For example, dashboards show employees' performance, the most required training courses, the

average length of a training session, the most common questions and issues posed by trainees, etc.

12. **Expanded Engagement by Virtual Tutors:** The virtual tutors support trainees at every step in discovering the relevant resources based on topics of interest and their profiles. This facility will optimize the learning process in terms of the time and effort required to perform the task manually. Virtual tutors will enhance the trainee's engagement level in learning.

1.6 SURVEY RESULTS ON THE POTENTIAL OF SUCH FRAMEWORKS

A survey was conducted to understand the potential of a few frameworks discussed in the chapter. A sample of 259 working professionals was considered for the study. A dichotomous (Yes/No) and 5-point Likert scale were used to mark response ratings (1-Strongly disagree to 5-Strongly agree). The study aimed to identify the awareness of e-learning platforms, usage, the generic framework of AI-based e-learning platforms, and their advantages.

The study depicted that 85% of the respondents were aware of the e-learning platform (Figure 1.1), and 15% were unaware of such e-learning platforms. The study focused on the most popular e-learning platforms' usage. It was observed that the most used e-learning platforms are Coursera, Udemy, Udacity, and Skillsoft compared to other available platforms in the market (Figure 1.2).

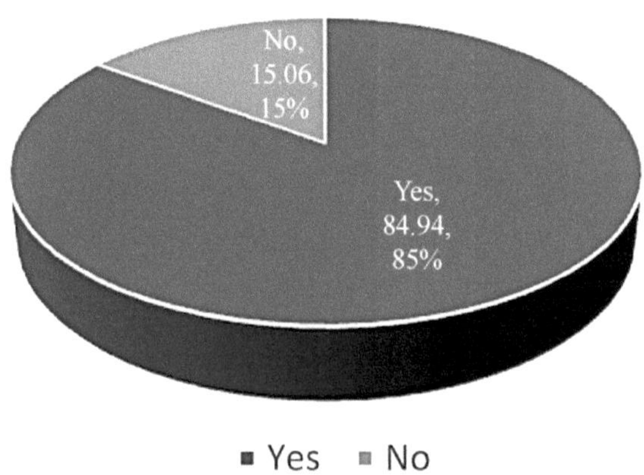

FIGURE 1.1 Awareness of e-learning.

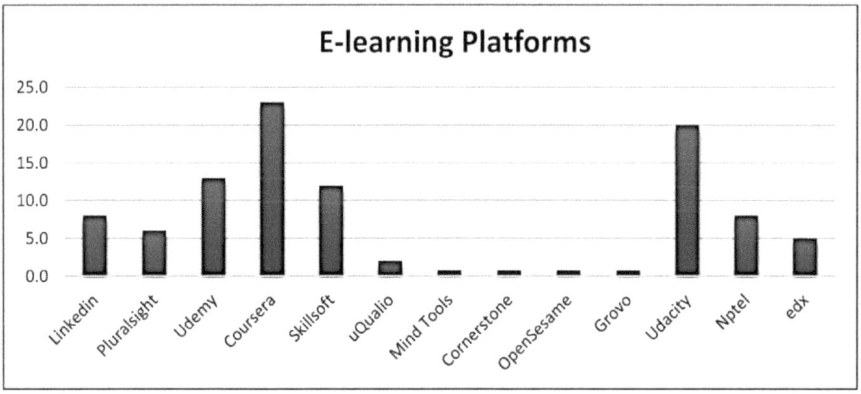

FIGURE 1.2 Usage of e-learning platforms.

The study reveals certain limitations of an e-learning platform, as shown in the graph (Figure 1.3). There is a lack of hands-on experience, no proper monitoring mechanism, too much internet dependency on the platform, and a lack of customized content from the e-learning platform (Figure 1.4).

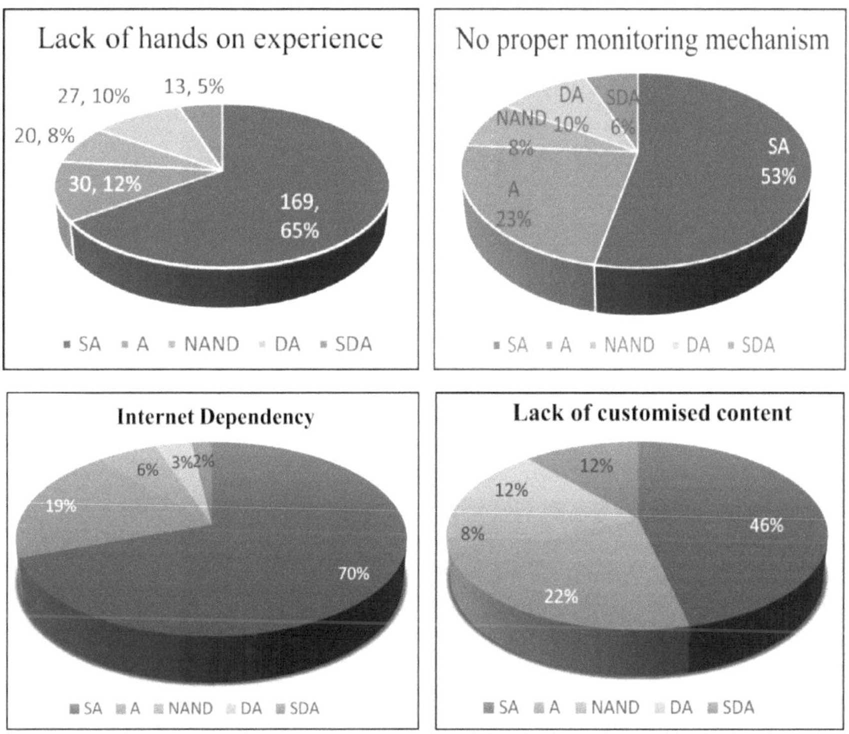

FIGURE 1.3 Limitations of e-learning platforms. (a) Lack of hands-on experience; (b) No proper monitoring mechanism; (c) Internet Dependency; (d) Lack of customized content.

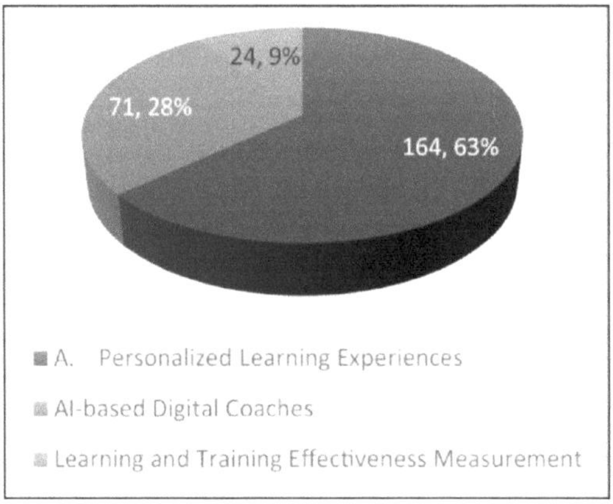

FIGURE 1.4 Framework of AI-based e-learning platforms.

From the above graph, it can be inferred that personalized learning experiences, digital coaches, and measurement aspects can facilitate a better AI-based e-learning platform (Figure 1.5).

It was found from the study that personalized sessions, deeper learning engagement, grading, gamification, and intelligent dashboards provide a lot of advantages for the trainees and give a quality experience when compared with other dimensions (Figures 1.5(a)–(d)).

1.7 CONCLUSION

The focus of the chapter is to identify some of the limitations of non-AI-based e-learning platforms and their impacts on the trainee's learning curve. The chapter attempts to showcase some advantages of enabling e-learning platforms with AI. It also covers some challenges and highlights salient features of the new-generation learning platforms. The study also highlights some popular e-learning platforms and their transformational challenges. Finally, the chapter concludes with the results of the opinion survey. In summary, AI-based e-learning platforms will add a lot of value additions for learners as against classical e-learning platforms and give a quality learning experience.

The chapter focuses on the following areas:

1. The Issues and limitations in non-AI-based E-learning platforms.
2. The non-AI-based E-learning to AI-based E-learning transformation challenges.
3. The generic framework for an effective AI-based E-learning platform and its functioning.

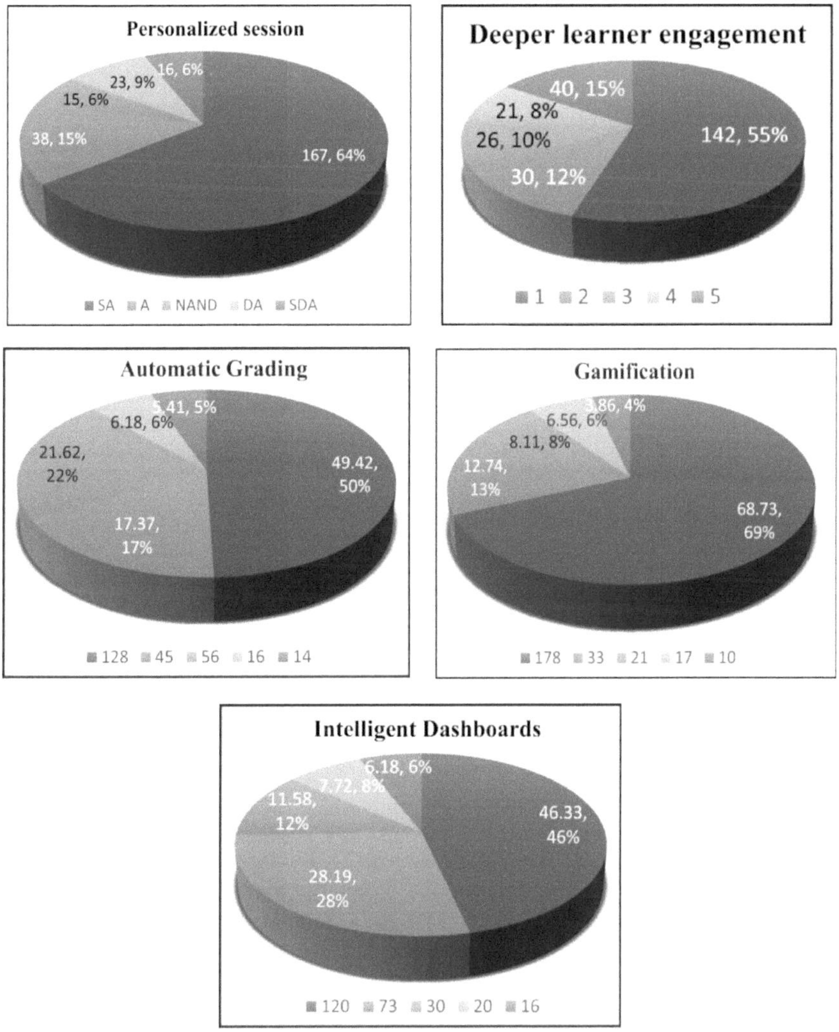

FIGURE 1.5 AI-based e-learning platforms' advantages. (a) Personalized session; (b) Deeper Learner Engagement; (c) Automatic Grading; (d) Gamification; (e) Intelligent Dashboards.

4. Impact of dynamic learning paths on the trainee.
5. Survey results on the potential of such frameworks.

Many learners and educators fear that AI technologies will replace humans. The study says that AI will serve as an excellent support system for human experts.

KEYWORDS

- **artificial intelligence**
- **dynamic learning**
- **e-learning**
- **e-learning transformation**
- **generic framework**
- **integrated workflow training**
- **quality learning experience**
- **universality**

REFERENCES

1. Kimwise, A. Adoption of e-learning technologies in education institutions/organizations: A literature review. *Asian Journal of Educational Research, 5*(4), ISSN 2311-6080.
2. Díaz Redondo, R. P., Caeiro Rodríguez, M., López Escobar, J. J., & Fernández Vilas, A. (2021). Integrating micro-learning content in traditional e-learning platforms. *Multimedia Tools and Applications, 80*(2), 3121–3151.
3. Benta, D., Bologa, G., & Dzitac, I. (2014). E-learning platforms in higher education: Case study. *Procedia Computer Science, 31*, 1170–1176.
4. Graf, S., & List, B. (2005). An evaluation of open-source e-learning platforms stressing adaptation issues. In *Fifth IEEE International Conference on Advanced Learning Technologies (ICALT'05)* (pp. 163–165). IEEE.
5. Freire, L. L., Arezes, P. M., & Campos, J. C. (2012). A literature review about usability evaluation methods for e-learning platforms. *Work, 41*(Supplement 1), 1038–1044.
6. Giannakos, M. N., Mikalef, P., & Pappas, I. O. (2021). Systematic literature review of e-learning capabilities to enhance organizational learning. *Information Systems Frontiers, 24, 619*–635.
7. Madani, Y., Erritali, M., Bengourram, J., & Sailhan, F. (2019). Social collaborative filtering approach for recommending courses in an E-learning platform. *Procedia Computer Science, 151*, 1164–1169.
8. Siddiqui, S. T., Alam, S., Khan, Z. A., & Gupta, A. (2019). Cloud-based e-learning: Using cloud computing platform for an effective e-learning. In S. (Ed.), *Smart Innovations in Communication and Computational Sciences* (pp. 335–346). Springer, Singapore.
9. Margalina, V. M., De-Pablos-Heredero, C., & Montes-Botella, J. L. (2017). Achieving quality in e-Learning through relational coordination. *Studies in Higher Education, 42*(9), 1655–1670.
10. Johnson, R. D., & Brown, K. G. (2017). *E-learning.* https://doi.org/10.1007/s11042-022-13076-8.

11. Sayed, W. S., Noeman, A. M., Abdellatif, A., Abdelrazek, M., Badawy, M. G., Hamed, A., & El-Tantawy, S. (2022). AI-based adaptive personalized content presentation and exercises navigation for an effective and engaging E-learning platform. *Multimedia Tools and Applications, 82, 3303*–3333.
12. Rana, H., & Lal, M. (2014). E-learning: Issues and challenges. *International Journal of Computer Applications, 97*(5), 0975–8887.
13. Banerjee, P. (2022). Corporate E-Learning Initiatives: A New Paradigm for Employee Development. *NHRD Network Journal, 15*(3), 345–352.
14. Greenhow, C., Graham, C. R., & Koehler, M. J. (2022). Foundations of online learning: Challenges and opportunities. *Educational Psychologist, 57, 131*–147.
15. Holohan, E., Melia, M., McMullen, D., & Pahl, C. (2005). Adaptive e-learning content generation based on semantic web technology. In International Workshop on Applications of Semantic Web Technologies for E-Learning (SW-EL 2005) at the 12th *International Conference on Artificial Intelligence in Education AIED 2005.* AIED.
16. My-Thanh Nguyen, T., Hai Diep, T., Bien Ngo, B., Bich Le, N., & Quy Dao, X. (2021). Design of online learning platform with Vietnamese virtual assistant. In *2021 6th International Conference on Intelligent Information Technology* (pp. 51–57).
17. Gartner. (n.d.). Five AI myths debunked. *Smarter With Gartner.* Retrieved from: https://www.gartner.com/smarterwithgartner/5-ai-myths-debunked (accessed on 27 May 2024).
18. Analytics Steps. (n.d.). Top 10 AI-based learning platforms. *Analytics Steps.* Retrieved from: https://www.analyticssteps.com/blogs/top-10-ai-based-learning-platforms-us (accessed on 27 May 2024).
19. Shift eLearning. (n.d.). Artificial intelligence & eLearning. *Shift eLearning.* Retrieved from: https://www.shiftelearning.com/blog/artificial-intelligence-elearning (accessed on 27 May 2024).
20. ColorWhistle. (n.d.). Impact of AI in eLearning industry. *ColorWhistle.* Retrieved from: https://colorwhistle.com/impact-of-ai-in-elearning-industry/ (accessed on 27 May 2024).

CHAPTER 2

AI-Based Stock Market Prediction During War Period

S. R. REEJA

Professor, School of Computer Science and Engineering (SCOPE), VIT-AP University, India

ABSTRACT

On the stock exchange, investors and traders can sell and purchase shares, changing the value of the stock. Because stock prices are determined by supply and demand, the ultimate purpose of stock shopping is to generate cash by purchasing assets that are predicted to increase in value (i.e., share price). Machine learning techniques are used in several research to forecast expenses in quantitative finance. Management and restriction of complete asset portfolios, as well as investing methods and a variety of other activities. Machine learning is a broad term that encompasses a variety of recursive tactics that employ algorithms to detect trends based solely on data rather than programming instructions. Many models in quantitative finance, notably in asset choice, provide a wide range of strategies that can be used to anticipate future asset values. Our paper's goal is to apply bidirectional LSTM recurrent neural networks to anticipate the adjusted final market amount for a portfolio of securities, the main goal here is to get the best skilled algorithmic software to predict future returns. LSTM gives an accuracy of 68%, Bidirectional LSTM gives an accuracy of 84%.

2.1 INTRODUCTION

Where stocks are traded is called a stock market [1]. It is regarded as a natural reflection of a nation's financial development. However, because of

Artificial Intelligence and Machine Learning for Business. Namita Mishra, A. V. Senthil Kumar (Eds.)

its diversity and unpredictability, its mechanism causes bewilderment and doubt. One of the most difficult jobs requiring human-computer interaction is predicting stock values. Stock prices are difficult to predict to the minute because of their dynamic character. Stocks never fluctuate by themselves. The movement of one stock has a cascading effect on multiple others [7–15]. This component can aid in the prediction of many shared values at once.

To anticipate stock values, a neural network will learn different scale features [5]. Through a self-learning process, they may detect hidden patterns, as well as remember earlier information. The data in the stock market is highly non-uniform. To represent this changing data, we need a framework that can identify patterns. Bi-directional LSTM networks will be looked into for stock price prediction. Following that, a comparison of accuracy with existing approaches is computed.

2.2 REVIEW WORKS

In this section, we describe the stock market forecasting literature. Finally, we also list the challenges of the existing systems that are still prevalent in stock market prediction. A similar project [2] was carried out by Mehar Vijha. This article describes methods for forecasting closing prices for the following day using random forest and ANN. In order to forecast the stock's following day closing price, ANN is employed, while RF is used for a comparative study. However, in data with a large number of parameters, ANN may have an overfitting problem and the solutions may fall into local minima. Undoubtedly, one of the world's most powerful political and economic powerhouses. Their capabilities typically become reduced by defense and paramilitary requirements during times of war. This forces them to reduce the amount they benefit the world market, and this adversely impacts equity markets. The number of deaths in a war reflects the seriousness of the situation that led to violence. They waste more money on the costs of the conflict, making the differences between the nations more important. As a result, the market's productivity declines as business investment is curtailed and frequently greatly diminished.

We also referred to a paper [3] by Richard Kyle. In this paper, a classifier machine learning model is discussed. Companies are connected using an undirected graph data structure and SSVM is applied to it to predict positive or negative movement in stock prices. But this model is correct 62% of the time, with a higher percentage of negative data being classified accurately than positive labels. We referred to a paper [4] that presents a solution using

SVM (support vector machine) and PSO (parameter swarm optimization). As a method for global optimization, PSO is used iteratively with LSSVM for stock price prediction [7–17]. In other works, RNNs (Recurrent Neural Networks) with a smaller number of layers were trained from scratch. The models achieved considerable accuracies. However, since the training was performed on a model with a smaller number of layers and the input dataset was too small, it led to the overfitting of data in the model. In datasets with a large number of parameters, ANN may face an overfitting problem and the solutions may converge to local minima.

2.3 RECURRENT NEURAL NETWORKS (RNNS)

Recurrent neural networks (RNNs) [6] are a kind of neural network where the input for one stage is the output from the previous one, as shown in Figure 2.1. In an RNN network layer, a neuron has two sets of weights: one for input and another for the preceding step's result, where 't' is the timestamp. The output of the recurrent layers for a minibatch can be computed immediately by placing all the inputs in a matrix of inputs Xt. The input data is then compiled into a function.

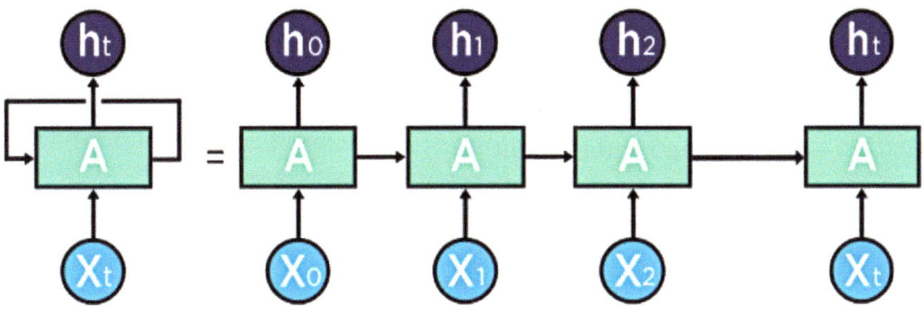

FIGURE 2.1 Recurrent neural networks (RNNs).

2.4 BIDIRECTIONAL-LSTM (BD-LSTM)

When LSTM is used to obtain, around the selective memory problem, it is easier to spot hard dependencies in data. The primary objective of the LSTM cell is for the neurons to be able to choose wanted and discard data. Gates are used for discarding or appending data to the cell state. As a result, they allow data through it on a case-by-case basis. A superior variant of LSTM is bi-directional LSTM. It processes the data in the following two ways: one starts from the past and ends in the future, and another one starts from the future and ends in the past. By doing this, information from both the future and past states is retained, as shown in Figure 2.2.

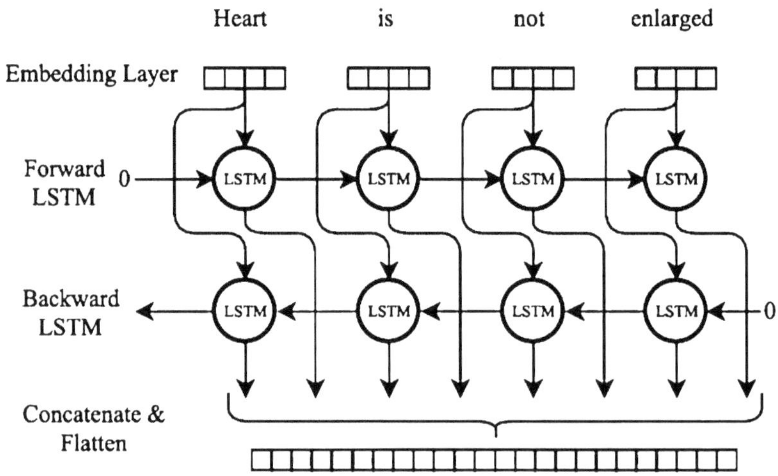

FIGURE 2.2 BILSTM.

2.5 PROPOSED MODEL

We present a neural network technique in Figure 2.3 for estimating a stock's end-of-day price using BDLSTM. We used a dataset taken from Finance-Yahoo. For the past four years, this information includes historical stock market data for Binge and Renault.

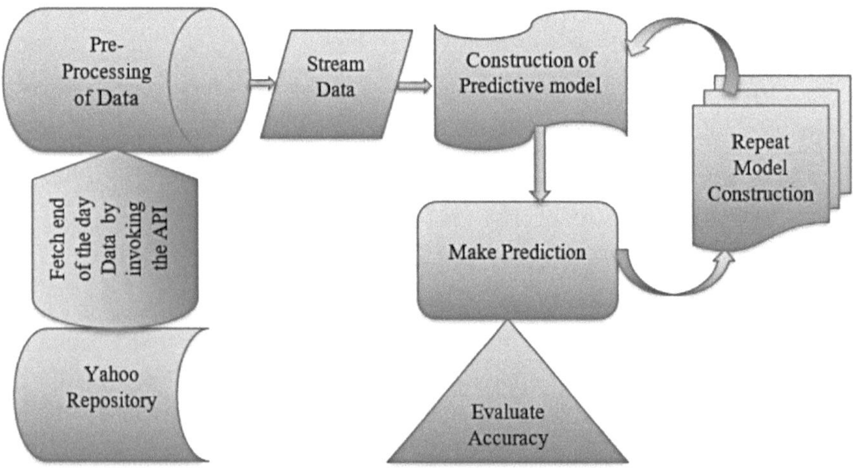

FIGURE 2.3 Workflow of the project.

2.5.1 DATA PRE-PROCESSING

Data modeling is a type of data pre-processing that reduces the size of the data collection to the point where the normalized data falls between 0 and 1. Our BD-LSTM model's [7] data frame comprises several dimensions, each with its own set of attributes. The volume is significantly more than the price of stock. Let's say we have a dataset where one of the vectors has a substantially larger magnitude than the others. As a result, the model's liking for these vectors increases dramatically. Furthermore, important data will be lost, which could alter the accuracy. To avoid these problems, normalization creates new data within a scale of values that preserves the dataset's overall distribution. As a result, seven eigenvectors must be normalized to ensure the accuracy of the results. The maximum and minimum methods for normalizing input data, as well as their formulas, are as follows:

$$X_{normalized} = \frac{X - X_{minimum}}{X_{maximum} - X_{minimum}}$$

To ensure that the company value of input and output data is consistent, the inverse action of normalization is required. A min-max scaler is used to solidify these components in the program.

2.5.2 INPUT LAYER

In Figure 2.4, we can see that Close, Open, Low, and High values have the same pattern, so we can choose any one of them. Therefore, we choose Close and Volume. Along with these two features, we use the RSI indicator, which is a momentum indicator used in technical analysis. It calculates the speed and amplitude of a security's price changes. RSI examines the amount of a security's average gains and losses over a defined time period.

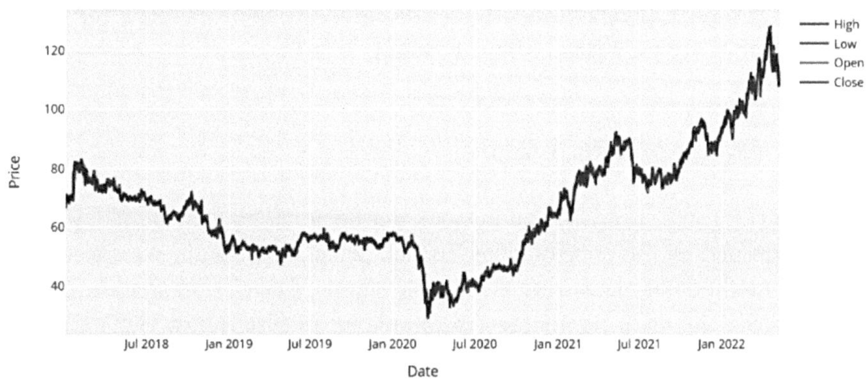

FIGURE 2.4 Comparing KPI values of binge stocks.

The input contains 3 features which consist of close, volume, and RSI Index as shown in Table 2.1.

TABLE 2.1 Input Matrix of First Five Values of Binge Dataset

Date	Close	Volume	RSI
2018-01-02	67.989998	9,44,500	68.7647
2018-01-03	69.449997	2,124,600	82.3478
2018-01-04	70.470001	2,026,900	87.2063
2018-01-05	69.940002	7,95,500	73.9808
2018-01-08	68.930000	1,041,200	54.3473

The output has a single feature called Close. In a 4:1 ratio, the data was separated into a training dataset and a test dataset. We turned each component of input data into a 0–1 interval after normalization. The previous thirty days are used as input for each entry in our dataset. It turns our input dataset into a three-dimensional form matrix (N, 30, 3).

2.5.3 IMPLEMENTATION OF THE BD-LSTM

The primary role of the BD-LSTM is to decide the data that is wanted to be held and the data that needs to be discarded.

The model is shown in Figure 2.5. This is the conclusion reached by the sigmoid layer. Data is either discarded if the output value is "0" or retained if it is "1." Choosing the data that will be kept in our Bi-LSTM cell comes next. We have an LSTM layer followed by a dropout of 30% for preventing complex co-adaptations on training data. Next, we have a few more layers of neural networks with "elu" activation (Exponential Linear Unit), which is a combination of tanh and relu activation. Finally, our output layer creates a more improved representation of our current input. In order to get the desired output value, we pass it *via* a linear model.

2.5.4 ERROR METRICS (EM)

Time series forecasting is used in stock market analysis. The next day's price is determined by the previous day's stock price. As a result, we can't utilize typical methods of measuring errors like standard deviation and variance. In our project, the error percentage is calculated to assess how our network is performing.

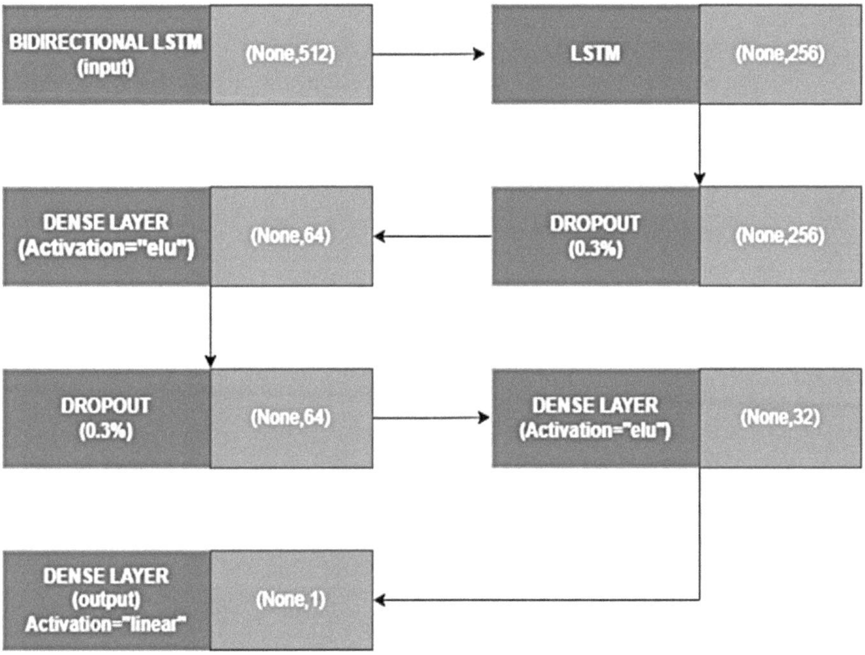

FIGURE 2.5 Model proposed.

The following two measures were used to compute the error percentage:

1. **Mean Absolute Deviation (MAD):** For n pieces of data, where Xi denotes the actual share value and m(X) denotes our anticipated price of the stock.

$$MAD = \left(\frac{1}{n}\right)\sum_{i=1}^{n}|X_i - m(X)|$$

2. **Mean Square Error (MSE):** For n data points, the real share price is Y_i, and the forecasted stock price is Y_i in the formula above.

$$MSE = \left(\frac{1}{n}\right)\sum_{i=1}^{n}(Y_i - \hat{Y}_i)^2$$

2.6 EXPERIMENTAL ANALYSIS

In our project, parameters are tuned in a way that ensures we don't overfit the training dataset and still get the required accurate output. As previously stated, we used a 4:1 split in our dataset. We discovered that 10 epochs and 100 units are the best values for both of them.

The financial sector is infamous for its fluctuation and lack of predictability. The stop-loss could be reached far before the target. As a result, being able to accurately estimate stock values is crucial. We want to improve the forecast model's accuracy by a few points. We were mostly successful in doing so. The accuracy gain is shown in Table 2.2.

TABLE 2.2 Error Metrics

EM	LSTM	BD-LSTM
Tr-D	0.68	0.84
Ts-D	0.72	0.86

For the Binge shares, we achieved an accuracy of 84.31% on the training dataset (Tr-D) and 86.621% on the test set (Ts-D). For Renault, the accuracy was 89.525% on the training dataset and approximately 88.58% on the test dataset. On average, it offers around 88% for Tr-D and 86% for Ts-D. Our model's accuracy is significantly higher than that of others, which was around 72%.

The utilization of the BD-LSTM layer contributed to the improved accuracy. Another factor in achieving good accuracy was fine-tuning the variables by matching them to a different set of data and then selecting the one that best suits our needs. The Relative Strength Index (RSI indicator) is an additional factor that is input into the neuron for comparison. By calculating their Relative Strength Index (RSI), these additional characteristics provide a better understanding of the financial exchange.

To begin, enter the trade ticker name in a designated field. Then, as shown in Table 2.3, we gather data such as the opening value, high value, and closing value as count, average, standard deviation, max, min, and other necessary information. Trades on the stock market occur within two-time intervals. The financial position at the opening and closing bells is referred to as the opening and closing, respectively. The open represents the stock amount at the starting phase, and the close represents the stock amount at the ending phase. Count indicates the number of records in that feature. Mean provides the average of all records. Min represents the minimum record value, and Max represents the maximum record value in that feature.

TABLE 2.3 Data Description

	Open	High	Low	Close	Adj Close	Volume
count	1009.000000	1009.000000	1009.000000	1009.000000	1009.000000	1.009000e+03
mean	666.801118	675.002200	658.994444	666.543113	629.899690	1.306047e+06
std	186.631073	184.852200	183.930170	186.839382	19.521213	7.471776e+05
min	30.030000	33.500000	29.000000	30.250000	28.398460	1.777000e+05
25%	53.453001	54.055200	52.945900	53.439999	48.976200	9.170000e+05
50%	64.900002	66.199997	63.749998	64.800003	57.092860	1.161900e+06
75%	77.945000	78.919998	76.794998	77.760002	75.900669	1.616900e+06
max	127.349998	128.949997	126.120003	126.760002	84.843300	8.434300e+06

A financial asset's share price is a measurement of the total amount that asset has been exchanged over a specified duration. Equities capacity is determined based on the overall number of sold shares. The stock's market interest and liquidity are determined by its volume. Figure 2.6 shows the close graph.

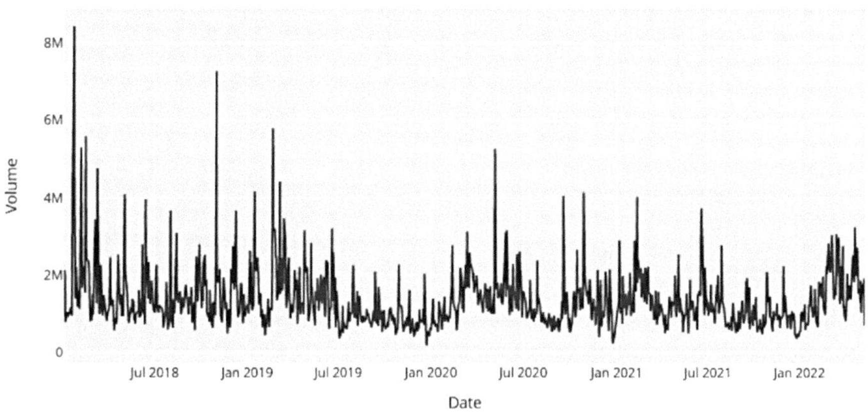

FIGURE 2.6 Volume graph.

Then we get the predicted graph (Figures 2.7 and 2.8). In the graphs, the red line indicates the expected equity value and the real stock level is depicted by the blue curve.

Now we have to enter a date in the future that predicts the stock price for the given date.

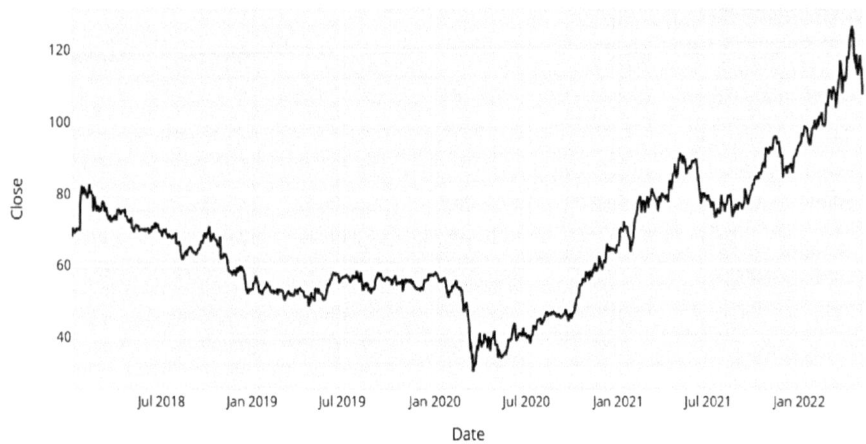

FIGURE 2.7 Close graph.

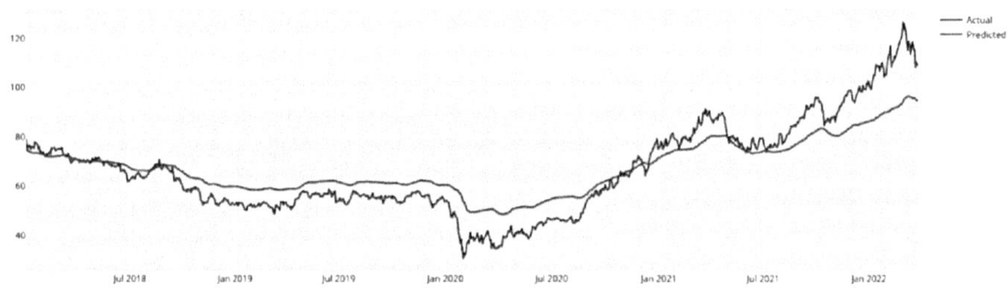

FIGURE 2.8 Predicted graph.

2.7 RESULTS

The purpose of the work was to create a technique for forecasting the closing prices of many stocks using the BDLSTM model. We observed that the outcomes were close and accurate when compared to the actual ones. With the help of this paper, we suggested integrating the attention mechanism, which relies on the scale of the provided receptive field. This was developed considering the numerous advantages DNNs have over conventional machine learning approaches. The graphs for Binge and Renault show the relationship between actual and predicted values. The Y-axis represents the current stock price, and the X-axis represents the timeframe for which we predict the stock value. In the training set, one unit on the X-axis corresponds to 100 days, while one unit on the Y-axis represents \$20. In the test dataset, one unit equals \$20 on the Y-axis and 20 days on the X-axis. The difference between the actual and predicted closing prices for Binge Company's shares is shown in Figure 2.9. The deviation between the actual daily closing price and the expected one for Renault's stock is displayed in Figure 2.10.

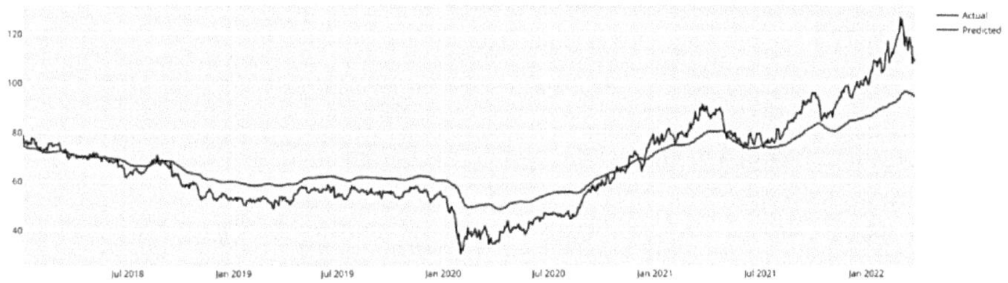

FIGURE 2.9 The discrepancy between what happened and what was expected closing prices for the shares of the Binge Company.

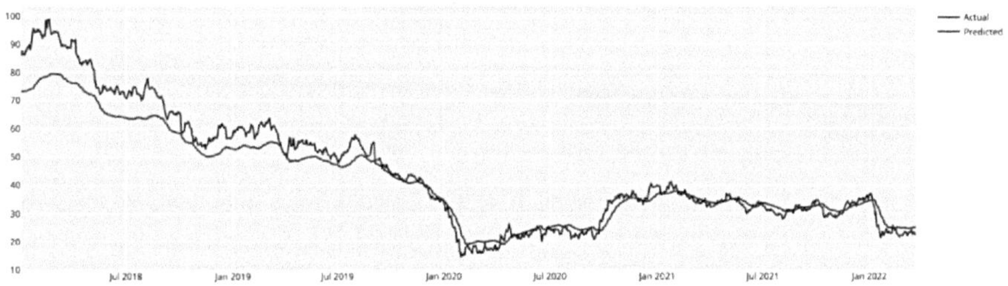

FIGURE 2.10 The difference between the actual and anticipated daily closing for the stock of the Renault firm.

2.8 CONCLUSION AND FUTURE WORK

With very few exceptions, the model suggested in this paper outperformed the usual models. In comparison to previous efforts, it appears to be quite promising. Big datasets allow our network to flesh out additional patterns, allowing the layer weights to do their best. Bi-LSTMs do well because they store data from both the previous and next states. When our algorithm is compared with others, we see a significant improvement in accuracy. We intend to continue investigating ways to substantially improve our model and its forecasts by advising improvements to the model's design and implementing new methods. Our model might have made a tradeoff in efficiency. More changes to the model will help to shorten the gradient's extensive dependency chain. We plan to use several technical indicators to analyze and improve the model. There are limitations to number crunching and price analysis. The addition of news stream analytics from the local financial community could enhance this method. It might be used in conjunction with trend analysis to gain a deeper comprehension of the feelings influencing pricing.

KEYWORDS

- **bidirectional LSTM**
- **error metrics**
- **LSTM**
- **machine learning**
- **quality learning experience**
- **stock exchange**

REFERENCES

1. Bustos, O., & Pomares-Quimbaya, A. (2020). Stock market movement forecast: A systematic review. *Expert Systems with Applications, 156*, 113464.
2. Vijh, M. (2020). Stock closing price prediction using machine learning techniques. *Procedia Computer Science, 167*, 599–606.
3. Choudhry, R., & Garg, K. (2008). A hybrid machine learning system for stock market forecasting. *World Academy of Science, Engineering and Technology, 39*(3), 315–318.
4. Reeja, S. R., & Yaseen, I. (2022). Object detection, tracking and behavioural analysis for static and moving background. *International Journal of Early Childhood Special Education (INT-JECSE). 14*(5), 788–795. DOI:10.9756/INTJECSE/V14I5.79.
5. Gandhmal, D. P., & Kumar, K. (2019). Systematic analysis and review of stock market prediction techniques. *Computer Science Review, 34*, 100190.
6. Kim, K., & Lee, W. B. (2004). Stock market prediction using artificial neural networks with optimal feature transformation. *Neural Computing & Applications, 13*(3), 255–260.
7. Pang, X., Zhou, Y., Wang, P., Lin, W., & Chang, V. (2020). An innovative neural network approach for stock market prediction. *The Journal of Supercomputing, 76*(3), 2098–2118.
8. Egeli, B., Ozturan, M., & Badur, B. (2003). Stock market prediction using artificial neural networks. *Decision Support Systems, 22*, 171–185.
9. Attigeri, G. V., Pai, M. M. M., Pai, R. M., & Nayak, A. (2015). Stock market prediction: A big data approach. In *TENCON 2015-2015 IEEE Region 10 Conference* (pp. 1–5). IEEE.
10. Hoseinzade, E., & Haratizadeh, S. (2019). CNNpred: CNN-based stock market prediction using a diverse set of variables. *Expert Systems with Applications, 129*, 273–285.

11. Hiransha, M., Gopalakrishnan, E. A., Menon, V. K., & Soman, K. P. (2018). NSE stock market prediction using deep-learning models. *Procedia Computer Science, 132*, 1351–1362.
12. Soja Rani, S., & Reeja, S. R. (2019). A Survey on Different Approaches for Malware Detection Using Machine Learning Techniques. In *International Conference on Sustainable Communication Networks and Application* (pp. 389–398). Springer, Cham.
13. Reeja, S. R., & Yaseen, I. (2022). Intelligent Music Genre Classification using CNN. *IJSTE, Volume 8*(10), ISSN (online): 2349–784X.
14. Reeja, S. R., & Yaseen, I. (2022). Emotion Detection for Live Video Face Expression – Standard Learning Techniques. *International Journal of Computer Applications, Volume- 184*(15), 4–7.
15. Parmar, I., et al. (2018). Stock market prediction using machine learning. In *First International Conference on Secure Cyber Computing and Communication (ICSCCC)*. IEEE.
16. Torres, P., & Edgar, P. (2019). Stock Market Data Prediction Using Machine Learning Techniques. In *International Conference on Information Technology & Systems*. Springer, Cham.
17. Leung, C. K. S., MacKinnon, R. K., & Wang, Y. (2014). A machine learning approach for stock price prediction. In *Proceedings of the 18th International Database Engineering & Applications Symposium* (pp. 274–277).

CHAPTER 3

Traffic Road Sign Detection and Recognition Approach Using OCR Based on Efficient DET and ROI Extraction

S. SUMATHY

Assistant Professor and Head, Department of Computer Science, Sir Theagaraya College, Shift II Chennai, Tamil Nadu, India

ABSTRACT

Object detection and identification of signboards are very significant and might hypothetically be used for driver support to lessen accidents and ultimately in driverless vehicles. In this paper, Efficient Det is used to develop a Road Traffic Signal Object discovery and acknowledgment classification (RTOA). The projected structure works in discovering and spotting traffic sign images. The involvement of this paper comprises developed Chinese traffic sign databases which encompass 6,164 traffic sign images comprising 58 sign groups and 10,000 traffic scene pictures encompassing various classes of signs. With this set of rules, the workstation knows how to categorize models of the annotations, facts, as well as additional designs, which might designate the prototype or further organization. The device spots numerous trials from the domain and offers possessions through or starved of elucidating the prearranged instructions. This work grants the acknowledgment of extracted version from the external surroundings concentrating on road signs. A background for text discovery and acknowledgment of the edition from the normal surroundings is offered. Primarily, the spitting image is apprehended from the external surroundings with an insolent ploy, monitored

Artificial Intelligence and Machine Learning for Business. Namita Mishra, A. V. Senthil Kumar (Eds.)

by the discovery of the boundaries of a road sign. The succeeding stage is the recognition and acknowledgment of the version using Efficient Det. An Artificial Neural Network is utilized for the ordering and acknowledgment of the text mined from the regular sights or exterior surroundings. In the final phase, extracted features are partitioned using regions of interest, and those segmented texts are given as input to OCR, i.e., signboards positioned sideways on the road. Residences are habitually identified by text or marks distributed all over the surroundings, through the concept of OCR, and word-based records can be extracted from the road signs. Object detection systems utilized in diverse color spaces are evaluated for effective, precise, and fast segmentation of the regions of interest. The Efficient Det structural design was used with varying constraints to achieve the best recognition results. Investigational outcomes show that the proposed design achieved an enhanced performance with an accuracy of 93% for text recognition and traffic road sign detection, respectively.

3.1 INTRODUCTION

Traffic road sign acknowledgment as a presentation of appeal acknowledgment has dual measures – sign discovery and Transcript discovery. This exertion emphasizes on the detection and acknowledgment of transcript on circulation road signs. Transcript on road transportation symbols records various evidence that know how to be very beneficial to drivers like promptness restrictions, accuracy of manner, cautions, and so forth. Acknowledgment of transcript as highway marks may remain predominantly challenging.

Experiments encompass type style dissimilarity, alignment, shades, low image tenacity, distorting, and added misrepresentation endorsed to the indication of the automobile. Numerous procedures have been recommended to discover visitors' signs [1].

Traditional strategies are commonly constructed on available-crafted structures such as color, texture, edge, and other low-level topographies to identify visitors' signs in a photograph [2]. In dynamic surroundings, due to the variety of the site visitors' signal appearance, the obstruction of road traffic signs by means of new objects, in addition to the outcome of illumination circumstances, outdated enactments for site visitors' signal detection exposed overall meager performance.

Artificial Intelligence (AI) is a use of man-made consciousness that gives the capacity to learn lacking involvement and vibrant program design. The primary reason permits a workstation to acquire and change its behavior as per humanoid interference [3]. Learning via machine permits studying big quantities of statistics. Mostly, rapid and more accurate results are obtained for design proof of identity. Spitting images, thumbprints, and others can be known as a design. Design acknowledgment is a process consuming instrument learning algorithms for the acknowledgment of design patterns. Together, machine learning algorithms and design discovery play a dynamic part in separating data from normal prospects [4]. Normal sights encompass supportive and valued data; separating text makes it straightforward to understand for individuals and supercomputers. This examination of separating text from ordinary divisions is extremely dynamic and stimulating in mainframe applications [5]. Construing the text of the extract offers numerous valuable claims dependent on geographical statistics.

In numerous earlier research focusing on traffic information sign detection [6, 7], determinations have been made to come across symbols and abstracts offered transcript in demand to put on ophthalmic character discovery structures. On the other hand, since old-fashioned OCR classifications are principally premeditated to understand and convert planar into digital form, paper-constructed manuscript imaginings, they are unfitted for the charge of handling textual content uncovering in regular sight pictures owing to the flexible in addition to composite contiguous surroundings [8]. In spite of the fact that there have been a few explorations pointed toward working on the capacity of OCR frameworks to perceive text embedded in normal extracts, it is to contemplate that the neural linkage would be likewise suitable for presentation to the text discovery in our review since they have demonstrated enormously effective in object location and grouping responsibilities. Existing pictures, comprising road traffic information symbols, were then verified using our prepared network prototypes. From those trials, high text discovery accuracy could be acquired utilizing artificial training data, which provided a technique to sequence neural linkage for practice in circumstances when gathering real data is difficult. A comparable accuracy can be attained even when text is not reduced in the realistic background pictures in the unreal dataset. The association between text and their circumstantial color is scrutinized and the reliance of color channels when the neural linkages identify text.

The overhead-mentioned competencies are convened in an added perspective in the succeeding regions. The rest of this work is systematized as a trail. In segment II, a survey of correlated works is briefly described. Segment III designates the anticipated approaches used for generating artificial information and distinguishing text on symbols. In segment IV, the datasets are presented, and afterward, the investigational technique is familiarized, and the outcomes are dissected. Lastly, segment V summarizes the system.

3.2 LITERATURE SURVEY

Piccioli et al. [9] accomplished street sign acknowledgment by ordering street signs according to their shapes, standardizing the sign to a size of 50x50 pixels by straight interpolation, and smearing cross-correlation between the street sign and the layout of the record correlated to the legitimate shape. Anil Kumar Meena et al. examined data abstraction from road signs, from this work we came to know about the extraction of statistics from the signpost and arrow detection [10]. Dahyot et al. [11] completed a pattern recognition framework centered on an appearance-based depiction of color images. Reina introduced a technique to separate transcripts from the road traffic symbol panels [12]. To sense the quadrilateral boards, color dissection, and contour arrangement are completed. Lim et al. proposed a vigorous discovery of the region of concern of signposts in a piercing atmosphere [13]. Lauziere et al. [14] identified traffic sign colors utilizing shading arrangement equations. The street signs' material spectral reflectance was estimated with a Spectrophotometer. In Ref. [15], Hanwell et al. projected a framework for perceiving and following the paths of streets. This is utilized to caution the motorists once they alter their paths. Md. Sadrul et al. proposed programmed signpost recognition from ordinary prospect pictures in this work and partook in the recognized discovery of the forename panel. The Bangladesh way sight signpost entities' picture records were utilized. This encompasses the appearance of certain style boards established in Bangladesh [16].

3.3 PROPOSED METHODOLOGY

The involvement of this work will be twofold; one is to foster another for the Chinese dataset of Traffic and Street Marks and the other is to progress and plan an Efficient Det structural design for Road traffic sign acknowledgment. The gathered informational collection is prearranged as a contribution to the projected Efficient Det design for preparation, approval, and testing. Once the Efficient Det is prepared, it is all set to be utilized for ordering new pictures that were not part of the gathered dataset. The TSOR framework relies upon a gathering of traditional Road traffic signs. Figure 3.1 illustrates the comprehensive description of the estimated structural design of the framework.

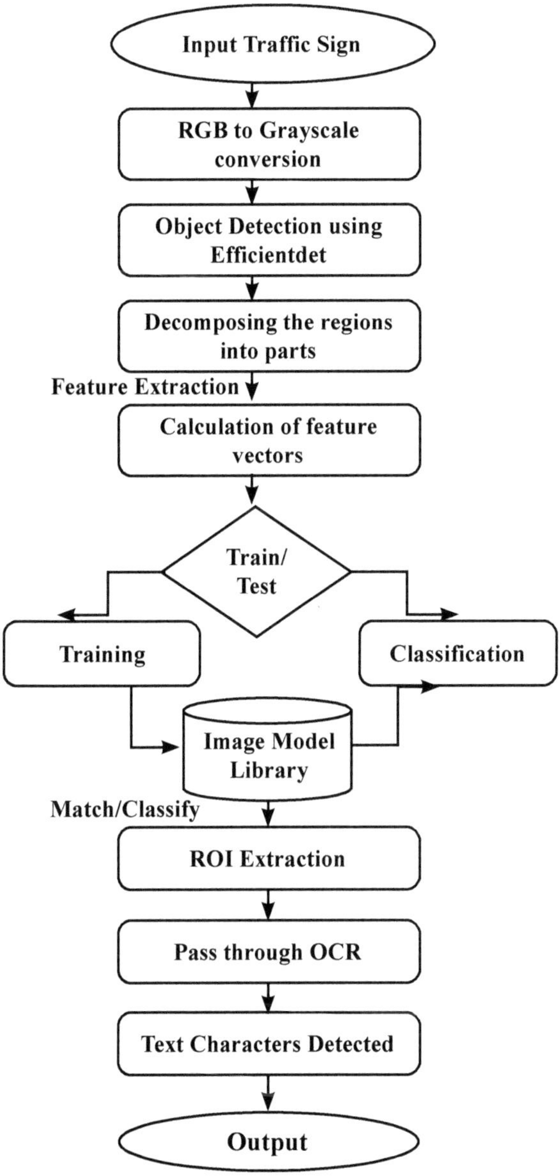

FIGURE 3.1 The overall flow of the proposed system.

3.3.1 OBJECT DETECTION UTILIZING EFFICIENT DET

Object recognition is a procedure of preparing computers to perceive objects from pictures or recordings; throughout the long term, there are various entity detection designs and algorithms produced by numerous enterprises and investigators. In this race to create the most reliable and efficient prototype, the Google Brain group recently released the Efficient Det prototype, which achieved the highest accuracy with the least training epochs in object recognition tasks.

Efficient Det was a benchmark network that achieved best-in-class precision of 84.4% and utilized an exceptionally active composite coefficient to enhance CNNs in a more organized way. Efficient Det proposed innovative optimization strategies to further improve efficacy, such as BiFPN and a new Computational Surmounting procedure, as shown in Figure 3.2.

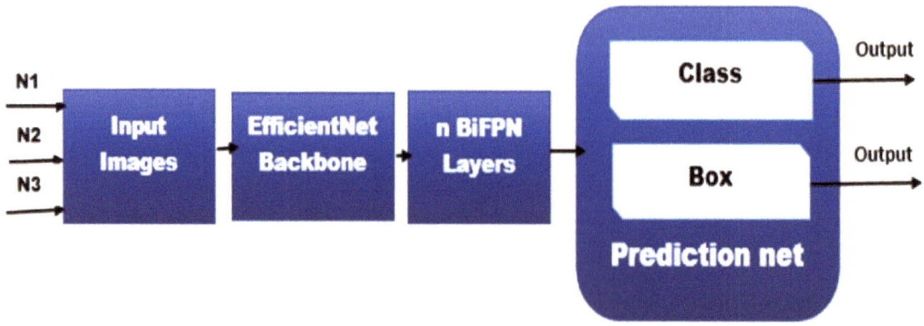

FIGURE 3.2 Efficient det architecture: BiFPN as the feature linkage.

Here we put forward BiFPN, a bi-directional element network improved with quick standardization, which empowers simple and quick feature combination, and for mounting a solitary composite scrambling factor to administer the profundity, width, and goal for all support, feature & likelihood networks is utilized. BiFPN as a multi-scale combination layer: when we have a sequencing linkage we are required to resourcefully abstract structures for the recognition phase. These two difficulties are tackled productively by utilizing the BiFPN layer. Two heads: at last, the whole thing is associated with two output linkages. One for anticipating the furthest probable mark and one for foreseeing the distinguished hurdling box.

The notion of Efficient Det emerged from our work to discover answers for improving computational effectiveness by leading a methodological investigation of earlier cutting-edge identification prototypes. In general, object finders have three primary constituents: a backbone that concentrates features from the given image; a component network that receives different levels of elements from the backbone as input and produces a list of combined elements that represent unique attributes of the image; and the last class/box network [18] that uses the combined features to predict the class and location of each object. By analyzing the design choices for these components, we identified several key innovations to further enhance performance and efficiency. By implementing an Efficient Det backbone, it is possible to achieve significantly improved efficacy. While the Efficient Det prototypes are primarily designed for object detection, we also evaluate their performance on other tasks [19], such as semantic segmentation. To perform segmentation tasks, we slightly modify Efficient Det-D4 by replacing the detection head and loss function with a segmentation head and loss, while retaining the same underlying backbone and BiFPN. Since Efficient Det utilizes both a powerful backbone and a new BiFPN, we need to understand how each contributes to the accuracy and efficiency improvements.

3.3.1.1 CLASSIFICATION MODULE

The fundamental undertaking of the discovery prototype is to preprocess the input picture and concentrate on the spaces that encompass street sign design. The identification module then advances this ROI to the grouping module for acknowledgment. The primary undertaking of the arrangement prototype is to group the removed regions of interest introduced to its input into the street sign class they belong to. Various methods in picture characterization like Artificial Neural Networks, Support Vector Machines [20], Ambiguous measures, Genetic Procedures, Ambiguous sustenance Direction Machines, and Genetic Procedures with Neural Linkages are being established for street sign acknowledgment and arrangement. Using neural linkages, the signboards can be arranged in the proposed work.

3.3.1.2 IMAGE SEGMENTATION USING ROI

Another strategy for an area of interest-based picture segmentation that utilizes a naturally motivated specific consideration model is presented. One of the most significant concerns in picture division dependent on a region of interest (ROI) is how to select a semantic entity locale according to a specific purpose. For the abstraction of components from the different Regions of

Interest, we train or test the determined element routes by considering those pixels from the picture model collection. The flow of information includes Region of Interest (ROI) division and pre-processing, followed by embedding the information into the ROI and concealing the picture feature bits in the background. Traditionally, a road traffic symbol board picture consists of an ROI and a background. For the ROI, enhance the contrast of the picture to visualize the details more clearly. For the background, the enhancement process is unnecessary. Therefore, a segmentation operation is first accomplished to divide the picture into the ROI and the background. A better description of the ROI division is specified in Algorithm 1 (Table 3.1).

TABLE 3.1 Procedure for ROI Segmentation

Input	:	A traffic Signboard Image, I
Output	:	Region of Interest and background of image, I
Step 1	:	Load Image, I
Step 2	:	Acquire the segmentation/threshold on image
Step 3	:	Transform image into a biner image by threshold
Step 4	:	Find the indices I_0 and I_1 equivalent to the pixels with the values of '0' and '1' of binary image respectively
Step 5	:	The background and Region of Interest of image are produced that corresponds to Image (I_0) and Image (I_1),

To identify the pixels inside the overlying intermissions, a double area map with a similar size to the picture is produced. We set 1s at the areas of the pixels inside the two interludes comprising the minutest amount of pixels and set 0s at any remaining areas.

3.3.1.3 OCR INTERPRETATION

OCR is the acknowledgment of composed or transcribed typescripts by a supercomputer. This includes photograph checking of the text character-by-character, investigation of the scanned-in picture, and then interpretation of the character picture into character programs, like ASCII, normally used in data processing. OCR is an invention that authorizes one to converse over countless kinds of documents, for instance, checkered paper documents, PDF files, or photographs captured by a digital camera into modifiable and manageable facts.

OCR is a huge investigation region in plan affirmation. The objective of an OCR structure is to see consecutive eruditions, quantities, or countless characters, which are modernized pictures, with next to no human interference [21] which is displayed in Figure 3.2. This is sophisticated by means of glancing through a contest amongst the places of interest detached starting from the specified atmosphere's picture and the collection of picture prototypes. OCR has been discussed fundamentally and has had extraordinary achievements recently, for instance, in tag recognition verification [22] and text archives [23]. In any case, the equivalence with the standard OCR, the substance of the ordinary possibility is invigorating of the arbitrary designs, light conditions, divergence in the enactment, and circumstantial entities that can strengthen complications and cannot be systematized. A signpost detection association extracts the signposts that are accessible at the boundaries of the streets, ascertains them, and displays them on the automobile's control panel [24]. In several circumstances, OCR in methodical situations is still extraordinarily challenging because of the many variables that occur, such as an extensive variety of manuscript font, size, lighting, impediment, incline, angle, and adjacent confusion clatter [25]. In the projected process, OCR for categorizing the transcript from the road sign was recycled.

Transcript acknowledgment segments are as trails:

- Viewpoint rectification;
- Ascertain text characters;
- Arrange typescripts into outlines;
- OCR.

The contemporary effort displays a complete background of text acknowledgment from the road sign. The picture first seized from the external surroundings. The projected exertion is in the stage of pre-processing; henceforth no limited outcomes can be exposed. Here, it grants the notion of idea and the predictable output. In the preparation stage of the procedure, the input pictures are made up of the training dataset images caught. These input images enclose both writings as well as secret messages.

3.4 EXPERIMENTATION AND ANALYSIS OF RESULTS

3.4.1 DATASETS

The Chinese Road traffic symbol records incorporate traffic sign acknowledgment records, traffic sign recognition database, and road traffic board dataset. All records are gathered by a camera under environmental sights or commencing from BAIDU Path Sight. The dataset likewise ensures that this present reality of road traffic representation occurrences is one of a kind inside the dataset i.e., each road traffic sign merely happens one time. Examining the pictures and their arrangement, every picture simply holds back one road traffic sign respectively.

In the projected exertion, the dataset utilized is the Chinese transportation symbol acknowledgment dataset displayed in Figure 3.3, which encompasses pictures of numerous road signs like a stopover, speediness boundary, km/hr, etc.

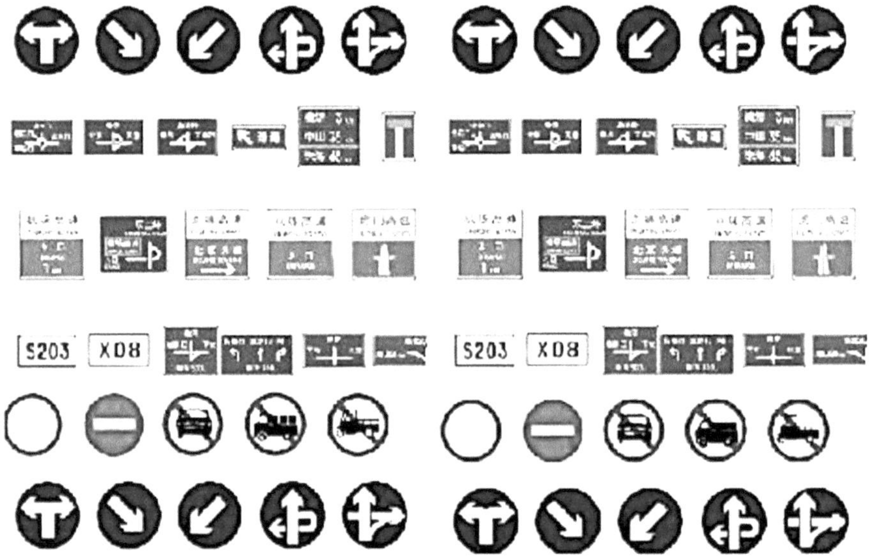

FIGURE 3.3 Chinese traffic sign dataset.

The Traffic Sign Recognition Database (TSRD) incorporates 6,164 road traffic symbol pictures comprising 58 sign classifications. The pictures are separated into binary sub-datasets as preparing datasets and challenging datasets. The preparing dataset incorporates 4,170 pictures while the testing one encompasses 1,994 pictures. All pictures are interpreted by the four synchronizes of the symbol and the class. The dissemination of the dataset can be well clarified with the assistance of Figure 3.4.

The Traffic Sign Discovery Database (TSDD) incorporates 10,000 road traffic sign pictures comprising numerous varieties of symbols as shown in Figure 3.5. The pictures are gathered under different times, weather circumstances, illumination situations, and moving obscuring.

FIGURE 3.4 Road traffic sign acknowledgment database.

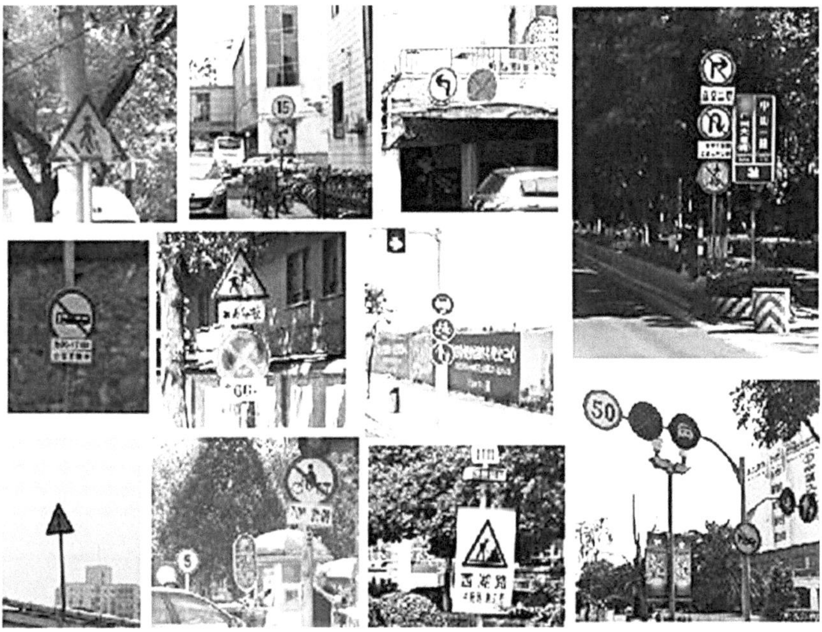

FIGURE 3.5 Traffic sign detection database.

The Traffic panel incorporates 2,329 road traffic pictures comprehending several sorts of road traffic boards. The pictures are gathered under an extensive assortment of diverse circumstances, like weather conditions, lighting, various environmental factors, incomplete obstruction, etc., as displayed in Figure 3.6.

FIGURE 3.6 Traffic panel.

3.4.1.1 *ACCURACY ANALYSIS*

All road traffic signs starting from the sidewalks are captured. These images are designated to contribute to the standard set of guidelines. The process is designed to recognize and interpret text and symbols from traffic signs. Test results showed improved performance, resulting in 78% to 93% accuracy for text recognition on signposts as shown in Table 3.2. This effort demonstrates that OCR aids in converting images into text, making it easier to understand. Through this process, the conversion from signpost to text is achieved, benefiting drivers by helping them navigate their route safely and avoid major accidents.

TABLE 3.2 Accuracy Analysis

Total Stages	Testing Samples	Recognition	Accuracy
Traffic signboard detection	1,000	931	93%
Text extraction	1,000	786	78.6%
Text recognition	1,000	760	76%

Here, 1,000 pictures are carefully chosen arbitrarily from ordinary divisions, and these example pictures were utilized for preparing and testing. For feature extraction, a modified version has been utilized. Neural Network has been chosen for the acknowledgment of these pictures. The purpose of this system is to distinguish and recognize road signs and measure the concert estimation. Table 3.2 displays the expected precision and the analysis test for acknowledgment of transcript abstraction and identification. The activation was carried out for the Chinese transportation symbol acknowledgment dataset. Testing model is the number of models engaged for analysis purposes, and acknowledgment would be exactly how many are appropriately accepted from the projected arrangement. The relationship between the challenging trial and acknowledgment is revealed in Figure 3.7. Accuracy is the proximity of a dimension to an explicit assessment, and in the planned work, 93% accuracy for road traffic sign recognition and 78.6% accuracy for text extraction is acquired as displayed in Figure 3.8.

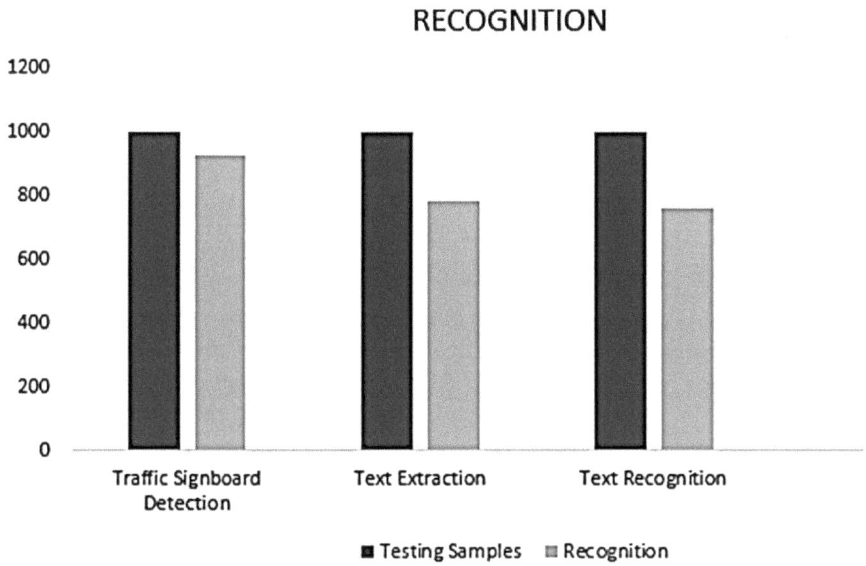

FIGURE 3.7 Text recognition.

The acknowledgement alongside training models is portrayed in Figure 3.7 and the efficacy is given in Figure 3.8. At this point, the trials and the precision have stood restrained by including the amount of appropriately acknowledged pictures.

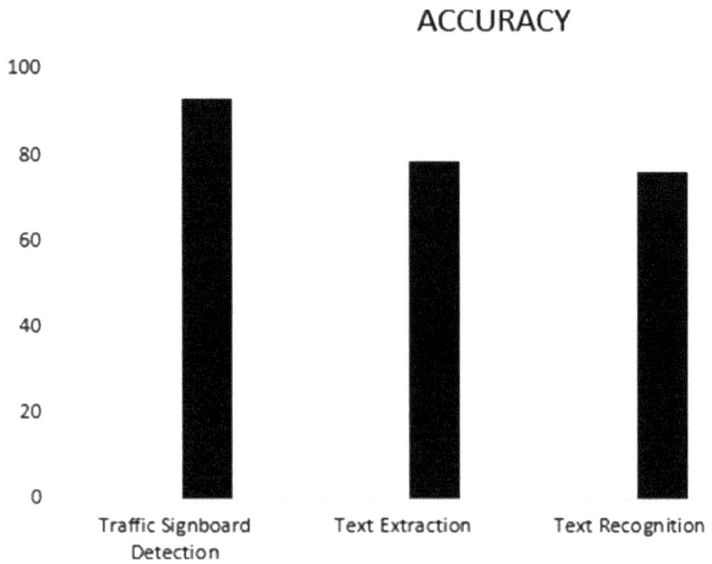

FIGURE 3.8 Accuracy analysis.

3.5 CONCLUSION

The work illustrates a complete background of text acknowledgment from regular prospects. The road traffic symbol discovery and recognition structure resolves the delinquency of classifying and understanding the road traffic symbol set on either sideways of the path. From side to side in this present work, it is probable to effectively convey on view the procedure of categorizing and understanding the road traffic symbol. The picture is first apprehended by the camera, from the outside environment, and then the method perceives the boundaries of a road sign from the datasets. The acknowledged street stream of traffic symbol is mined from the environment. A neural network is used for recognition. Each message of the script in the road transportation symbol panel is recognized and nursed into the OCR for understanding. Viewpoint presentation and sequential combination of applicant areas of the transcript were utilized to progress OCR outcomes. OCR distributes improved consequences for text acknowledgment. Investigational results designated improved enactment and ensued in 76% to 93% for text recognition road traffic signboard detection correspondingly. In forthcoming, OCR knowledge can be more enhanced so that typescripts can be discovered without normalization.

KEYWORDS

- **accuracy analysis**
- **efficient det**
- **optical character recognition**
- **road traffic signal object discovery and acknowledgment classification**
- **road traffic symbol discovery**
- **segmentation**
- **typescripts**

REFERENCES

1. Liu, C., Li, S., Chang, F., & Wang, Y. (2019). Mach vision-based traffic sign detection methods: Review, analysis and perspective. *IEEE Access, 7*, 86578–96.
2. Berkaya, S. K., Gunduz, H., Ozsen, O., Akinlar, C., & Gunal, S. (2016). On circular traffic sign detection and recognition. *Expert Systems with Applications, 48*, 67–75.
3. González, A., Bergasa, L. M., Member, IEEE, & Yebes, J. J. (2014). Text detection and recognition of traffic panels from highway flat images using visual appearance. *IEEE Transactions on Intelligent Transportation Systems, 15*(1), 228–238.
4. Jaderberg, M., Simonyan, K., Vedaldi, A., & Zisserman, A. (2016). Reading text in the wild with convolutional neural networks. *International Journal of Computer Vision, 116*(1), 1–20.
5. Greenhalgh, J., & Mirmehdi, M. (2015). Recognizing text-centered traffic flow signs. *IEEE Transactions on Intelligent Transportation Systems, 16*(3), 1360–1369.
6. Zhu, Y., Zhang, C., Zhou, D., Wang, X., Bai, X., & Liu, W. (2016). Traffic sign detection and recognition using fully convolutional networks guided proposal. *Neurocomputing, 214*, 758–66.
7. Baran, R., & Partila, P. (2018). Automated text detection and character recognition in natural sights based on local image topographies and contour processing performances. In *International Conference on Intelligent Human Systems Integration* (pp. 42–48). Springer, Cham.
8. Sahare, P., & Dhok, S. B. (2017). Review of text extraction algorithms for scene text and document images. *IETE Technical Review, 34*(2), 144–64.
9. Piccioli, G., De Micheli, E., Parodi, P., & Campani, M. (1996). Robust methods for sign detection and recognition. *Journal of Image and Vision Computing, 14*, 209–223.
10. Meena, A. K. (2019). Info from Signboards (Doctoral dissertation, IIT Delhi India).
11. Dahyot, R., & Charbonnier, P. (2000). Robust visual recognition of color images. Paper presented at *IEEE Conference on Computer Vision and Pattern Recognition*, Hilton Head Island, SC, USA.

12. Vazquez-Reina, A., Sastre, R. J. L., Arroyo, S. L., & Gil-Jimenez, P. (2006). Adaptive traffic șroad sign panels text extraction. In *Proceedings of the WSEAS International Conference on Signal Processing, Robotics and Automation* (pp. 295–300).
13. Wu, I. Z., & Chang, H. C. (2015). Signboard optical character recognition. *Tech. Rep.*, Stanford University, https://web.stanford.edu/class/ee368/Project_Autumn_1516/Reports/Wu_Chang.pdf.
14. Lauziere, Y. B., Gingras, D., & Ferrie, F. P. (2001). A model-based road sign identification system. Paper presented at *IEEE Computer Society Conference on Computer Vision and Pattern Recognition*, Kauai, Hawaii.
15. Hanwell, D., & Mirmehdi, M. (2009). Detection of lane departure on great speediness roads. In *Proceedings of the International Conference on Pattern Recognition Applications and Methods (ICPRAM)* (pp. 529–536).
16. Toaha, S. I., Asad, S. B., Rahman, C. R., Haque, S. M. S., Proma, M. A., Shuva, A. H., Ahmed, T., & Basher, A. (2020). *Automatic Signboard Detection and Localization in Densely Populated Developing Cities.* https://arxiv.org/pdf/2003.01936.
17. Naddaf-Sh, S., Naddaf-Sh, M., Kashani, A. R., & Zargarzadeh, H. (2020). An Efficient and Scalable Deep Learning Approach for Road Damage Detection. *2020 IEEE International Conference*.
18. Elfwing, S., Uchibe, E., & Doya, K. (2018). Sigmoid weight linear units for neural network function approximation in reinforcement learning. *Neural Networks, 107*, 3–11.
19. Ghiasi, G., Lin, T. -Y., Pang, R., & Le, Q. V. (2019). Learning scalable feature pyramid architecture for object detection. In *Proceedings of the IEEE/CVF Conference on Computer Vision and Pattern Recognition (CVPR)*.
20. Huang, J., Zhou, J., & Zheng, L. (2020). Support Vector Machine Classification Algorithm Based on Relief-F Feature Weighting. In *2020 International Conference on Computer Engineering and Applications (ICCEA)*.
21. Wu, I., & Chang, H. C. (2017). *Signboard Optical Character Recognition. 10*(7), 73–84 DOI:10.14257/ijsip.2017.10.7.07.
22. Wanniarachchi, W. K., Sonnadara, D. U. J., & Jayananda, M. K. (2007). License plate identification based on image processing techniques. In *2007 International Conference on Industrial and Information Systems* (pp. 373–378). IEEE.
23. Amin, A. (2015). A robust system for thresholding and skew detection in mixed text/graphics documents. *International Journal of Image and Graphics, 5*(02), 247–265.
24. Madre, S. C., & Gundre, S. B. (2018). OCR Based Image Text to Speech Conversion Using MATLAB. In *2018 Second International Conference on Intelligent Computing and Control Systems (ICICCS)* (pp. 858–861). IEEE.
25. Bissacco, A., et al. (2013). Reading text in abandoned circumstances. In *Proceedings of the IEEE International Conference on Computer Vision* (pp. 785–792).

CHAPTER 4

Recent Trends and Future Prospects of AI and Machine Learning in Decision Making

A. MUTHUSAMY,[1] S. MAHESWARI,[2] and S. ANITHA[3]

[1]*Assistant Professor, Department of Computer Technology (UG), Kongu Engineering College, Perundurai, Erode, Tamil Nadu, India*

[2]*Associate Professor, Department of Computer Science and Engineering, Faculty of Engineering and Technology, SRM Institute of Science and Technology, Tiruchirappalli, Tamil Nadu, India*

[3]*Assistant Professor, Department of Computer Applications, Faculty of Science and Humanities, SRM Institute of Science and Technology, Tiruchirappalli, Tamil Nadu, India*

ABSTRACT

Artificial Intelligence (AI) is currently advancing swiftly and is once again a popular academic topic. A wide range of cutting-edge technologies that continue to have an impact on daily life are included in AI. It improves decision-making by providing trustworthy information. This book chapter addresses the challenges associated with the application and impact of reviving AI and Machine Learning (ML)-based systems for decision-making in order to offer information systems researchers a set of research recommendations. The general use of AI and ML for decision-making is then discussed, along with issues relating to AI's interaction and integration with human decision-makers or to assist them in order to advance the study of AI application to decision-making in the ML and predictive analytics era.

Artificial Intelligence and Machine Learning for Business. Namita Mishra, A. V. Senthil Kumar (Eds.)

This chapter delves into some of the outlines and summaries of Artificial Intelligence and Machine Learning in Decision Making.

4.1 INTRODUCTION

Artificial Intelligence (AI) advocates for constructing smart machines competent in performing tasks that normally necessitate human intelligence. AI is employed to implement huge applications like Siri, Alexa, and other virtual assistants, self-driving cars, e-mail spam filters, and recommendation systems. LISP (List Processing) and PROLOG (Programming Logic) are the two leading AI languages. AI plays a vital role in all domains like Healthcare, Agriculture, Marketing, Banking, Finance, Gaming, Retail, and Self-Directed Vehicles [2]. Moreover, AI can be easily integrated with emerging technologies like Edge Computing, Soft computing, and Wireless technologies to implement intelligent applications. Alan Turing discussed the "Turing test" in 1950, which validates the performance of a machine. AI consists of two main categories, namely Machine Learning and Deep Learning as depicted in Figure 4.1. Machine learning makes computers perform tasks like human beings without explicit programming. ML predicts the future with the help of past historical data. Deep learning performs predictive analysis based on the algorithms related to the human brain's neural networks. For analyzing the massive amount of data, especially image data, deep learning (DL) is employed.

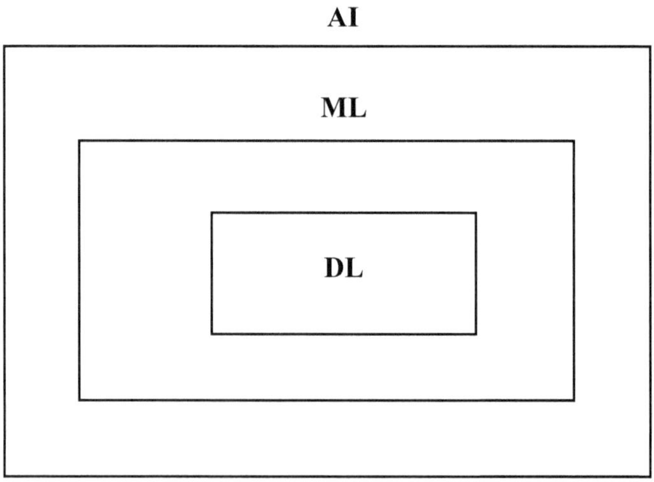

FIGURE 4.1 Association with AI, ML, and DL

4.1.1 NEED OF AI

AI advocates for businesses to increase their performance and profit. For example, Natural Language Processing (NLP)-based chatbots provide efficient customer service. AI can be easily integrated with other technologies like edge, fog computing, soft computing, mobile computing, NLP, and robotics to develop intelligent applications, as shown in Figure 4.2. Deep learning handles image data and also provides more accuracy than machine learning [1].

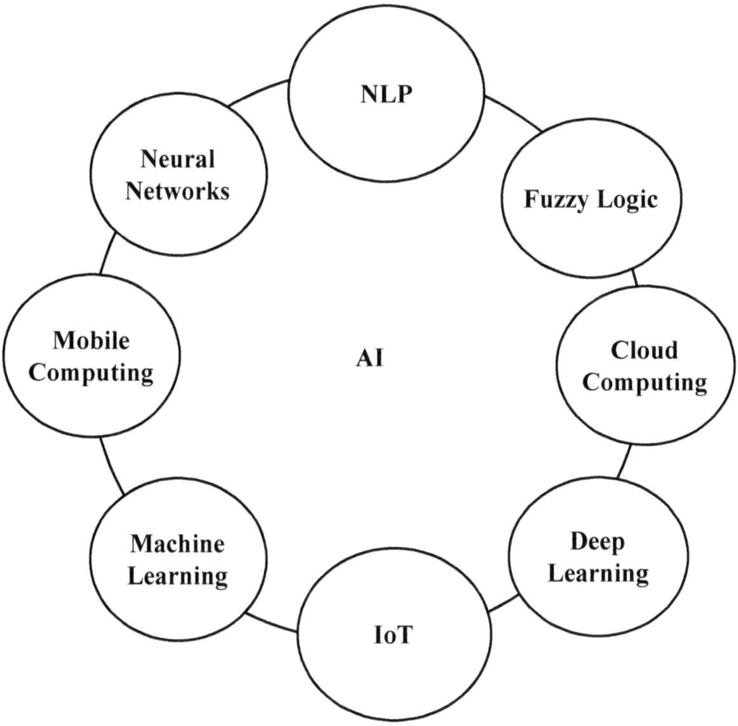

FIGURE 4.2 Interfacing AI with other technologies.

4.1.2 AI APPLICATIONS

Even though AI applications [3, 4] are difficult and expensive, industries are adopting AI-based technologies. For example, security systems, prediction and forecasting, product recommendation systems, and customer support for online stores. AI plays a vital role in Netflix for giving trends and suggestions.

Google Maps exploits AI to suggest an optimal route. The main difference between human intelligence and artificial intelligence is depicted in Table 4.1:

1. **AI in Marketing:** AI is exploited to attract more customers. For example, showing related advertisements on social media based on the searched item on any e-commerce store. In addition to these product recommendations, suggesting movies based on customers' reactions to movies and shows.
2. **AI in Banking:** Intelligent systems are offering customer support and detecting deceptive transactions. HDFC Bank is using an Artificial Intelligence-based bot termed EVA (Electronic Virtual Assistant) to give responses to customers' queries.
3. **AI in Finance:** AI advocates identify forthcoming trends in the stock market by examining a huge amount of historical data.
4. **AI in Healthcare:** AI systems aid doctors in diagnosing diseases quickly and reducing the Length of Stay (LOS) of patients in hospitals. Health monitoring systems and telemedicine help mitigate the mortality rate of patients.
5. **AI in Agriculture:** AI plays a vital role in precision agriculture for efficient crop cultivation and livestock management. For example, Plantix is an intelligent application to detect deficiencies in the soil.
6. **AI in Gaming:** AI makes games incredibly challenging and requires players to frequently change their movements and be cautious.
7. **AI in Autonomous Vehicles:** AI can be implemented as a digital transformation by integrating intelligent automation and data science, for example, driverless vehicles and digital manufacturing.
8. **AI in Virtual Assistants:** Text and voice-based chatbots are the most widely used technologies. AI is applied to convert human language into desirable actions. NLP (Natural Language Processing) helps machines understand human languages. For example, Siri, Alexa, and Google Assistant help make calls, book a vehicle, order food, and control household devices, in addition to simply playing favorite kinds of music.
9. **AI in Food Technology:** AI aids food processing companies in automating activities like selecting the size, shape, and color of chips.

10. **AI in Energy Generation:** AI technologies are employed for efficient and economical power generation and utilization, for example, continuous fine-tuning of turbines.
11. **AI in Oil and Gas Production:** AI promotes the performance and efficiency of oil & gas wells and also reduces hidden waste by analyzing underperforming wells and drilling operations. AI-based modeling mitigates downtime and equipment failure.
12. **AI in Security:** AI helps detect threats well in advance and also predicts future crime spots quickly. Moreover, it gives alerts and notifications to organizations at regular intervals.

TABLE 4.1 Human Intelligence vs. Artificial Intelligence

Parameters	Human Intelligence	Artificial Intelligence
Creativity	Higher due to natural thinking	Inferior to human intelligence
Decision making	From experience	From training data sets
Accuracy	Low and chance of committing errors	More accuracy than human intelligence
Social interaction	Better interaction	Poor social interaction due to the absence of emotions

4.2 SUMMARY OF AI AND ML IN DECISION-MAKING

- More and more often, businesses opt for solutions powered by big data, AI, and ML. These systems have the ability to combine data from several organizational operational areas, such as economics, organization, consumer service, etc.
- Automated cognitive and physical tasks are used by AI in decision-making. It is strong and supports the resolution of difficult issues. Making simple decisions, resolving complicated issues, launching strategic changes, assessing risks, and evaluating overall business performance are all made easier by it.
- Machine learning analyzes information using numerical metrics. The plan is to discover useful patterns (associations or connections) between different substances of facts.
- By utilizing datasets, AI and ML support the decision-making process and enable the company to get accurate and dependable conclusions.

- The analysis of huge datasets using AI and ML is error-free. Business teams can better focus on tasks relating to their areas of expertise thanks to this.
- AI and ML are able to train themselves to create models from data sets. These models can make precise classifications and decisions based on the given data. Similarly, the models make predictions, classifications, and recommendations based on the data in real time.
  - **Business Problem:** AI and ML on their own are not worth it. To be valuable, they have to be applied to a specific problem or goal.
  - **Choose a Metric to Optimize:** It can be measured by tenure, higher revenue, lower costs, customer acceptance, and sales churn.
  - **Select System Type and Applicable Events:** Develop decision support to determine which predictive models should be used to make these decisions.
  - **Process:** Apply the decision-making guidelines and predictive models.
  - **Automation Poses Ethical and Legal Risks:** If you are using automation to make judgments about people, you should test it first to ensure it does not have any unfair or illegal biases against specific groups.
  - Make the data scientist submit a checklist for each piece of information that appears in their models so that you can be sure the implementation platform has it.
  - A real-time system requires a monitoring process to assess it and compare the actual benefits to the forecasted ones.
  - As time goes on, the system may need to be modified or even completely redone due to new data, rules, changing business requirements, etc.
  - The core components that drive most AI and ML applications are Data input, Data pre-processing, Predictive models, Decision rules (rule sets), and Output.
  - **Data Input:** Sensory inputs from cameras, microphones, or other sources might be considered data input. Additionally, it contains pre-processed data, such as the data gathered when a person fills out a form online, information about purchases made with a credit card, or a person's credit history as provided by a credit reference service.

- **Data Pre-Processing:** Before being used, the raw data input needs to be transformed into a standard format.
- **Predictive Models:** These are created by the ML process employing historical knowledge or vast volumes of data. To provide new forecasts moving forward, pre-processed data for new cases is supplied into the algorithms.
- **Decision Rules or Rule Sets:** By itself, a prediction has no significance. Use rule sets or decision-making guidelines instead. Decision rules are coupled with data inputs, predictive model scores, and results to arrive at decisions. Sometimes the ML algorithm generates these rules automatically, but more often than not they also contain additional rules that have been defined by experts or business users in the actual world.
- **Output:** The conclusions that have been prepared require action to be taken.

4.3 RESEARCH IDEAS FOR AI AND ML IN DECISION-MAKING

Businesses are currently experiencing digital disruption, according to Gartner, due to the enormous amount of data they must handle. However, with the help of artificial intelligence (AI) and machine learning (ML), they are now able to transform all of that data into usable outcomes, from supply chains and demand planning to sales and marketing.

- **Decision-Maintain:** Analyzing data using various AI and ML techniques provides critical insights. The final decision is a combination of data-driven insights, human experience, emotion, and intelligence.
- **Decision Extension:** AI and ML can quickly analyze large amounts of complex data and recommend decisions. People can accept or reject AI recommendations based on their knowledge and expertise.
- **Decision Automation:** AI and ML predictive capabilities are accurate, consistent, and trusted enough to make decisions autonomously. The system can make its own decisions without human intervention.
- Operations are expected to be more important than profit and revenue growth. They are used in executive-level meetings to assist executives in making important decisions. The innovations of smart intelligent systems in various businesses are,
- In banking and financial services, incorporate AI & ML-based decision-making systems to identify fraud activities during the

processing of loan applications. This rigorous model analyzes loan applications from companies and efficiently predicts credit risk.

- AI and ML are involved in creating and marketing various products as automated and optimized ad campaigns with high conversion rates.
- Demand forecasting will be used for automated inventory management, and AI and ML will help retailers develop better strategies for checking product availability using intelligent shelving. This helps detect missing or unreadable barcodes. It also helps retailers increase margins and predict top-selling products by recognizing voice and gestures to interact with customers and make informed decisions throughout the product lifecycle.

The most common challenges in implementing the AI & ML are:

- Determining the correct dataset with transformation;
- Data storage and security;
- Infrastructure;
- AI integration into existing systems;
- Complex ML algorithms and training of AI models.

4.4 CASE STUDY: HEALTH CARE SYSTEMS-BABY MONITORING SYSTEM

For automated, intelligent, and smart systems to meet contemporary expectations, AI and ML-based modeling is required [5]. Utilizing systematic, practical, connected, lexical, illustrative, and different varieties of Artificial Intelligence can enhance an application's intelligence and capabilities. As a result, the major objective of Artificial Intelligence is to make it possible for machines and computers to carry out cognitive tasks including decision-making, observation, and comprehension of human communication. Understanding the principles of diverse AI approaches is essential to improving computers and decision-making to fulfill the demands of the Fourth Industrial Revolution as shown in Figure 4.3.

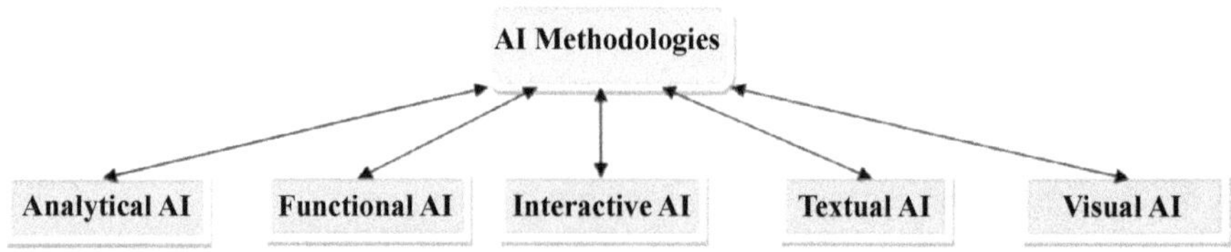

FIGURE 4.3 AI methodologies.

4.4.1 AI METHODOLOGIES

1. **Analytical AI:** Analytics is typically used to describe the procedure for locating, understanding, and sharing significant patterns in data. Systematic AI seeks to find fresh insights, patterns, correlations, or dependencies in data to aid in data-driven decision-making.

   An analytical AI version may be created using a number of machine learning and deep learning techniques to address a specific real-world issue. For instance, a data-driven analytical model may be used to assess business risk.

2. **Functional AI:** It works similarly to analytical AI, as it searches for patterns and dependencies in vast amounts of data. On the other hand, functional AI takes action rather than just offering suggestions. A functional AI model, for instance, might be used in robotics and Internet of Things applications to make quick decisions.

3. **Interactive AI:** Communication automation is often a conversational success, and conversational AI is firmly established in many areas of everyday life, especially in the business world. For example, interactive AI models can help develop chatbots and intelligent personal assistants.

4. **Textual AI:** Enterprises can benefit from the content generation capabilities of text recognition, speech-to-text, machine translation, and text analysis or natural language processing, a subset of artificial text intelligence. For example, companies can use Text AI to internally manage their corporate knowledge store to provide useful services such as answering client inquiries.

5. **Visual AI:** This often has the ability to perceive, classify, organize things, and draw conclusions from images and videos. As a result, visual AI can be viewed as a branch of computer science that teaches robots to acquire knowledge through images and visual information similar to humans.

4.4.2 FUNCTIONAL AI – CASE STUDY BASED ON DECISION-MAKING AND REASONING SYSTEMS IN HEALTHCARE

In India, both the mother and father want to work and look after their infants/ toddlers, so there is more workload and pressure on such families, especially on female counterparts. If a system is developed that constantly provides updates about their toddlers during illness or regular routines, it will be of great help to such individuals as they can work in a less stressful environment, giving more fruitful output. Also, urgent situations can be quickly identified and treated in less time. Usually, when a young child cries, the reason is one of the following things, i.e., they are hungry, tired, not feeling well, or need their diaper changed. So, we developed a prototype that can monitor the activities of the infants and/or toddlers along with identifying one of the above reasons and providing this information to their parents.

Women now make up a larger percentage of the labor force in wealthy nations than they did a few decades ago. As a result, many families now face a daily challenge in caring for infants. Moms are constantly concerned about their child's well-being. For such families, especially female coworkers, there is more work and stress since, as we have seen in India, both parents must work and care for their infants or toddlers. Such members will benefit much from the creation of a system that maintains the baby current in the face of illness and everyday life since they will be able to work more effectively in a stress-free setting. Additionally, emergencies are rapidly identified and may be handled. Small babies typically cry for one of the following reasons: A further benefit is that the configurable alarm state might lessen the errors brought on by typical sensors. The GSM interface is used for communication, and SMS (Short Messaging Service) is a crucial component of both the original GSM system and subsequent improvements.

4.4.2.1 PROBLEM DEFINITION

There are many home care systems available; however, the majority of these systems are created specifically for seniors and patients. These systems can perform a number of tasks, including automatically sending out emergency signals and monitoring their state of health. Infants are not cared for in the same ways, though. Adults and children need different types of care because they are completely dependent on others for their daily tasks. Infants cannot communicate their illnesses and health problems. When a child develops a fever, for example, he or she can only show their distress by crying. Infants cannot articulate themselves like older people can. Therefore, a system of home care specifically created for infants is necessary today and would greatly lessen the load on parents, especially mothers. Numerous research articles and patents for healthcare applications [6, 7] are examined in support of this requirement with the goal of finding potential solutions to care for infants.

4.4.2.2 OBJECTIVES

- To design and develop a cost-effective health monitoring system for babies/ patients using IoT.
- Wearable device is designed with RF or Biosensors.

In order to improve society, we may need to provide new technologies in our lives that can consume much less power and save precision and time. One such technology is the Internet of Things (IoT), which in a number of ways is ultimately aimed at improving life, saving energy and resources, and reducing time for seemingly unimportant tasks. Thanks to the Internet, we have been able to connect in ways we never imagined. As depicted in Figure 4.4, the Internet of Things will push us beyond linking and integrate us into a dynamic, living global system. The objective is to design and develop a cost-effective health monitoring system for babies/patients using IoT. Wearable devices are designed with RF or Bio sensor systems as shown in Figure 4.4.

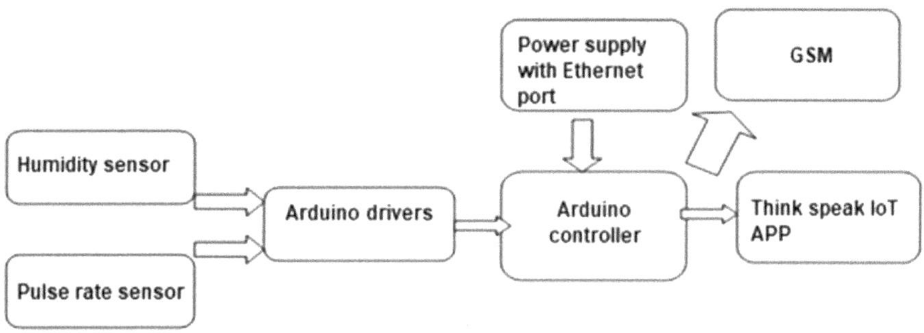

FIGURE 4.4 Overall design for proposed work.

1. **Humidity Sensor:** The environmental sensor picks up on the humidity, noise levels, and temperature of the baby's room. Pulse rate sensor interface with Arduino Uno. Connect Arduino analog pin A0 with the data out pin of the pulse rate and connect 5V and ground pin. A pulse sensor is attached to the child's finger and measures the child's heart rate before sending the information to the giant controller. The giant controller sends data to the cloud and stores it online in the appropriate fields. A text editor for script code, a communication area, a manuscript console, a toolbar with buttons for important operations, and several menus are all included in the Arduino-incorporated progress location. Connect to Arduino and Genuino hardware to download and operate programs (Figure 4.5).

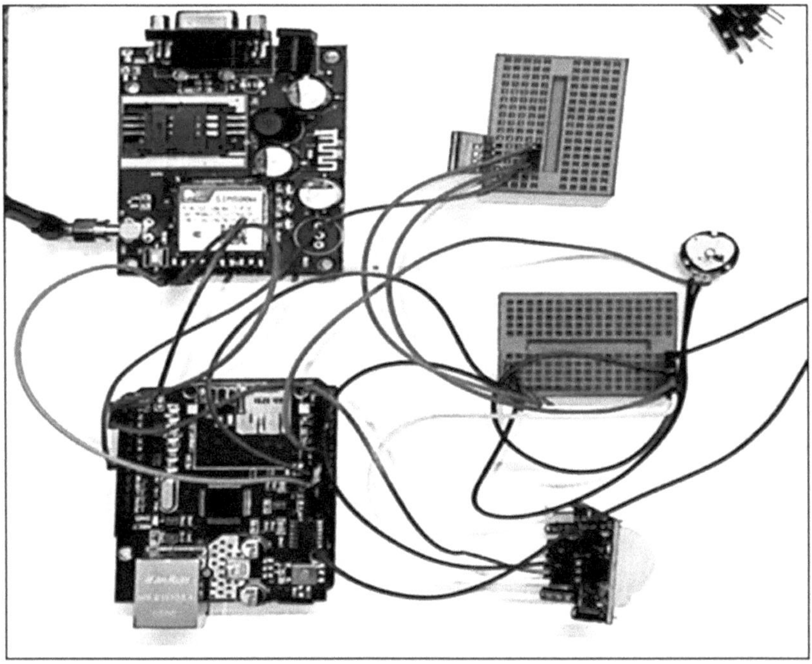

FIGURE 4.5 The complete structure of the cost-effective and compact design.

2. **Ethernet:** The library allows the Arduino board to connect to the Internet. It can act as a client that initiates connections or as a server that accepts incoming connections. The libraries can handle up to four connections at once (incoming outgoing or a combination). The W5100 chip is managed by the Ethernet library (Ethernet.h), while the W5500 chip is managed by the Ethernet2 library (Ethernet2.h); all the functions are the same in both libraries. The same code can be transferred from an Arduino Ethernet Shield to an Arduino Ethernet 2 Shield, an Arduino Leonardo Ethernet, and vice versa by changing the library That is being used. For mobile communication, there is the GSM global system. Global system controlled only by the parents. By the use of thingspeak, we can monitor a child's health condition anywhere in the world. So we can easily predict their situation. If anything goes wrong with their health condition, we will take action immediately with the help of the corresponding person by sending a message through the GSM as shown in Figure 4.5.

4.5 CONCLUSION AND DISCUSSION

The proposed infant monitoring system is an inexpensive and easy-to-use device that can improve the quality of communication between children and parents. This system gives parents a sense of security. Continuous recording of some of the baby's biological parameters and analysis of general health will help the mother understand the baby's internal condition. It uses GSM technology, allowing users to communicate over long distances. This is a convenient system for monitoring your baby's health from anywhere. Therefore, we propose a "baby health monitoring system." Using the Internet of Things and Hardware is more beneficial to all working parents and is useful for observing every movement of the baby along with their health. To overcome all the shortcomings of existing systems, parents can track their current location and have remote access over long distances. Therefore, the proposed system is much more efficient than the existing system.

KEYWORDS

- **Arduino ethernet 2 shield**
- **artificial intelligence**
- **baby health monitoring system**
- **decision-making**
- **internet of things**
- **machine learning**
- **mobile communication**

REFERENCES

1. Finlay, S. (2018). *Artificial Intelligence and Machine Learning for Business* (3rd ed.). ISBN: 978-1-999-73034-5.
2. Ghosh, B., Daugherty, P. R., Wilson, H. J., & Burden, A. (2019). *Taking a Systems Approach to Adopting AI,* Harvard Business Review, May 9, 2019.
3. Nair, S., Augustine, N., & Varghese, L. (2020). Smart health monitoring system. *International Journal of Engineering Research and Technology, 9*(6), 1–6.

4. Zhao, H., Chen, P. -L., Khan, S., & Khalafe, O. I. (2021). Research on the optimization of the management process on internet of things (IoT) for electronic market. *The Electronic Library, 39*(4), 526–538.
5. Raisch, S., & Krakowski, S. (2021). Artificial Intelligence and Management: The Automation-Augmentation Paradox. *Academy of Management Review, 46*(1), 192–210.
6. Devine, J. K., Schwartz, L. P., Chounowski, J., & Hursh, S. R. (2022). Expert Demand for Consumer Sleep Technology Features and Wearable Devices: A Case Study. *IoT, 3*(2), 315–331.
7. Hossain, J., Bari, A., & Monirujjaman Khan, M. (2022). Development of an IoT Based Health Monitoring System for e-Health. *IEEE 12th Annual Computing and Communication Workshop and Conference (CCWC).*

CHAPTER 5

Socio-Economic Impact Analysis of Russo-Ukrainian War Based on Tweets Using Opinion Mining

DESAI KARANAM SREEKANTHA,[1] R. S. KAMATH,[2] and R. K. KAMAT[3]

[1] *Professor, Department of Computer Science and Engineering, NMAM Institute of Technology, Nitte (Deemed to be) University, Mangalore, Karnataka, India*

[2] *Associate Professor, Chhatrapati Shahu Institute of Business Education and Research, Kolhapur, Maharashtra, India*

[3] *Vice Chancellor, Dr. Homi Bhabha State University, Mumbai, Maharashtra, India*

ABSTRACT

The antagonistic relationship between Russia and Ukraine dates back in history. Russia considers the objective of Ukraine joining the North Atlantic Treaty Organization (NATO) as a risk to Russia's internal safety, so they are opposing Ukraine's move from joining NATO. Ukraine has not accepted Russia's proposal. Russia attacked Ukraine on 24th February 2022. The European Union (EU) and the USA have imposed severe sanctions on Russia as a countermeasure. The current Russia-Ukraine war is the most significant after World War II. This war has an immense influence on the global economy, oil prices, and other important sectors such as health, finance, geopolitics, a swift refugee crisis, and infrastructure. The imports and exports of goods and services across the world are seriously disturbed. The International Organization for Migration has predicted that about seven million people will

Artificial Intelligence and Machine Learning for Business. Namita Mishra, A. V. Senthil Kumar (Eds.)

be displaced because of this war. There is a huge requirement for military and humanitarian needs. The African and Middle Eastern countries that were importing grains from Ukraine and Russia are now facing shortages. This chapter reviews the literature on the impact of war to present a sector-wise analysis. Social media is a real-time platform for sharing/posting opinions. The author's objective is to analyze the socioeconomic impacts of the Russia-Ukraine war by analyzing opinion-based tweets across the world. The authors analyzed the tweets using various machine-learning techniques and compared the results. The visualization of results is represented as graphs to help the administration implement appropriate policies.

5.1 INTRODUCTION

The Russia-Ukraine war has influenced many economic, infrastructural, social, health, and geopolitical aspects across the world. The world has witnessed severe disruptions in the supply of essential goods such as food, and oil, and services such as healthcare, resulting in steep hikes in prices.

The geographical position of Ukraine has gained importance for the stability of the region because it is between Russia and Central Europe. Ukraine's main exports are mainly minerals, gas, and oil. Ukraine's black soil is highly fertile in the world. The opposition between Ukraine and Russia started in 1954. The invasion of Ukraine by Russia has compelled a large number of people to leave Ukraine and move to surrounding countries such as Romania, Moldova, Poland, Hungary, Belarus, Russia, and Slovakia. Severe restrictions on imports, payments, and exports of goods and services are implemented in Russia. The refugee agency of the United Nations has estimated that about 8.3 million citizens might be displaced from Ukraine and need all humanitarian support from the rest of the world. Refugees need money, food, education, housing, and transportation. Russia and Ukraine are mainly exporting fertilizer, cooking oil, corn, barley, and wheat to Middle Eastern and African countries. The interruptions in the supply chain of goods and services are leading to hikes in prices, forcing several million people to starve. Nations such as Afghanistan, North Africa, West Africa, Congo, Syria, Iraq, and Lebanon are consuming large quantities of food grains from Ukraine and Russia. Gas prices across the globe are at an all-time high. Ukraine has created about six thousand Nigerians because of the war. International bodies such as UNESCO, UNICEF, UN, Red Cross, other local governments, and civic bodies are providing humanitarian support to refugees.

5.2 REVIEW OF RECENT LITERATURE

The public healthcare services and supply of medicine are seriously affected in Ukraine because of the war [1]. Ukraine's population is 44.1 million and 4.99 million people are suffering from COVID-19 infection and one hundred thousand people have died by 22nd April 2022. The tourism and hospitality industries, companies, and businesses using gas are severely affected by the lack of supply of gas and the hike in prices resulting in the loss of jobs across Europe. Nigerian refugees have acknowledged the receipt of financial, social, and moral support received from the world. Mounting disputes in Russia and Ukraine have posed an urgent and increasing risk to the life and safety of 7.5 million children and women [2]. Humanitarian demands are ever-increasing. Many children have died and been injured. Children are severely frightened by the savagery going around them. Millions of citizens are displaced and children and women are isolated from their family members. The prevailing conflict of the previous eight years in the east region of Ukraine has led to a long-term adverse impact on the children of Ukraine and Russia. UNICEF is helping in enhancing the delivery of humanitarian services in the affected regions. Thousands of houses have collapsed and public infrastructure such as hospitals, schools, and roads have been damaged, leaving millions of people unsafe and unhygienic without basic services. The Ukrainian government has declared that thousands of people have been killed since the civil war started. The United Nations (UN) stated that about 7.5 million children have faced difficulties during the war. This paper has studied the application of social media by the refugees of Nigeria who are affected by the Russia and Ukraine wars [3]. The authors explored the parameters to express their gratitude for the aid received.

The data was collected using a well-designed online questionnaire. The outcome of this survey revealed a result of the study that showed an important affirmative association between help-seeking methods in social media and the help they received. The gratitude was effectively communicated for macro-level help received compared to micro and medium-level support received. The authors have revealed the results effectively. There was huge public demand for imposing severe sanctions on businesses and corporations to quit Russia after its invasion [4]. The authors studied the decisions of multinational corporations and the behavior of the markets between 3rd February to 8th March 2022. This period represents the beginning of the invasion by Russia of Ukraine on 24th February and a couple of prominent news declarations in public newspapers about companies that remained in and the companies that left Russia during the period 28th February and 3rd March 2022. Many companies preferred to maintain Russian business.

The authors investigated the stock market reflections on imposing sanctions on those companies that remained in Russia even two significant weeks after the invasion. Investors imposed significant market penalties on those companies that stayed in Russia. There is enough evidence to show the high volume of trading and the pressure to sell the stock of those companies that remained in Russia. These findings revealed that a portfolio of those companies that stayed in Russia underperformed compared to those companies that left Russia. This study suggests that stock markets are very responsive to the decisions of corporations when political problems prevail in the country. Apart from this, hundreds of very rich people had their assets seized who had good relations with the government of Russia. Many companies suspended their commercial operations in Russia in response to social media warnings from customers banning their products (e.g., Coca-Cola). Despite this, only a few companies remained in Russia despite sanctions, troubles in banking transactions, and negative public sentiment. The authors identified the remaining companies based on a day-to-day revised list of companies and cross-referenced them with other public sources like CNN and Business Insider. The authors noted twenty-two stocks, six of which traded on NASDAQ and the rest on NYSE. A total of twenty companies remained as of March 10th, continuing their operations and business in Russia even after two weeks of the invasion.

The authors matched the list of twenty-eight companies that remained in Russia with the corresponding companies that left Russia. Special focus is on two dates, i.e., 28th February and 3rd March 2022. Some companies were selected for imposing sanctions, and other firms were criticized on many news channels for keeping quiet. The healthcare ecosystem in Ukraine is already under severe pressure because of an increasing amount of fatalities and adverse consequences due to the war on the social and economic front [5]. The shortage of clean drinking water and sanitation facilities, lower COVID-19 vaccine coverage, excess crowds, and non-availability of basic health facilities are anticipated to aggravate the conditions.

UN children's agency UNICEF states that several hundred thousand refugees from Ukraine are youth. Anxiety, social withdrawal, and depression are some of the mental and physical health issues that will affect people in the long term. There is a challenge for hosting EU nations to maintain the good mental and physical well-being of refugees. A few problems arising from the war include radioactive materials, heavy metals, and chemical wastes penetrating natural water bodies from damaged industries, water dams, gasoline sites, hydrocarbon leakage from war-affected areas, weapons fires, and leakages in coal mines. The authors estimated the mental and social effects of war on the children of Ukrainian patients and their family members who are suffering from cancer. These patients left Ukraine before the invasion [6]. The family members have expressed their concerns after the Russian-Ukraine war. The problems of cancer patients can be outlined in four categories: 1. Mental pressure faced by the patients, children, family relatives, members, and relatives due to the dangers of war. 2. Problems faced in accessing past health records in Ukrainian hospitals. 3. Support for health expenditure. 4. Unpredictability related to the patients' and their families' lives in the year to come and the uncertainty of children returning home. Mental stress regarding how long this war will continue and when the families will reunite and return home. Financial and property concerns about leading a life in war-affected Ukraine. The transfer of health records from Ukraine was very difficult because of the damage caused to cancer treatment centers. Loss of jobs and income is a big concern for refugees to return to their homeland and continue their medical treatment because of the extensive damage caused to civil and health infrastructures by war.

The people of Ukraine have shown exceptional resilience to the ongoing war [7]. The effect of war on patients was very significant. The method of integrating the wisdom of the crowd to solve a particular problem is called crowdsourcing. This community-based problem-solving approach was applied to solve the problem of access to healthcare services. The production of sufficient medicine for consumption to treat opioid disorders and HIV was not possible during the war period. The crowdsourcing method applied to procure the medicine from countries outside Ukraine was very much needed at the hour. This approach has saved the lives of seventeen thousand opioid patients in Ukraine, with one-half of these also suffering from HIV. This crowdsourcing method helped the patients to improve their health and reduce the public health burden in Ukraine.

Forty-four million is the population of Ukraine, out of which about 1.3 million are suffering from cancer [8]. Every year, about 160,000 new cases of cancer are registered. There are local cancer treatment centers in every region, and there are sophisticated oncological centers in big cities. Patients can access all advanced facilities for cancer treatment. Cardio-oncology was also set up in Europe and Ukraine recently. War has damaged the advanced cancer healthcare ecosystem. Medical care systems and services are completely stopped in war-affected zones. Excessive pressure and life threats prevail on medical professionals and patients. The stocks of medicine were partially damaged. A shortage of medicines exists, particularly in the Eastern and Southern parts of Ukraine.

The EU and WHO have teamed up to shift patients from Ukraine for medical treatment. The WHO is helping the refugees by providing healthcare free of cost. New legislation was enacted to help refugees migrating to Romania to take advantage of healthcare even for cancer. The Czech Republic has set up a contact center with Ukrainian language support for refugees to seek help and visit cancer centers. Hungary has also set up a central interpreter point for cancer patients. The happiness levels of the people drastically reduced in areas directly affected by a war based on the survey from the Journal of Economic Behavior and Organization [9]. The areas that are not directly involved in the war are primarily as happy as they were before the start of the war. The children in Germany which are highly war-affected areas have minimum schooling, grow less physically, and have less self-confidence and less satisfaction [10]. During the Eritrean-Ethiopian war also the children from highly impacted regions had lesser age-for-height points when compared to children from less affected regions. The study of the war in Bosnia and Herzegovina revealed that even several years after the end of the war, people living in municipalities which are heavily affected by the war were less satisfied with their lives than people living in municipalities that were not heavily affected by war. Russia's invasion of Ukraine has further worsened the conditions, creating threats on to what degree South Caucasus nations can depend on the Western world [11]. Now, Azerbaijan, Armenia, and Georgia have distinct demographic policies. Georgia has joined the Euro-Atlantic track, and Armenia stuck to the Russian-led Eurasian Union in January 2015. Last year, Russia's unlawful occupation of Crimea and its current backed war in the eastern part of Ukraine raised concerns and well challenged the accepted world order and the understanding not to redefine the boundaries of the EU. It has also questioned the EU as an external threat in its next region. Russia invaded Georgia in 2008 without any loss.

This reaction of Russia reinforced that it paid no price for its invasions. In hindsight, this was a serious mistake, as Russia believes that the EU and NATO are weak and will perish. The EU appeared to test Ukraine's dedication to the EaP partnership and its capability to handle Russia. The former Soviet Union was threatened by the South Caucasus as a very complicated and unsafe area because of its demographic position in Europe and Central Asia. The future of the South Caucasus was influenced by many foreign nations such as the Russian, Persian, and Ottoman empires. Georgia's external strategy is bound to Euro-Atlantic integration and EU membership in full. The authors surveyed the history of financial sanctions and their role in theories of disincentives and settling disputes [12]. The authors have presented a few strategic inferences that can be generic to strengthen previous research. The banks heavily rely on transactions in dollars in Russia. The systematic policies implemented by Russia have promoted its financial supremacy for extended economic inclusion. The authors believed that financial sanctions have influenced the Russian budget and that this impact was aggravated by the Covid-19 pandemic. The debt placements are made very tactically to delay the exacerbation of sanctions. Russia has reinforced its defense program, invading Crimea and promoting proxy war in Ukraine's eastern regions.

The selected economic sanctions were imposed in 2014 to be in effect up to 2021. Some political observers believe that Russia's reactions are self-destructive and still operational as of 2021. Russia's choice of action initially appeared to be economically self-destructive. Russia believed that Ukraine was willing to become a member of the EU and it would be a threat to Russia's supremacy and security. So Russia invaded to bear the cost of the invasion of Ukraine. The financial sanctions imposed on Russia by the US and EU in July 2014 were created to have an accruing impact on the Russian stock market by restricting its entry to banks and companies of Russia for a long period. The authors have reviewed the impact of sanctions on the Russian economy after seven years. President Vladimir Putin suggested in November 2019 that the damages brought to the Russian economy by sanctions were below 50 billion USD, and he has also stated that these lost business dollars were completely regained by regional Russian companies. Many estimated that the impact of the sanctions on Russian GDP was between 0.5 to 1.5% of GDP yearly in the medium term, and found a simultaneous oil shock in the short term. These total losses account for 40 to 120 billion USD between 2014 and 2018. This loss is not small and cannot be neglected, which is opposite to President Putin's statement.

Some reviewers felt that these sanctions were not very effective because they could not change Russian foreign policy. Russian companies that issued securities on the euro-bond stocks have shown a steep increase in corporate interest rates by 0.5 to 1.0% points. There are many instances of Russian firms losing business after being targeted by American sanctions, such as Rosneft Trading in 2020 and Rusal in 2018, and these instances have confirmed quick and important strategic issues for Russian policymakers compared to the progressive sanctions on the internal bank and state-sponsored debt markets that author emphasized studying. The sanctions have the effect of reducing competitors' abilities without imposing concessions. The sanctions on Russia have progressed in many stages. In July 2014 many serious financial sanctions were imposed on access to credit to Russian banks and companies. In April 2018, severe sanctions were imposed on many Russian companies, blocking them from world-dollar business transactions and restricting them from carrying out business with non-Russian counterparts. Russia has introduced a de-dollarization plan to counter the impact of the sanctions. The initial set of US financial sanctions imposed on Russia involved small banks being stopped from dollar transactions with US companies such as Visa and Mastercard. This event revealed that Russian banks depend on clearing and processing systems executed by Western firms, quickly having political influence. Russia intended to worsen the conflict by the summer of 2014. As a result, the West imposed severe sanctions focusing on the financial sector after July 15, 2014. Oil prices decreased and began to impact the financial sector, creating a crisis in the fall of 2014. Russia started experiencing a severe economic slowdown. Two out of three major credit rating agencies reduced their rating for Russia's government debt to non-investment grade. This marked the beginning of Russia being removed from Western bond markets as expected. Russia's debt strategy was integrated into the entire government's way of confronting the West. The Trump administration (2017–2021) displayed less political will for sanctions on Russia. The Trump administration's unwillingness to impose sanctions on Russian debt forced a few Russian finance officials to comment that the liberalization policy of the early 2000s had proven fruitful since it provided Russia with some protection against severe sanctions. However, the US has imposed many new sanctions focusing on specific people and companies in 2018. Russia's financial integration has helped Eurobonds trading through the Russian framework and OFZs trading on the international framework. The outcome shows a severe impact because of the war, especially from the first two weeks after the invasion of Ukraine on 24 February 2022 [13]. The response from global stock markets was not strong after the invasion. Only those countries sharing borders with Ukraine and Russia, and members of the UN have shown strong market reactions. The New York Times and the S&P 500 index reported on the day of the attacks and fell by more than 10% from its recent peak as its first correction since October 2020.

The authors studied the data of stock market returns on a day-to-day basis from 94 countries' data samples from 22nd January 2022 to 24th March 2022. This paper showed a negative and prominent impact of the armed battle between Russia and Ukraine on the global stock market. Data related to the Ukraine-Russia war was captured from Wikipedia Trends using panel data. The results showed that the conflict between Russia and Ukraine has a crucial negative effect on the world stock market performance indices. This study showed a stronger impact on the stock market at the start of the war (especially two weeks after the invasion), this effect became fragile after three to four weeks, thus emphasizing a setback in global stock markets. However, the effect was considerably higher for the nations that opposed the invasion.

About 3 million refugees have entered Poland seeking help, which accounts for about 56% of total refugees [14]. There were thousands of refugees, mostly women and children, waiting at very low temperatures before the war broke out with their animals and some luggage. Refugees' capital and skills have determined the level of help they receive in the host country for several weeks. Refugees who knew several languages could receive better aid. Those who had friends and relatives found better places to stay and felt more comfortable in the host country. In the end, many services were also provided online. Online networks offered information on the availability of food, shelter, products, and medicines as immediate relief. Several hotels, pubs, and other food establishments served good meals and drinks. Three weeks after the invasion, Poland enacted a special act to help refugees access social services and healthcare, and children who were admitted to Poland attended schools. Poland provided financial assistance to citizens who accommodated refugees in their homes. Many volunteers supported refugees through language interpretation and provided information to those who had lost family members and were confused.

Police and the army also provided food and shelter to refugees. Refugees are helped less and unable to make any decisions. Volunteers help refugees by providing all necessary information and answering their questions. The refugees are expecting that war will come to an end and they will return to their land to rebuild their houses, and some are planning to settle in host countries only. The paper studied the problems faced by Ukraine after President Yanukovich left Ukraine and the induction of a pro-European and pro-NATO Union government [15]. Russia's reactions are understood in the broad context of the political changes in the Soviet space, the enlargement of the European Union, and the expansion of NATO. Russia's economic and defense strengths and weaknesses are compared in the context of the developments in the Eurasian Economic Union. Russian policy by President Putin was defensive and reactive. Russia has displayed its geo-political objectives by geographical expansion through invasion. The Western countries are facing a major warning from the Eastern countries in the form of a cold war. President Putin's objective is to safeguard Russia's supremacy, culture, and national interests, and he wants to have a monopoly on power. Putin is opposed to Western dominance, and his interest in state supremacy is only a way to empower Putin personally. The Russian Federation projects as an "active" problem to the international order.

The European Union would like to expand its influence by imparting economic wealth and democratic values to Europe. The oil market prices always influence other financial services and commodity prices. Escalating oil prices created huge instability in the global economy during the war period [16]. The authors studied fluctuating oil price data related to major financial elements, namely stocks, the U.S. dollar, gold, bitcoin, and bonds before and during the war. Oil became a net transmitter of spillovers during the war period. The world economy was just recovering after the COVID-19 pandemic, and this war has created a major problem in the process of recovery [17]. At this moment, food ecosystem management is very urgent and should be taken up due to the ongoing Ukraine war. Russia and Ukraine are major producers of fuel, fertilizer, and growers of wheat, maize, and oilseeds in the world. Exports are seriously disturbed because of the war. Africa and the Middle East heavily rely on grain imports from Russia and Ukraine. Ever-increasing grain prices could force millions of people in these countries into starvation.

The expected shocks to food markets have also called for short-sighted suggestions like pausing sustainable agricultural methods that are part of the EU's Farm2Fork policies and enhancing Europe's grain production capabilities to ensure animal feed supply. A new trend toward more human consumption of fruits, legumes, and vegetables, and fewer animal products in Europe could considerably increase pressure on the world grain supply chain. Energy-intensive nitrogen fertilizers are extensively used in European agriculture. Russia is one of the largest producers of fertilizer and natural gas in the world. The supply chain of gas and fertilizers is highly affected by war.

Europe has implemented a Farm2Fork agriculture policy that would enhance soil quality and make biodiversity stronger in lands supporting sustainable agriculture. Reducing the quantity of food waste globally by 2030 is also an integral part of the sustainable development goals. European countries should modify their policies to ensure that poor, food-importing countries do not become food insecure. Food banks and social security systems in EU countries aim to prevent the adverse effects of increasing food prices for poor people. The adverse effects of war on children are terrible and manifold. War affects children in attacking and attacking countries, as well as children in countries not actively involved in the conflict [18]. Children of countries under attack bear the adverse effects of war. They endure severe injuries and extensive burns, leading to higher mortality rates. Healthcare services are disrupted, causing a shortage of medicines and halting regular preventive care, such as childhood vaccinations. During times of war, violence against children and child labor increase in refugee conditions. Many children become separated from their families and friends. Poverty, security issues, lack of access to education, and inadequate sanitation facilities represent additional burdens and can result in post-traumatic stress disorders.

This paper examines the perceptions of the current political and military conflict in and around Ukraine by political and policy observers from the United Kingdom, the United States, France, Germany, Poland, Italy, and Greece [19]. By incorporating strategic descriptive reports and theoretical concepts, the authors outline the main aspects of the conflict, identify the structural policies of each narrative, and analyze their implementation. The authors propose six key interpretations of the Russian–Ukrainian conflict based on their understanding of the events and their proposed solutions. In each country, the predominant policies demonstrate a certain level of alignment between political interests, priorities, and academic/analytical ideologies. The first interpretation focuses on Russia's deliberate aggression, illustrated by a series of events including the annexation of Crimea, support for separatist movements in the southeast, and direct involvement in the conflict in the Donbas.

It projected the dispute as international, and its main policies are Russia's complete responsibility for the militant action and its infringement of international law, which should be responded to by suppression. Hence, the West has intensified its actions to oppose the aggression by imposing harsh sanctions on Russia. The EU has provided much help to Ukraine in a short time and supported its democracy and European integration over the long term. Russia's actions are perceived as a legal reaction to a warning from the West approaching its conventional areas of influence and/or irrational strategies of the post-Euromaidan state of Ukraine. This narrative transfers the basic responsibility to the West and Ukraine, from Russia, and considers Russian reactions as an expected opportunistic move rather than a strategy in its own right. Russia's main objective was to fight with Ukraine in the eastern and southern regions.

This narrative revolves around the intentionally irreconcilable identity differences between Kyiv and/or essentialized "Western Ukraine," on the one hand, and the east-southern regions of Ukraine, on the other. The perceived differences between Russian speakers and Ukrainian speakers or pro-Europeans and pro-Russians. At the outset, there is equal responsibility on all sides. The conversation between all parties is essential to bring an end to the suffering of the affected populations. Also, extra pressure is exerted from the national interest perspective, be it the perceived priority of maintaining political/economic/energy relations with Russia or the wish to weaken US hegemony. This study analyzed various trends in tweets, emotions, and polarity. The tweets for the current analysis are retrieved from Kaggle, an online data science platform, and also by accessing Twitter APIs using a Twitter app [20, 21]. Thus, the derived dataset is analyzed using open-source packages provided in Python and R to identify the prevailing opinion expressed in the tweets. The dataset has a standard set of features extracted, such as user details, date of the tweet, URLs, tweet text, re-tweet details, hashtag, source, etc. This dataset contains 50,000 tweet records for the period from 24th February 2022 to 5th March 2022. As Russia invaded Ukraine on 24th February 2022, the tweets from this date are considered for analysis. The analysis of war-based tweets revealed a mixed opinion of the public toward war. Thus, the present exploration concludes that opinion mining of Twitter data has the potential to be a suitable tool for analyzing public opinions on the Russia-Ukraine war.

5.3 PROPOSED METHODOLOGY

Twitter is a social networking and micro-blogging platform that allows users to express their views openly. Opinion mining is the practice of monitoring emotions in posts on social media platforms to gain insights into the public's opinions [22]. This is a key strategy used in social media analysis. The experiment carried out to accomplish the tweet analysis is shown in Figure 5.1. To use the Twitter API, an application on developer.twitter.com is created. Then, the Python libraries are used to access its functions. The app keys and tokens are used to access the data. The Python package "tweepy" is used to extract tweets made with the #Ukraine War hashtag. Hashtags are used to group tweets so they can be more easily searched.

FIGURE 5.1 Flowchart of war-based tweets analysis.

The step-by-step procedure for conducting tweet analysis is shown in Figure 5.1:

1. An application named "Russia Ukraine War Disaster" was created on developer.twitter.com to use the Twitter API.
2. The app keys (API key, Secret) and tokens (access token, secret) are used for Twitter authentication.
3. The "tweepy" package was used to extract tweets made with the #Ukraine War hashtag. Hashtags are a way to group tweets so that they can be more easily searched.
4. Authors have used the tweets dataset from Kaggle [20]. The dataset includes a standard set of features like user details, tweet date, URLs, tweet text, retweet details, hashtags, source, etc. The dataset used for analysis comprised 50,000 tweet records from February 24, 2022, to March 5, 2022.
5. Data pre-processing was carried out by converting raw data into lowercase and removing punctuation, numbers, and URLs.
6. Tokenization is the process of breaking up a sequence of strings into individual pieces, called tokens.
7. Python libraries such as Seaborn, NLTK, and WordCloud are used to analyze the tweets, distribute the sentiments, identify sentiment polarity, and construct the word cloud [24].
8. "syuzhet," an R library used to get emotions and details from the NRC vocabulary [25]. The NRC sentiment dictionary can be accessed using the "get_nrc_sentiment" function.

9. The emotions expressed in tweets are analyzed using a function to determine their relative weight [26].
10. A polarity score is assigned to each of the components. The sentiment of the text is then calculated by summing up the score for each component. The content of the figure has been named positive, negative, and unbiased based on the score.

5.4 RESULTS AND DISCUSSIONS BASED ON TWEET ANALYSIS

The intention of analyzing tweets was to understand the views of the writer. The reported study of war-based tweet analysis was carried out in R tools and a Python programming environment. About fifty thousand tweets with the hashtag "Ukraine War" posted during the period from 24th February to 5th March 2022 are considered as a dataset for the present analysis. The open-source tweet analysis packages of R and Python are used for the analysis of war-based tweets.

5.4.1 STEMMING AND WORD CLOUD CONSTRUCTION

When we looked into how many tweets are posted in different languages, it was found that 47,501, i.e., the majority of tweets are in English, 1,566 tweets in Portuguese, 500 in Italian, and the rest are in other languages. The pie plot given in Figure 5.2 explains this.

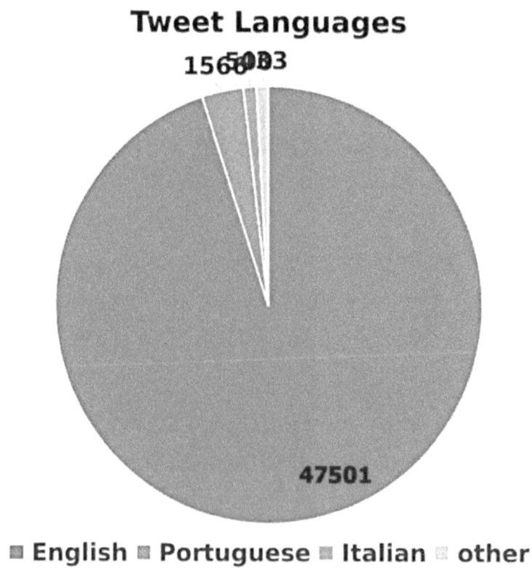

FIGURE 5.2 Tweet languages.

The tweet contents are cleaned by removing links, punctuation, symbols, and other linguistic problems for opinion mining. The 'stopword' package from 'nltk' Python was applied. The tweet texts are cleaned by removing '\ [.*?\],' 'https?://\S+|www\.\S+,' '<.*?>+,' '\n' and '\w*\d\w*' as they don't convey any sentiment of the text.

The word cloud was constructed that display the most commonly used words in tweets by people expressing their thoughts and updates on the Ukraine-Russia conflict. Wordcloud is a visual representation of a text for the useful analysis of unstructured data. Here the words 'invade,' 'Ukraine,' and 'Russia' appear bigger as more often they are mentioned in the tweets (Figure 5.3).

FIGURE 5.3 Word cloud for war-based tweet contents.

5.4.2 POLARITY CLASSIFICATION

The function sentiment intensity analyzer () was used to calculate the sentiment scores, and these scores were added to each tweet. Figure 5.4 illustrates the sentiment scores added to tweets based on the tweet content.

	content	Positive	Negative	Neutral
49995	floofydalton send american troop europ recip d...	0.104	0.19	0.706
49996	russia need invad america ukrain	0.000	0.00	1.000
49997	richardengel proudliberalmom oh well good thin...	0.366	0.00	0.634
49998	russia olympicrussia olymp russianparalymp mid...	0.000	0.00	1.000
49999	kremlinrussia claim ukrain nazi presid jewishw...	0.336	0.00	0.664

FIGURE 5.4 Tweets' text is augmented with sentiment scores.

The polarity classification compares the number of positive tweets, negative tweets, and neutral tweets. The sentiment polarity is considered positive, negative, and neutral if the polarity score is greater than 0, less than 0, and equal to 0 respectively. The derived polarity distribution is shown in Figure 5.5, where the majority of the tweets exhibit neutral polarity.

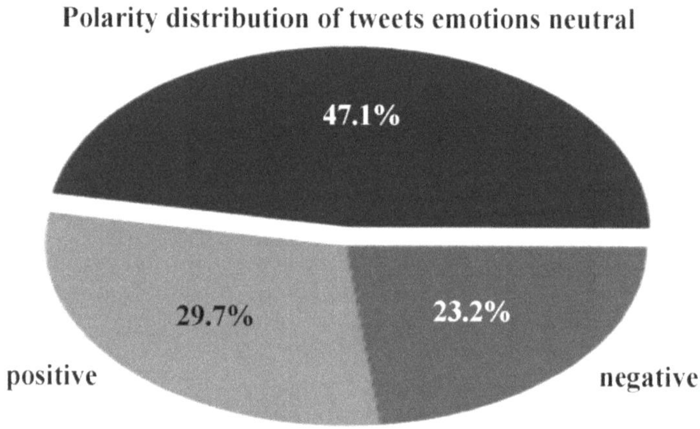

FIGURE 5.5 Polarity distribution of tweets' emotions.

The authors have also compared the tweet lengths of positive, negative, and neutral tweets. Figure 5.6 shows the distribution of tweet lengths of positive and negative neutral tweets.

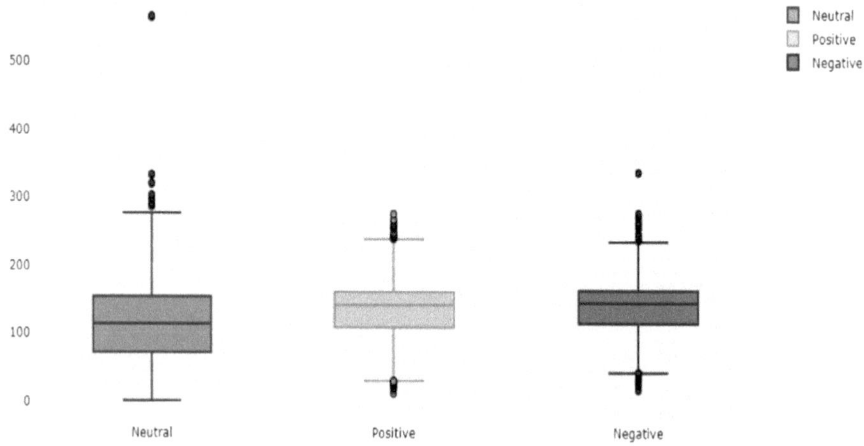

FIGURE 5.6 Distribution of tweet lengths.

5.4.3 OPINION MINING

As per the NRC dictionary, the eight different emotions are anger, anticipation, disgust, fear, joy, sadness, surprise, and trust. "syuzhet," an R library used to get emotions and details from the NRC vocabulary [8]. The emotions that are expressed in tweets are analyzed using the "get_nrc_sentiment" function to determine their relative weight. The infographic highlights the comparison between eight types of emotions. Figure 5.7 presents the proportion of the different emotions in the war, and the same is summarized in Figure 5.8. The proportion of fear, anger, and disgust is maximum, revealing disapproval of the war. Also, a significant proportion of tweets contained emotions of surprise and trust.

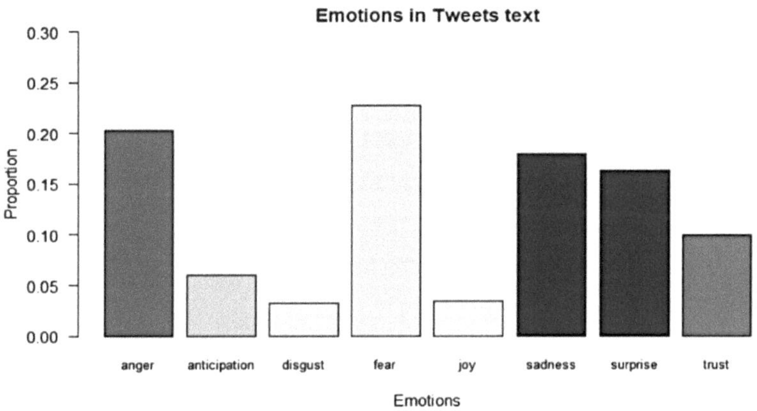

FIGURE 5.7 The proportion of the tweets' emotions.

```
> summary(tweetSentiment)
     anger         anticipation        disgust            fear
 Min.   :0.000   Min.   :0.0000   Min.   :0.000   Min.   :0.00
 1st Qu.:1.000   1st Qu.:0.0000   1st Qu.:0.000   1st Qu.:1.00
 Median :1.000   Median :0.0000   Median :0.000   Median :1.00
 Mean   :1.482   Mean   :0.4399   Mean   :0.238   Mean   :1.66
 3rd Qu.:2.000   3rd Qu.:1.0000   3rd Qu.:0.000   3rd Qu.:2.00
 Max.   :8.000   Max.   :6.0000   Max.   :7.000   Max.   :9.00
      joy            sadness         surprise          trust
 Min.   :0.0000   Min.   :0.000   Min.   :0.000   Min.   :0.0000
 1st Qu.:0.0000   1st Qu.:1.000   1st Qu.:1.000   1st Qu.:0.0000
 Median :0.0000   Median :1.000   Median :1.000   Median :0.0000
 Mean   :0.2498   Mean   :1.313   Mean   :1.186   Mean   :0.7222
 3rd Qu.:0.0000   3rd Qu.:2.000   3rd Qu.:1.000   3rd Qu.:1.0000
 Max.   :5.0000   Max.   :7.000   Max.   :5.000   Max.   :8.0000
    negative         positive
 Min.   : 0.000   Min.   :0.000
 1st Qu.: 1.000   1st Qu.:0.000
 Median : 2.000   Median :1.000
 Mean   : 2.023   Mean   :1.011
 3rd Qu.: 3.000   3rd Qu.:2.000
 Max.   :10.000   Max.   :8.000
```

FIGURE 5.8 Summary of sentiments revealed in war-based tweets.

5.5 CONCLUSION

This study aimed at a socio-economic impact analysis of public opinion that is being expressed in tweets on the Russia-Ukraine war. The authors presented the findings from the literature survey on how people have suffered and markets are affected because of war. A Twitter application is created to ingest data by calling Twitter APIs and also the required data is retrieved from Kaggle. This experiment was carried out by utilizing open-source packages of the R and Python platform. This study looked into various trends, emotions, and polarity of the tweets about the issue. This exercise revealed a mixed opinion toward war. The present exploration concludes that opinion mining of Twitter data has the potential to demonstrate a suitable tool for analyzing public opinions on the Russia-Ukraine war. At the outset, the authors conclude that this war has tremendous adverse impacts on the people, prices, and markets across the world. Such wars should be prevented by multilateral negotiations in the future.

KEYWORDS

- **opinion mining**
- **polarity classification**
- **Russo-Ukrainian war**
- **socio-economic impact analysis**
- **tweet analysis**
- **word cloud construction**

REFERENCES

1. Choudhary, O. P., Saied, A. A., Priyanka, Ali, R. K., & Maulud, S. Q. (2022). Russo-Ukrainian war: An unexpected event during the COVID-19 pandemic. *Travel Medicine and Infectious Disease, 48*, 102346. DOI: 10.1016/j.tmaid.2022.102346.
2. Gonçalves Júnior, J., de Amorim, L. M., Neto, M. L. R., Uchida, R. R., de Moura, A. T. M. S., & Lima, N. N. R. (2022). The impact of "the war that drags on" in Ukraine for the health of children and adolescents: Old problems in a new conflict? *Child Abuse & Neglect, 128*, 105602. DOI: 10.1016/j.chiabu.2022.105602.

3. Talabi, F. O., Aiyesimoju, A. B., Lamidi, I. K., Bello, S. A., Okunade, J. K., Ugwuoke, C. J., & Gever, V. C. (2022). The use of social media storytelling for help-seeking and help-receiving among Nigerian refugees of the Ukraine–Russia war. *Telematics and Informatics*, *71*, 101836. DOI: 10.1016/j.tele.2022.101836.
4. Tosun, O. K., & Eshraghi, A. (2022). Corporate decisions in times of war: Evidence from the Russia-Ukraine conflict. *Finance Research Letters, 48*, 102920. DOI: 10.1016/j.frl.2022.102920.
5. Dhawan, M., Choudhary, O. P., Priyanka, & Saied, A. A. (2022). Russo-Ukrainian war amid the COVID-19 pandemic: Global impact and containment strategy. *International Journal of Surgery*, *102*, 106675. DOI: 10.1016/j.ijsu.2022.106675.
6. Ugurluer, G., Ozyar, E., Corapcioglu, F., & Miller, R. C. (2020). Psychosocial Impact of the War in Ukraine on Pediatric Cancer Patients and Their Families Receiving Oncological Care Outside Their Country at the Onset of Hostilities. *Journal of Clinical Oncology, 38*, 954–962. DOI: 10.1016/j.adro.2022.100957.
7. Altice, F. L., Bromberg, D. J., Dvoriak, S., Meteliuk, A., Pykalo, I., Islam, Z., Azbel, L., & Madden, L. M. (2022). Extending a lifeline to people with HIV and opioid use disorder during the war in Ukraine. *The Lancet Public Health*, *7*(5), e482–e484. DOI: 10.1016/S2468-2667(22)00083-4.
8. Coupe, T., & Obrizan, M. (2016). The impact of war on happiness: The case of Ukraine. *Journal of Economic Behavior & Organization*, *132*, 228–242. DOI: 10.1016/j.jebo.2016.09.017.
9. Islam, A., Ouch, C., Smyth, R., & Wang, L. C. (2014). The Long-Term Effects of Civil Conflicts on Education, Earnings and Fertility: Evidence from Cambodia. *SSRN Electronic Journal*. DOI: 10.2139/ssrn.2473143.
10. Paul, A. (2015). The EU in the South Caucasus and the Impact of the Russia-Ukraine War. *The International Spectator, 50*(3), 30–42. DOI: 10.1080/03932729.2015.1054223.
11. Andermo, E., & Kragh, M. (2021). Sanctions and dollar dependency in Russia: resilience, vulnerability, and financial integration. *Post-Soviet Affairs*, *37*(3), 276–301. DOI: 10.1080/1060586X.2021.1913932.
12. Boungou, W., & Yatié, A. (2022). The impact of the Ukraine–Russia war on world stock market returns. *Economics Letters, 215*, 110516. DOI: 10.1016/j.econlet.2022.110516.
13. Byrska, O. (2022). Civil Crisis Management in Poland: The First Weeks of the Relief in Russian War on Ukraine. *Journal of Genocide Research. 25*, 463–470. DOI: 10.1080/14623528.2022.2079196.
14. Lane, D. (2016). The International Context: Russia, Ukraine and the Drift to East-West Confrontation. *International Critical Thought, 6*(4), 623–644. DOI: 10.1080/21598282.2016.1242084.
15. Adekoya, O. B., Oliyide, J. A., Yaya, O. S., & Al-Faryan, M. A. S. (2022). Does oil connect differently with prominent assets during war? Analysis of intra-day data during the Russia-Ukraine saga. *Resources Policy*, *77*, 102728. DOI: 10.1016/j.resourpol.2022.102728.
16. Shafiee-Jood, M., & Cai, X. (2016). Reducing food loss and waste to enhance food security and environmental sustainability. *Environmental Science and Technology, 50*(16), 8432–8443. DOI: 10.1021/acs.est.6b01993.
17. Lava, S. A. G., de Luca, D., Milani, G. P., Leroy, P., Ritz, N., & de Winter, P. (2022). Please stop the Russian-Ukrainian war – children will be more than grateful. *European Journal of Pediatrics, 181*, 2183–2185. DOI: 10.1007/s00431-022-04444-5.

18. Koval, N., Kulyk, V., Riabchuk, M., Zarembo, K., & Fakhurdinova, M. (2022). Morphological Analysis of Narratives of the Russian-Ukrainian Conflict in Western Academia and Think-Tank Community. *Problems of Post-Communism, 69*(2), 166–178. DOI: 10.1080/10758216.2021.2009348.
19. Purtova, D., et al. Russia-Ukraine War Tweets Dataset (65 days). Retrieved from: https://www.kaggle.com/datasets/foklacu/ukraine-war-tweets-dataset-65 days?resource=download&select=Ukraine_war.csv, Kash, Twitter data extraction; https://www.kaggle.com/kaushiksuresh147/twitter-data-extraction (accessed on 27 May 2024).
20. Kamath, R. S., et al. (2017). Analysis of Twitter Data on Demonetization in India: An Opinion Mining Approach. In *International Conference on Demonetization and Remonetization: Issues and Challenges for Global Business*, organized by CSIBER, Kolhapur, 4th and 5th August 2017 (pp. 75-84). ISBN – 9789385381461. .
21. How to Do Twitter Sentiment Analysis with Machine Learning. Retrieved from: https://monkeylearn.com/blog/sentiment-analysis-of-twitter/ (accessed on 27 May 2024).
22. Tonmoy, T. Are we heading towards World War III? Retrieved from: https://www.kaggle.com/code/towhidultonmoy/are-we-heading-towards-world-war-iii/notebook (accessed on 27 May 2024).
23. Jockers, M. Introduction to the Syuzhet Package. Retrieved from: https://cran.r-project.org/web/packages/syuzhet/vignettes/syuzhet-vignette.html (accessed on 27 May 2024).
24. Mohammad, S., & Turnel, P. (2010). Emotions Evoked by Common Words and Phrases: Using Mechanical Turk to Create an Emotion Lexicon. In *Proceedings of the NAACL-HLT 2010 Workshop on Computational Approaches to Analysis and Generation of Emotion in Text*, June 2010, LA, California. Retrieved from: https://saifmohammad.com/WebPages/NRC-Emotion-Lexicon.html (accessed on 27 May 2024).
25. Gaur, L. (2017). Text Mining for unstructured data on Twitter hashtags using R. *Australian Journal of Basic and Applied Sciences, 11*(8), 49–55.

CHAPTER 6

Robotic Process Automation in Business Management Using Machine Learning Algorithms

P. GAYATHIRI

Department of Information Technology, Nirmala College for Women, Coimbatore, Tamil Nadu, India

ABSTRACT

Robotic process automation bots try to mimic how people communicate with computers. RPA bots may handle activities that include document scanning and conversion into a machine-readable format thanks to optical character recognition. Most document automation tasks performed by RPA bots, including billing, screening resumes, inventory management, and other processes, rely on OCR. Poor handwriting and inconsistent text are common in handwritten documents. Before supplying a word to the RPA system, OCR technologies may be combined with a neural network whale optimization algorithm to accurately read the word depending on the overall content of the text. The primary objective of the research is to focus on the Robotic Automation Process in Invoice documents used in Business. The main challenge is implementing machine models that are lacking in accuracy, to overcome this challenge neural network whale optimization is to enhance the accuracy of optical character recognition.

6.1 INTRODUCTION

Robotic Process Automation is a set of techniques relating to the operation and the execution of multiple tasks in place of humans [1] and can be defined

Artificial Intelligence and Machine Learning for Business. Namita Mishra, A. V. Senthil Kumar (Eds.)

as industrial applications like administrative, scientific, or industrial tasks. In a nutshell, the RPA tools are a collection of methods that, by automating as many repetitive processes as possible, seek to enhance the quality of the work [2]. Process automation utilizing robots Automation of service tasks that mimic human labor is known as robotic process automation [3]. Software robots or artificial intelligence workers who are capable of doing repetitive tasks with accuracy are used to automate processes. These behaviors include logging into the program, copying and pasting data, opening emails, and completing forms [4]. RPA, according to Van der Aalst et al. [3], is a fine tool that interacts with other user interfaces. Although more conventional techniques of process automation. The role of RPA is to identify the element and coordinate XPath selections. We can observe some studies where these technologies are utilized for automating digital forensics, auditing [5], and industry, while commercial providers of RPA solutions indicate a rise in demand since 2016.

The development of the fourth industrial revolution of Industry 4.0 is opening up new RPA tools on data gathered from smart devices to automate routine rules-based business activities [6]. RPA refers to the robotization of repetitive operations carried out by human workers in commercial processes. This can externally replace people with automation. As compared to previous methodologies, RPA rests on top of the information infrastructure rather than being integrated into it, indicating a lower rate of loss of privacy [7] and potentially lowering expenses. The usage of RPA technology has been shown in certain surveys to reduce operational costs of transactional tasks inside shared services by 30% to 60% [8]. This research aims to present a study of the AI-related RPA technologies that can aid in Industry 4.0 organizational process improvement. It appears that the capability of RPA tools increases when the objectives of AI are broadened through the use of neural networks and whale optimization techniques.

6.2 MACHINE LEARNING AND INDUSTRY 4.0

AI is applied in a variety of fields such as robotics and natural language processing. A set of fundamental concepts that support many of these applications is the best approach to comprehending AI as it exists now [9]. The fundamental idea behind smart factories and Industry 4.0 is that machines will use AI to complete difficult jobs, save costs, and improve the quality of products and services [10]. Through the use of AI, the industrial sector becomes more knowledgeable and better equipped to deal with modern concerns, including configurable requirements and the number of sensors used in RPA [11]. The implementation of robotics and AI simplifies the wide range of goods. Artificial intelligence approaches can be used to analyze a large amount of data collected from various sensors [12].

6.3 OPTICAL CHARACTER RECOGNITION IN ROBOTIC PROCESS AUTOMATION

A layout-based OCR model is built for a particular receipt design. Input courses are set up for the bills, the information is separated, and the extracted information is then combined with a structured data collection. Fixed-format reports can have field-specific data extracted from them using a semi-automated process. Data separation from invoices can be difficult because no two bills are the same. The robotic process extracts the information from invoices, and programs must be modified to ensure double-dealing layouts processing data as follows:

1. **Image Pre-Processing:** In this stage, PDF invoices that have not been scanned are scanned and converted into JPG documents with a resolution of 600x600x3 and 300 DPI. This stage involves the use of several pre-processing techniques. Following the processing of all the images, a device learning model is trained using the information from the parsed images.
2. **Text Detection:** After the information has been processed, it is sent to the text detection version so that it can recognize the tables, paragraphs, and documents in the input photos.
3. **Text Recognition:** During this phase, one or more objects or textual content chunks are positioned, and the volume of each is indicated by bounding boxes.
4. **Texts/Information Extraction:** To extract information from the invoice bills, Tesseract-OCR is currently being used. There are several different ways in which OCR invoicing can be accomplished:
    - Machine learning-based method of detecting regions.
    - Using OCR to extract text from found areas.
    - Using text analysis to identify the connections between captured texts and save them as a dataset.

In Figure 6.1, OCR translates printed or handwritten texts into machine-readable characters by converting them into unstructured data. OCR patterns are light and dark that make up the various letters and numbers in various languages.

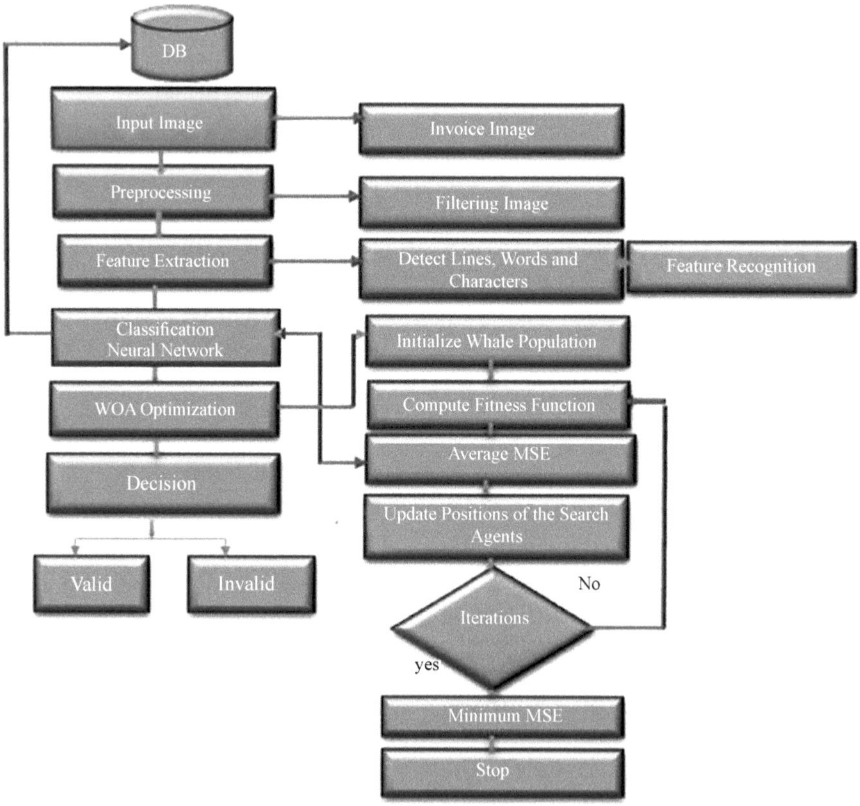

FIGURE 6.1 Architecture of OCR in RPA.

Systems for payments may be able to automatically extract relevant information from invoices using optical character recognition. The information on various invoice types must be properly isolated from crucial fields on each of them, such as Address, Name, and Total. The accuracy of the final method will be incorrectly identified. The AI and machine learning algorithms differ from traditional algorithms in that they completely rely on their initial training data and understand the input to automatically process the output.

6.4 MULTILAYER PERCEPTRON NEURAL NETWORK

One of the most challenging problems in machine learning is the lack of accuracy. The learning process of artificial neural networks has recently drawn the attention of many academics. The main challenges in training a neural network are its nonlinear character and the lack of knowledge about the ideal set of primary governing parameters: weights and biases. Local optima stagnation and sluggish convergence speed are the fundamental drawbacks of conventional training techniques or feedforward neural networks. The neurons are spread throughout layers, with each layer being completely linked to the one below it. The most prevalent and well-known neural network is the multilayer perceptron. Neurons are linked together in MLP in a one-way, one-directional manner. Weights, which are real values falling within the range [–1, 1], serve as a representation of connections. MLP typically has just one hidden layer. There are two phases involved in calculating each node's output in the network. Equation 1 calculates the weighted sum of the input, where I_i is the input value and w^{ij} is the weight between the input layer and the hidden neuron j. The output of neurons is then triggered by an activation function based on the result of the summation function. The output layer is shown in Equation 2 as:

$$S_j = \sum_{(i=1)}^{n} w_{ij} I_i + \beta_j \tag{1}$$

$$f_j(x) = \frac{1}{1+e^{-S_j}} \tag{2}$$

The output Sas given in Equation (3).

6.5 META-HEURISTIC ALGORITHM

The Whale Optimization Algorithm is more efficient than other existing algorithms. The whale optimization algorithm is a stochastic optimization algorithm recently proposed by Mirjalili and Lewis. The meta-heuristic algorithm can reduce population size and find the best solution to improve accuracy. The optimization problems are solved by the search agents [13]. The other existing optimization algorithms are not random search agents [14].

6.5.1 BUBBLE NET ATTACKING METHOD

The bubble-net hunting is a hunting behavior of humpback whales attacking prey shown in Figure 6.2. A humpback whale creates a spiral around prey and makes bubbles along the way. The encircling process is another simulated humpback [16]. Two methods are designed to mathematically method as follows:

FIGURE 6.2 Bubble net hunting behavior.

6.5.1.1 ENCIRCLING MECHANISM SHRINKING

Equation 4 has decreased the path of the random value with the interval of [–a, a] gradually decreasing from 2 to 0 over the number of iterations. By using random values for A in [–1, 1], the new position of a whale reaches the new best agent position. Figure 6.3 represents the different positions that 0 >A ≤1 from (X1, Y1) to (X1*, Y1*).

The vectors $A^{\rightarrow}$ and $C^{\rightarrow}$ are as follows:

$$A^{\rightarrow} = 2a^{\rightarrow}.\, r^{\rightarrow} - a^{\rightarrow} \tag{4}$$

$$C^{\rightarrow} = 2.\, r^{\rightarrow} \tag{5}$$

6.5.1.2 SPIRAL UPDATING POSITION

The whale at (X1, Y1) and the prey at (X1*, Y1*). spiral equation.6 is the position of whale and prey as follows:

$$X^{\rightarrow\rightarrow}(t+1) = D^{\rightarrow\rightarrow}.\, ebl.\, \cos(2\pi l) + X^{\rightarrow\rightarrow}*(t) \tag{6}$$

Bubble Net Hunting method the Humpback whale to start hunting them. D1 = |X1∗(t)–X1(t)| and is the distance between the whale and prey, During the optimization process, the shrinking encircling changes the position of whale optimization.

6.5.2 PREY SEARCH

The exploration may use the same as the exploitation phase depending on the A vector. Humpback whales search positions at random. As a result, |A1| with random values greater than or equal to 1, the search agent moves away from the reference whale. In comparison to the exploitation method, the exploitation is in equations 7 and 8.

$$^{\to}D^{\to}\ C^{\to}.^{\to}X^{\to\to\to}r^{\to\to\to}a^{\to\to}n^{\to\to}d^{\to\to}-X^{\to\to\to\to\to}A^{\to\to}| \tag{7}$$

$$X^{\to\to}(t+1)=X^{\to\to\to\to\to}r^{\to\to}a^{\to\to}n^{\to\to}d^{\to\to\to}o^{\to}m^{\to\to\to}-A^{\to}D^{\to\to} \tag{8}$$

where; $X^{\to\to\to\to\to}r^{\to\to}a^{\to\to}n^{\to\to}d^{\to\to}$ is a random vector 's' shown in Eqns. (8) and (9) calculate the possible positions with A > 1. At the end of each iteration, it finds the best solution, and the parameter is decreased from 2 to 0. Since it has the potential to explore and exploit methods, the WOA can be referred to as a global optimizer.

The WOA is divided into two-step processes: the encircling mechanism and the bubble-net technique [17]. The search agent equations are in Figure 6.3. The Neural Network weights and Biases tune the parameters and enhance the result [18].

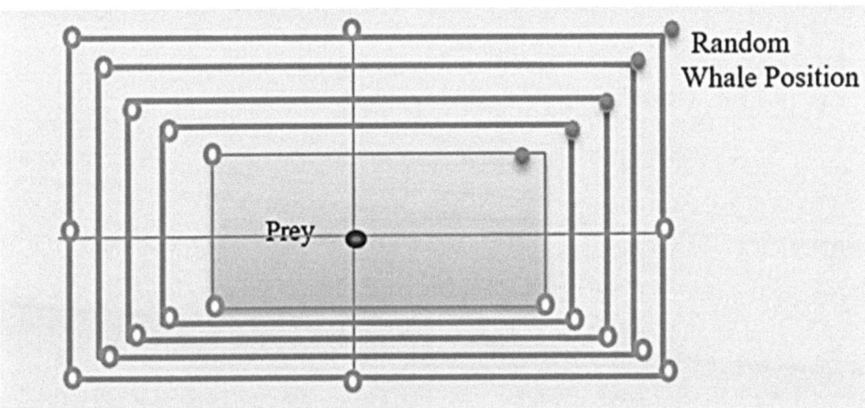

FIGURE 6.3 Encircling bubble-net hunting.

To update the positions of search agents $|X1| > 1$ otherwise $|X1| \leq 1$, in Refs. [19, 20].

6.5.3 TRAINING MLP USING WOA

Figure 6.4 illustrates the proposed method for training the MLP network with WOA [19]. The WOA method is used to train a single hidden layer MLP network. The neural network is connected to the input and output layers. The total number of weights and biases in the network is calculated in Equation 10.

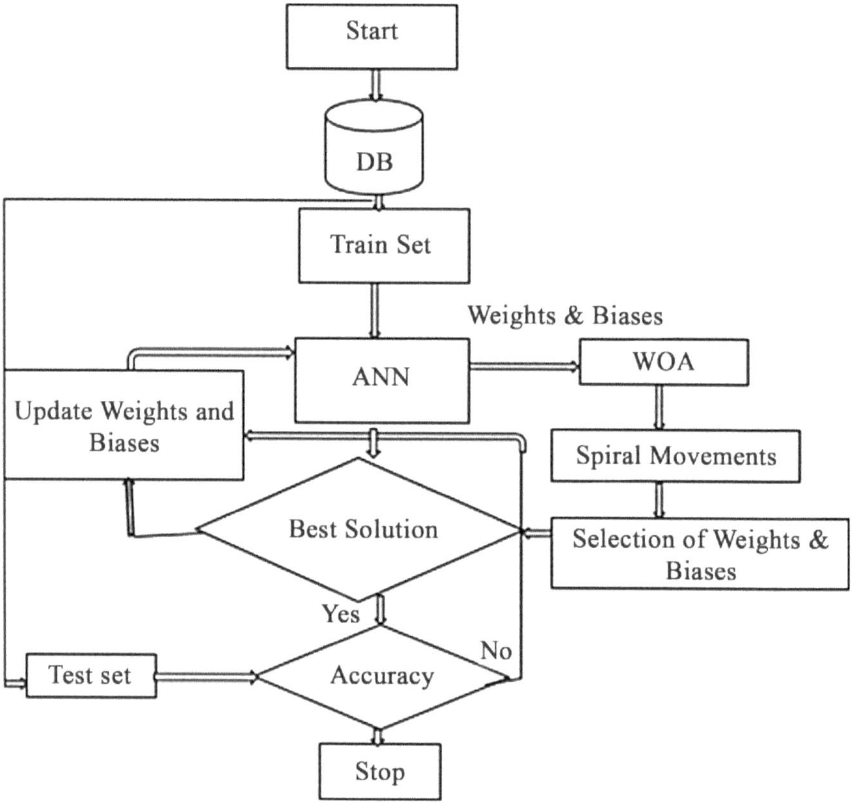

FIGURE 6.4 Architecture of neural network WOA.

$$individuallength = (n * m) + (2 * m) + 1 \tag{10}$$

Mean Square Errors are shown in Eq. (11) where y_1 is the actual value, $\hat{y_1}$

$$Mean\ Square\ Error = \sum_{1}^{n} (y_1 - \hat{y}_1) \quad (11)$$

6.5.4 *WHALE OPTIMIZATION ALGORITHM IN ARTIFICIAL NEURAL NETWORK*

Optical character recognition is a classification problem. It classifies the data as a valid invoice or an invalid invoice, represented by 0 and 1. This is illustrated in Figure 6.5.

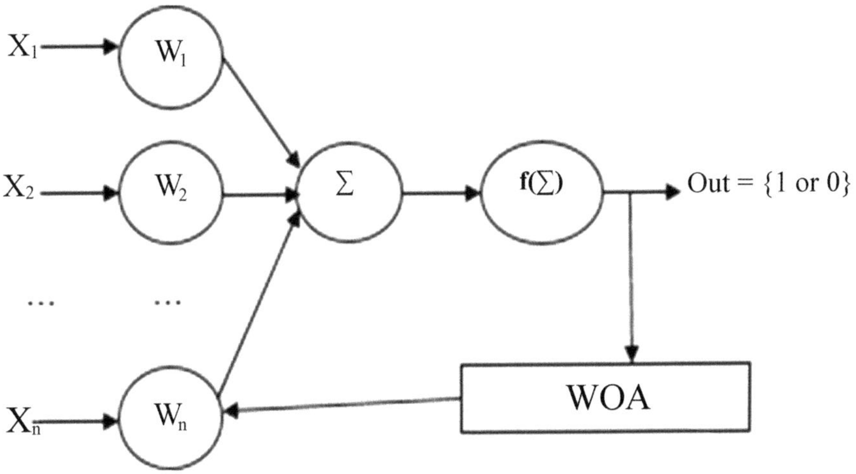

FIGURE 6.5 WOA optimal weights and biases for ANN.

The ANN consists of 49 input neurons in the first and second layers, as well as two hidden layers of Sigmoid activation functions. Weights and biases are considered attributes of the whale population, and they are modified at each step of the algorithm to achieve their best values. As a result, the WOA performs in ANN to increase classification accuracy. The above hybrid method, neural network, is used to classify the data into 0 and 1 classes as shown in Figure 6.5. The ANN and whale optimization communicate the best weights and biases in two-way communication. The role of the ANN is to minimize the Error.

6.6 RPA IN OCR USE CASES

RPA bots can use OCR to extract text from scanned documents and images. As a result, it serves as the basis for many RPA use cases. Consider the subsections.

Algorithm 1: The Whale Optimization-based Neural Network Algorithm

Input: Train and Test Image

Output: Minimum

- **Step 1:** begin
- **Step 2:** Load samples of data
- **Step 3:** Initialize search agents randomly by MLP network
- **Step 4:** The network calculated by

$$\text{Individual length } 1 = (n \times m) + (2 \times m) + 1 \qquad (1)$$
$$w_{ij} = W_I X_I + \beta_I$$

- **Step 5:** While iterations <maxite do
- **Step 6:** For each search agent I do
- **Step 7:** For each data agent x do
- **Step 8:** A fitness function calculated by:

$$fitness = \sum_{i=1}^{n} \sum_{j=1}^{n} \left(x(x_2 - x_1)\right)^2 + \left(y_2 - Y_1\right)^2 = \begin{cases} 1, x < 0 \\ 0, x \leq 0 \end{cases}$$

- **Step 9:** X1 is the best search agent
- **Step 10:** Update a, A, C, I and p
- **Step 11:** if $p < 0.5$ then
- **Step 12:** if $|A| \leq 1$ then
- **Step 13:** Update the position of the current search agent by the equation

$$\vec{X}(t+1) = \overrightarrow{X^*}(t) - \vec{A}.\vec{D}_1$$

- **Step 14:** else if $|A| \geq 1$ then
- **Step 15:** select a random search agent S
- **Step 16:** Update the current search
- **Step 17:** minimum error value is tested
- **Step 18:** end if
- **Step 19:** else if p >= 0.5 then
- **Step 20:** update the position of the current search agent by:

$$\vec{D}^{r} = |\overrightarrow{X^*}(t) - \vec{X}(t)|,$$
$$\vec{X}(t+1) = \vec{D}'.e^{bl}.\cos(2\pi l) + \overrightarrow{X^*}(t)_1$$

- **Step 21:** end if
- **Step 22:** end for
- **Step 23:** t = t + 1
- **Step 24:** end while
- **Step 25:** return X^*

6.6.1 FINANCE

According to estimates, the correct technologies can automate 42% of financial procedures. Using RPA and OCR together, financial directors can automate processes like:

- **Invoices:** To help RPA robots match invoices to purchase orders and gather invoice data by extracting pertinent fields including vendor data, VAT ID, address, and purchasing information of the customer.
- **Insurance Documents:** To extract insurance-related data like passports, birth certificates, driving licenses, previous medical records, voter IDs, etc., using optical character recognition. To process claims and check whether it is original or fake information.
- **Credit Scoring:** Data for generating credit reports can be captured using OCR. Client payment histories, tax returns, credit card debt, mortgages, loans, and other financial records can all be used to extract this information. These data are processed by RPA bots for managing credit and debit cards, processing loans, and validating loans.

6.6.2 HUMAN RESOURCE

- **Resume Screening:** The RPA automatically checks the information of the candidate, and OCR collects candidate data from hard copies of resumes, letters, and certificates.
- **Travel and Expense Management:** Cash register receipts, boarding passes, account statements, and other expenses can be scanned and processed using OCR. To ensure compliance, RPA can check individual costs against corporate policies and industry expenditures.
- **Document Management:** HR generates many documents for tasks such as hiring, payroll, employee archives, company regulations, etc. OCR enables RPA to retrieve the information and automatically send it to the HR department.

6.6.3 HEALTHCARE

According to statistics, in 2020, the global healthcare business produced 2.3 bytes of data. Healthcare staff can automate the following tasks by combining RPA and OCR:

1. **Patient Registration:** Before entering a healthcare facility, a patient must fill out a patient entry form containing personal information that will be physically entered into the system by a healthcare worker. The RPA enters the data without the need for human interaction and OCR extracts the information of the patient.
2. **Patient Entry:** This form to be manually filled.
3. **Electronic Records:** These are digitalized in the healthcare system. OCR is the first step in converting paper records to electronic records. It extracts information from the paper that is pertinent to the transition, such as patient information, to an RPA that can enter the data into the healthcare record system, and process, and retrieve the patient information.
4. **Clinic:** Pathology reports and unstructured doctor's notes can be digitized and fed into Natural Language Processing algorithms for clinical trial matching using OCR. Following that, data can be automatically uploaded to the trial master file by RPA.

6.7 CHALLENGES

As a result, the data used in RPA must be accurate as it is unlikely that a human user will double-check it. The purpose of automating processes with RPA is to reduce human interference and errors. The biggest issues with OCR integration with RPA are listed below:

1. **Position of the Page:** Due to the difficulties that skewness and improper page arrangement bring for OCR, it is essential to combine the OCR configuration with a picture adjustment tool to fix and de-slant the picture.
2. **Risky Text:** Many composed by hand unique duplicates contain mistakenly spelled words and messy handwriting. To unequivocally grasp a word considering the entire context of the text preceding dealing with it in the RPA structure, OCR techniques may be used connected with NLP and ML estimations.
3. **Blurred Documents:** ID cards, and driver's licenses, blurred images, when snapped with a smartphone's camera, increase the likelihood of OCR errors. Many OCR programs include light bouncing and

blurriness correction to get scans with improved quality. Limited Dataset: Initially, we included a fourth category made up of images of newspapers to examine how goods performed in images of written materials. However, the excess text in these images made it difficult to establish the actual situation. So, we made the decision not to use them.

4. **Inaccuracies in the Output:** Only a few pictures contain instances where there are distinct texts on the left and right sides. Despite the texts being precisely detected, the result records differ because the items eliminate these texts in different sequences. As a result, we were only able to compute text rightness and were therefore unable to use alternative distance metrics, like Levenshtein distance.

6.8 CONCLUSION

The majority of OCR calculations can be made with great precision. The importance of transformation precision for OCR is obvious. This shows that the characters will match exactly for a website with 1,000 users. Most of the time, this level of accuracy is sufficient. The question is whether full-page information extraction from these distributions is possible. You should keep in mind that scores for page-level exactness are frequently determined by unusual sweeps. By removing handling delays and error rates for solicitations, brain network whale streamlined computation increases precision. Extricate information gradually from a large number of requests using sophisticated OCR technology, with greater than practically 100% accuracy. The proposed research uses special payment terms robotics to find duplicate payments, identify errors, and thwart potential fraud. Make your back office more affordable, lower by up to 50% of the cost of document processing and back-office activities. Employing the neural network whale optimization method for document classification, the identification of crucial qualities, and data verification, reduces onerous paperwork and reduces the number of paid hours they previously spent on these responsibilities. It has an accuracy rate of at least 99%. You can automate tasks that need almost high accuracy.

KEYWORDS

- **artificial intelligence**
- **automation**
- **business management**
- **machine learning**
- **neural network**
- **robotic process automation**
- **whale optimization algorithm**

REFERENCES

1. Infopédia. (2020). *Dicionário Infopédia da Língua Portuguesa, 2020.* Retrieved from https://www.infopedia.pt (accessed on 27 May 2024).
2. Aguirre, S., & Rodriguez, A. (2017). Automation of a Business Process Using Robotic Process Automation (RPA): A Case Study. 65-71. DOI: 10.1007/978-3-319-66963-2_7. Retrieved from https://www.researchgate.net/publication/319343356_Automation_of_a_Business_Process_Using_Robotic_Process_Automation_RPA_A_Case_Study (accessed on 27 May 2024).
3. van der Aalst, W. M., Bichler, M., & Heinzl, A. (2018). Robotic Process Automation. *Business & Information Systems Engineering, 60*, 269–272. DOI: 10.1007/s12599-018-0542-z
4. Asquith, A., & Horsman, G. (2019). Let the robots do it!–Taking a look at Robotic Process Automation and its potential application in digital forensics. *Forensic Science International: Reports, 1*, 100007.
5. Moffitt, K. C., Rozario, A. M., & Vasarhelyi, M. A. (2018). Robotic process automation for auditing. *Journal of Emerging Technologies in Accounting, 15*(1), 1–10.
6. Madakam, S., Holmukhe, R. M., & Jaiswal, D. K. (2019). The future digital workforce: robotic process automation (RPA). *JISTEM – Journal of Information Systems and Technology Management, 16*, e201916001.
7. Enríquez, J. G., Jiménez-Ramírez, A., Domínguez-Mayo, F. J., & García-García, J. A. (2020). Robotic Process Automation: A Scientific and Industrial Systematic Mapping Study. *IEEE Access, 8*, 39113–39129.
8. Williams, D., & Allen, I. (2017). Using artificial intelligence to optimize the value of robotic process automation. Retrieved from: https://www.ibm.com/downloads/cas/KDKAAK29 (accessed on 27 May 2024).
9. Nilsson, N. J. (2014). *Principles of artificial intelligence.* Morgan Kaufmann Editors.
10. Bahrin, M. A. K., Othman, M. F., Azli, N. N., & Talib, M. F. (2016). Industry 4.0: A review on industrial automation and robotics. *Jurnal Teknologi, 78*(6–13), 137–143.

11. Zheng, P., Sang, Z., Zhong, R. Y., Liu, Y., Liu, C., Mubarok, K., Yu, S., & Xu, X. (2018). Smart manufacturing systems for Industry 4.0: Conceptual framework, scenarios, and future perspectives. *Frontiers of Mechanical Engineering, 13*(2), 137–150.
12. Ustundag, A., & Cevikcan, E. (2017). *Industry 4.0: managing the digital transformation.* Springer Editors. Retrieved from: https://www.springer.com/gp/book/978331957869 (accessed on 27 May 2024).
13. Jiang, Q., Guo, Y., Yang, Z., Wang, Z., Yang, D., & Zhou, X. (2020). Improving the performance of whale optimization algorithm through OpenCL-based FPGA accelerator. *Complexity, 2020*(1), 8810759.
14. Gharehchopogh, F. S., & Gholizadeh, H. (2019). A comprehensive survey: Whale Optimization Algorithm and its applications. *Swarm and Evolutionary Computation, 48*, 1–24.
15. Kaur, G., & Arora, S. (2018). Chaotic whale optimization algorithm. *Journal of Computational Design and Engineering, 5*(3), 275–284.
16. Aljarah, I., Faris, H., & Mirjalili, S. (2018). Optimizing connection weights in neural networks using the whale optimization algorithm. *Soft Computing, 22*(1), 1–15.
17. Nasiri, J., & Khiyabani, F. M. (2018). A whale optimization algorithm (WOA) approach for clustering. *Cogent Mathematics & Statistics, 5*(1), 1483565.
18. Rana, N., Latiff, M. S. A., Abdulhamid, S. I. M., & Chiroma, H. (2020). Whale optimization algorithm: a systematic review of contemporary applications, modifications, and developments. *Neural Computing and Applications, 32*(20), 16245–16277.
19. Mohammed, H. M., Umar, S. U., & Rashid, T. A. (2019). A systematic and meta-analysis survey of the whale optimization algorithm. *Computational Intelligence and Neuroscience, 2019*, 8718571.
20. Mirjalili, S., & Lewis, A. (2016). The whale optimization algorithm. *Advances in Engineering Software, 95*, 51–67.

CHAPTER 7

Contemporary Inclinations and Forthcoming Solicitations of AI and ML in Business Transformation

PRIYANKA SHARMA[1] and AJAY BHARDWAJ[2]

[1]*Department of Computer Science and Engineering, Swami Keshvanand Institute of Technology, Management & Gramothan, Jaipur, Rajasthan, India*

[2]*Department of Electrical Engineering, Swami Keshvanand Institute of Technology, Management & Gramothan, Jaipur, Rajasthan, India*

ABSTRACT

Over the last few years, a huge number of vicious goods/services, their availability in the market, and their socio-economic impact have raised the issue of whether the present state of development of AI truly has the strength to revolutionize the world or if it's just hype. In today's era, developments and innovations happen in the blink of an eye, making this the most exciting period in human history. In this article, we'll talk about how the business sector is expanding and how entrepreneurs are adopting AI technology and its different applications. In addition to this, the impacts of AI technologies on the global marketplace are also examined. Utilizing Artificial Intelligence in business could push the sector to rely on quicker, less expensive, and more precise marketing strategies. Furthermore, it has the capacity to revitalize businesses with fresh concepts. Additionally, it provides solutions for challenging problems, aiding in the enormous corporate expansion. AI's involvement in many aspects of the business is also discussed, where AI has

Artificial Intelligence and Machine Learning for Business. Namita Mishra, A. V. Senthil Kumar (Eds.)

been shown to have a positive effect on all business activities, as it enhances sustainability and market dominance.

7.1 INTRODUCTION

To give learners knowledge of both known and new advancements in AI for business, the Artificial Intelligence for Business has evolved. AI is anticipated to significantly increase business value and worker skills. The application of AI in business can lead to faster, less expensive, and more precise marketing techniques. Artificial intelligence is a term that is becoming more and more common but doesn't have a clear, concise explanation [1]. It is the activity focused on artificial intelligence, where intelligence can be seen as a distinction that allows a unit to function in its environment wisely and appropriately. Technically stated, artificial intelligence is a process of integrating cloud computing, computers, digital content generation, robots, network devices, and other daily operations, systems, and business processes. There have always been artificial intelligence computers, and they will continue to exist. Future marketing initiatives must include the growth and development of artificial intelligence [2].

Businesses use artificial intelligence software on a daily basis to streamline operations, cut costs, speed up turnaround, and increase output. Technology is developing at an unusually rapid rate and businesses that have already transitioned to AI marketing software will be well-positioned to take advantage of the next breakthrough. A study says the increased AI adoption in organizations will generate $2.9 trillion in corporate value and 6.2 billion hours of worker productivity in 2021 [3]. AI and ML are transforming how corporations can interact with customers and deliver better results in less time, from deep learning and predictive analytics to image recognition and chatbots. This transformation is evident in a wide range of industries, including HR, marketing, healthcare, technology, manufacturing, and operations (Figure 7.1).

AI technology can be put to use in a wide range of diversifications. Some technological autonomy and self-driving cars, the Internet of Things (IoT), robotic manufacturing assistance, purchasing without contact, choosing candidates for positions, and medical evaluations are several instances of AI use cases that are explored very frequently. The world is full of unlimited business possibilities. However, we need staff that is trained to handle the technology so that machine learning and artificial intelligence can be integrated into business [4] (Figure 7.2).

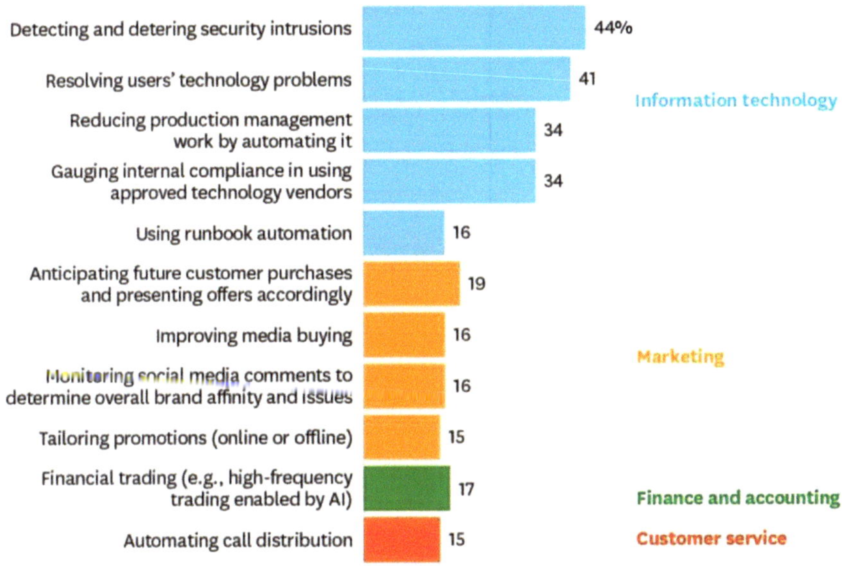

FIGURE 7.1 The way companies around the globe use AI nowadays [1].

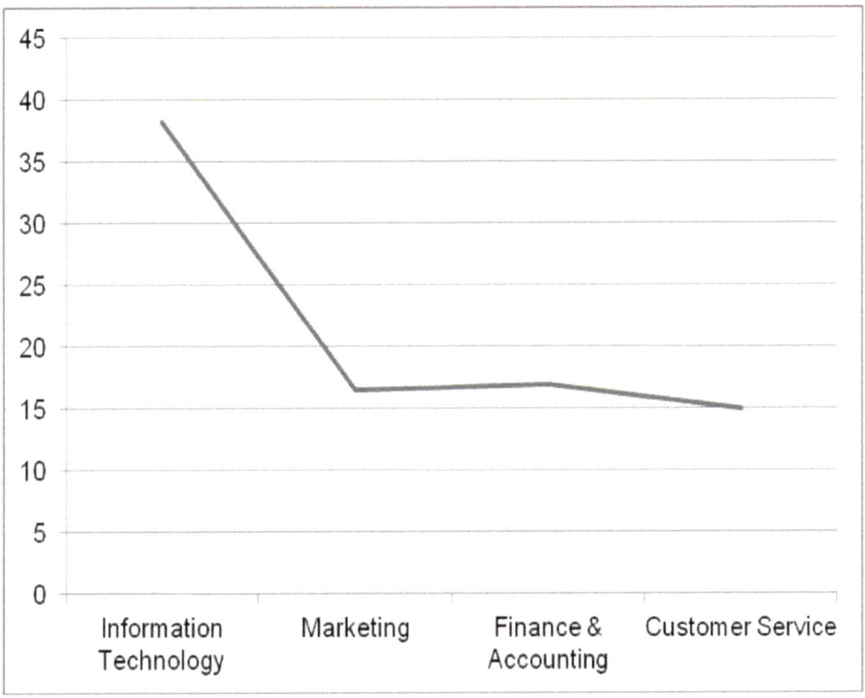

FIGURE 7.2 The way companies around the globe use AI nowadays [6].

7.1.1 HOW ARE BUSINESSES UTILIZING AI?

There are many business applications for AI software. Contrary to what is depicted in movies, AI has instead emerged as a supporting actor in the background of enterprises to help improve productivity, streamline workflows, and increase efficiency.

1. **Personalization:** AI enables the improvement of the consumer experience through personalization. For shops, artificial intelligence technologies can offer products based on past interests and purchases. Nowadays, social media platforms are using AI to determine the type of content people want to see. Amazon uses natural language processing for people to interact with Alexa [5]. Netflix, a dominant player in the media streaming industry, is well known for using AI to suggest shows to viewers and to dynamically fill in content based on their preferences.
2. **Process Automation:** Robotic process automation, which uses AI to automate specific business processes, is particularly useful (RPA). Leading businesses like IBM, LinkedIn, Deloitte, Microsoft, and frequently automate repetitive processes using RPA.
3. **Customer Service:** Contactless alternatives and research available on the internet are now the main driving forces behind the purchasing process. Many businesses have adopted Artificial Intelligence to offer a more efficient method of customer service as a result of several e-commerce consumer trends including shopping for comparison, simplicity of purchase, and hyper-personalization [6]. AI is regularly employed to deliver an improved client experience, from chatbots to multi-channel interactions. Amazon is among the top companies that employ AI to enhance customer service.
4. **Boost Output:** Several top businesses are accelerating the production process to offer greater results in less time by utilizing AI and robotics. According to Forbes, Nissan is testing AI to build new models in an effort to accelerate the launch date of new models.
5. **Analysis of Data:** It is among the most frequently used applications of AI in modern industry. Right now, Google is capable of carrying out tasks with the help of AI that depend on the examination of information by using data from several sources and predictive analytics. For example, Google can now also suggest a departure time for the

journey based on information like maps, calendar entries, flight details, and home addresses.

7.1.2 AI BUSINESS IMPLICATIONS

7.1.2.1 A BUSINESS NLP

With the aid of language interpretation, Natural Language Processing (NLP) – a division of artificial intelligence, facilitates communication between people and machines by assisting computers in reading, comprehending, and interpreting human languages. Massive amounts of unstructured data are produced daily by enterprises. Such data, often known as free text, is extremely difficult for organizations to analyze and interpret [7]. Even the most disorganized data structures can have meaning derived from them using NLP, which can recognize important phrases and categories in the free text.

7.1.2.2 TYPES OF AI

Businesses would benefit from considering AI from a business capabilities standpoint as opposed to a technological one. In general, AI can assist 3 crucial business requirements: outsourcing company activities, learning from data, and interacting with clients.

7.1.2.2.1 Process Automation

The majority of the 152 projects we looked at included employing RPA technologies to outsource physical and digital tasks, usually financial functions and back-office administrative tasks. Robotic Process Automation is more sophisticated than prior business-process automation solutions as the "robots" (which are pieces of server-side code) behave like people while entering and using data from various IT systems [8]. The tasks consist of using several systems to manipulate records, reading legal/contractual documents to extract provisions, updating customer files with address manipulations, replacing lost credit/debit cards, sorting out failures to charge for services across billing systems by extracting information from multiple document types, working on customer communications, etc. Of the cognitive technologies we'll explore here, RPA is the least expensive and easiest to install, and it often has a good return on investment. It works particularly effectively when interacting with various back-end systems.

7.1.2.2.2 Cognitive Perspectives

In our survey, the second most frequent project type (38% of the total) employed algorithms to find patterns in massive amounts of data and decipher their significance. It's like "analytics on steroids," so to speak. These ML techniques are employed to detect credit fraud and insurance claim fraud in real-time, predict what a specific buyer will probably buy, examine warranty data to identify any quality or safety concerns, etc. [9]. Three things that set cognitive insights apart from standard analytics are as follows: The models are often trained on a subset of the dataset, are normally far more complex and data-intensive, and they get better over time—that is, they get better at using fresh data to generate predictions or categorize things.

7.1.2.2.3 Cognitive Participation

The least frequent type of projects in our analysis used ML to engage staff and clients, intelligent agents, chatbots, etc. This group comprises: Service and product recommendation systems to be used for retailers that boost sales, personalization, and interaction, and include images/rich language, and recommendation systems for medical treatments that assist providers in developing individualized care strategies that consider each patient's medical history, intelligent agents who provide round-the-clock customer service and deal with a diverse range of concerns, internal websites that provide information to employees on issues including IT, employee perks, and HR policies [10].

7.1.2.3 TOOLS FOR AI IN BUSINESS

1. **Communication:** Utilize these tools to improve processes and promote better internal and external communication by reducing errors and misconceptions.
2. **Data Analysis:** These AI-powered data analysis solutions make it simple to aggregate, consolidate, and use information to improve both the internal business processes and the consumer experience.

3. **Organization:** To save critical time and resources, automate and streamline a range of internal procedures using these technologies.
4. **Security:** To keep business operations operating smoothly, cutting-edge security measures like these shield your data and assets (as well as those of your customers) against cyberattacks (Figure 7.3).

FIGURE 7.3 AI business benefits [8].

7.1.2.4 APPLICATIONS OF AI

7.1.2.4.1 Sales Using AI

The ratio of humans to machines in sales is currently being reevaluated by seasoned salespeople and sales organizations. Sales are already being impacted by automation AI and will continue to be. According to a Harvard Business Review study, businesses employing AI for sales are able to increase leads by more than 50%, cut call times by 60% to 70%, and reduce costs by 40% to 60%. These figures make it abundantly evident that business owners looking to increase their bottom line should investigate artificial intelligence [11]. Current applications of AI in sales include – demand forecasting, a sales representative chat or email bot, and lead scoring.

7.1.2.4.2 Automated Customer Service

Businesses put a lot of effort into making sure that customers value their interactions with them and want to recommend them to others [12]. One of the best methods to keep consumers satisfied is to promptly address problems. But when more and more demands come in, this could be difficult for businesses that are growing. Many firms are integrating AI into customer support teams for improving the customer service experience. A few recent applications of AI in customer service include Voicebots that lower the quantity of calls and front-line customer support representatives as chatbots.

7.1.2.4.3 Accounting Using AI

As was already mentioned, AI has the potential to automate tedious processes, improve accuracy and efficiency, and uncover hidden trends. It is capable of reading, categorizing, and uploading files using the proper accounting codes. AI never makes mistakes and is always awake [13]. Therefore, it is not surprising that AI is making progress in this complex area. The following are a few recent applications of AI in accounting: performing routine activities and partially automating complicated procedures, such as payroll, etc.

7.1.2.4.4 Human Resources AI in an Earlier

Professionals in human resources are working in an entirely different manner than they used to before the COVID-19 outbreak. Virtual recruiting, with a stronger focus on diversity and inclusion, has added new dynamics and strengthened old ones as hybrid and remote workforces continue to grow in size. To remain competitive, new platforms and technologies are needed, and AI is driving this development [14]. Current applications of AI in human resources include Organization Network Analysis and candidate profile analysis.

7.1.2.4.5 Contact Centers Using AI

Every customer interaction at a contact center either strengthens customer loyalty or drives them away. Therefore, effective customer service is a top priority. AI can help businesses better understand their customers due to the abundance of data held in contact centers [15]. The use of virtual agents powered by AI that are, in theory, indistinguishable from people has generated a lot of attention. But for now, these are the practical and well-liked applications of AI in contact centers: identifying the most critical consumer inquiries and conducting outreach initiatives.

7.1.2.4.6 AI Currently in Use

Numerous businesses receive assistance from AIOps, or the application of AI to business operations, on their path to a successful digital transformation. As a result of the need for organizational agility, operations also advanced, making it challenging for individuals to stay up [16]. By automating particular processes and assigning staff time to projects with a higher priority, AIOps helps with this. Here are a few instances of how AI is currently applied in business: enhanced IT operations and digital transformation.

7.2 LITERATURE REVIEW

Marketing potential seems to be endless thanks to AI and machine learning in particular. However, developing individualized and human experiences has always been essential for marketing success [17]. Studying AI and ML in marketing management is therefore both promising and difficult. Both have a measurable impact on marketing effectiveness. There are several potentials to use AI technologies in marketing, such as recognizing and comprehending current clients, drawing conclusions from data on customer purchases, identifying present rivals, and segmenting and targeting future clients. All four pillars of marketing, including product (like Amazon Echo or Google Home) and service (like autonomous shopping cart Dash by Walmart), price (like auction sniper by eBay), place (like driverless semi-truck by Tesla or Softbank Robotics' Pepper), and promotion (like Nike's Chalkbot), have been shown to be covered by AI, ML, and robotics. To get in-depth knowledge, AI and ML aid in the analysis of substantial data from diverse media (such as: visual/textual/vocal) and sources (such as: mobile, web, in-person) [18]. These insights assist entrepreneurs in developing decision-making skills, which is essential for business success. The previous two decades have seen significant progress in the use of artificial intelligence and machine learning in decision-making, which will further affect how marketers make decisions.

Modern AI systems can enhance decision quality by supporting human judgment and minimizing human mistakes. It's no longer a question of whether to use AI and ML to gain a competitive advantage, but rather how much. Despite this, research demonstrates that people often reject algorithms and AI, particularly when errors are made [20] or people feel less accountable. Only under specific circumstances, such as with objective or numerical tasks, do humans typically favor algorithmic guidance over human judgment. Thus, despite their potential, a lot of marketing managers are still wary about using AI and ML fully in decision-making. Because computers don't provide justification for their choices, some marketing managers find it challenging to trust AI and ML advice. Computer performance may be excellent, but not for the right reasons. Data may inherit an unrevealed bias, or the model may also not work at all when there is even a small departure from the norm. Additionally, excessive and disproportionate use of big data, ML, and AI can cause conflicts for AI and inferior managers, who may notice it underappreciated and misunderstood [21]. In the end, these responses to AI and ML may even cause people to worry about robots taking their jobs.

Although these instances show issues with employing AI and ML inside (to enhance workflows, cooperation, and choices), marketing must discover methods to apply these technologies outside (customer interactions). There is continuing discussion about automation and AI technology enhancements rather than detract from the consumer experience as marketing strives to create distinctive, value-creating experiences through interpersonal connections. There is an inherent threat that these technologies will objectify customers and disrupt the customer-employee relationship [22]. If perceived as human-generated, computer-based communication that is identical is assessed as much more enjoyable, underscoring the significance of interpersonal connections in a service setting.

Additionally, if a consumer strongly identifies with a product and if automation hinders them from showcasing their abilities, they may reject automated and AI-based items (such as robotic surgery, and robotic advisory for experienced financial investors). This begs the question of when and whether AI, machine learning, and automation can lead to business losses and the loss of their most coveted clients. Last but not least, businesses must modify their practices to prevent infringing data privacy if ML and AI are used to target, identify, and keep important consumers through personalized offers. Therefore, managing potential disputes between humans and AI/ML is necessary on a domestic and international level in marketing [23].

Marketers must take strategy, ethics, and psychology into account along with technology if they are to truly benefit from AI. This necessitates interdisciplinary collaboration and a reconsideration of the obligations placed on humans and robots. Therefore, a two-fold (behavioral and strategic) focus was put as well as a coupled perspective to investigate the function of ML and AI in marketing (inward and outward) as done [24]. In order to generate study proposals meant to inspire additional research aimed at assisting businesses in overcoming the current obstacles of AI and ML, we have investigated managerial responses and studied the management duties of AI and ML. Making machines intelligent with artificial intelligence is an art. Since AI is a general word used for a range of indications, it is the most widely used definition, as well as the most appropriate one. ML and DL are two branches of AI that develop real-world AI applications, such as virtual assistants, image recognition, voice recognition, search suggestions, etc. Artificial intelligence (AI) is the name given to the analytical method supported by computers that aims to create intelligent systems. The automated system is what enters data so that intelligent beings can carry out jobs with a higher success rate [25].

AI can be viewed as an amalgamation of several technologies because it encompasses a wide variety of different sorts, as described by IBM's head of AI research Guruduth Banavar. These technologies perform a variety of tasks and are available in a range of pricing points, but they all aim to imitate human intellect in order to give their functions intelligence. The development of AI technologies that are relevant and advantageous for marketing professionals is the outcome of the advancements made in AI and its applications in numerous industries [26]. There is a lot of data available for the use of AI technologies because digital marketing is prioritized more than traditional marketing techniques. Marketing managers can benefit from AI technologies in a variety of ways, including social media management, lead generation, and customer experience customization. It is helpful to have a framework to comprehend how AI has an impact on marketing tactics in general and consumer behavior in specific. He came to the following conclusion: If AI enhances managers, it might have a more immediate and minimal influence [27]. With rising computer power, falling hardware costs, easy access to big data, and improving ML models and algorithms, AI's role in marketing is currently on the rise. We observe widespread AI uses across various marketing domains. The academic research on AI in marketing can be divided into a few different categories, such as consumer psychological responses to AI, AI's influence on jobs and the domain [15], and problems in management and policy related to AI algorithms in specific marketing issues.

Despite some modern efforts to use AI to address strategic marketing concerns, algorithmic themes still predominate most of the research. Additionally, AI is designed to process data to generate fresh interpretations or judgments [28]. The data is frequently unorganized. One of the modern types of ML is the way AI processes data in its reasoning. AI is employed singly or in concert with other technologies during marketing efforts to further standardization, customization, and renationalization. The usage of AI intelligence in marketing must be decided by marketers. For instance, standardization might be advantageous for mechanical AI activities like automatic payment and delivery tracking in the supply chain. Digital marketing can gain from personalization with the help of AI-based thinking systems, such as different recommendation systems. By utilizing customer service and initial consumer interaction, such as social robots welcoming clients and services with conversational AI, users of Feeling AI can profit from renationalization. In contrast to AI-powered advertising, past marketing uses traditional channels to reach consumers, such as the press, television, and face-to-face interactions [29]. These marketing tactics can have a unique element that enables one or two-way encounters and have varying effects and life spans.

AI is seen as a marketing element that develops with time and saves data for an unlimited amount of time, providing a larger foundation for marketing that uses fewer resources. In the era of globalization, AI has matured as a boon to small businesses since it gives them the opportunity to go global online. Indeed, AI has become incredibly successful and lucrative in today's international economic environment [30]. The software framework provides assistance when marketing is carried out online. The analysis was based on the actual and potential uses of AI in marketing. The study examines how artificial intelligence is now being used in marketing with the intention of evaluating prospective applications, identifying potential growth areas, and putting the research's conclusions into practice. By efficiently evaluating, gathering, and generalizing data that yields better and more satisfying results for businesses, marketers, and customers, AI was built to offer customers individualized service. All members of the business community benefited greatly from AI. The efficiency of a company's work has been improved by AI [31]. The strategic application of AI is organized in terms of marketing's 4 P's and 4 C's in order to strike a balance between advertisers and consumers. Logical AI can be applied to categorize competitors in a finely defined market with the flexibility to learn more about the competitive advantages of the product [24]. The main distinction between client comprehension and market research is the emotional content present in consumer attitudes, ideas, desires, and feelings. The Feeling AI can consequently comprehend clients more effectively than the Mechanical AI because it can measure emotional data [32]. When consumers have distinct preferences and desire to use gender, a market should be segmented. The Mechanical AI is capable of spotting new data trends, particularly those using mining and grouping methods.

The market can be segmented by AI into a single group (each customer is its segment) and has the ability to combine various lengthy sides into a single segment. AI-based segmentation is flexible. With such flexibility in breakdown and aggregation, advertisers can choose the ideal size of a segment [33]. Marketers can utilize the sensing AI to inquire about present consumers' contentment and the reasons behind it. Past clients' expectations are quite predictable, and the company provides transaction records for a greater awareness of present and past events. Marketers may utilize AI to think about their expectations from prospective clients and the reasons customers are happy with the current. Potential consumers' expectations are much more unpredictable, and there is less information available about their emotional state. In reality, algorithmic AI-driven marketing tools are utilized to identify high-potential customers and find and target new consumers [34]. There are numerous academic study methods for employing AI to understand customers, according to recent studies. The interaction between customers and conversational IC can also be reinforced using a scientific methodology, in the sense of interpreting client replies using their language.

For instance, language and speech models can convey both explicitly and indirectly the consumer sentiments expressed in social media platforms like online reviews and tweets. To predict erratic consumer dynamics and diverse client preferences, marketers also utilize predictive analytics [35]. Marketing research (targeting, positioning, and segmentation) and activities (4 P's and 4 C's) both require strategic marketing planning that incorporates AI. The fundamental AI-enabled commercial model is concentrated on a more intricate understanding of AI technologies, current AI literature, and potential uses of AI that can be used to organize ongoing AI marketing research, identify AI marketing research gaps, and create strategic marketing plans. Using AI to segment data is flexible as it divides the market into individual segments (each client is its segment) and can assemble various long sides into a single segment [36]. The optimal segment size can be chosen by advertisers thanks to the flexibility in aggregation and breakdown. The Feeling AI can be used by marketers to find out why current customers are happy and how satisfied they are. Existing consumers' expectations are easier to foresee, and a business may better grasp both the past and the present thanks to transaction data. Marketing is a practical field that uses in-depth literature for practice. In addition to this, it is the crucial duty of the marketing academy. By methodically and carefully addressing scientific gaps that link AI marketing strategies and research, this paper also advances the field of strategic marketing research [37].

Marketing-related AI technologies can be widely divided into software-as-a-service (SaaS) and vendor-provided solutions that integrate AI elements, as well as customized AI systems for tailored utilization. Customized and genuine AI technologies may be produced by a company's internal AI division, third-party vendors, or a combination of the two [38]. Additionally, many AI vendor-provided solutions require adaptation for individual usage scenarios. Many software companies and service providers have invested heavily in AI, and tech companies like IBM are offering their personal marketing computerized quick fixes with IBM Watson Campaign Automation [39]. AI is a standard feature of IBM Watson Campaign Automation and is included in the program. Salesforce, regarded as the top supplier of customer relationship management (CRM) software, has started to offer AI services along with Salesforce Einstein implemented in the solution. The structure for marketing AI (5P's) was developed by Paul Roetzer. The building was created to make the ground simpler and easier to see, and it is persistent with various AI businesses demonstrating how marketing can get potential gains from AI. Nowadays, artificial intelligence (AI) [40] is utilized to assist marketing managers in a variety of jobs and operations, such as SEO, social media monitoring, external email marketing, digital marketing, A/B testing, lead generation, and web construction. Nowadays, artificial intelligence (AI) is utilized to assist marketing managers in a variety of jobs and operations, such as SEO, social media monitoring, external email marketing, digital marketing, A/B testing, lead generation, and web construction.

7.3 PROPOSED METHOD

The study done here employs a qualitative research methodology to answer the research question and to understand the motivations and points of view of the participants. The use of a qualitative technique is essential because the research's objective is to enlighten marketing experts about how AI affects marketing. Data is gathered using both primary and secondary sources. The initial information gathered with the use of the interviewing approach is the main data. Many additional sources including blogs, books, websites, and different articles are used as secondary data. In Jaipur, a number of marketing specialists are interviewed. At first, 15 individuals were picked and 25 Jaipur, Rajasthan business owners were interviewed. The purpose of the methodology was to hold candidates accountable for the study in the context of their firms, which were implementing AI as a marketing tactic. Marketers who participated in the adoption of AI would be more knowledgeable about how AI will impact firms.

There were some unresolved questions in the interview process. To follow the inductive research approach, the researcher was prepared to ask extra questions during the interview based on the situation, which does not limit the use of existing theories. The researcher used a qualitative research approach to carry out this study. The primary purpose of the qualitative technique is exploratory research revised to understand the viewpoints, motivations, and perspectives to answer the research question. Qualitative research is the best option as the objective of the study is to incorporate the viewpoints of marketing experts to understand the influence of AI on marketing. The research is using both primary and secondary sources for data collection. To address the research problem for the first time, the researcher collected primary data using the interview approach. As a secondary data source, additional publications, journals, books, websites, and blogs are also included.

Interviews are conducted with marketing executives from Jaipur-based businesses. Twenty entrepreneurs from Jaipur, Rajasthan were interviewed with a sample size of 25 participants. The respondents were included in the study for a specific reason as part of the researcher's purposive sampling technique. The main requirement for inclusion as a respondent in the study was that they work for an organization that uses AI in the marketing field. A series of open-ended interview questions was prepared for the respondents. Since we have followed the inductive research approach, the researcher was prepared to add more questions to the interview based on the context without being limited by the current hypotheses.

7.3.1 SAMPLE INTERVIEW QUESTIONS

Sl. No.	Interview Questions
1.	What effect does artificial intelligence have on the corporate world?
2.	What is the advice for utilizing AI technologies in a company effectively?
3.	What are the many obstacles to using AI technologies in the workplace?
4.	What are intelligent Agents, and how do they function in marketing-related AI?
5.	How does Machine Learning relate to AI?
6.	What are some typical misconceptions concerning AI?
7.	What distinguishes the strong AI from the Weak AI?
8.	Describe Q-learning.
9.	How AI can accelerate your efforts for digital transformation?
10.	Is the Digital Marketing sector being transformed by AI?
11.	What role do disruptive technologies play in achieving strategic objectives?
12.	How can personalization in marketing be enhanced?

Given the cross-sectional nature of the study, a month has been set aside for gathering data from the respondents. According to the aforementioned statistic, of the entire sample, 55% were male entrepreneurs and 45% were female entrepreneurs (Figure 7.4).

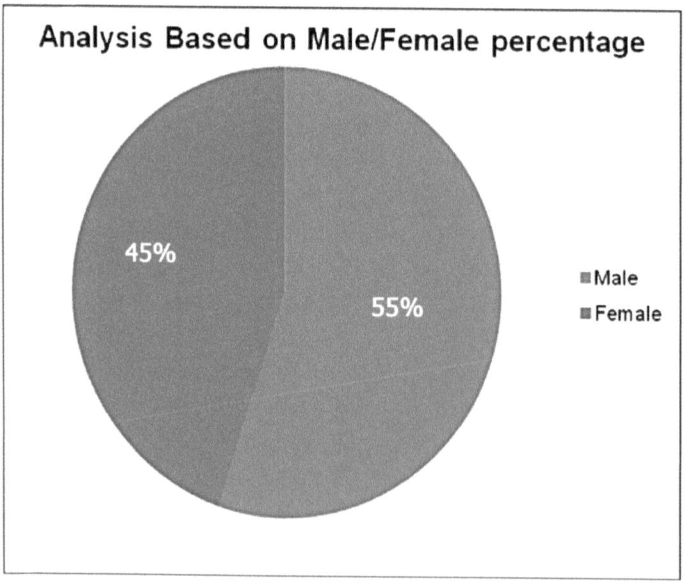

FIGURE 7.4 Data analysis.

The analysis done here leads to the conclusion that women are interested in becoming entrepreneurs. These participants are business owners from Jaipur. About 80% of them have been successful in their various businesses for more than five years, with just 10% of them just starting, as seen in Figure 7.5.

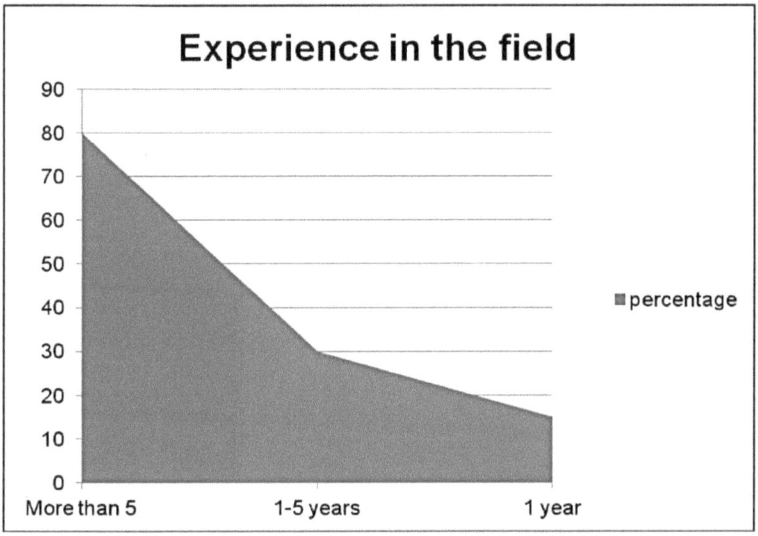

FIGURE 7.5 Participant categorization according to their business experience.

Only 5% of the participants in the study reported using AI in their place of work, according to the survey analysis and Table 7.1. As a result, an additional analysis of AI business was done on 20 respondents.

TABLE 7.1 AI Wisdom-based Categorization

Basics of AI	Number of Participants	Percentage (%)
No	08	40%
Yes	12	60%
Total	20	100%

7.3.2 *SAMPLE INTERVIEW QUESTIONS*

7.3.2.1 ANALYZING DATA

The analysis of the data received from the study's respondents is presented in this part. The interviews included fifteen company owners from ten various Jaipur groups. This experiment aims to evaluate AI usage in the business world.

7.3.2.2 ANALYZING THE INTERVIEW

An extensive analysis of the interview is provided in this section. The key inquiries and thoroughly examined questions from the interview are the deciding considerations, the main advantages, the biggest obstacles, the ethical implications of integrating AI, the uses of AI in the firm's marketing functions, the pre- and post-AI marketing plan, and the influence on the spending of the company before and after AI.

7.3.2.2.1 Influential Elements for Implementing AI in Business

Competitive pressure (50%) is the main element driving the integration of AI in marketing, as per the information collected from the respondents (Figure 7.6). Many businesses experience pressure from rival corporations to implement AI in marketing.

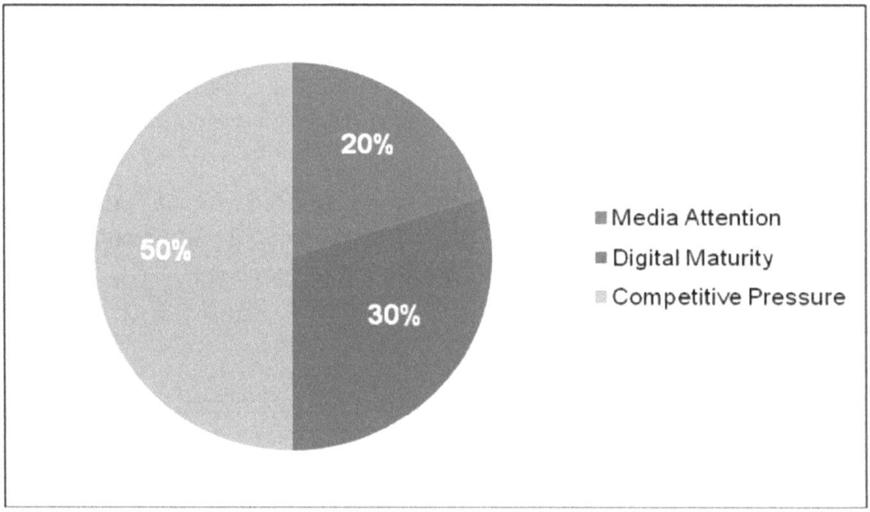

FIGURE 7.6 Influential elements for implementing AI in business.

The management of the organization has begun to promote the use of AI in marketing and is motivated to do so by digital maturity, media attention, and competitive pressure. Since the organization understood it needed to include AI in its business processes in order to set itself apart from other rival companies, pressure from competitors is the main factor. The business felt the need to incorporate AI-related technologies since it understood that clients sought out businesses with the finest products and performance.

7.3.2.2.2 Advantages of Applying AI to Marketing

Different comments were received from the respondents when they were asked about the advantages of incorporating AI in marketing. About 30% of businesses anticipated that incorporating AI into marketing tasks would increase productivity and save time, but it is now clear that AI aided the business in streamlining its marketing procedures. It contributed to increasing conversion rates, a superior comprehension of client data, and more practical marketing choices. Most importantly, it contributed to raising ROI. The AI-based software's findings can be applied to a variety of tasks that include new product development and pricing. The main benefit of using AI-oriented application software in marketing is that it enables businesses to offer clients better service and greater value, both of which increase customer happiness to the highest possible level. As a result, 40% of businesses now use AI to develop marketing strategies. Improved data analysis and efficient management of marketing procedures are other advantages, which is why 30% of businesses have turned to AI for decision-making (Figure 7.7).

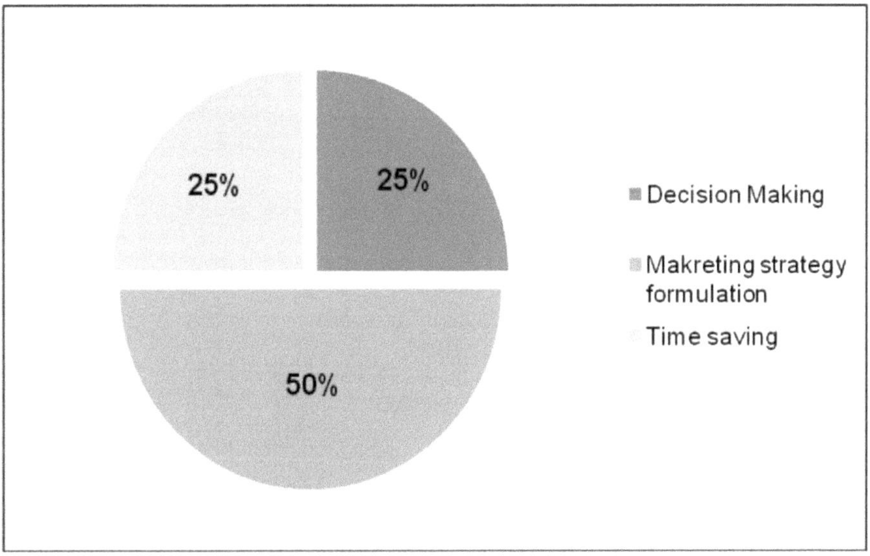

FIGURE 7.7 Advantages of applying AI to marketing.

7.3.2.2.3 The Biggest Obstacles to AI Integration in Business

Technical compatibility is regarded by 75% of respondents as the main obstacle to AI integration, according to the respondents (Figure 7.8). In order to address the compatibility issue, the company attempted to make it simple to integrate the system with the primary customer relationship management. It continues to be the company's biggest difficulty, and the business has been working nonstop to improve the procedure. According to 25% of respondents, the biggest barrier to overall functions following the integration of AI is the team's lack of technical expertise. It is true that implementing new technology within an organization involves change, and it is crucial to recognize and successfully address any issues upfront. To gain a competitive advantage, businesses should not be reluctant to adopt new technology. As the most crucial component of AI, respondents have demonstrated that it is crucial to have data in place. However, they also claimed that data is the biggest problem.

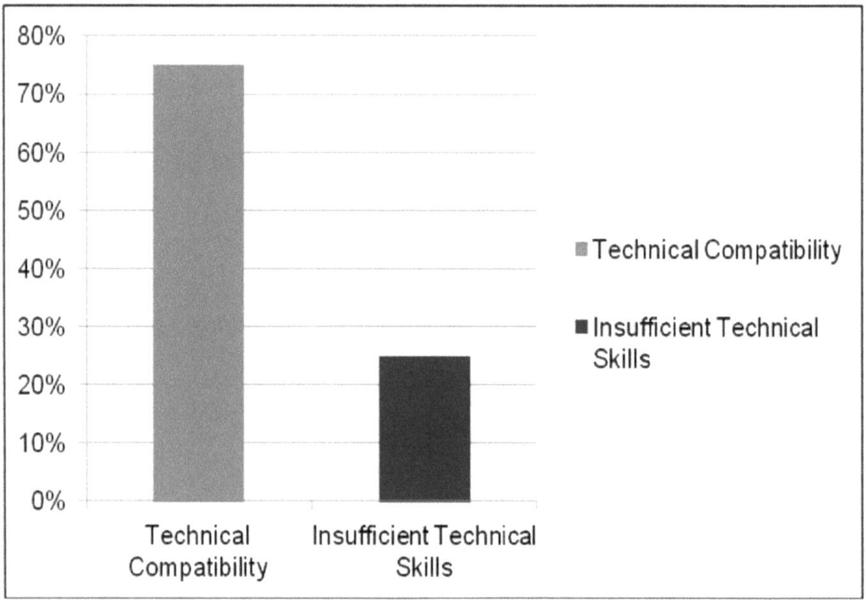

FIGURE 7.8 Obstacles in AI business integration.

7.3.2.2.4 AI's Ethical Implications for Business

The main ethical consideration for customers, in the opinion of the respondents, is data. Respondents claim that even the development team finds it difficult to grasp the decisions surrounding the selection of AI. If a corporation does not take into account the unethical decisions taken, it may become the biggest obstacle.

7.3.2.2.5 *Using AI for Marketing Purposes*

The respondents claim that AI has increased the effectiveness of the marketing function and that it is applied in nearly all significant marketing roles. They claimed that AI aids in the creation of sales and marketing strategies that significantly enhance company performance. The planning and creation of products, as well as pricing, promotion, and distribution, have all been aided by artificial intelligence. Digital platforms, advertising functions, and customer relationship management all heavily utilize AI. Digital marketing extensively uses digital advertising, AI, predictive analysis, web design, chatbots, and email marketing.

7.3.2.2.6 *Marketing Approach Before and After AI*

AI application in marketing does alter the trends of the entire industry. Similar to that, it also modifies the company's strategies. Before the adoption of AI in marketing, initiatives aimed to expand product offerings and enhance marketing resources. Following the use of AI, business intelligence drew the attention of marketing managers and gave them a deeper grasp of trends in marketing, sales, and operations. They created predictive models from the data to foresee future tactics. It contributed to increased responsiveness and productivity. Additionally, the corporation will be selecting future AI investments. The company began focusing on improved data collection, SEO, social media reach, sales, payment processes, and personalization with the deployment of AI. All of the company's tactics are now directed towards these goals.

Given that it exceeds the table value of 2.565 for df-17, the estimated "t" value of 4.06 is significant at the level of 0.01. Therefore, the theory is disproved. This shows that the two business methods are very different from one another. Table 7.2 leads to the conclusion that using AI in business will improve both the marketing strategy and the bottom line.

TABLE 7.2 Hypothesis Evaluation

Method	N	Mean	SD	SE	't'	Significance Level
Pre	10	18.9	4.28	1.98	4.06	0.01
Post	10	24.7	2.76			

7.3.2.2.7 Impact of AI on the Company's Marketing Volume and Spending

Although the adoption of AI in business has increased the company's acquisition marketing costs, it has also greatly decreased those costs. After AI, data attainment to make various marketing decisions was simpler. It not only assisted in lowering marketing expenses but also in attaining marketing goals. After AI was adopted, it assisted in reducing various costs, improving efficiency, and achieving marketing goals. It has simplified tasks and reduced marketing expenses significantly. Additionally, it contributed to the company's entire sales and future marketing strategy having a defined direction.

7.4 CONCLUSION

The goal of the research was to determine how AI is affecting business by integrating the viewpoint of a Jaipur entrepreneur. Various actions were taken to accomplish the research's goal and respond to its research questions. An extensive literature study was first highlighted, providing a thorough grasp of AI and its application in business by including the viewpoint of various academics. Second, the investigator employed a qualitative research approach, handling partially structured interviews with 15 different entrepreneurs from 10 distinct Jaipur-based businesses. The main conclusions of the study indicated that media attention, digital maturity, competitive pressure, and customers are the main influencing variables in incorporating AI in business areas. Different replies were received from the respondents on the results of the advantages of AI integration in marketing. According to marketing experts, the main advantages are increased productivity, time savings in marketing tasks, higher conversion rates, a better knowledge of consumer data, more feasible decision-making, increased ROI, insights, improved service, and customer pleasure. According to the answers, the main obstacle to AI integration is technological compatibility.

Additionally, respondents felt that having data in place is crucial because it is the most critical component of AI and, as a result, data is also the biggest barrier. According to the respondents, the main ethical consideration to be made with regard to customers is data. Respondents claimed that AI has increased the business's effectiveness in response to the question about AI usage in the organization. AI is said to help create sales and marketing strategies that greatly improve company performance. The findings discussed above show how crucial AI is to businesses. Major obstacles, ethical concerns, and applications also gave businesses guidance on how to implement AI. It is advised that businesses consider the advantages and disadvantages of integrating AI into their operations.

KEYWORDS

- **artificial intelligence**
- **cognitive engagement**
- **cognitive insights**
- **entrepreneur**
- **intelligent systems**
- **machine learning**
- **marketing intelligent system**

REFERENCES

1. Martínez-López, F., & Casillas, J. (2013). Artificial intelligence-based systems applied in industrial marketing: An historical overview, current and future insights. *Industrial Marketing Management, 42*(4), 489–495.
2. Volkmar, G., Fischer, P. M., & Reinecke, S. (2022). Artificial Intelligence and Machine Learning: Exploring drivers, barriers, and future developments in marketing management. *Journal of Business Research, 149*, 599–614.
3. Torra, V., Karlsson, A., Steinhauer, H. J., & Berglund, S. (2019). Artificial Intelligence. In A. Said & V. Torra (Eds.), *Data Science in Practice* (Vol. 46, pp. 269–272). Springer.
4. van Osselaer, S. M. J., Fuchs, C., Schreier, M., & Puntoni, S. (2020). The Power of Personal. *Journal of Retailing, 96*(1), 88–100.
5. Wright, L. T., Robin, R., Stone, M., & Aravopoulou, E. (2019). Adoption of Big Data Technology for Innovation in B2B Marketing. *Journal of Business-to-Business Marketing, 26*(3-4), 281–293.
6. Loureiro, S. M. C., Guerreiro, J., & Tussyadiah, I. (2021). Artificial intelligence in business: State of the art and future research agenda. *Journal of Business Research, 129*, 911–926.
7. Xiao, L., & Kumar, V. (2021). Robotics for Customer Service: A Useful Complement or an Ultimate Substitute? *Journal of Service Research, 24(1), 9–29.*
8. Du, S., & Xie, C. (2021). Paradoxes of artificial intelligence in consumer markets: Ethical challenges and opportunities. *Journal of Business Research, 129*, 961–974.

9. Duan, Y., Edwards, J. S., & Dwivedi, Y. K. (2019). Artificial intelligence for decision making in the era of Big Data – evolution, challenges and research agenda. *International Journal of Information Management, 48*, 63–71.
10. Liu, Y., & Li, Z. (2021). Application Analysis of Artificial Intelligence Technology in Brand Marketing Strategy. In *2021 International Conference on Forthcoming Networks and Sustainability in AIoT Era (FoNeS-AIoT)* (pp. 120–124). IEEE.
11. Li, C. (2022). The Impact and Response of Artificial Intelligence on the Theory of Enterprise Management. In *2022 3rd International Conference on Electronic Communication and Artificial Intelligence (IWECAI)* (pp. 314–317). IEEE.
12. Vishnoi, S. K., Bagga, T., & Tripathi, A. (2021). Exploring Technology and Organizational Capability from the Perspective of Marketing Intelligence. In *2021 9th International Conference on Reliability, Infocom Technologies and Optimization (Trends and Future Directions) (ICRITO)* (pp. 1–7). IEEE.
13. Tanveer, M., Khan, N., & Ahmad, A. -R. (2021). AI Support Marketing: Understanding the Customer Journey towards Business Development. In *2021 1st International Conference on Artificial Intelligence and Data Analytics (CAIDA)* (pp. 144–150). IEEE.
14. Liu, Y. (2021). Enterprise Brand Marketing Strategy under the Background of Artificial Intelligence. In *2021 International Conference on Forthcoming Networks and Sustainability in AIoT Era (FoNeS-AIoT)* (pp. 115–119). IEEE.
15. Singh, N., & Chouhan, S. S. (2021). Role of Artificial Intelligence for Development of Intelligent Business Systems. In *2021 IEEE International Symposium on Smart Electronic Systems (iSES)* (pp. 373–377). IEEE.
16. Agrawal, A., Gans, J. S., & Goldfarb, A. (2019). Artificial intelligence: The ambiguous labor market impact of automating prediction. *Journal of Economic Perspectives, 33*(2), 31–50.
17. Gursoy, D., Chi, O. H., Lu, L., & Nunkoo, R. (2019). Consumers acceptance of artificially intelligent (AI) device use in service delivery. *International Journal of Information Management, 49*, 157–169.
18. Huang, M. H., Rust, R., & Maksimovic, V. (2019). The feeling economy: Managing in the next generation of artificial intelligence (AI). *California Management Review, 61*(4), 43–65.
19. Zhao, X., Wang, C., Su, J., & Wang, J. (2019). Research and application based on the swarm intelligence algorithm and artificial intelligence for wind farm decision system. *Renewable Energy, 134*, 681–697.
20. Paliukas, V., & Savanevičienė, A. (2018). Harmonization of rational and creative decisions in quality management using AI technologies. *Economics and Business, 32*(1), 195–208.
21. Mogaji, E., Soetan, T. O., & Kieu, T. A. (2020). The implications of artificial intelligence on the digital marketing of financial services to vulnerable customers. *Australasian Marketing Journal (AMJ)*.
22. Bostrom, N. (2017). Strategic implications of openness in AI development. *Global Policy, 8*(2), 135–148.
23. Hasan, M. (2016). Roles of digital marketing communications over conventional marketing: A perspective on Ogilvy & Mather Communications (Pvt.) Ltd.
24. Vinuesa, R., Azizpour, H., Leite, I., Balaam, M., Dignum, V., Domisch, S., Fekkander, A., Langhans, S. D., Tegmark, M., & Nerini, F. F. (2020). The role of artificial intelligence in achieving the Sustainable Development Goals. *Nature Communications, 11*(1), 1–10.

25. He, J., Baxter, S. L., Xu, J., Xu, J., Zhou, X., & Zhang, K. (2019). The practical implementation of artificial intelligence technologies in medicine. *Nature Medicine, 25*(1), 30–36.
26. Liophanich, C. (2017). Knowledge management success factors: Human perspective. *Interdisciplinary Research Review, 12*(4), 32–43.
27. Sterne, J., & Razlogova, E. (2019). Machine Learning in Context, or Learning from LANDR: Artificial Intelligence and the Platformization of Music Mastering. *Social Media+ Society, 5*(2), 2056305119847525.
28. Canhoto, A. I., & Clear, F. (2020). Artificial intelligence and machine learning as business tools: A framework for diagnosing value destruction potential. *Business Horizons, 63*(2), 183–193.
29. Camilleri, M. A. (2018). Market segmentation, targeting and positioning. In *Travel Marketing, Tourism Economics and the Airline Product* (pp. 69–83). Springer, Cham.
30. Lashgari, M., Sutton-Brady, C., Søilen, K. S., & Ulfvengren, P. (2018). Adoption strategies of social media in B2B firms: a multiple case study approach. *Journal of Business & Industrial Marketing, 33*(5), 730–743. https://doi.org/10.1108/JBIM-10-2016-0242.
31. Kang, J. Y. M., & Kim, J. (2017). Online customer relationship marketing tactics through social media and perceived customer retention orientation of the green retailer. *Journal of Fashion Marketing and Management: An International Journal. 21*(3), 298–316. https://doi.org/10.1108/JFMM-08-2016-0071.
32. Toncar, M., & Munch, J. (2001). Consumer responses to tropes in print advertising. *Journal of Advertising, 30*(1), 55–65.
33. Timoshenko, A., & Hauser, J. R. (2019). Identifying customer needs from user-generated content. *Marketing Science, 38*(1), 1–20.
34. Tirunillai, S., & Tellis, G. J. (2014). Mining marketing meaning from online chatter: Strategic brand analysis of big data using latent dirichlet allocation. *Journal of Marketing Research, 51*(4), 463–479.
35. Stone, M., Aravopoulou, E., Ekinci, Y., Evans, G., Hobbs, M., Labib, A., Laughlin, P., Machtynger, J., & Machtynger, L. (2020). Artificial intelligence (AI) in strategic marketing decision-making: a research agenda. *The Bottom Line*.
36. Bauer, J., & Jannach, D. (2018). Optimal pricing in e-commerce based on sparse and noisy data. *Decision Support Systems, 106*, 2018, 53–63, ISSN 0167-9236, https://doi.org/10.1016/j.dss.2017.12.002.
37. Chester, R., Jerosch-Herold, C., Lewis, J., & Shepstone, L. (2018). Psychological factors are associated with the outcome of physiotherapy for people with shoulder pain: a multicentre longitudinal cohort study. *British Journal of Sports Medicine, 52*(4), 269–275.
38. Arlitsch, K., & Newell, B. (2017). Thriving in the age of accelerations: a brief look at the societal effects of artificial Intelligence and the opportunities for libraries. *Journal of Library Administration, 57*(7), 789–798.
39. Soni, N., Sharma, E. K., Singh, N., & Kapoor, A. (2020). Artificial Intelligence in Business: From Research and Innovation to Market Deployment. *Procedia Computer Science, 167*, 2200–2210.
40. Paliwal, M., Patel, M., Kandale, N., & Anute, N. (2021). Impact of artificial intelligence and machine learning on business operations. *Journal of Management Research and Analysis, 8*(2), 70–75, https://doi.org/10.18231/j.jmra.2021.015.

CHAPTER 8

Climate Smart Agriculture Analysis of Soil Properties and Weather Parameter Using Artificial Intelligence and Machine Learning

RAMDAS GORE, MINAKSHI SONAWANE, and BHARTI GAWALI

Department of Computer Science and Information Technology, Dr. Babasaheb Ambedkar Marathwada University, Aurangabad, Maharashtra, India

ABSTRACT

Soil, rainfall, humidity, and temperature have been significant factors in minimizing losses not only for companies, corporations, and politicians but also for farmers. Other atmospheric characteristics, such as soil and climate, are important for agriculture. To provide trustworthy weather predictions, atmospheric procedures must be understood, measurements must be improved, and research and development must continue. In India, the Ministry of Earth Science (MoES) strives to enhance forecasting through distinct programs and departments such as the India Meteorological Department (IMD) and the Indian Council of Agriculture Research (ICAR), as well as agricultural institutions. We obtained 160 soil samples from the Aurangabad district and a climate database from 1952 to 2017 (66 years) from IMD in Pune, Maharashtra, India.

This study intends to improve forecast accuracy in a variety of geographical locations ranging from weather subdivisions to agro-climate zones and soil property analyses. We also investigated the relationship between climatic parameters and soil qualities. Artificial intelligence and machine

Artificial Intelligence and Machine Learning for Business. Namita Mishra, A. V. Senthil Kumar (Eds.)

learning approaches have been used to develop extensive experimental location of soil analyses and projections for the Aurangabad region of Maharashtra, India. We employed pre-processing techniques for normalization, outliers, and database strategies. Using machine learning approaches, we created a prediction model for the Marathwada area. We forecasted using Holt Winter's methodologies for additive and multiplicative seasonality and trend. The consequence of additive seasonality and trend is favorable. The mean absolute percentage error (MAPE) values are 14.87, 11.38, 13.01, and 2.34 for total month rainfall, heavy rainfall, number of rainy days, and temperature respectively.

8.1 INTRODUCTION

Due to the consequences of harsh weather, diminishing soil quality, drying up places, and collapsing ecosystems, farmers have recently found it difficult to produce adequate food [1]. Artificial intelligence (AI) helps a wide range of sectors, including agriculture, and its primary aims are to increase production, and efficiency, and discover answers to long-standing difficulties related to critical agricultural jobs. AI has a tremendous impact on agriculture, assisting farmers in increasing output while reducing negative environmental consequences. Furthermore, the agriculture business openly and forcefully employs AI technology to change the ultimate result. Machine learning, a type of artificial intelligence, is critical to combating global warming and reducing greenhouse gas emissions [2]. It helps to design more efficient power systems, monitor agricultural emissions and deforestation, create novel low-carbon materials, anticipate extreme weather occurrences, and manage stubble [3].

According to scientific data, the climate is changing faster than predicted, which will have a negative impact on the socioeconomic growth of developing countries (Intergovernmental Panel on Climate Change (IPCC), 2018). Climate-sensitive industries like agriculture and forestry may suffer disproportionately as a result of changing weather patterns and rising temperatures.

In order for climate information or forecasts to be useful to smallholder farmers, they require agronomic assistance to help them manage their fields to avoid the consequences of climate risks. Climate data will only be useful in combating climate change issues if it can be accessed in a format that smallholder farmers can understand. However, the availability of climate data is usually limited by a number of socio-economic and technical challenges, limiting the use of climate data for effective decision-making. As a result, assessing the primary obstacles that prohibit smallholder farmers from successfully utilizing climate information is crucial [3].

Historically, smallholder farmers depended on their agro-ecological understanding to forecast rainfall patterns using a range of meteorological indicators. Smallholder farmers have developed complex mental models of the environment to guide their adaptation efforts, which include tree flowering and the arrival of specialized birds. With such agroecological knowledge, making critical climate change adaptation decisions, such as when to plant or harvest, becomes easier. However, smallholder farmers' dependence on local traditional knowledge has come under criticism since climate change is likely to exacerbate in the future, along with the possibility of catastrophic weather occurrences. Because of the effects of climate change, traditional indicators are either becoming less reliable or have vanished entirely. As a result, smallholder farmers must have ready access to fact-based climatic information such as temperature and rainfall in order to adapt to climate change [4].

It is critical to have current climate information in order to make informed decisions about how to deal with climate shocks in Maharashtra and India. There is still a scarcity of empirical evidence in the Marathwada region on the benefits of climate information and the barriers to smallholder farmers using these services more regularly, limiting their capacity to adapt to climate threats. The goal of this article is to examine soil features and climatic factors for smallholder farmers' resilient agricultural systems. This study report will offer the following responses: i) The kind of soil and climatic data analyses are accessible to smallholder farmers for use in making agricultural management decisions. ii) The agricultural systems in the Marathwada region use AI technology to provide climate information.

8.2 STUDY AREA AND METHODS

The three primary seasons in the Marathwada area are summer (pre-monsoon), monsoon (rainy), and winter (with post-monsoon). The summer season begins in March and continues until May. The season's sweltering heat. Temperatures vary from 35 to 42 °C. The rainy season, which lasts through September, begins in June. During this monsoon season, the kharif season also begins. There is a lot of humidity. In the fall, the monsoon season returns. It occurs during the winter season, and farmers harvest crops such as wheat, barley, oats, chickpeas or gram (pulses), linseed, mustard (oilseeds), and so on. The season is known as rabi.

There is less rain, and the vegetation begins to dry up. This time period marks the transition from wet to dry seasonal conditions in the bulk of India. The sky is normally clear for most of this season. The months of October and November 2019 had a lot of rain. Farmers spread kharip during the coldest months of the year. Recent cross-sectional research studies have mostly focused on how farmers are responding to climate change by changing crop varieties, using soil management practices, and implementing water conservation strategies. Adaptation, according to the research, increases household welfare when it is not hampered by financial access constraints and a lack of environmental knowledge. It helps determine how technologically successful agriculture is under changing climatic conditions and how this impacts food safety more easily.

8.2.1 CLIMATE AND SOIL DATABASE

The Indian Meteorological Department (IMD) in Pune, under India's Ministry of Earth Sciences, has provided the climate database. Data from IMD station index 43014 (Chikalthan, Aurangabad) from 1952 to 2018 was utilized. Meteorological variables such as temperature (in degrees Celsius), rainfall (in millimeters), relative humidity, the number of rainy days (RD), and mean wind speed (MWS, in kilometers per hour) were included in our forecast models. Additionally, 150 soil samples were collected from the villages of Chikalthan and Andhaner.

8.2.2 PRE-PROCESSING

The raw climate data was converted into an Excel file. Missing days, months, and years were identified. Soil samples were collected using zigzag methods and a 2 mm sieve for sample processing. Soil samples were examined at the Agriculture Engineering, MIT, CARS lab in Satara Parishar, Aurangabad [5].

8.2.2.1 OUTLIERS IN THE DATASET

Outliers were identified to detect low and extreme values in the database. Histograms and box plots were used to identify outliers, which can impact the prediction model.

We have removed the outliers from the dataset, it shown in Figure 8.1.

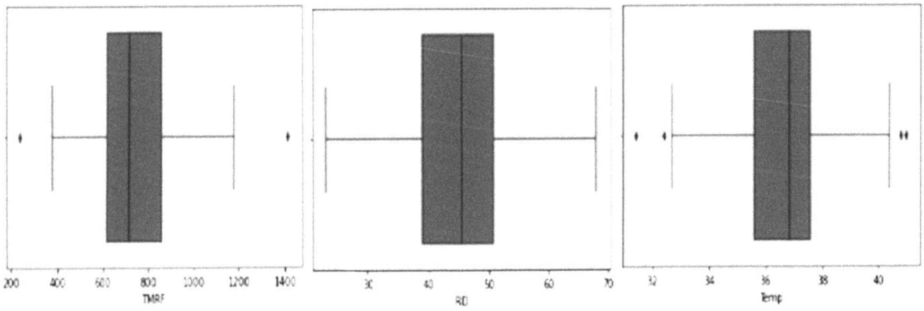

FIGURE 8.1 Outliers in the dataset.

8.3 TECHNIQUES

8.3.1 CORRELATION

Correlation is integrally connected to the statistical metrics of mean, standard deviation, variance, and covariance. Relationships between two or more variables (or features) of a dataset are widely explored in statistics and data science [6]. The features are the characteristics or properties of the observations, and each data point in the collection is an observation. We utilized variables and observations in every dataset we used. The dataset displays the characteristics or variables (temperature, total monthly rainfall, heavy rainfall in 24 hours, number of rainy days, mean wind speed, relative humidity).

When data is displayed in a table, the columns usually correlate to the characteristics, while the rows usually reflect the observations.

Each entry in this table represents a single observation or piece of data regarding a certain weather element (either month of Jan, Feb, Mar, etc.). Each column displays one feature from the whole collection of weather data (Any two characteristics in a dataset that we have evaluated have some kind of relationship). The pair diagram below depicts the pairwise relationship between these closely linked qualities [7] (Figures 8.2 and 8.3).

Each of these plots shows one of three different forms of correlation:

1. **Negative Correlation:** In a negative correlation plot, the y values normally fall as the x values increase. According to studies, large values of one quality are highly adversely connected with small values of the other, and vice versa.

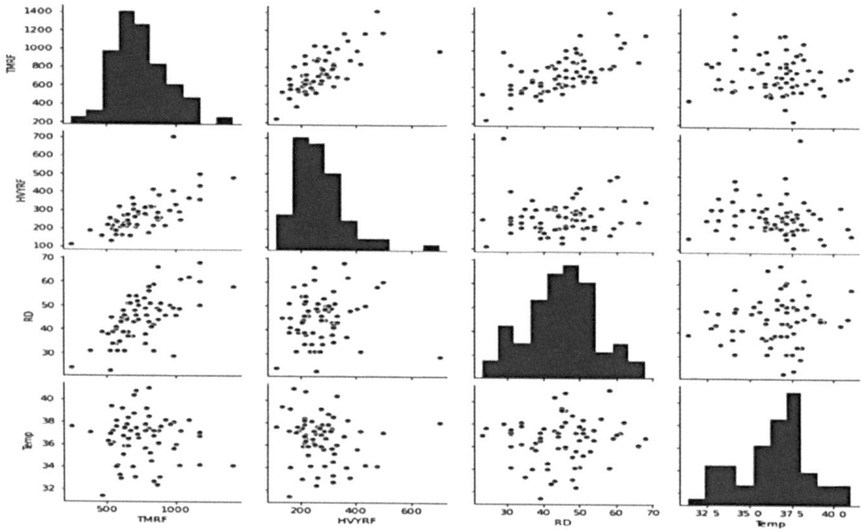

FIGURE 8.2 Correlation of weather parameters.

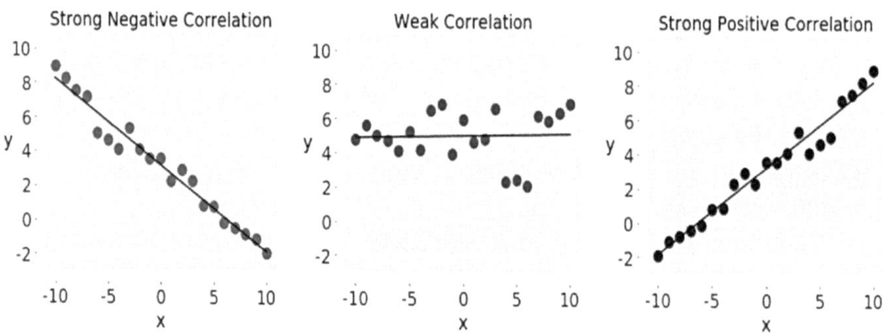

FIGURE 8.3 Three different forms of correlation.

2. **Weak or No Correlation:** The central figure shows no discernible trend. When there is no apparent or hardly noticeable link between two characteristics, this type of weak correlation arises.
3. **Positive Correlation:** When there is a large positive correlation, the y values frequently rise in tandem with the x values. There is a significant positive relationship when large values of one property match large values of the other, and vice versa [8].

8.3.2 *HEAT MAP OF WEATHER DATASET*

A correlation matrix is a table that shows how two variables in a dataset are related to one another. The rows and columns of this matrix each represent a variable, and each value in the matrix indicates the correlation coefficient between the variables represented by the relevant row and column. The correlation matrix is an important data analysis statistic used to summarize data so that consumers may better understand the link between various aspects and make educated decisions. When dimensionality reduction on huge volumes of data is necessary, the correlation matrix is a crucial pre-processing step in machine learning pipelines. Each cell in the correlation matrix represents the correlation coefficient between the two variables given by the row and column of the cell [9] (Figure 8.4).

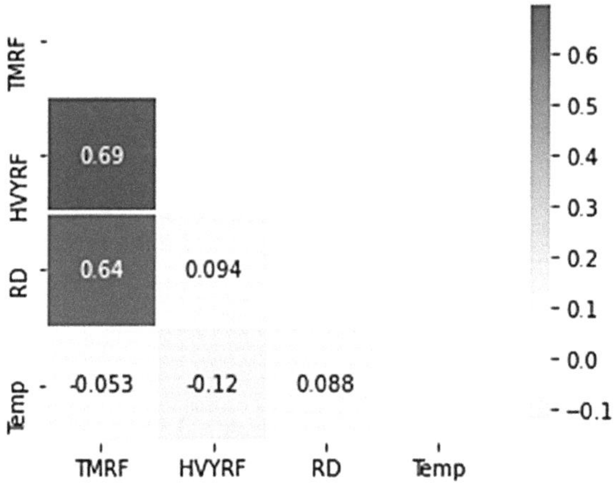

FIGURE 8.4 A correlation matrix of data.

8.3.3 *TIME SERIES ANALYSIS FOR CLIMATE*

It is the most widely used branch of data science, and machine learning, and analyzes historical data to uncover patterns, seasonality, and noise to forecast future trends. It is a type of predictive analysis in which previous data is extrapolated to estimate the value of a variable in hypothetical future situations. Because of outside factors, also known as independent variables, the projected values may differ from the actual values. The temperature on a given day, for example, may change based on the quantity of rain, humidity, wind speed, and so on [10].

A data scientist has access to a number of time series forecasting methodologies, but the algorithm they choose will be determined by the business problems they are attempting to address and the data they have available.

In addition to this algorithm, hybrid forecasting approaches that incorporate new procedures that have been developed to generate more exact prediction results are used. Hybrid forecasting approaches combine two or more forecasting methodologies [11].

8.3.4 HOLT WINTER'S METHOD

In the real world, demand data from any industry often demonstrates substantial seasonality and patterns. Models that take the trend and seasonality in the data into account are required when predicting demands in these scenarios because the business's option will be dependent on the model's output. It is one of several time series prediction methods, applied in such cases.

Holt-Exponential Winter's Smoothing is used as one of the first time series analytic approaches to forecasting that took trend and seasonality into account. This method is used to make predictions in three different ways based on trend and seasonality; it has an average value. For each of the three characteristics, there are three types of exponential smoothing, and Winter's method is also referred to as triple exponential smoothing for analysis [13]. As the name implies, simple exponential smoothing is used to anticipate when the data set lacks patterns or seasonality.

8.3.5 LIMITATIONS OF HOLT-WINTER'S TECHNIQUE

Even if the Holt-Winters approach delivers the best forecast for winter, it has certain downsides. One of the algorithm's key weaknesses is the multiplicative component of seasonality. The multiplicative seasonality issue concerns how the model behaves during periods of low rainfall. Seasonality, which is defined as a relative term, varies dramatically and is taken into account when developing the model. A time period with a data point of 10 or 1 might have an actual difference of 9, but a relative difference of around 100% [14].

8.3.6 MEAN ABSOLUTE PERCENTAGE ERROR (MAPE)

MAPE is a metric that measures how accurate a forecasting system is. The accuracy is expressed as a percentage. It is calculated using the following formula.

$$MAPE = \frac{1}{n} \Sigma_{(t=1)}^{n} \left| \frac{e_t}{Y_t} \right| \quad (1)$$

where; 'n' denotes the number of data points; and 'e_t' denotes the forecast error from $Y_t - \hat{Y}_t$.

8.4 RESULT AND DISCUSSION

There are two types of models: multiplicative and additive. The key principle of the additive model is that each data point's predicted value is the total of its baseline, trend, and seasonality components. Similarly, to forecast the value for each data point, the multiplicative model computes the baseline values, trend, and seasonality components (Table 8.1).

The additive seasonality gives good results for climate trends, and seasonal and forecast errors (Table 8.2).

The temperature and rainfall have increased in the last decade and are expected to increase in the next decade (2018–2027). The number of rainy days has decreased in the last decade. Heavy rainfall has increased during the monsoon season, occurring over 3–4 days and covering the total monthly average rainfall. This indicates wet droughts. The simple exponential method has provided better results for total monthly rainfall, heavy rainfall, and the number of rainy days parameter. The Holt method has yielded good results for temperature (1.97). The MAPE values for total monthly rainfall, heavy rainfall, and the number of rainy days are 14.87, 11.38, and 13.01, respectively. We have analyzed the soil properties and found the soil texture of samples (Table 8.3).

The identification of sand, silt, and clay is based on size:

- Sand 0.05 to 2.00 mm in diameter;
- Silt 0.002 to 0.05 mm in diameter;
- Clay < 0.002 mm in diameter.

Most of the soil sample texture is silt clay loam. Narshingpure village soil sample is sandy loam. Chikhalthan and Andhaner village soil sample texture is clay loam. Silt soil texture is high in all soil samples. As per the soil sample recommended the following crops are in Table 8.4.

Table 8.5 shows statistics on land (soil) usage, and the most significant crops cultivated in six primary climatic zones.

Crop development is influenced by both climatic (most notably temperature) and non-climatic variables, such as the availability of appropriate soils.

TABLE 8.1 Holt-Winters Exponential Smoothing with Additive and Multiplicative Seasonality and Trend

Additive Seasonality	Multiplicative Seasonality
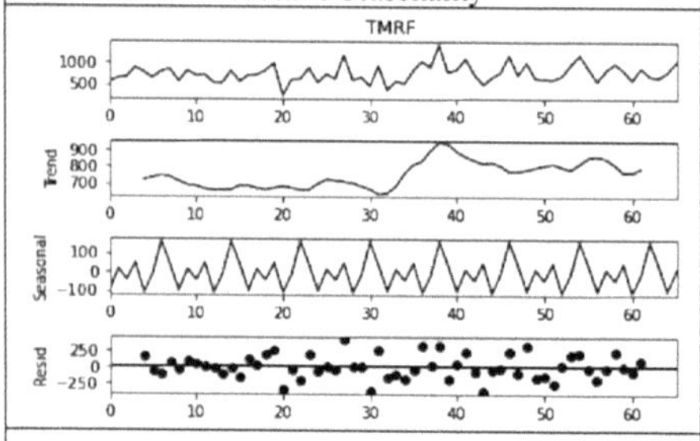	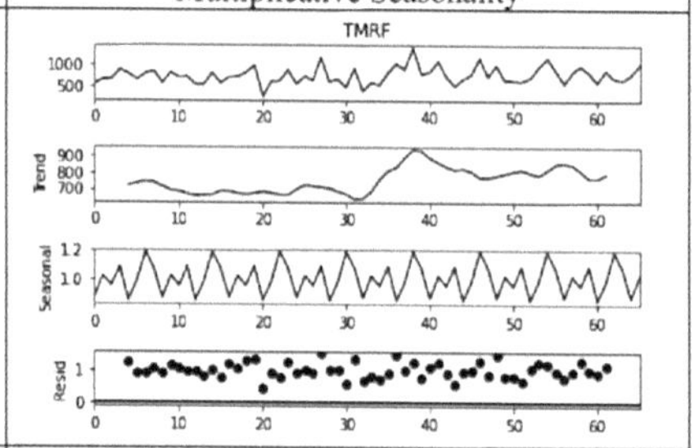
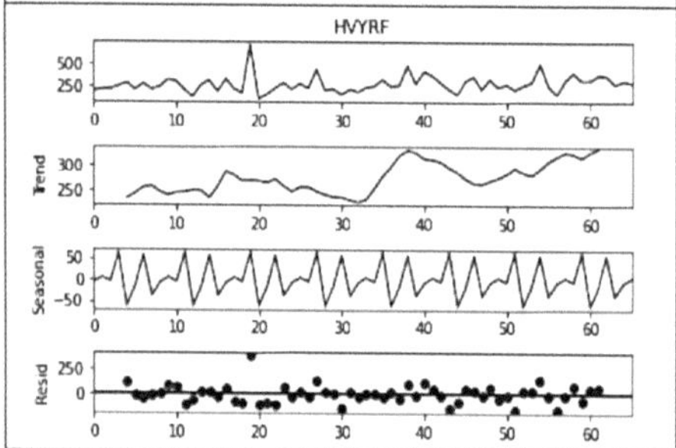	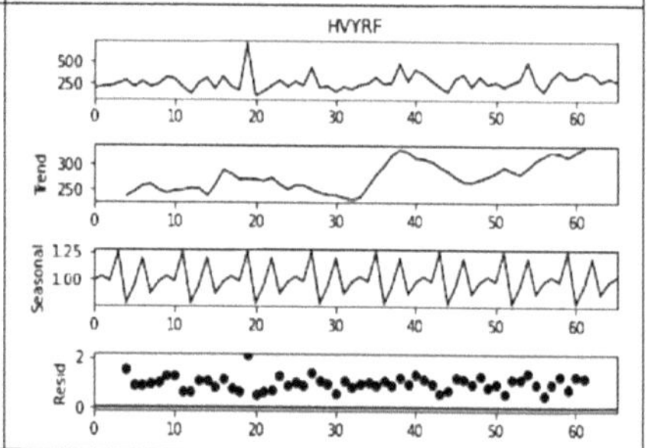
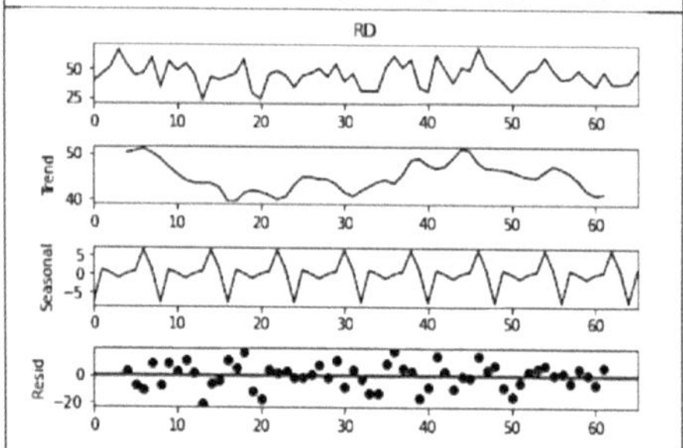	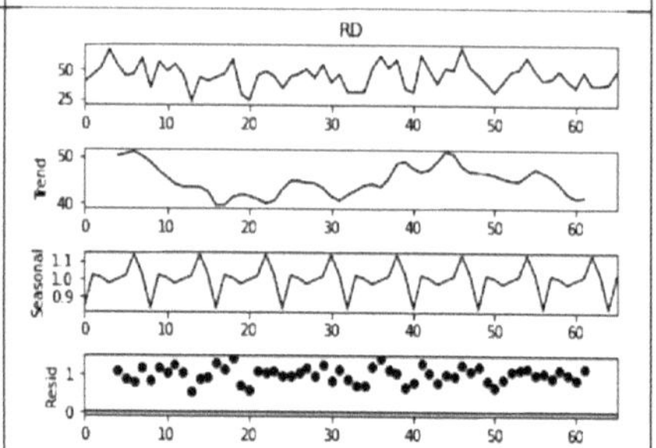
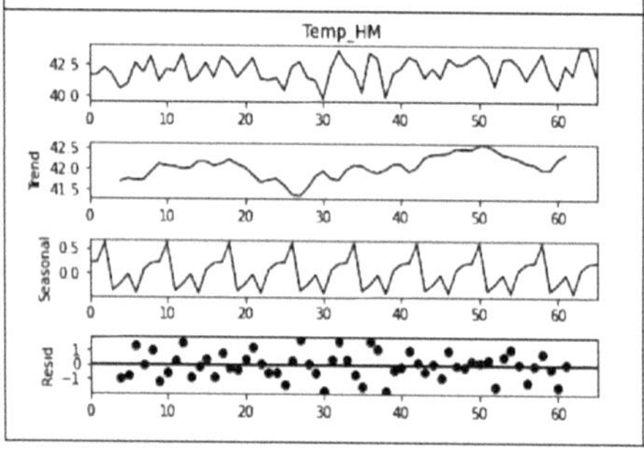	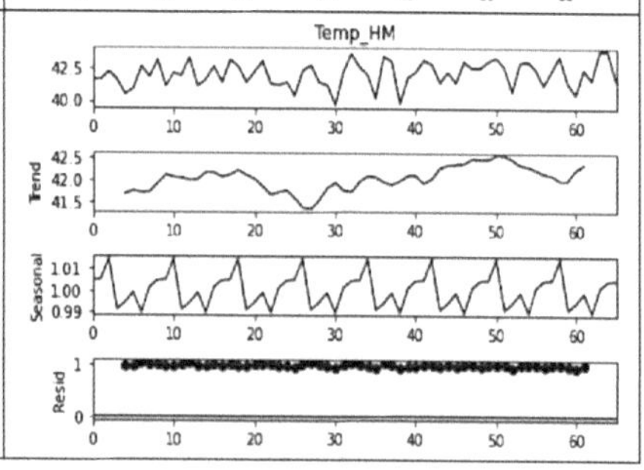

Crop development is hampered by low temperatures at certain times of the year (winter season) or at high elevations (mountainous places). Due to extreme temperatures, other places are not suited for some crops.

TABLE 8.2 Result of Methods and Moving Average for the Time Series

Parameter of Database	Simple Exponential Method	Holt Method	Holts Winter with Additive Seasonality and Trend	MAPE
TMRF	17.44	21.76	32.14	14.87
HVYRF	19.67	26.94	20.48	11.38
RD	14.91	44.48	26.96	13.01
Temp.	2.17	1.97	1.99	2.34

TABLE 8.3 Soil Textures of Samples

Name of Village/ City	Sand (%)	Clay (%)	Silt (%)	Total	Texture Class
Chikhalthan	23	37	40	100	Clay loam
Andhaner	20	29	51	100	Clay loam
Rithi	9	28	63	100	Silt clay loam
Aurangabad	13	26	61	100	Silt clay loam
Khultabad	15	27	58	100	Silt clay loam
Ellora	18	26	56	100	Silt clay loam
Mulwadi	17	52	31	100	Clay
Narshinpure	29	22	49	100	Sandy loam

8.5 CONCLUSION

Holt Winter's method has numerous applications. It is used in a variety of research and business problems for two reasons: first, it has an easy implementation approach, and second, the model will adapt as our research and company demands change.

Holt Winter's time series model, despite being one of the simplest, provides a powerful prediction algorithm. It can manage seasonality in the data set by calculating the central value and adding or multiplying it by the slope and seasonality. If the correct set of parameters is dialed in, the best-fitting model is all that is necessary. Always remember to use the MAPE or RMSE (Root Mean Squared Error) numbers to assess the model's efficacy. The accuracy of the model will vary based on the research or commercial challenge at hand, as well as the data collection utilized to construct and evaluate it. In the pairwise correlation, TMRF, HVYRF, and RD have a strong correlation, while rainfall and temperature have a negative correlation, and RD and temperature have a weak correlation.

The amount of rain falls differently from year to year. The Marathwada region as a whole is impacted by the fact that certain areas receive more

TABLE 8.4 Soil Health Recommendation for Crops

Name of Crop	Vegetative Stage	Flowering Stage	Maturity Stage	Post-Harvest
Cotton	To avoid surface ponding, open field canals to drain surplus water. After the rain has stopped, apply a foliar spray containing 2% urea. To promote soil aeration, intercultivate at optimal soil wetness.	To avoid surface ponding, open field canals to drain surplus water. To encourage flowering, use a multi-nutrient or hormonal spray.	To avoid surface ponding, open field canals to drain surplus water. Cotton harvesting on time.	Protect harvested cotton against soaking and soiling in storage. Wet cotton drying and marketing.
Pearl millet	Drain any extra water as soon as possible. Inter-cropping with a hoe. After draining any extra water, add 20 kg more nitrogen per hectare.		Remove any excess water as quickly as possible. Harvest, when physiological maturity is reached. Green cobs from uprooted plants, should be harvested for immediate sale. Use an ear head dryer to fully dry the ear heads before harvesting them.	Harvest the cobs after they are dried up properly. Dry the grain to optimum moisture content before storage.
Maize and sorghum	Drain any extra water as soon as possible. Inter-cropping with a hoe and apply 25 kg additional N / ha after draining of excess water.			
Soybean	Any excess water should be drained as quickly as feasible.		Harvesting of mature crops on time.	Moving to a safer location and drying the veggies.
Green gram/black gram-chickpea			Any excess water should be drained as quickly as feasible. Before harvesting, let the crop dry.	Threshing after quick drying.

*N: Nitrogen.

TABLE 8.5 Major Climatic Zones and Land Use

Climatic Zone	Land (Soil) Use (Major Crops)
Desert	No rainfed agriculture, hunters and gatherers, nomadic pastoralists, or stationary irrigators near an oasis.
Arid	Extensive grazing, and flood irrigation of millet and sorghum in damp depressions.
Semi-arid	Nomadic pastoralists as well as cultivators grow millet and sorghum, which are the most common crops, but short-cycle cowpea, phaseolus beans, and groundnuts are also grown. There is no fodder or pasture. Maize is grown in colder climates.
Sub-humid	In dry season and drought years, traditional nomadic pastoralists. Settlement crops included millet, sorghum, maize, and groundnuts, as well as cassava, cowpeas, cotton, sweet potatoes, tobacco, rainfed rice, soybean, mango, and cashew nuts. Possible fodder and planted pasture.
Moist sub-humid	Agriculture's transition zone: too moist for seasonal crops, too dry for tree crops. Tropical crops include maize, cassava, yams, bananas, pineapple, sugarcane, and rice. Wheat and barley are grown in winter rainfall zones.
Humid	Tree crops such as oil palm, rubber, and cocoa are featured. It is altering farming to include root crops like yams and cassava, as well as sorghum, maize, banana, sugarcane, rice, and tropical hardwoods.

rain than others. As a result of the high temperatures and low rainfall, the Marathwada area endures drought conditions for most of the year. Therefore, it is vital to switch the crops planted in this area to those that are temperature-resistant.

KEYWORDS

- **artificial intelligent**
- **climate parameter**
- **forecasting model**
- **machine learning**
- **prediction model**
- **rainfall**
- **soil properties**
- **temperature**
- **time-series trend**
- **weather**

REFERENCES

1. Lakhiar, I. A., Jianmin, G., Syed, T. N., Chandio, F. A., Buttar, N. A., & Qureshi, W. A. (2018). Monitoring and control systems in agriculture using intelligent sensor techniques: A review of the aeroponic system. *Journal of Sensors, 2018*(1), 8672769.
2. Liakos, K. G., Busato, P., Moshou, D., Pearson, S., & Bochtis, D. (2018). Machine learning in agriculture: A review. *Sensors, 18*(8), 2674.
3. Dheeraj, A., Nigam, S., Begam, S., Naha, S., Devi, S. M., Chaurasia, H. S., & Kumar, V. V. S. (2020). Role of Artificial Intelligence (AI) and Internet of Things (IoT) in mitigating climate change. In *Climate Change and Indian Agriculture: Challenges and Adaptation Strategies* (pp. 465–472). ICAR-National Academy of Agricultural Research Management, Hyderabad, Telangana, India.
4. Antwi-Agyei, P., Dougill, A. J., & Abaidoo, R. C. (2021), Opportunities and barriers for using climate information for building resilient agricultural systems in Sudan savannah agro-ecological zone of north-eastern Ghana, *Climate Services, 22*(2021), 100226. https://doi.org/10.1016/j.cliser.2021.100226
5. Abhilash, Alka Rani, Arti Kumari, Ram Narayan Singh, & Kavita Kumari. (2021). Climate-Smart Agriculture: An Integrated Approach for Attaining Agricultural Sustainability. In *Climate Change and Resilient Food Systems* (pp.141–189). Springer, Singapore.
6. Alreshidi, E. (2019). Smart sustainable agriculture (SSA) solution underpinned by internet of things (IoT) and artificial intelligence (AI), *International Journal of Advanced Computer Science and Applications, 10*(5), 93–102, *arXiv preprint arXiv:1906.03106.*
7. Bannerjee, G., Sarkar, U., Das, S., & Ghosh, I. (2018). Artificial Intelligence in Agriculture: A Literature Survey. *International Journal of Scientific Research in Computer Science Applications and Management Studies, 7*(3), 1–6.
8. Bose, B. K. (2017). Artificial intelligence techniques in smart grid and renewable energy systems-Some example applications. *Proceedings of the IEEE, 105*(11), 2262–2273.
9. Chostner, B. (2017). See & Spray: the next generation of weed control. *Resource Magazine, 24*(4), 4–5.
10. Grieve, B. D., Duckett, T., Collison, M., Boyd, L., West, J., Yin, H., Arvin, F., & Pearson, S. (2019). The challenges posed by global broadacre crops in delivering smart agri-robotic solutions: A fundamental rethink is required. *Global Food Security, 23*, 116–124.
11. McGovern, A., Elmore, K. L., Gagne, D. J., Haupt, S. E., Karstens, C. D., Lagerquist, R., Smith, T., & Williams, J. K. (2017). Using artificial intelligence to improve real-time decision-making for high-impact weather. *Bulletin of the American Meteorological Society, 98*(10), 2073–2090.
12. Maspo, N., Harun, A. N., Goto, M., Nawi, M. N. M., & Haron, N. A. (2018). Development of Internet of Thing (IoT) technology for flood prediction and Early Warning System (EWS). *International Journal of Innovative Technology and Exploring Engineering (IJITEE), 8*(4S), 219–228.
13. Gore, R. D., & Gawali, B. W. (2021). Vulnerability Assessment of Climate-Smart Agriculture. In *Recent Trends in Image Processing and Pattern Recognition: Third International Conference, RTIP2R 2020, Aurangabad, India, January 3–4, 2020, Revised Selected Papers, Part II 3* (pp. 290–301). Springer Singapore.
14. Vincent, D. R., Deepa, N., Elavarasan, D., Srinivasan, K., Chauhdary, S. H., & Iwendi, C. (2019). Sensors driven AI-based agriculture recommendation model for assessing land suitability. *Sensors, 19*(17), 3667.

CHAPTER 9

A Novel Approach to Monitor Garbage System by Using LORA Technology

P. SALEEM AKRAM and M. LAKSHMANA KUMAR

Department of ECE, Koneru Lakshmaiah Education Foundation (Deemed to be University), Guntur, Andhra Pradesh, India

ABSTRACT

The current state of the world's population expansion poses a significant challenge to the garbage disposal and maintenance systems. In this article, we propose an IoT-LoRA-based smart garbage monitoring and notifying alarm system, where a buzzer would be used to notify the amount of waste currently in the bin. People receive the status of garbage bin full to avoid overflow of garbage bins. The sensor in the bin monitors the garbage level after it has been disposed of and intimates people to utilize those particular bins. In the event that the trash level exceeds the permitted threshold, a notice is issued to the concerned authorities to dispose of the garbage at the earliest. A clearing alert notification is sent to the concerned authorities if the trash level is under the threshold level but not cleared for more than two days. The LoRA nodes play a vital role in the information distribution system of central IoT monitoring through gateways. The advantages of LoRA nodes are providing long-range communication, easy installation, low power requirement, and low cost. The presented proposal provides a robust solution to manage potential hazardous garbage and waste management systems. In this proposal, we also suggest potential hardware and software to construct the technologically advanced solution. This detailed reference is intended to provide a platform with a better design and implementation.

Artificial Intelligence and Machine Learning for Business. Namita Mishra, A. V. Senthil Kumar (Eds.)

9.1 INTRODUCTION

Overpopulated towns face everyday issues owing to the overpopulated population. Every day these cities produce enormous amounts of rubbish. Overflowing public dustbins cause the foul smell of healthy environments. Solid residues Pollution of garbage is one of the hazards to human survival. This occurs when waste products like food leftovers, paper, plastic, glass, iron, canned goods, animal bones, and vegetable peels [1] are dispersed in the open areas, as shown in Figure 9.1, leading to rotting, odor dispersion, and air contamination, and spread when waste is consumed in the surrounding areas with the threat of living things. Solid waste management is one of the most exemplary initiatives performed by municipal authorities to keep urban centers clean. The authorities have provided area-specific incentives for the regular collection of rubbish. Figure 9.1 depicts the unrecovered waste divided on highways, causing significant health hazards in cities. The rubbish collected is eventually thrown inside and outside the town and incinerated into open spaces or dumps. Burning problems generate harmful gases that provide terrible smells in the surrounding places that impair the health of the living. The cities are confronting solid waste management challenges with their rising population. According to the report, over 377 million urban inhabitants live in 7,935 cities each year, producing 62 million tons (MT) of solid municipal trash. 11.9 MT is recycled, and 31 MT is thrown out of so much garbage gathered. News about Vijayawada City states that the city produces an average of 0.5 kilograms tons/day, with a population of roughly 10.18 million, municipal solid waste each day. The Bengaluru Bruhat Mahanagará Palike (BBMP) is a leading member of the municipal solid waste management sectors of health and engineering [2, 3].

The Ministry of Health collects, transports, and disposes of solid waste. Built and demolition debris is available to the Engineering department. Different researchers have conducted several actions and architectural solutions for waste management [6] in clever urban areas mentioned in genuine parts.

9.2 RELATED WORK

One of the main issues for a healthy urban environment is solid waste management. Solid waste management has become both necessary and difficult with rapid urbanization and population growth. The environment would be polluted and dirty if garbage were not handled and collected on time. A better waste management strategy might boost general well-being and help to establish a better community. Many IoT-based waste management

FIGURE 9.1 Garbage collection.

solutions are now being developed to enhance the trash collection process and provide a healthier and more efficient environment for the green planet [4, 5]. Municipalities wishing for cleaner urban environments can use a system based on IoT [6, 7]. Some Internet of Things-based waste management systems [8–10] When a garbage bin has reached its full capacity, send a message alarm. An IoT system that monitors typical garbage and is cost-effective. A smart city's solid waste management system based on IoT allows garbage bin monitoring, dynamic programming, and vehicle routing [11, 12]. To integrate the most modern solution for self-powered solutions, an analysis of existing IoT-enabled solutions in trash management by smart cities is carried out [13, 14]. IoT is a revolutionary new platform that will benefit the entire world's population. The Internet of Things (IoT) lies at the heart of the impending engine revolution.

The phrase "Internet of Things" is widely employed to refer to a system in which objects are embedded with sensors and use an Internet connection to broadcast their "digital voice" to the outside world. IoT is feasible with enough electricity and an internet connection [15]. IoT has developed into a purpose-built network aggregation in recent years. [16, 17]. Blynk, Ubidots,

IBM Bluemix, and Devicepilots were the IoT platforms used for this project. In this case, we are using IoT-based LoRa technologies to transfer data to the cloud in an efficient [18] manner. Ubidots is a simple, user-friendly cloud service that allows users to communicate with devices ranging from their smartphones and PCs to an embedded system [19]. A computer is available from Ubidots. Ubidots is a platform that can link various device types to a cloud database and record variables [20, 21] that may be expressed and represented quickly and securely.

This article shows how to use IoT – LoRa technology on Ubidots Cloud to create a Smart Waste Collection Monitoring and Alert System [22, 23]. LoRa nodes are important in sending and collecting data in this scenario. Each smart dustbin has a LoRa node, an ultrasonic sensor, a motor, and other components [24, 25]. It means regular dust bins without the proposed model with LoRa technology can be called smart dust bins, as shown in Figure 9.1.

9.3 METHODOLOGY

The trash bins are changed into smart rubbish bins under the practical technique of monitoring the waste management system. These trash cans can also connect with the sweeper surveillance area to update their status in real time by implementing the suggested IoT-LoRa protocol. Updating status information allows a sweeper to gather waste after filling with LoRaWAN nodes in all the city's waste bins into the principal internet surveillance desk. The handling of municipal trash management is made easier and more accessible by having and arranging all the information required on a dashboard.

9.3.1 PROPOSED MODEL

This part gives a brief overview of the project's development and approach. This proposal presented a technique for controlling waste material from waste bin overflows, and the warning was sent to the waste collecting cleaner. Monitoring the state of the garbage collection might be successfully controlled using the expected system. This study suggests a methodology in which the waste level might be monitored regularly to avoid overflowing the bin. The filling level of the garbage and the initial level can be detected/monitored using an ultrasound sensor. Arduino UNO programming takes place to deliver the information message to the user asking that the dustbin be cleaned once a specified amount of fullness has been noticed. The LoRa Transmitter Block is shown in Figure 9.2(a) as a reference to the block design, and Figure 9.2(b) shows the LoRa Receiver Block Smart Trash.

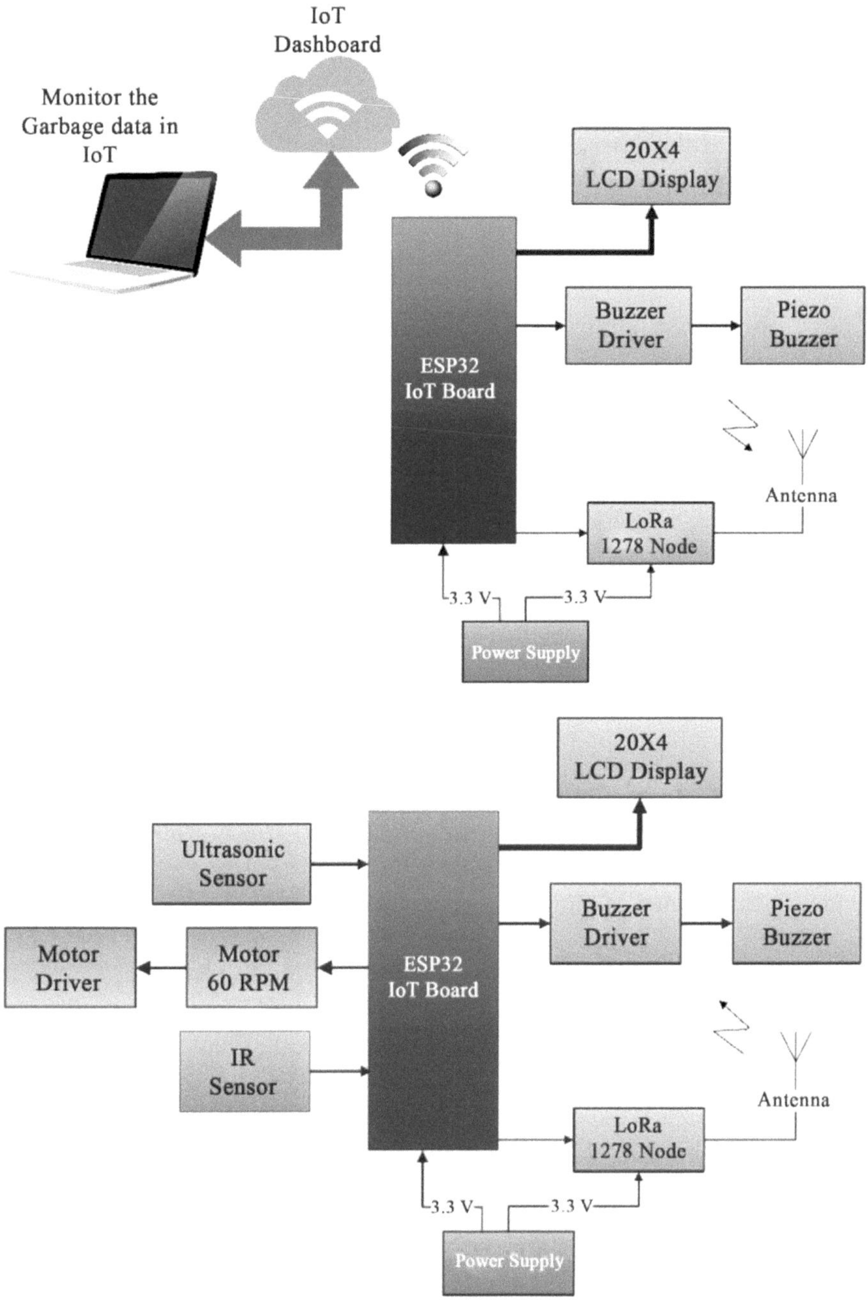

FIGURE 9.2 (a) Smart garbage LoRa transmitter block; and (b) smart garbage LoRa receiver block.

The hardware components in the transmitter/receiver scheme will now investigate each module:

1. **System Monitor:** The Garbage data with IoT is monitored through smart Internet connections.
2. **IoT Dashboard:** A data visualization tool that converts, displays, and organizes a data collection that the network-linked devices gather and broadcast. The fundamental objective of the IoT dashboard is to provide legible human information to monitor historical and real-time IoT data remotely.
3. **ESP32 IoT Board:** This is utilized as an interface between the IoT dashboard's genuine data collecting. It offers Bluetooth dual-mode interaction with embedded devices through Wi-Fi (and in some variants). While ESP32 is only a chip, it is commonly called "ESP32" by the manufacturer. The modules and development boards include this chip. With a clock rate above 240 MHz, the ESP32 device contains a Tensilica Xtensa LX6 microprocessor with dual-core and single-core versions.
4. **LCD Display:** We're using the 20X4 LCD here to get dustbin messages like "FULL," and 'NOT FULL' along with the dustbin percentage filled threshold values like 50, 60, 70, etc.
5. **LoRa 1278 Node:** The central portion transmits the complete information and is passed on to the monitor. The LoRa module we use in this case is the 433 MHz Sx1278 Ra-02. I come from India, and the frequency range without a license goes from 865MHz to 867 MHz. So, for some time, not for educational purposes, I have been legally permitted for the 433 MHz frequency module. Check the permitted ranges in your country and make sure that you utilize this specific frequency range. The LoRa modules have various frequencies; the 433 MHz, 915 MHz, and 868 MHz are more frequent. At the module's rear is the frequency at which your module functions. Figure 9.3 represents the transmitting/receiving LoRa side related to Arduino UNO.
6. **Buzzer Driver and Piezo Buzzer:** We'll use the buzzer to warn that the dust bin is full, that no more waste should be added, and to prompt you to check if another bin is nearby. The Driver Buzzer is used to operate the buzzer circuit.

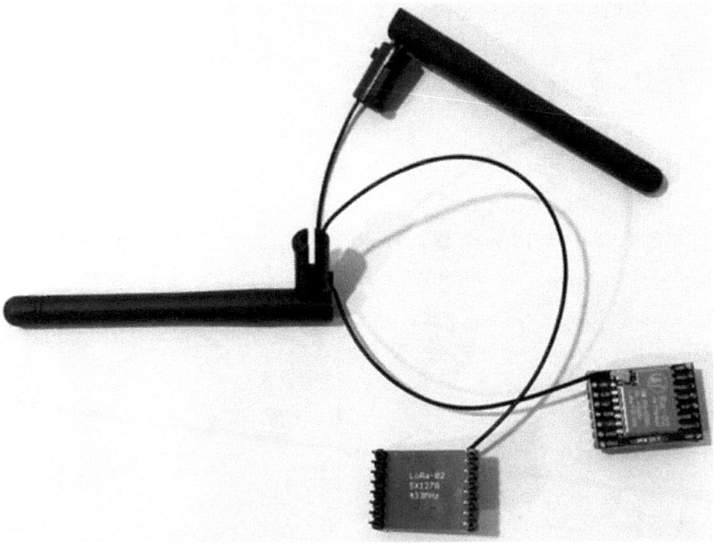

FIGURE 9.3 SX1278 with Arduino UNO.

7. **Power Supply:** This is a crucial component in the entire circuit diagram that provides power to all the components in the circuit. It typically takes a 230 V input power and steps it down to the required power supply for each component, such as 3.3 V, 3.5 V, etc.

   Now, we will describe the hardware equipment of the receiver, where we install the setup in the smart dust bins shown in Figure 9.4. We will discuss other hardware components in addition to those mentioned earlier as part of the Transmitter. These components perform similar functions on both the transmitter and receiver sides. The hardware components used in the transmitter part will be discussed below.

8. **Ultrasonic Sensor:** These are placed on the top of the bin or the deck of the waste bin, as shown in Figure 9.4(a)–(c). As the trash accumulates, the ultrasonic sensor emits sound waves. There is a transmitter and a receiver that calculate the distance using sound waves at a specific frequency. To determine the distance between the ultrasonic sensor and the target, the time taken for the sound waves to be emitted and received is measured. It consists of a Receiver sensor and an ultrasonic transmitter. Distance can be measured using the following formula:

$$\text{Distance } L = [(½) \times T \times C] \quad (1)$$

were; 'L' is the distance; 'T' is the time from issue to receipt; and 'C' is the sonic speed. (The value is doubled by 1/2 since "T" is the time to spin back and forth).

In Figure 9.4, the garbage container with sensors can be located at the top edge of the container. The way waste bin model stages of information collection are repeated in the same way. The collected data or information is passed on to the Ubidots Platform. The prototype diagram of the smart bin is illustrated in Figure 9.4.

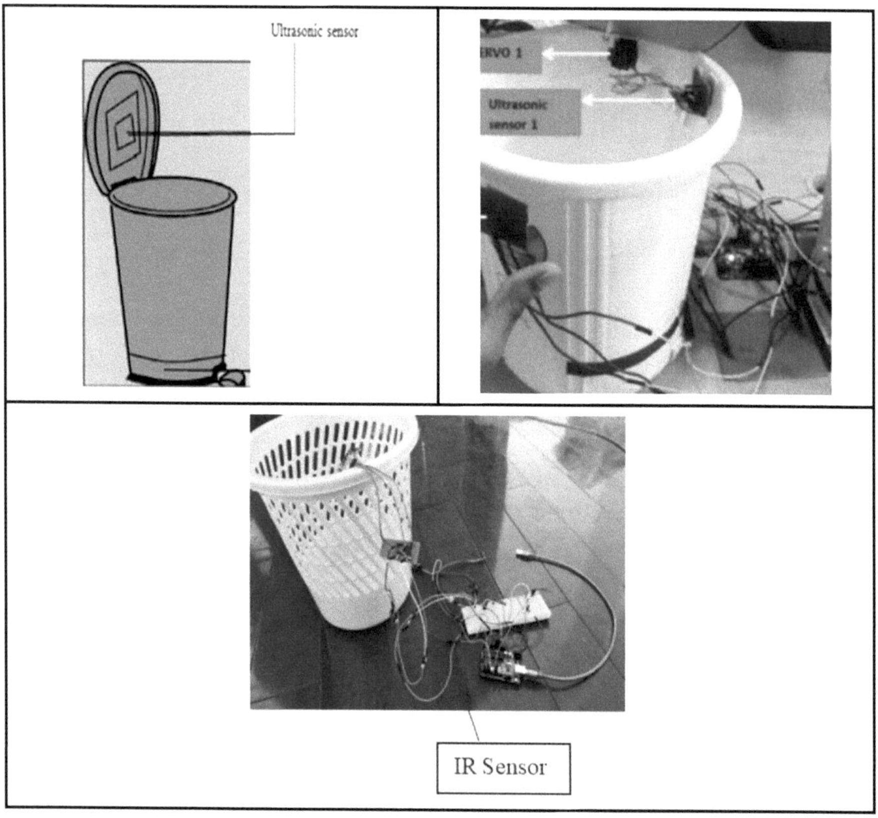

FIGURE 9.4 (a) Proposed model with ultrasonic sensor; (b) smart dust bin with ultrasonic sensor and servo motor; and (c) smart dust bin with ultrasonic sensor and servo motor and IR sensor.

A motor will be connected to the smart dustbin to open/close the lid of the dustbin when someone approaches the bin. A motor with 60 RPM will be connected and operated with an IR sensor.

9. **IR Sensor:** The smart bin's IR sensor detects any person approaching or leaving near the dust bin. Whenever it identifies any person near the bin, it sends a signal to the motor driver, which operates the motor to open/close the lid.

9.3.2 *CONFIGURATION AND DEVELOPMENT OF SOFTWARE*

During the software development and setup phase, the sensor node's MAC and IP addresses should be configured in Arduino to send the garbage bin's depth level to the Ubidots IoT cloud (Figure 9.5).

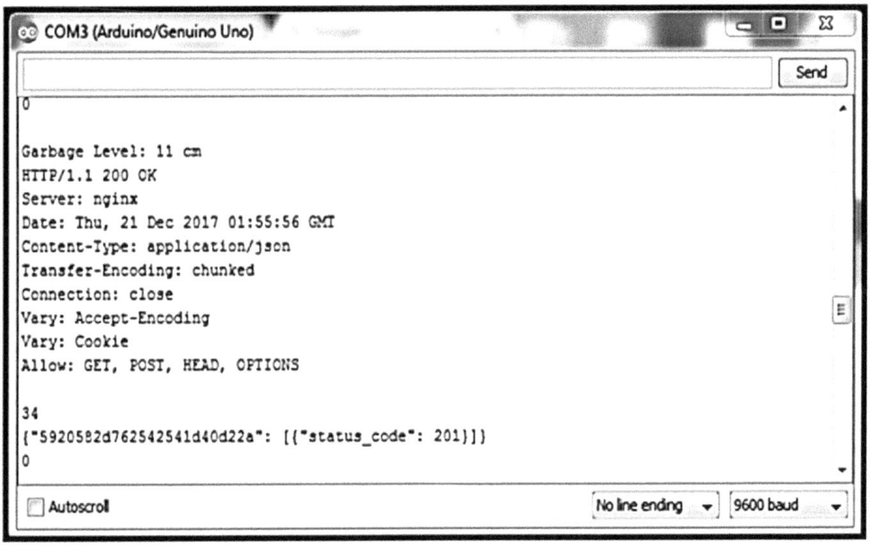

FIGURE 9.5 Data from ultrasonic sensors is uploaded to the Ubidots cloud.

The data collected from a sensor node using the MQTT protocol connection to Arduino IDE's Ubidots platform is presented in Figure 9.5. Figure 9.5 shows that the transmission encoding, acceptance, and cookie are altered for this project. The connection is provided through a connection between the Arduino IDE and Ubidots Websites. After numerous rounds of medication coding, Arduino, Node configuration, and Arduino Ethernet Shield configuration, the data will be collected and transferred to Ubidots IoT Cloud. The project began with the establishment of the Ubidots Platform's IoT structure.

9.4 RESULTS

This section displayed the data acquired during the project in Vijayawada, Andhra Pradesh, India. The gathered pieces of information were utilized to assess the system's performance, and those results are shown in two parts. The garbage bin depth data is presented on the Arduino IDE serial monitor from the distance measuring data from the Ultrasonic sensor. The IoT Cloud Platform Ubidots dashboard displays the status of garbage content in bin results covered in the second section.

9.4.1 *SMART GARBAGE SYSTEM MONITORING SYSTEM LAYOUT ARCHITECTURE*

Figure 9.6 depicts the model architecture of the data acquisition working process involving smart bins' status data collection and transfer to the cloud through the LoRa gateway to display the bins' status on a monitor. First, we will replace the bins with smart bins using LoRa technology across the whole city. In Figure 9.6 the Node1 and Node2, the recipient sections, i.e., data from two distinct smart bins, are represented. The message on an LCD attached to the smart bin will appear when the smart bin is emptied and ready for the rubbish initially. It also automatically opens the deck to take waste employing a linked motor, depending on the IR sensor inputs that can detect anybody coming close to it. When the smart bin is filled, the notification on the LCD will show as 'Smart bin is full, choose another smart bin nearby.' At the same time, its alarm sounds like a buzzer so that people can notify themselves and avoid getting close to the trash. The LoRa node is linked with Arduino and will send the same information to the cloud and monitor through the internet via a LoRa gateway, where all primary and current data are stored. The central city office monitor can recognize the smart bin threshold levels in different areas, stop the buzzer, and promptly inform the cleaning personnel of the empty bin by determining the site on the monitor. Data is collected and monitored similarly to Node 2. In this essay, we have tracked and observed data from 5 smart bins in the town of Vijayawada.

9.4.2 *UBIDOTS DASHBOARD RESULTS*

We can now examine the results of the Ubidots Dashboard using Figures 9.8(a) below 9.8(c). The raw data bits on the Ubidots Dashboard are presented in Figure 9.7. Here the data reveals the numerical value of the smart bins.

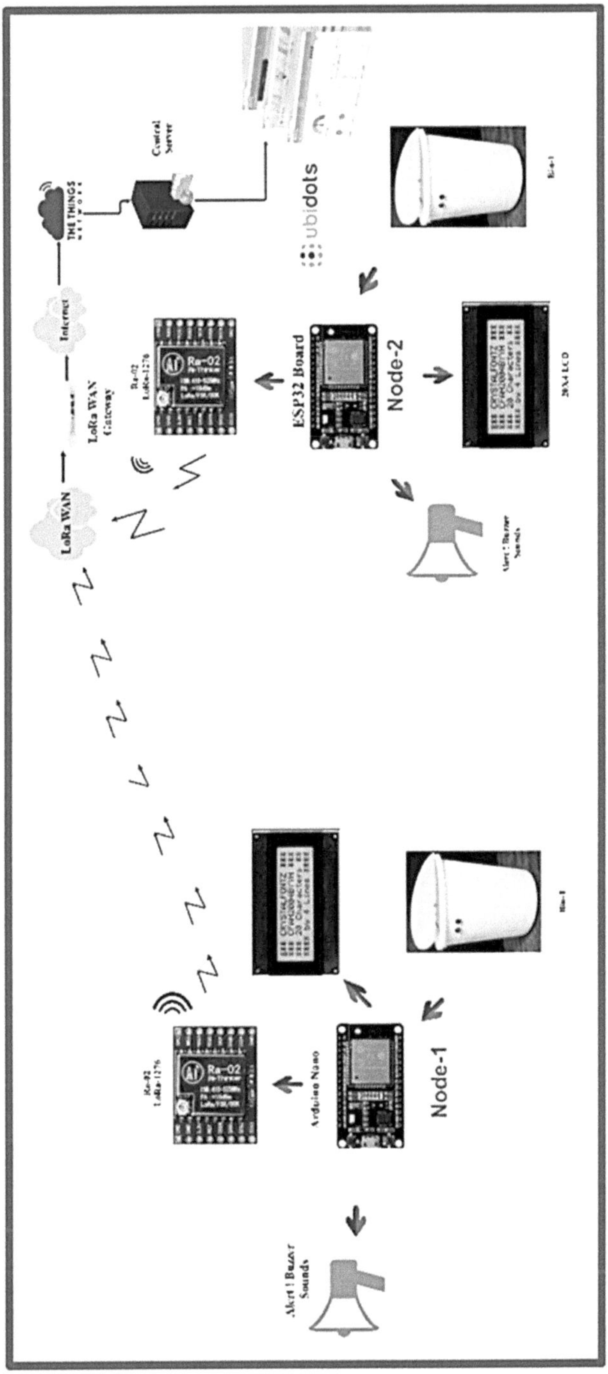

FIGURE 9.6 Smart garbage system monitoring system layout architecture.

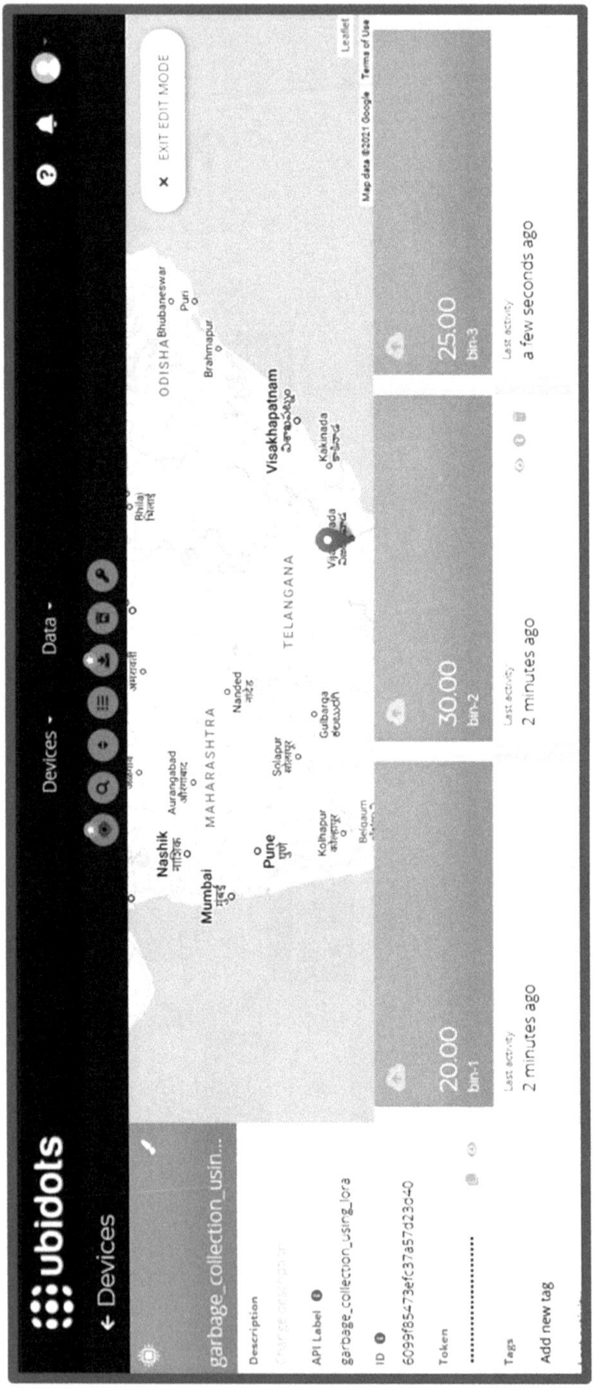

FIGURE 9.7 Raw data of dust bins storage filled data at a different place in the city.

The dust container (stabilization of dust container – the proportion of powder in a container). Ubidots Dashboard can monitor the functioning of this garbage collection system. The distance value data or information may be seen as raw, medium, and overall. The obtained data and information are from the rubbish container at the chosen place. The data should be transmitted to constructed Ubidots devices using the Arduino Ethernet Shield from the sensor node. Figure 9.8 (a,b,c) displays the diagram of the data gathered from the distance between the waste and the trash bin lid when the value of the trash depth is nearly full, as shown in Figure 9.8c. As the volume of trash increases, the distance between the ultrasonic sensor deck is lowered. Ubidots will notify if the distance level is less than the specified value (4 cm).

Figure 9.8(a)–(c) above illustrates smart waste collection monitoring in different places in the town of Vijayawada for five smart bags named BIN-1, BIN-2, BIN-3, BIN-4, and BIN-5. The varying storage levels of the smart bin are visible on display and collected from the many smart tanks of the city via LoRa nodes. By seeing the bins as RED, almost complete, YELLOW, to fill, GREEN, free, and no need to replace the bin. This monitor's alarm system displays for easy tracking in the main municipal office. If the smart dustbin is full, the buzzer module will provide you with an alarm, so no other person will be able to fill the bin with waste. With this smart waste system, any resident can quickly determine where waste may be placed. The finest WIFI models LoRa based on compared to all other models of the smart trash system that function with GPS, GSM is at least cost.

9.5 CONCLUSION

The Arduino Uno with Arduino Ethernet Shield module, ultrasonic sensor depth measurement systems, and LoRa technology with IoT interface were suggested in this article as innovative techniques for successful garbage collection. This proposed methodology can prevent trash overflow and correctly treat garbage. The waste management system and garbage collection facilities are currently non-compliant with current regulations. As a result, improved waste collection and transportation facilities should be made available. Because it provides suggestions on how to fill a bin, the arrival time of the garbage collection vehicle is cut in half and alerts the public when the smart bin is full of a buzzer.

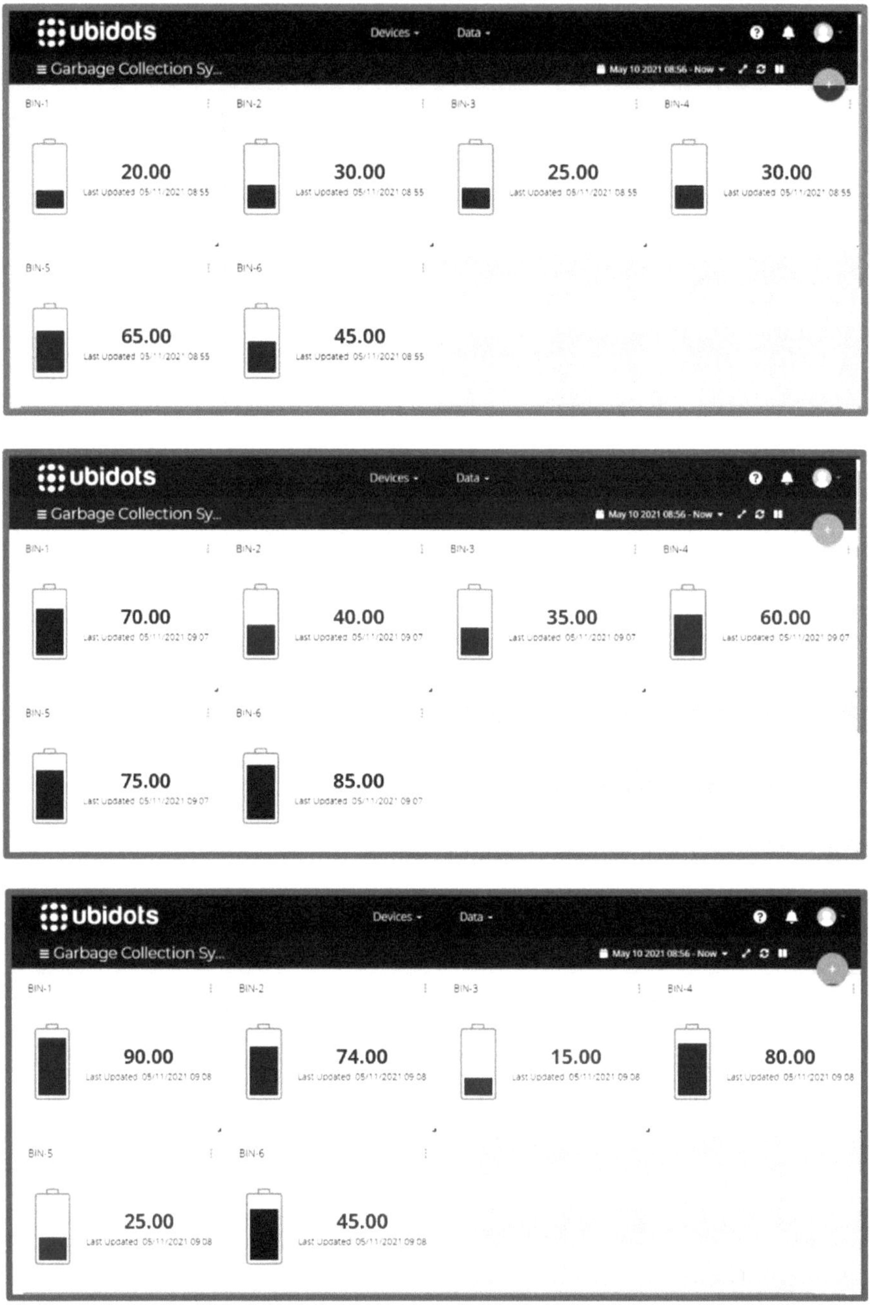

FIGURE 9.8 (a)–(c) Status of smart waste collection monitoring of five smart bins on monitoring.

KEYWORDS

- **garbage disposal**
- **gateway**
- **internet of things**
- **LoRA**
- **LoRA node**
- **smart garbage system**
- **ultrasonic sensor**

REFERENCES

1. Chandramohan, A., & Mendonca, J. (2014). Automated Waste Segregator. In *2014 Texas Instruments India Educators' Conference (TIIEC)* (pp. 1–6). Bangalore.
2. Okasha, M. E., Adam, M. et al. (2018). Waste Management System Using IoT. *2018 International Conference on Computer, Control, Electrical, and Electronics Engineering (ICCCEEE)*, Khartoum, Sudan, 2018, pp. 1-4, DoI: 10.1109/ICCCEEE.2018.8515871.
3. Aleyadeh, S., & Taha, A. M. (2018). An IoT-Based Architecture for Waste Management. In *2018 IEEE International Conference on Communications Workshops (ICC Workshops)* (pp. 1–4). Kansas City, MO.
4. Shyam, G. K., Manvu, S. S., & Bharti, P. (2017). Smart waste management using Internet-of-Things (IoT). In *2017 2nd International Conference on Computing and Communications Technologies (ICCCT)* (pp. 199–203). Chennai, India.
5. Chen, W., Wang, Y., Huang, P., Huang, Y., & Tsai, M (2018). A Smart IoT System for Waste Management. In *2018 1st International Cognitive Cities Conference (IC3)* (pp. 202–203). Okinawa.
6. Bhole, V. Y., & Chaudhari, S. S. (2018). Solid Waste Collection as a Service using IoT-Solution for Smart Cities. In *2018 International Conference on Smart City and Emerging Technology (ICSCET)* (pp. 1–5). Mumbai.
7. Al-Masri, E., Diabate, I., Jain, R., Lam, M. L., & Nathala, S. R. (2018). Recycle.io: An IoT-Enabled Framework for Urban Waste Management. In *2018 IEEE International Conference on Big Data (Big Data)* (pp. 5285–5287). Seattle, WA, USA.
8. Banerjee, S., & Paul, S. et al. (2018). Smart Garbage Monitoring Using IoT. In *2018 IEEE 9th Annual Information Technology, Electronics and Mobile Communication Conference (IEMCON)* (pp. 1181–1185). Vancouver, BC.
9. Saha, H. N., Gon, S., Nayak, A., Kundu, S., & Moitra, S. (2018). IoT Based Garbage Monitoring and Clearance Alert System. In *2018 IEEE 9th Annual Information Technology, Electronics and Mobile Communication Conference (IEMCON)* (pp. 204–208). Vancouver, BC.

10. Memon, S. K., Shaikh, F. K., Mahoto, N. A., & Memon, A. A. (2019). IoT based smart garbage monitoring & collection system using WeMos & Ultrasonic sensors. In *2019 2nd International Conference on Computing, Mathematics and Engineering Technologies (iCoMET)* (pp. 1–6). Sukkur, Pakistan.
11. S, S. K., Suvidharbabu, T., & Subrahmanian, R. N. (2017). Smart Bin using IoT with Fog Computing. *International Journal of Emerging Technology in Computer Science & Electronics, 24*(6), 13–16.
12. Ganapathy, V., & Murugaanandam, S. (2018). Efficient IOT Based Smart Bin for Clean Environment. In *2018 International Conference on Communication and Signal Processing (ICCSP)* (pp. 0715–0720). Chennai.
13. Alsbou, N., Samad, M. A., Alhashem, M., & Abuabed, A. S. A. (2018). Developing a Self-Powered Enlarging Smart Waste Bin. In *2018 14th International Wireless Communications & Mobile Computing Conference (IWCMC)* (pp. 683–689). Limassol.
14. Mdukaza, S., Isong, B., Dladlu, N., & Abu-Mahfouz, A. M. (2018). Analysis of IoT-Enabled Solutions in Smart Waste Management. In *IECON 2018 – 44th Annual Conference of the IEEE Industrial Electronics Society* (pp. 4639–4644). Washington, DC.
15. Evans, D. (2011). The internet of things, how the next evolution of the internet. *Cisco Internet Business Solutions Group (IBSG)*. Retrieved from: http://www.cisco.com/web/about/ac79/docs/innov/IoT_IBSG_0411FINAL.pdf (accessed on 27 May 2024).
16. Kanakaraja, P., & Kotamraju. (2021). IoT enabled ble and lora based indoor localization without GPS. *Turkish Journal of Physiotherapy and Rehabilitation, 32*(2), 642–653.
17. Akram, P. S., Ramesha, M., & Ramana, T. V. (2021). SIMULATION AND ANALYSIS OF SMART HOME ARCHITECTURE. *ARPN Journal of Engineering and Applied Sciences, 16*(6), 280–286.
18. Ashok, G. L. P., & Saleem Akram, P. (2020). Implementation of smart home by using packet tracer. *International Journal of Scientific and Technology Research, 9*(2), 678–685.
19. Gopal, S. R., & Akram, P. S. (2019). Design and analysis of heterogeneous hybrid topology for VLAN configuration. *International Journal of Emerging Trends in Engineering Research, 7*(11), 487–491.
20. Suresh, N., & Kiran, K. U. (2021). Node mcu and lora based temperature monitoring with OLED. *Turkish Journal of Physiotherapy and Rehabilitation, 32*(2), 1167–1172.
21. Kanakaraja, P., & Sairamnadipalli, L. S. P. (2021). Industrial parameters monitoring with lora technology in next generation wireless communications. *Turkish Journal of Physiotherapy and Rehabilitation, 32*(2), 805–815.
22. Komalapati, N., & Yarra. (2021). Smart Fire Detection and Surveillance System Using IOT. *Proceedings – International Conference on Artificial Intelligence and Smart Systems, ICAIS 2021*, 1386–1390.
23. Nanda, I., & Chadalavada. (2021). Implementation of IIoT based smart crop protection and irrigation system. *Journal of Physics: Conference Series, 1804, 12206.*
24. Nidhya, R., & Kumar, M. (2020). Enhanced Route Selection (ERS) algorithm for IoT enabled smart waste management system. *Environmental Technology and Innovation, 20*, 101116.
25. Sowmya, K. V., & Teju, V. (2020). Energy monitoring and management in smart home using IoT. *Journal of Green Engineering, 10*(10), 9543–9556.

CHAPTER 10

Applications of AI-Based Decision Support System in Business Management

K. SAMPATH KINI,[1] B. H. KARTHIK PAI,[2] and R. P. PUNEETH[1]

[1]*Department of CSE, N.M.A.M. Institute of Technology, Nitte, Karkala, Karnataka, India*

[2]*Department of ISE, N.M.A.M. Institute of Technology, Nitte, Karkala, Karnataka, India*

ABSTRACT

An intelligent decision system processes huge amounts of heterogeneous data to extract useful and interesting insights by applying advanced computing techniques such as machine learning and big data analytics. These intelligent systems are capable of providing recommendations to enable effective decision-making in business management. It achieves this by analyzing multiple input data sources and determining useful patterns, trends, and correlations on par with human decision-making abilities. Traditional methods involve processing data organized in a structured manner, which is stored as rows and columns. It is used to generate knowledge and apply intelligence from data sources. Traditionally, analytics such as real-time analytics and sentiment analysis were not performed. Now, with the help of advanced techniques such as big data analytics and natural language processing, we are able to extract meaningful information from a huge amount of both structured and unstructured data in a faster manner. In this paper, we are going to present various AI techniques, tools, and approaches that need to be followed to visualize the business performance of any organization and make effective decisions in business management. We are going to discuss techniques for

Artificial Intelligence and Machine Learning for Business. Namita Mishra, A. V. Senthil Kumar (Eds.)

information repositories, applications of AI (artificial intelligence), and information visualization techniques across various domains. We are also going to present the results after running AI techniques on various business scenarios. In this paper, we are going to showcase how various visualization techniques can be used during the business decision-making process. As data size grows or scales up, how usage of big data analytics methods are introduced to meet the needs of advanced analytics. This paper also describes a full-fledged design that is used for AI-based decision-making processes in the management of the business. The design comprises of various software components such as knowledge sources, information management software, machine learning models, and visualization methods.

10.1 INTRODUCTION

This research work discusses innovative methods that are utilized in AI-based decision support systems (DSS) in business management. AI-based decision support systems have emerged as one of the most relevant technologies that have the power to change the way organizations use information to enhance the customer experience and transform their business processes. The major challenge for any company is utilizing data to its best advantage. Companies would like to apply computer technologies to process large data into useful insights and apply intelligence in their business management [1]. In this chapter, we describe how the usage of AI and machine learning technology realizes data evolution in a meaningful way.

Artificial Intelligence-based DSS comprises evolving technologies for managing dynamic data. AI-based decision support systems enable organizations to manage and maintain large chunks of data. They achieve this at the right speed and also at the right time in order to gain interesting insights. Many organizations have initiated their journey with AI-based DSS systems. These organizations are conducting experiments with AI techniques. The goal of these experiments is to see if they allow them to analyze ever-growing data and to check whether interesting information exists. It can be an early indication of a key change required if interesting information and insights are found within the data. Data may indicate that customer preferences are changing. We may have to add new elements to the business process before it is too late.

We discuss the below analytical queries. This will help us understand AI case studies and the influence it has on business:

- What is the usage of AI techniques in business management?
- How can we enable organizations with their right decisions at the right time?
- What are the advantages of various data analytics?
- When are we supposed to consider it to be used in decision-making strategy?

Data analytics-based applications are being created now to make it easier for organizations to assist them in deciding on plans and growth. Data analytics-based applications are used across most problem domains such as healthcare, agriculture, governance, sports, and education. A data analytics system is a system that takes input in the form of raw data, processes it, and outputs interesting, useful, and meaningful patterns for knowledge workers to help them make business decisions.

We divided our chapter into various parts to organize the contents. Section I: Glance at Artificial Intelligence. In this section, we cover the key concepts of AI and machine learning techniques. This will help us understand AI from both technical and business perspectives. We introduce the technical components of AI-based Decision Support Systems. Section II: Architecture Foundations for AI-based DSS. This section is intended for technical and business experts as well. It will help them understand the various components and the underlying technology features of the architecture being used. Section III: Data Analytics and DSS Methodology. This section discusses methods to analyze large data that are part of heterogeneous data infrastructure. We also highlight the kinds of analytics that are helpful in getting true meaning from raw data. It also helps to go about ways using which we can transform data into action needed for any kind of business. Section IV: Experimental results using AI-based DSS in the Real World. Here, we are going to have an understanding of how AI-based DSS is being used in various business case studies to enhance their business operations.

10.2 GLANCE AT ARTIFICIAL INTELLIGENCE

Organizations and industries have seen bigger challenges with the storage of diverse data. They also have gained bigger benefits from analyzing the diverse data using techniques of data analytics such as AI. Business vendors have come across challenges in coming up with effective procedures for capturing information, which includes information about their customers, products, and services. In today's dynamically evolving world, the business scenarios we deal with are more sophisticated. To gain a competitive advantage with consumers, organizations introduce more product lines and diversify their products. Struggles with data persist in business.

Simulation of human intelligence processes by machines is termed Artificial Intelligence. This simulation is performed by computer systems. Applications of AI include DSS, expert systems, speech recognition, and natural language processing. As the usage of AI has increased, vendors are keen to promote business products and services with the help of AI. AI is a technique that uses machine learning as a key component [2]. AI requires a foundation of hardware and software for building and training machine learning algorithms.

10.3 ARCHITECTURE FOUNDATIONS FOR AI-BASED DSS

Here we present a high-level architectural model for building technology foundations for AI-based DSS. In today's world, where we need to manage and maintain data effectively, we need to address the design challenges for developing an architectural model, as we are seeing ever-growing, dynamic, and diverse data. In this section, we examine the architectural requirements needed for AI-based DSS. We also delve into the AI-based technology stack shown in Figure 10.1.

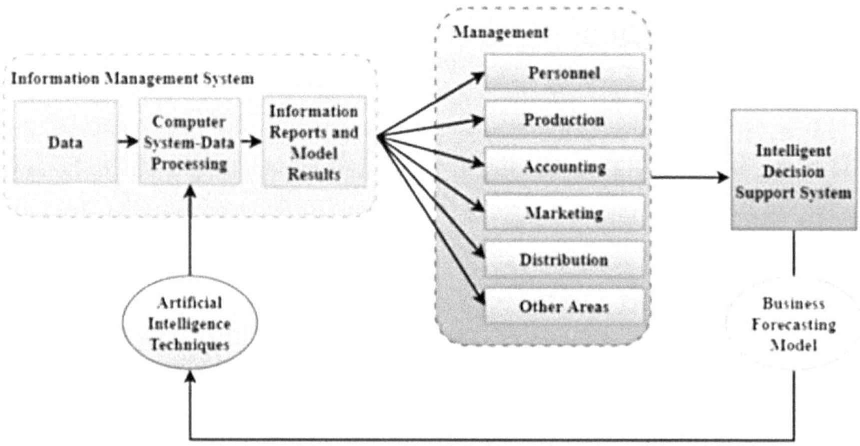

FIGURE 10.1 AI-based DSS technology stack.

We would need to have a full-fledged design that can take care of the broad functions of the entire DSS consisting of different parts. The design would make sure that these parts come together with minimal hurdles. It is going to save much effort during the subsequent implementations. AI-based DSS is treated as a strategy. When we deal with storage, analytics, and reporting of evolving data, we need to have a robust design that follows tested design principles. This would provide a suitable environment to support DSS. This design environment would consider prerequisites of hardware infrastructure, software, operational software, management software, and software developer tools as well. This design will be able to address all the prime requirements of data capture, data integration, data analysis, visualization, and decision making as depicted in Figure 10.1. It can be used as a framework for DSS technologies that can meet functional requirements for AI-based DSS projects. AI-based DSS consists of different parts: An information management system, an AI module, management software, and intelligent DSS.

10.3.1 INFORMATION MANAGEMENT SYSTEM

It is the heart of DSS and functions as a knowledge source. It makes an integral part of a decision support system. It contains data from both internal and external knowledge sources. It is a warehouse of information from the perspectives of different subjects. This is part of a decision support system that will persist information for a longer period of time. This is going to be used by the reasoning component to determine a course of action needed in business scenarios.

10.3.2 AI MODULE

With the help of an AI module, intelligence provided by machine learning techniques will be used in decision support systems. In this intelligent decision support system, the AI module pulls and processes huge amounts of data to extract insights. These meaningful insights will be used to make recommendations for better decision-making. It performs by analyzing a variety of data sources. To mimic human decision-making capabilities, it will identify patterns, trends, and associations within data.

10.3.3 MANAGEMENT SOFTWARE

This software component takes care of management activities. It is about bringing out real-world use cases with the goal of determining how various organizational departments are performing, and providing guidance on ways they can be further improved. Organizations utilize this component's features to predict the impact of outcomes.

It can be useful for understanding and determining the potential risks of fully exploring our real business life. It is used for managing research, marketing, accounting, human resources, and predicting business growth.

This system can also be used to prototype and explore systems that do not currently exist. It can be used to experiment with proposed new technologies, factory plans, or supply chains. Businesses also use it to anticipate the outcomes of various changes made to a business system, such as changes in policies and regulations.

10.3.4 INTELLIGENT DSS

The purpose of this module is to have a consultant like an intelligent human. It makes decision-makers jobs smarter by gathering and analyzing data. It is capable of identifying and troubleshooting problems and evaluating feasible solutions. The AI component of this decision support system mimics human brain capabilities very closely. It processes and analyzes information as a computing system more efficiently. It includes advanced functional components like knowledge sources, machine learning, and data analytics. Intelligent marketing decision support systems, medical diagnostic systems, and smart production systems are a few examples of these.

10.4 DATA ANALYTICS AND DSS METHODOLOGY

Companies like Amazon and Google are great players in performing data analysis using AI techniques. These players use the resulting knowledge to gain a sustainable benefit in the real world. Amazon's recommendation system pulls all of our purchasing history. It collects our data to understand our purchasing patterns. It is a marketing machine for them. Its AI analytical features have successfully placed it in the winner's circle. In this section, our focus is mainly on the methodology of data analysis using AI techniques, as captured in Figure 10.2.

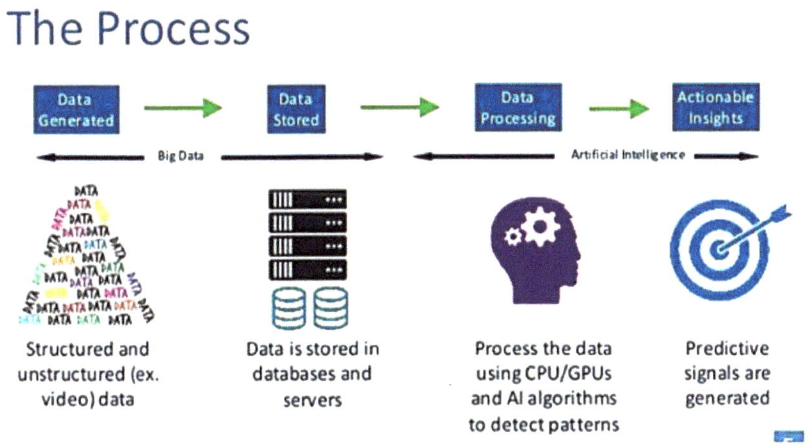

FIGURE 10.2 AI-based DSS process.

Decision support systems perform analytics involving key steps such as data generation, data storage, data processing, and pulling actionable insights. In the data generation step, a variety of sources such as sensor devices, computer applications, social media applications, satellites, RFIDs, and many other sources generate huge chunks of both structured data and unstructured data. Later, data is further processed using various AI algorithms such as supervised learning and unsupervised learning algorithms. The data processing step will detect useful information and interesting patterns. These insights are further analyzed and visualized by decision-makers and applied in various business cases.

10.4.1 EXPERIMENTAL RESULTS USING AI-BASED DSS IN THE REAL WORLD

Here, we are going to showcase experimental results obtained from applying AI techniques across different business problem scenarios.

10.4.1.1 TOURIST BEHAVIOR ANALYSIS

Tourism is one of the key sectors contributing significantly to the growing economy of India. In recent times, AI-based data analysis has been used in the tourism sector. It is used for activities such as demand forecasting, predicting the interests of tourists, identifying tourist attraction items, and behavioral analysis. Three large groups of people who can benefit from the analytical results are tourists themselves, managers of the public sector, and business people. It makes it easy for tourists to decide whether to visit a place they have not seen before. It promotes marketing tactics and answers the question of why people from different countries visit India. It also indicates where India stands in tourism. This data analysis has been conducted using Python and its analytical library functions on the Jupyter Notebook development tool. Please refer to Figure 10.3 to understand India's tourism rank in the world. Please refer to Figure 10.4 to understand the percentage shares of countries in Indian tourism. Please refer to Figure 10.5 to understand the purpose of the visit of tourists from 5 countries to India. Please refer to Figure 10.6 to analyze the monuments visited by tourists.

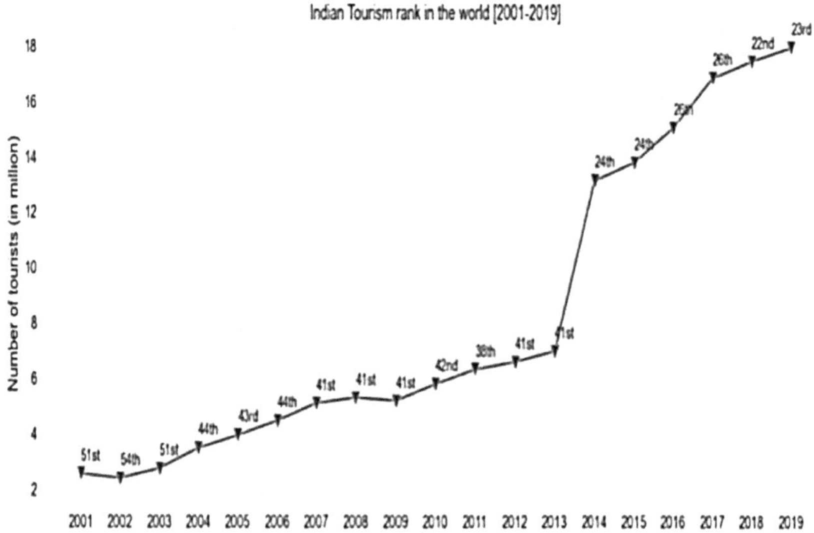

FIGURE 10.3 Indian tourism ranks in the world.

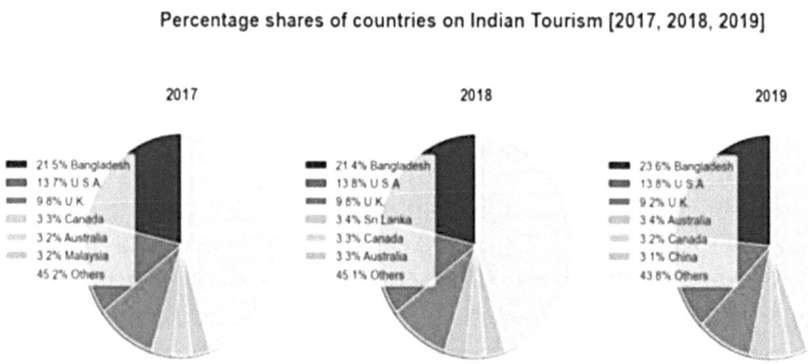

FIGURE 10.4 Percentage shares of countries on Indian tourism.

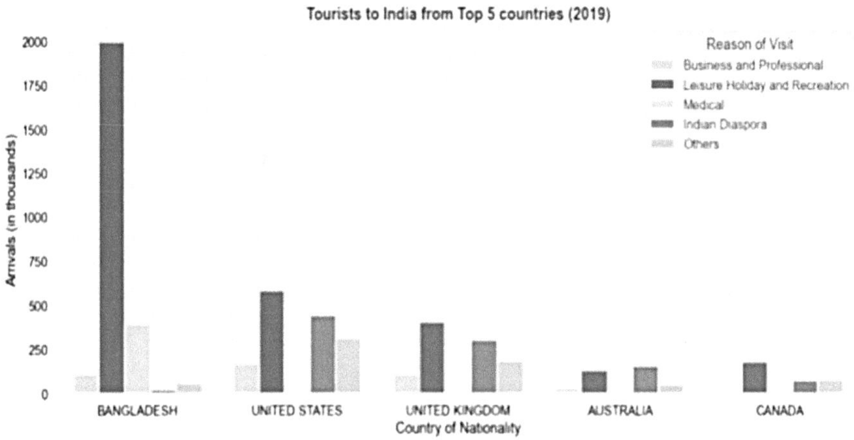

FIGURE 10.5 Purpose of visit of tourist from 5 countries to India.

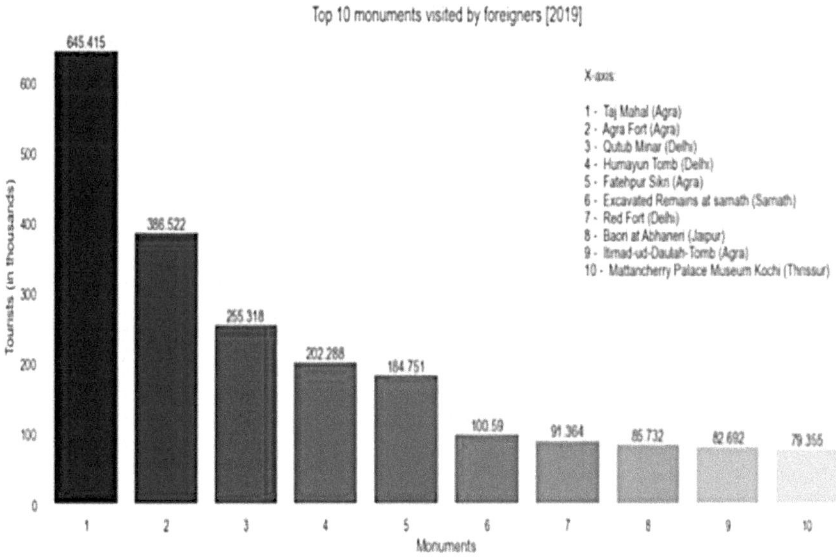

FIGURE 10.6 Monuments visited by tourists.

10.4.1.2 GOOGLE PLAY STORE APPS ANALYSIS

The Google Play Store is one of the biggest and most popular Android app stores. The dataset we processed contains different interesting features [3]. These features can be used to predict if a mobile app can succeed or not. There are three phases in this analysis: data extraction, data processing, and data visualization. Data analytics here aim to show the distribution of app ratings, which will help users find the popularity and profitability of the apps, derive insights on how the app features are correlated with each other to assist users in choosing between apps with similar functionality, compare different categories of apps based on their size and price, determine top-rated, expensive, top-reviewed, and most installed apps. We have used a Kaggle dataset for performing the above-mentioned analytics [4]. Please see Figure 10.7 to understand the Analysis of Apps categories. Please see Figure 10.8 to understand the app ratings analysis. Please see Figure 10.9 to understand the analysis of the apps in the Play Store, i.e., Free apps vs. paid apps.

10.4.1.3 CUSTOMER SEGMENTATION ANALYSIS

The process of separating customers into different groups is called customer segmentation [5]. This separation is based on certain properties such as personality, interests, habits, and factors related to demographics, domain, and income. Here we are performing various segmentation tasks using the K-means clustering algorithm to segregate customers based on

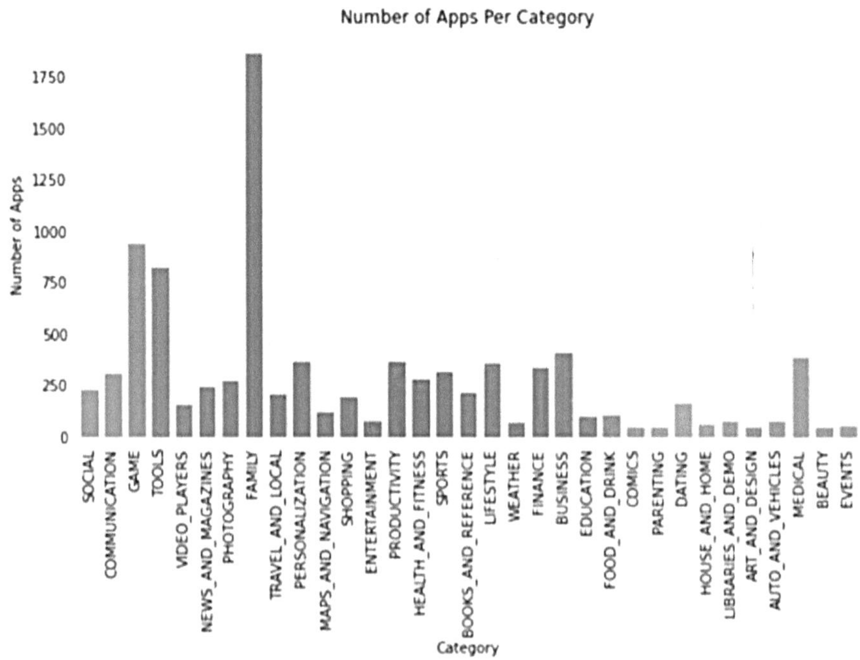

FIGURE 10.7 Analysis of app categories.

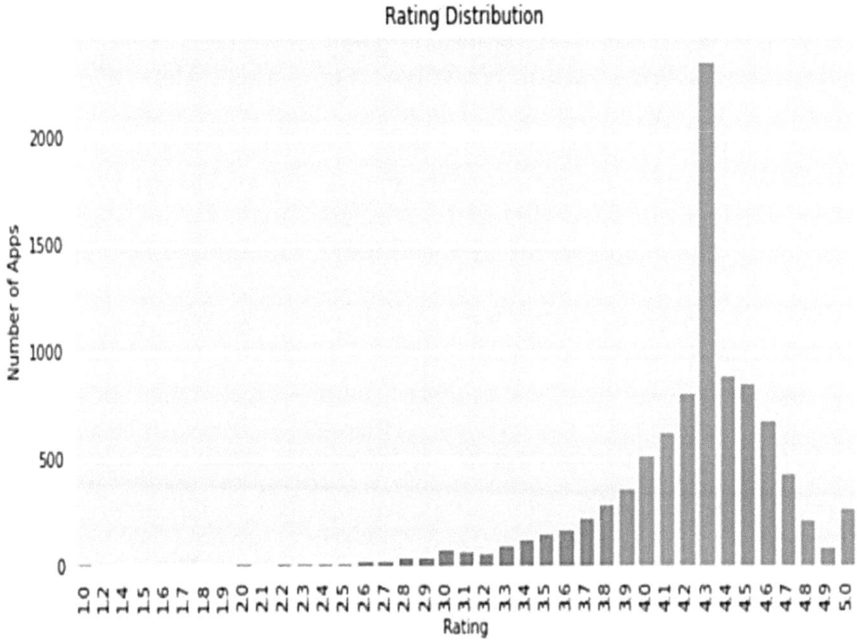

FIGURE 10.8 Apps ratings analysis.

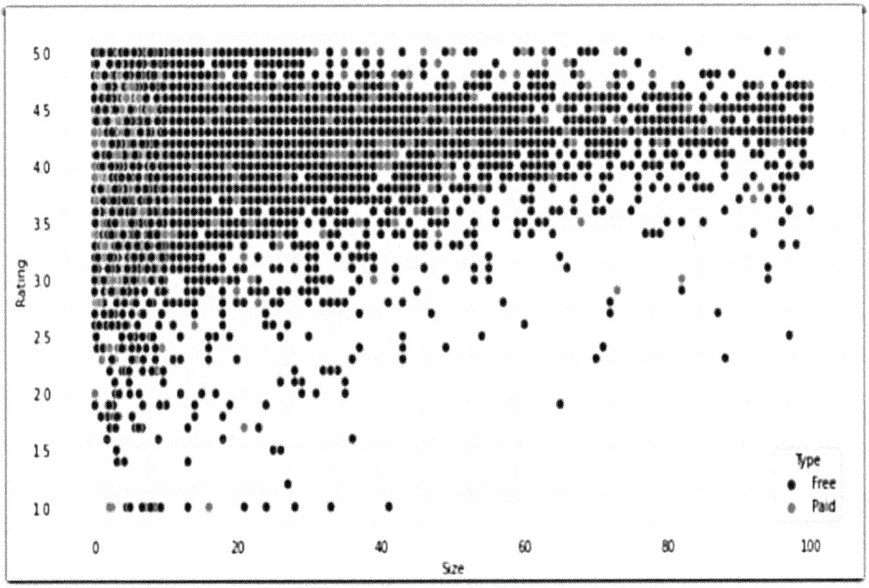

FIGURE 10.9 Analysis of the apps in the Play Store: Free apps v/s paid apps.

their traits [6]. This helps to boost customer loyalty and behavior. This analysis makes it simple to tailor and personalize marketing of business needs, service, and sales efforts involved. The marketing team can assist in identifying and exhibiting various types of customer segments. Customer segmentation can find groups that think differently and follow different purchasing patterns. Customer segmentation can also be used to find out the customers who vary with their preferences, expectations, desires, and attributes. The main purpose of performing customer segmentation is to make different groups of people with similar interests [7]. This will be beneficial for the marketing team to converge on an effective marketing plan.

The analysis of the customers based on their age, annual income, and spending capabilities is depicted below. Please see Figures 10.10 and 10.11.

10.5 CONCLUSION

This section provides concluding remarks on AI-based DSS systems used in business management. Tourist behavioral analysis makes it easier for tourists to decide whether to visit a place they have not seen before. It

FIGURE 10.10 Analysis of the customers based on age and spending score.

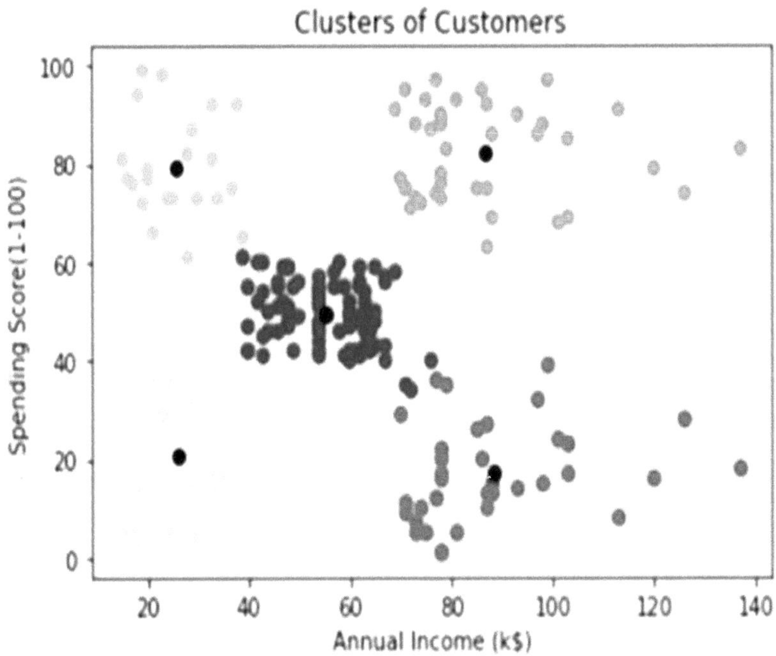

FIGURE 10.11 Analysis of the customers based on annual income and spending score.

promotes marketing tactics and answers the question of why people from different countries visit India. It also indicates where India stands in terms of tourism. Play Store app analysis has huge potential to drive business success by creating successful apps. Insights derived from the analysis can be used by developers to target the Android market effectively. Various visualization techniques have been used on different features in the dataset to derive meaningful insights that can help business people quickly understand the details of Play Store apps. A machine learning model can be developed for future developers and the Google Play Store team to analyze the market and determine which app categories will keep Google Play Store popular in the future. Customer segmentation helps identify groups with diverse thoughts and purchasing behaviors. It can also reveal customers with varying preferences, expectations, desires, and attributes. The primary goal of customer segmentation is to group people with similar interests, aiding the marketing team in creating an effective marketing plan.

KEYWORDS

- **analytics**
- **artificial intelligence**
- **business management**
- **clustering techniques**
- **data analytics**
- **data mining**
- **decision-making process**
- **decision support system**
- **expert systems**
- **index terms**
- **insights**
- **K-means clustering**
- **machine learning**

REFERENCES

1. Han, J. (2005). *Data Mining: Concepts and Techniques*. San Francisco: Morgan Kaufmann Publishers Inc. ISBN 1558609016.
2. Wu, A., Wang, Y., Shu, X., Moritz, D., Cui, W., Zhang, H., & Qu, H. (2021). Ai4vis: Survey on artificial intelligence approaches for data visualization. *IEEE Transactions on Visualization and Computer Graphics. 28*(12), 5049–5070.
3. Islam, M. R. (2014). Numeric rating of Apps on Google Play Store by sentiment analysis on user reviews. In *International Conference on Electrical Engineering and Information & Communication Technology, IEEE* (pp. 1–4).
4. Kaggle. (n.d.). Play Store Analysis dataset. Retrieved from: https://www.kaggle.com/datasets/madhav000/playstore-analysis (accessed on 27 May 2024).
5. Berkhin, P. (2016). A survey of clustering data mining techniques. In *Recent Advances in Clustering* (pp. 25–71). Springer, Berlin.
6. Xu, D., & Tian, Y. (2015). A comprehensive survey of clustering algorithms. *Annals of Data Science, 2*(2), 165–193.
7. Sampath Kini, K., & Karthik Pai, B. H. (2021). Enhanced Processing of Input Data in Clustering Techniques of Data Mining Algorithms. In N. Chiplunkar & T. Fukao (Eds.), *Advances in Artificial Intelligence and Data Engineering* (Advances in Intelligent Systems and Computing, vol. 1133). Springer, Singapore. https://doi.org/10.1007/978-981-15-3514-7_38.

CHAPTER 11

Current Trends and Future of AI in Sales and Marketing

SUNANDA VINCENT JAIWANT and G. S. SAI KRUTHI

CHRIST (Deemed to be University), Bangalore, Karnataka, India

ABSTRACT

Industry 4.0 has been fueling the growth of Artificial Intelligence owing to the expanding progress of data produced by the Internet and IoT devices and the computation of this enormous quantity of data. Artificial Intelligence has revolutionized the business world. AI technology has had a striking influence in the field of finance and accounting. As the market is becoming increasingly competitive, AI-empowered finance and accounting structures are making the business organization sturdy competitors as AI technologies and tools help in saving time and extracting deeper understandings. Today, companies use AI to predict customer behavior, serve more people, better target campaigns, forecast trends, etc.

It goes without question that AI could improve the productivity of marketing teams. For example, location, age, and other essential information can lead to more personalized content. Along with big data, AI can undoubtedly provide businesses with a powerful means to engage and convert potential customers. This chapter aims to study the use of artificial intelligence in sales and marketing. The chapter also studies the role of AI in the sales and marketing field. This chapter also describes the benefits and current trends of AI applications in sales and marketing operations. This chapter includes the fundamental and theoretical base. It attempts to analyze the key practical applications of AI in the very specific work of the sales and marketing field.

Artificial Intelligence and Machine Learning for Business. Namita Mishra, A. V. Senthil Kumar (Eds.)

11.1 INTRODUCTION: AI IN SALES AND MARKETING

In today's evolving, fast-paced world, people try to complete their work in the least amount of time and effort. A tremendous increase in gadget usage has led to the generation of a large amount of data. Detailed studies are being conducted in the field of technology. Great improvements have been noticed in the fields of augmented reality, data collection and computation, computer visualizations, and other areas.

Among these fast-developing and widely utilized technologies, artificial intelligence is leading the way. Research dependent on artificial intelligence combines passive data, sales figures, social media statistics, and other familiar factors. Research conducted through artificial intelligence has produced results with a high level of accuracy in a short period. As more organizations have started utilizing AI, development in the AI spectrum is also fast-paced.

The world of sales and marketing is constantly changing. While some firms are failing as they are unable to catch up, others are adapting to the market and flourishing. The usage of AI has increased drastically in the past few years as it has proved to be beneficial to many organizations. AI will be essential for firms to improve their ability to compete. The initial expectancy for AI started with doing repetitive and slow-paced tasks but now marketers are starting to depend on it for market analytics. All the trailblazers in the industry have already started improving their analysis and forecasting accuracy through AI. The tools that are being used by marketers are combined with AI and made better.

Artificial intelligence is a term that encompasses all the intelligence-based functional capabilities of a machine that resembles human intelligence. AI is widely used in the present day to perform myriads of activities in different industries. Artificial intelligence is used in the forms of virtual assistants (e.g., Amazon Alexa), product recommendations (e.g., Netflix suggestions), search engine optimization, self-driving cars (e.g., Tesla), service robots, AI-based customer support, and personalized healthcare guidance.

In the last decade, AI has strongly established itself in the marketing sphere. The number of businesses utilizing AI grew by 270% in the last four years. Marketing and sales enterprises are identifying and capitalizing on significant opportunities through the adoption of AI.

AI records consumer behavior and activity on the internet to create an assortment of personalized advertisement portfolios. AI identifies preferences, tracks purchase patterns, and optimizes search results. Product recommendation is one of the most utilized attributes of AI. Product recommendation is closely connected to search engine optimization. The AI predicts what kind of information the consumer would like to see based on their previous search patterns. Similarly, AI predicts which products the consumer would like to buy next based on their previous purchases. Pay-per-click advertising has also gained popularity in the last few years. AI tools help discover new advertising avenues instead of depending on consumers to search for required information continually. Language translators and processors have allowed businesses to take advantage of potential demand in foreign countries with language barriers, and outsourcing male talent has also become convenient. AI also assists marketers in eliminating predictions and creating accurate content clusters and product libraries. Identifying potential consumers in the market and confirming sales was always an obstacle-ridden path in the past, but with AI, businesses can pave direct routes toward assured sales. The efforts of the sales professionals in adopting an AI-oriented approach have already started bearing fruit. AI-based chatbots are available all day, every day. They create new possibilities to capture leads by communicating with potential consumers even when the inbound team is unavailable. AI is widely used in the customer care sector as it curates suitable responses based on the keywords used by the customers.

AI is more reliable in the sales department as it forecasts future figures based on previous sales and present market trends, instead of blindly selling. It also helps identify the lacking areas, so that the executives can plan accordingly and set new corrective measures and goals. AI technology informs marketers about the untapped potential in the market based on the prospect's past performance, return on investment, and prominence in the sector.

E-commerce giant players like Amazon, JD.com, Alibaba, and Suning.com are adopting AI for implementing end-to-end solutions to give a comprehensive retail experience both online and offline. E-commerce uses AI-enabled applications in different phases from carrying the product from its inception to the post-purchase stage. AI is used for the entire marketing of the product or service, automating manufacturing, transportation, delivery, promotional campaigns, sales forecasts, etc. (Figure 11.1).

L'Oréal retail outlets allow their customers to try out various cosmetic products virtually with the help of their smartphone applications and an interactive smart mirror technology developed by Alibaba. The technology gives customers the ability to sample a range of products before they buy and supplies L'Oréal with data they can use to better match a user's facial features and appearance to their products. Monolith AI specializes in using AI-supported applications to design products across industries, focusing

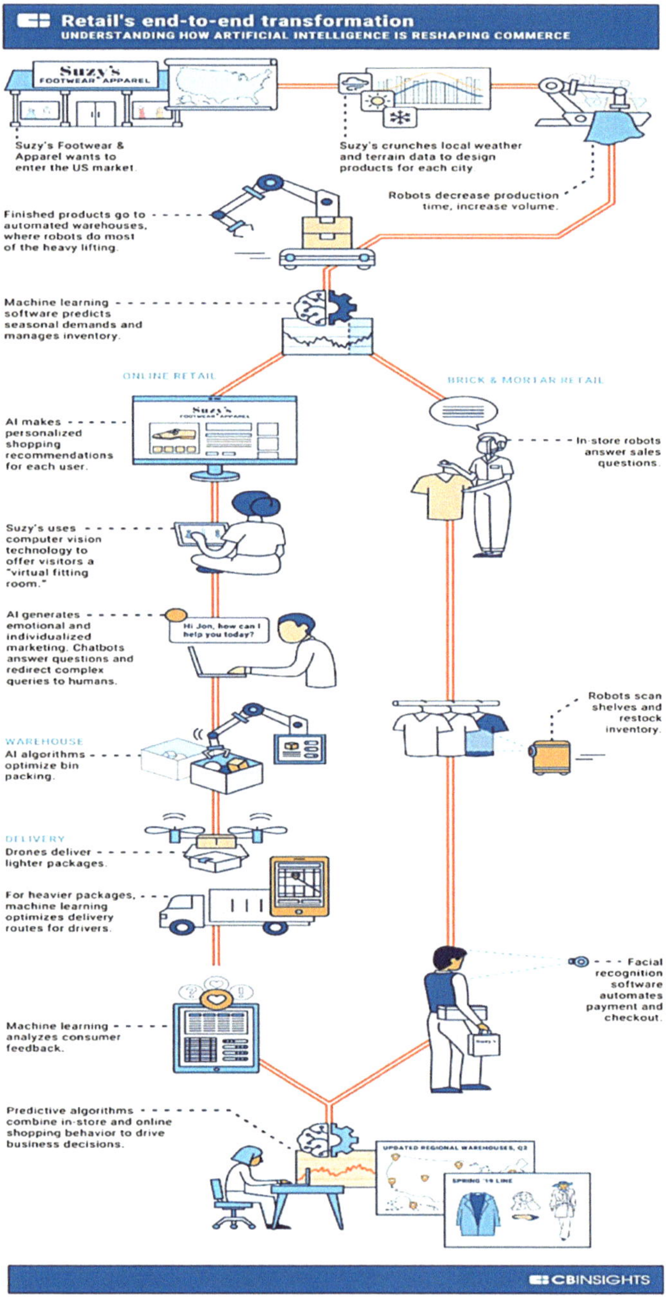

FIGURE 11.1 AI transforming retail.

Source: CBINSIGHTS. https://www.cbinsights.com/research/artificial-intelligence-reshaping-commerce.

mainly on sectors like automotive, aerospace, and consumer packaging. To address the constantly changing customer needs, retailers try to minimize production lead time using robotics, machine learning, and computational analytics. For example, Adidas uses production automation and AI technologies in its assembly operations [1].

11.2 LITERATURE REVIEW

Artificial intelligence is transforming the markets, marketing strategies, and behaviors of consumers [2]. This research study proposed a multidimensional context to understand the influence of artificial intelligence. AI can be used by organizations to understand what their consumers will purchase. This aids the firms in improving their predictive skills and refining their predictions about future demands. Business models can be changed by organizations based on their AI-driven predictions, leading to better performance for their customers. The researchers recommend that AI should be introduced and used in organizations to enhance human efforts and performance and not to replace human involvement [3]. Artificial intelligence is making inroads into every sphere of life. There are cars that use artificial intelligence to enhance their driving performance, and stock markets are also using AI technologies. Schools and colleges are also employing AI technologies to provide a better education platform for their students. Restaurants and hotels are using AI tools and technologies to offer an enhanced experience to customers. AI can help in reducing the cost of the prediction process. AI helps in prediction analysis by bringing the cost of prediction much lower. AI acts like prediction machines that facilitate seamless and smooth decision-making, which is very strategic for better organizational performance.

The researcher suggested a framework for gaining a deeper understanding of AI in retail operations [4]. The model suggests that producers and retailers need to be in constant connection and exchange information about customers' attitudes and behavior. This information can be accessed from various sources and channels. Algorithms can then be used to identify patterns and make predictive decisions regarding customer demands in the future. Retailers benefit from AI technologies in numerous aspects. AI technologies help retailers predict buyer behavior, recommend products, and manage customer relationships, sales, stores, transactions, and media, among others.

AI has also revolutionized the banking sector [5]. AI-supported systems and technologies are helping banking professionals personalize their product offerings. Chatbots, robotic automation, and machine learning are enhancing banking performance and offering customers a more personalized service tailored to their specific needs. AI algorithms are facilitating quicker fraud detection, reducing transaction times, automating routine tasks, and leading to more optimal, resourceful, and efficient performance.

Artificial Intelligence emerged as a catalyst for the entire business, changing the industry panorama [6]. The most noteworthy aspect of Artificial Intelligence in the marketing profession is the improvement in marketing performance. The study attempted to examine the influence of AI on marketing operations by conducting interviews with marketing professionals in Pakistan. An inclusive literature assessment revealed a comprehensive insight into the role and usage of AI in the field of marketing. The study recommends integrating AI into all marketing operations to be more competitive, enhance overall output, and increase the revenues of organizations.

The future of all businesses will be remarkably impacted by the increased use of AI technologies [2]. AI will significantly transform both marketing approaches and customer behaviors. The current research has established an extensive study and comprehensive communications with marketing professionals, proposing a multi-dimensional model to understand the effect of AI in marketing. The study also addresses future policy-making, ethical, and privacy issues related to AI involvement.

11.3 AI RESHAPING SALES AND MARKETING FUNCTION

Even in the neonatal stages, AI has assisted organizations in improving efficiency and increasing profitability. Yet the percentage of organizations that own and utilize AI technology is quite small. AI possesses immense growth potential. By 2030, AI is estimated to contribute nearly $15.7 trillion to the global economy.

AI is being used in new and more creative ways across both sales and marketing in facets such as:

1. **Facial Recognition:** This software is implemented to take image identification to the next level. This feature can recognize and differentiate between first-time customers and pre-existing customers, through these personalized offers can be curated to attract them and build loyalty.

2. **Advanced Content Creation:** AI-oriented content creation has developed to an extent where it can mimic human language. This conserves time, money, and effort.

3. **Voice-Enabled Applications:** The voice assistants market is slowly reaching its saturation point. This provides an excellent opportunity for marketers to create voice-based advertisements to attract new customers.

   eBay is one of the initial companies that began to employ AI-supported systems for its online processes. eBay first cited machine learning in its Q3'15 earnings calls. eBay instructed its traders to describe products' details and used machine learning to analyze the data to discover comparable goods in the catalogs. AI was used in ad placements, personalization, visual search, and delivery approvals for customer-to-customer operations [1] (Figure 11.2).

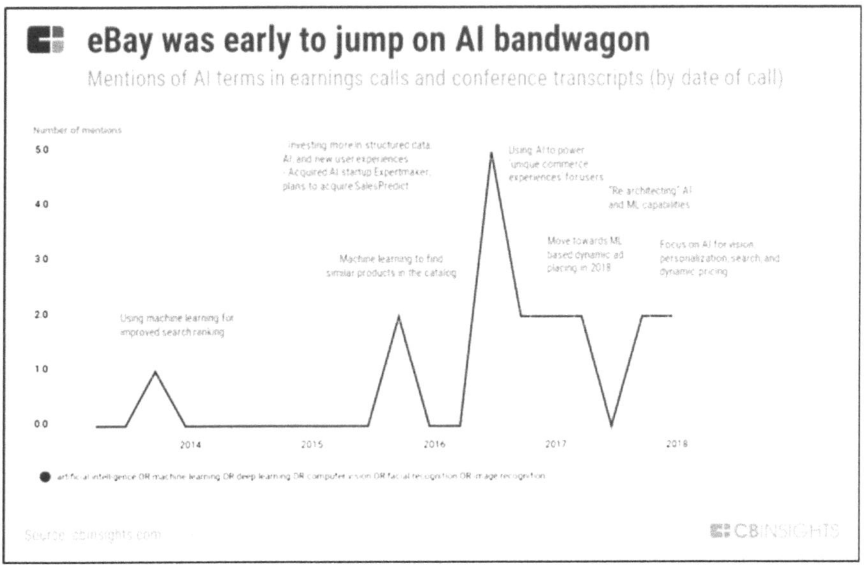

FIGURE 11.2 Retailers using AI.

Source: CBINSIGHTS. https://www.cbinsights.com/research/artificial-intelligence-reshaping-commerce.

In this digital era, marketing functions depend hugely on data, digital approaches, and datasets. Beginning with buyer communication to intention to purchase, all is calculated and examined using advanced machine learning tools that reduce a large quantity of data to access useful insights about the customers. AI-enabled systems aid marketing to segment the market and target the specific segment. It helps in decreasing cost-per-click (CPC) costs, which helps in designing better advertisement budgets. AI provides detailed information for analyzing a customer's communication with the products and with the competitors as well. A few AI-supported systems provide organizations the capability to compare their viewers with their rivals and arrive at customers' details.

11.4 USING AI TO INFORM AND TRANSFORM SALES AND MARKETING DECISIONS

Technological advancements like artificial intelligence have created newer and easier solutions for present-day problems. AI presents a competitive advantage for organizations by reducing the workforce and effort required for a task, allowing employees to focus on learning and development. Though AI in sales and marketing is still in the introduction stages, it is growing at a rapid pace. AI has developed the ability to mimic human behavior with greater efficiency rates. Everything that the customer searches for, views, and buys is influenced by the AI algorithm. From search engine optimization where goods related to the customer's interest are displayed to the location tracking on the Uber app, everything is AI-based. AI can be used to predict which consumer group will react to which strategy or offer and thus push sales. AI studies the different datasets with respect to the multiple consumer bases to forecast the product life cycle in a certain market. This will help companies to improve sales and take measures to elongate the growth and maturity stages. A common term used among marketers is STP – segmentation, targeting, and positioning.

Here, an organization segments the potential consumers into suitable categories, produces a commodity that is targeted to satisfy their needs, and sets a position that it desires to occupy in the customer's mind. When done without the help of a computer, this process can be time-consuming and tedious. AI, on the other hand, stores results from the previous market study so that only necessary alterations can be made and results can be generated in minutes. Any market can be studied and analyzed with ease due to AI. The next biggest task in marketing is pricing; it requires extensive research and experimentation to arrive at the right prices. But with AI, the pricing scenarios can be tested out with real-time augmentation to arrive at beneficial price points. AI considers a myriad of factors such as demand, cost, competition, target customers, etc., while deciding the pricing strategies. AI also helps generate customer feedback and estimate the efficiency rate of the product in satisfying the consumer's needs.

AI helps standardize and automate the distribution process, thus reducing the burden on the staff to perform this repetitive task. In the past year, the retail giant Amazon has utilized AI and started using drones for deliveries.

In terms of promotion, AI allows marketers to personalize responses to customers. Content analysis is an effective strategy to make the customers feel noticed. AI customizes search results and replies based on the customer's previous purchase patterns and consumption behavior.

11.5 AI TRENDS IN SALES AND MARKETING

As man evolves, he builds newer and more sophisticated technology to make his life easier. Taking that into consideration, the evolution of artificial intelligence is no different from the evolution of man. It is a never-ending process with infinite potential for improvements. Each day there is a new development and only the fittest survive. Marketers have to learn to wield the double-edged sword of AI in their favor. The recent pandemic has shaken a lot of organizations from their roots. While some crumbled to the ground, others came back stronger than before with a better understanding of the market and its reaction to stimuli.

AI has been prominently used in the present day for customer targeting, mainly with 'What if?' analysis. This analysis is being used more extensively to derive results for future pandemic situations. AI also provides lead generation and lead nurturing. The AI algorithm observes consumer behavior and generates a set of leads who can be turned into customers. This is then followed by another AI algorithm which curates personalized responses for the customers to build brand loyalty.

Another strength that AI has recently improved on is psychographics. AI has mastered the art of mimicking human behavior. With this, the information gathered from the market study is segregated and customized human-like responses are presented to the customers. AI not only studies customers' ideas, interests, values, preferences, and goals but also mimics them to show that the organization will be helpful to them in achieving their goals.

While many AI instruments are used by marketers, the most famous AI algorithms are voice assistants and image search. From setting an alarm to digging out research articles on the internet, Google Home, Alexa, and Siri have done it all. Marketers can also optimize voice assistants to study the customers and provide accurate responses. Amazon shopping app is connected to Alexa, so customers can place orders via their assistant, which boosts sales tremendously. Similarly, every time a customer searches for a dress they like but cannot find the same style, they can use an image search. Fashion retail brand Myntra scans the pictures uploaded by the customer and shows them clothes of similar styles. Spectacle sales giant Lenskart allows customers to try out frames on their mobile pictures. Online educational industry leader Byju tracks customers who have searched for educational content on the network and sends them convincing offer-based advertisements to capitalize on the untouched segments of the market. AI has been consistently used for marketing to understand customers. The results obtained through AI are accurate and more reliable than manual studies. The functionality is the reason why AI is growing at such a rapid pace.

11.6 INHERENT CHALLENGES OF ADOPTING AI IN SALES AND MARKETING

The use of AI receives a lot of denials because employees tend to assume that AI will replace the labor force in the organization. But in reality, AI just aids the employees to finish slow and repetitive tasks. Machines cannot replace man in terms of creativity or emotional intelligence. These two traits are essential for any business organization, so being completely capital-intensive is not possible.

One of the main differences between man and machine is judgment. AI can mimic human behavior efficiently but the problem with AI is that not all questions require the same solution. Sometimes, a salesman will be able to understand customers' concerns just by their tone or body language, AI cannot do this. AI cannot comprehend human emotions and thus cannot take actions based on them. It can only work based on the pre-programmed methods.

The primary problem with the data being used by AI in the present age is the poor quality. AI requires high-quality data to produce better outcomes, if the data provided is poor, the outcomes will be poor too. This poor quality of data is due to the lack of developed infrastructure in IT. The equipment required to run an AI-oriented unit requires a large amount of investment, updates, and maintenance. So, smaller firms are advised to use cloud technology that is connected to a well-established AI-oriented firm.

The problem with organizations being able to collect data about customers is that their privacy will be compromised. The man strongly advocates freedom; the fact that every move of his is influenced by a profit organization scares him. Customers become conscious and uncomfortable when they know that their actions are being noticed. Storing data poses a myriad of problems; data possessed by the organization might be personal and secretive, data about one person might have details about another, and inexpensive storage might encourage the organization to retain the data longer than intended, and data can be misused. So, rules must be established for AI data analysis. The rules must not be too rigid and prevent creativity, and they must not be so flexible that the customers are scared to adapt to AI. Personalization should be carefully drafted by AI so that the customer feels special and not scared. Like all the other new technologies, AI is also being accepted with hesitance. The growth of AI might be slow-paced due to fear, but it will be an asset once accepted.

11.7 ADAPTATION TO AN AI MARKETING LANDSCAPE: AN AI FUTURE

As long as human beings have needs and wants, business organizations will continue to exist. But existence is not enough to grow; existence must be combined with improvements for prosperity. With AI growing consistently each day, its use in business organizations will increase manifold.

In the future, AI will be able to curate human-like responses efficiently, and organizations will primarily utilize AI bots to associate with leads and promote sales. Marketers are also trying to promote the ship-and-shop model. As the ability of AI to predict future sales becomes more accurate, firms can ship the product even before receiving an official order, allowing the customer to enjoy instant delivery and return products they do not intend to buy. AI will affect the sales process in the future; most marketers rely on telephone, television, and social media marketing to promote brand awareness in the present day, but this will soon change. AI will monitor customer activity and patterns of purchase and predict underlying issues that are preventing the customer from making purchases. Marketers can help resolve these issues and promote sales. This scheme is presently on the rise in the finance sector.

Payment companies are utilizing an instrument called BNPL, buy now and pay later. The AI algorithm studies their present customer database and their financials to offer loans for small amounts when the customer is running low on funds in their account. Payment applications have started earning additional income through BNPL interest. With the development of AI in the future, the number of defaulters will be reduced to less than half the present rates due to better predictions.

Another development in the world of technology is 5G. While the connection between AI and 5G is not established strongly yet, the combination of both will be a game-changer in terms of online marketing and sales. With the simultaneous development of AI and 5G, organizations will be able to understand the customers faster and better. With everything at the end of their fingertips within seconds, customers will be more enthusiastic than before to improve their quality of life. The main hindrance faced by online platforms is the time duration between the order and delivery. With the combination of AI and 5G, this wait duration can be reduced.

5G is estimated to reach even the smallest nooks and corners of the world. This will increase the consumer base for the market. The accumulation of consumers will lead to the multiplication of data. Without the help of AI, the huge magnitude of data will be difficult to analyze.

11.8 CONCLUSION

The prominence of AI in the sales and marketing industry has increased in the past few years. AI is necessary for firms to build competitiveness. The adoption of AI will require companies to redesign their structures, improve their employees' skills, and enhance the quality of data obtained. AI is a very powerful tool, but there are organizations that have used AI and failed. AI is a high-caliber weapon, but without the right operator, it is still useless. Marketers need to understand AI and use it to their advantage; otherwise, any advancements in AI will be irrelevant.

Once people realize that AI is meant to work alongside humans and not replace them, AI will be more widely utilized. Employees can focus on developing their creativity and leadership skills, while AI handles slow and repetitive tasks. AI is the key to surviving in the next generation by increasing human productivity through reducing the time spent on each task. Innovative tools like data analytics, augmented reality, artificial intelligence, etc., are transforming the way organizations function. Organizations will need to learn to use these advancements efficiently and effectively to thrive in the market. With new AI developments emerging daily, the sales and marketing industry will reach new heights.

KEYWORDS

- **artificial intelligence**
- **automation**
- **machine learning**
- **marketing**
- **marketing strategy**
- **robots**
- **sales**

REFERENCES

1. Retail's Adapt-Or-Die Moment: How Artificial Intelligence Is Reshaping Commerce. (2019, July 18). Retrieved from CBINSIGHTS: https://www.cbinsights.com/research/artificial-intelligence-reshaping-commerce/
2. Davenport, T., Guha, A., Grewal, D., & Bressgott, T. (2020). How artificial intelligence will change the future of marketing. *Journal of the Academy of Marketing Science, 48*, 24–4
3. Agrawal, A., Gans, J., & Goldfarb, A. (2018). Prediction Machines: The Simple Economics of Artificial Intelligence. *Harvard Business Review.* https://hbr.org/2016/11/the-simple-economics-of-machine-intelligence.
4. Shankar, V. (2018, December). How Artificial Intelligence (AI) is Reshaping Retailing. *Journal of Retailing, 94*(4), 6–9. doi:10.1016/S0022-4359(18)30076-9.
5. Jaiwant, S. V. (2022). Artificial Intelligence and Personalized Banking. In R. G. Vikas Garg (Ed.), *Handbook of Research on Innovative Management Using AI in Industry 5.0* (pp. 74–87). IGI Global.
6. Shahid, M. Z., & Li, G. (2019). Impact of Artificial Intelligence in Marketing: A Perspective of Marketing Professionals of Pakistan. *Global Journal of Management and Business Research, 19*(E2), 27–33. Retrieved from https://journalofbusiness.org/index.php/GJMBR/article/view/2704.
7. Antonio, V. (2018). How AI Is Changing Sales. *Harvard Business Review.* Retrieved from https://hbr.org/2018/07/how-ai-is-changing-sales.
8. Verma, S., Sharma, R., Deb, S., & Maitra, D. (2021). Artificial intelligence in marketing: Systematic review and future research direction. *International Journal of Information Management Data Insights, 1*(1), 100002. https://doi.org/10.1016/j.jjimei.2020.100002.

CHAPTER 12

Predicting Precious Metal Markets Using Custom Deep-Learning NARX Network: A Portfolio Application

STEPHANIE A. TJENDRA[1], FILBERT H. JUWONO[2], DHANUSKODI RENGASAMY[3], JOBRUN NANDONG[4], and ANDREW J. BRENNAN[5]

[1]*Department of Economics and Finance, Curtin University Malaysia, Sarawak, Malaysia.*

[2]*Department of Electrical and Electronics, Xi'an Jiatong – Liverpool University, Suzhou, China*

[3]*Department of Accounting, Finance, and Economics, Curtin University Malaysia, Sarawak, Malaysia*

[4]*Department of Chemical and Energy Engineering, Curtin University Malaysia, Sarawak, Malaysia*

[5]*Department of Accounting, Finance, and Economics, Curtin University, Perth, Western Australia*

ABSTRACT

Precious metals such as gold, silver, platinum, and palladium represent beneficial investments due to their haven characteristics. Including these metals in portfolios can avoid substantial losses, especially during a financial crisis. Constructing and implementing efficient portfolios for financial markets requires advanced statistical data analysis, including studying external impact, predictive analysis, and risk-return investigation. This

Artificial Intelligence and Machine Learning for Business. Namita Mishra, A. V. Senthil Kumar (Eds.)

chapter presents the construction and examination of diversified precious metal portfolios representing a three-month (July - September 2021) investment during the coronavirus pandemic economic downturn. A total of 58 assets from global futures, equity, and Exchange-Traded Fund (ETF) markets were investigated as potential investment targets by conducting preliminary research to identify factors affecting asset prices. The correlations among these factors were examined using historical data from July 2016 to June 2021 (5-year period) using an Elastic Net (EN) feature selection method. The dataset was filtered by removing features representing low correlations with the selected assets. Relationships among 17 assets could not be confirmed due to low performance of EN, leading to speculation regarding the widely discussed haven behavior of precious metals. The updated dataset from EN was utilized for training a deep learning neural network called Nonlinear AutoRegressive with eXogenous input (NARX), which has proved to be effective for time series predictions. The performance of NARX model was optimized via a One-Factor-at-a-Time (OFAT) approach by utilizing step changes in a training parameter called Learning Rate (LR). The optimum configuration achieved was implemented to generate multi-step price predictions over the selected period. Forecast errors from each asset were compared through average percentage error and maximum deviations, where the total sum should be less than 10% for assets to exhibit high performance. Further optimization of NARX performance was suggested by employing multi-objective approaches requiring a higher degree of complexity. Based on their prediction error, a portfolio set representing nine assets was chosen for further examination to measure risk-return levels. Portfolio returns were optimized through Mean-Variance (MV) and Conditional-Value-at-Risk (CVaR) strategies by comparing their results with actual data. Both strategies produced positive returns, although predicted MV outperformed CVaR by a minor margin. The predicted CVaR did not include three target assets in the actual portfolio due to relatively high error deviations. A refined maximization of portfolio returns was suggested by improving prediction performance and modifying target returns. The findings suggest that portfolio performance is susceptible to prediction accuracy, implicating that neural network optimization is crucial. This study contributes towards data analytics within precious metal markets using deep learning artificial intelligence. Furthermore, it reveals valuable information regarding the behavior of these markets during a recession. These revelations allow investors to develop reliable diversification strategies to safeguard their assets amid a plunge in the market.

Contents of this chapter include:

- Introduction;
- Market review and external influence;
- Prediction using deep learning;
- Portfolio optimization;
- Conclusion.

12.1 INTRODUCTION

Investors are always looking for methods to expand their financial potential and search for strategies that suit their financial interests based on their ability to tolerate risk. Investing can be lucrative but requires extensive research to identify a favorable asset. A pandemic caused by the Coronavirus disease 2019 (Covid-19) outbreak has substantially impacted the world's economy. These events triggered a global slump among exchanges, signifying the importance of risk management (Mazur, Dang, and Vega 2021; Mishra and Mishra 2021). Therefore, uncertain conditions urge investors to identify safer markets to protect their wealth (Maram Al and Qasim 2022). Discovering safe investments during downturns requires detailed analytical investigations of trends and external influence (Hamad et al. 2021). Moreover, market research and reliable forecasts can assist investors in developing successful strategies to avoid losses and even generate steady profits during the bear market.

Precious metals are commodities sought by investors due to their evident haven behavior during the financial crisis (Low, Yao, and Faff 2016; Klein 2017; Li and Lucey 2017; Rehman and Vo 2021). Furthermore, gold, silver, platinum, and palladium represent vital assets, considering their rarity. Exceptional physical properties of these metals prove suitable for commercial applications, establishing vast industrial demand (Sensoy 2013; Sverdrup, Koca, and Ragnarsdottir 2014; Oktay, Öztunç, and Serin 2016). These commodities offer monetary advantages such as high liquidity, making them valuable protective assets (Hammoudeh, Malik, and McAleer 2011; Zhu, Chen, and Zhong 2015; Eryiğit 2017; Wang et al. 2019). Therefore, including precious metals in a diversified portfolio has proven to be a reliable risk reduction strategy during uncertainties (Li and Lucey 2017; Alkhazali and Zoubi 2020; Salisu, Raheem, and Vo 2021).

Precious metals are traded globally, with assets available to be purchased through several financial markets, including futures, equity, and Exchange-Traded Funds (ETFs). Yielding favorable returns from these markets requires comprehensive investigation and precise investment decisions. With the rise in technological usage, selecting an investment relies immensely on predictions, describing a challenging component of financial data analysis. The importance of forecasts utilizing complex statistical modeling techniques is highlighted in the literature addressing these challenges (Nti, Adekoya, and Weyori 2020). Machine Learning (ML) is a commonly employed prediction approach that has the ability to process and compute large financial datasets (Obthong et al. 2020; Vijh et al. 2020). Recent financial decision-making applications involve the use of Artificial Intelligence (AI) systems due to technological advancements (Farooq and Chawla 2021). Artificial Neural Networks (ANNs) are computational models inspired by AI, capable of outperforming the accuracy of conventional ML models (Wanjawa and Muchemi 2015; Xiao, Xia, and Jiang 2020; Yun, Yoon, and Won 2021). ANNs can incorporate multiple 'thinking layers', providing a Deep-Learning Neural Network (DLNN). The DLNN structures can tackle problems with high nonlinearity, suitable for dynamic datasets (Nikou, Mansourfar, and Bagherzadeh 2019; Mehtab and Sen 2020). Recurrent Neural Networks (RNNs) are a class of ANNs employed specifically for dynamic time-series data, such as forecasting financial asset price movements (Yu et al. 2019). RNNs can achieve high accuracy for estimating time-varying data, representing a suitable prediction model for future price projection (Zhao et al. 2021). RNN applications could be beneficial for accurately forecasting precious metal markets, particularly under unforeseeable economic conditions. These predictions could assist investors in developing effective diversification strategies and avoiding significant losses amid downturns.

This chapter demonstrates a short-term precious metal investment portfolio during the Covid-19 recession. A dataset containing 58 assets from global precious metal markets has been selected for analysis under a five-year historical period (July 2016 - June 2021). Factors influencing asset prices are reviewed through market research to compute future price estimations. The complexity of prediction dataset requires employing a feature selection algorithm known as Elastic Net (EN) to remove uncorrelated inputs. Filtered data from EN is then employed to predict the selected assets for three months ahead (July - September 2021). The RNN model, known as Nonlinear AutoregRessive with Exogenous input (NARX), is adopted to obtain accurate forecasts, attributing to its superior memory characteristics (Miky et al. 2021; Kuranga and Pillay 2022). The performance of NARX-RNN is further enhanced by optimizing a training parameter called Learning Rate (LR) in a One-Factor-At-a-Time (OFAT) approach. The predicted assets are curated for inclusion in a portfolio, which is sorted based on a defined error threshold ($< 10\%$). Assets depicting reliable predictions are analyzed through portfolio optimization method to measure risk-return levels. Mean-Variance (MV) and Conditional-Value-at-Risk (CVaR) strategies are employed to construct diversified portfolios, generating possible returns during the forecast period. This study contributes towards precious metal market prediction during uncertain financial conditions, which is less acknowledged within the literature. Moreover, this research proves the effectiveness of precious metals as an investment and assesses their speculated haven characteristics.

12.2 MARKET REVIEW AND EXTERNAL INFLUENCE

A comprehensive market review for precious metals is necessary to develop a general understanding of their fluctuations and investment potential. Precious metals are commonly traded within futures, equity, and ETF (Mensi et al. 2021). Among these exchanges, 58 assets were selected for the current investigation (Table 12.1) based on their performance criteria (highest production or market capitalization) in 2021. The assets are traded in the corresponding country's primary commodity market and national stock exchanges. The daily historical price data between July 2016 – June 2021 were accessed from trading websites1,2. These assets represent a foreign portfolio investment that is diversified across 12 countries. Expanding investments to the international market provides risk mitigation during downturns within certain countries (Oloko 2018; Thomas et al. 2022).

Further in-depth analysis of the selected assets includes anticipating factors driving the movements in price. The literature review indicates several factors influencing precious metals, such as economic variables, oil prices, and stock indices (Lili and Chengmei 2013; Apergis, Christou, and Payne 2014; Balcilar and Ozdemir 2019). Correlations between the selected assets and identified factors could be utilized to assess market conditions and forecast their value. It is noteworthy that financial relationships exhibit reccurence, implying that relationships vanish and reappear under different periods (Hammoudeh, Araújo Santos, and Al-Hassan 2013). Recurrence signifies that the speculated influence of factors over specific investment periods must be re-examined. The presence of uncorrelated inputs also deteriorates the performance of predictive models such as ANNs by altering their learning process (Ghasemi et al. 2018). These immense data-driven models represent higher complexity, which might result in lower performance (Barbedo 2018). Therefore, eliminating low-impact components can decrease the computational load on the system and enhance neural network performance.

[1] www.finance.yahoo.com
[2] www.investing.com

12.2.1 FEATURE SELECTION

Analyzing and removing input data requires feature selection through regression-based algorithms. Regression is a method to estimate numerical values of coefficients (β) describing input-output relationships within a dataset. The Mean Squared Error (MSE) over the estimations describing output (z) as a function of any number of inputs (x) can then be computed through *equation* 1 (Bun and Harrison 2019).

$$MSE = \frac{(\sum_{(i=1)}^{n} (z_i - \sum_{j=1}^{k} \beta_j x_j)^2}{n} \tag{1}$$

where n denotes the number of data points; k states the number of input features, and z_1 represents the actual values of the output. The summation of terms $\beta_j x_j$ represents the ordinary least squares (OLS) regression model [41]. Feature selection models update the MSE correlations by adding a minor penalty to reduce coefficients for elimination.

12.2.1.1 LASSO

The Least Absolute Shrinkage and Selection Operator (LASSO) is a unique feature selection algorithm adopting *the L1* penalty function with a shrinkage coefficient (λ) described within *equation 2* (Çiftsüren and Akkol 2018).

$$L1 = \lambda \sum_{j=1}^{k} | \beta_j | \tag{2}$$

The *L1* term can be added to the right-hand side of *equation 1*, reducing the overall coefficient value within the system. The rate of coefficient reduction in the updated MSE function (*equation 3)* serves as criteria for feature elimination, where values of β approach zero.

$$MSE_L = \frac{(\sum_{(i=1)}^{n} (z_i - \sum_{(j=1)}^{k} \beta_j x_j)^2}{n} + \lambda \sum_{j=1}^{k} | \beta_j | \tag{3}$$

In *equation 3*, higher values of λ will induce significant shrinkage in the OLS term, leading to reduced model fit over the data. Such inaccuracies are observed within LASSO estimations among data exhibiting inter-correlations and high variance, resulting in reduced model performance [43]. This issue is called multicollinearity and requires conservative estimates of λ to improve fit.

12.2.1.2 RIDGE

Tackling multicollinearity by employing ridge feature selection utilizes the *L2* penalty term defined in *equation 4*. Notice here that the squared coefficient sum is incorporated, which forces the algorithm to limit the shrinkage [42].

$$L2 = \lambda \sum_{j=1}^{k} \beta_j^{\,2} \tag{4}$$

The squared term in *L2* produces another challenge where most input correlations do not approach 0, indicating feature selection performance limitation despite the improved regression. This problem represents a trade-off issue between regression and feature selection performances.

12.2.1.3 THE ELASTIC NET

The issue highlighted above requires consideration of tuning parameters describing both performances. Such application is available in the EN algorithm, representing a LASSO-ridge hybrid system through the updated *L3* penalty in *equation 5*. Furthermore, this algorithm can significantly improve the overall performance by balancing the ratio of *L1* and *L2* penalties [44].

$$L3 = a\lambda \sum_{j=1}^{k} |\beta_j| + (1-a)\lambda \sum_{j=1}^{k} \beta_j^{\,2} \tag{5}$$

Where the term α represents the weight of LASSO in the system ($0 < \alpha < 1$), and the ridge ratio is computable through the balance ($1 - \alpha$). This tuning parameter can be tested over the defined range to conduct a sensitivity analysis concerning the model error.

The EN algorithm can be implemented within our current case study to detect correlations of the identified factors with the selected assets, and a set of 17 features representing possible correlations with precious metals are listed in *Table 12.1*. The dataset for the selected assets is standardized in US dollars, and the commodity prices in futures market are quoted as US dollars per troy ounce. The closing price is the output for futures, along with the adjusted closing prices for ETF and equity. Missing data are imputed using a quadratic extrapolation approach known as Modified AKIMA piecewise cubic hermite interpolation (MAKIMA). This method helps achieve low deviations in nonlinear estimations, as proven in previous literature for data filling (Ren et al. 2022; Panda and Meher 2022). Removing missing values in financial data can result in the loss of valuable correlations, making

TABLE 12.1 Results from Feature Selection

Asset Name	Alpha	MSE	R^2	Feature Selected*
Gold Futures				
[USA] Gold Futures (GC = F)	0.5	0.0009	0.9746	1,9,12,14,16,17,18,19,20
[CHINA] Gold Futures (SHAUc1)	0.5	0.0038	0.9765	5,9,12,14,16,18,19
[INDIA] Gold Futures (MGPLc1)	0.1	0.0022	0.9915	1,2,5,6,8,9,10,11,12,13,14,15,16,17,18,19,20
Gold ETF				
[USA] SPDR Gold Shares (GLD) – [Commodities]	0.5	0.0009	0.9746	1,9,12,14,16,17,18,19,20
[USA] iShares Gold Trust (IAU) – [Commodities]	–	–	(Negative)	–
[INDIA] Nippon India ETF Hang Seng BeES (HNGS) – [Equity]	–	–	(Negative)	–
[CHINA] Huaan Gold ETF Fund (518880) – [Commodities]	0.3	0.0026	0.97489	2,5,6,8,9,10,12,14,16,17,18,19
Gold Equity				
[USA] Newmont Corporation (NEM)	0.7	0.0038	0.9857	1,2,3,4,6,7,8,10,12,15,16,17,18,19,20
[USA] Barrick Gold (GOLD)	0.8	0.0039	0.8349	1,2,6,8,9,10,11,12,13,14,15,16,17,18,19,20
[RUSSIA] Polyus PAO (PLZL)	1	0.0051	0.9716	1,2,5,6,8,9,10,11,12,13,14,15,16,17,18,19,20
[USA] AngloGold Ashanti Ltd. (AU)	–	–	(< 0.7)	–
[USA] Gold Fields Limited (GFI)	1	0.0045	0.9402	2,6,8,9,10,11,12,14,15,16,17,18,19,20
[USA] KIndiaoss Gold Corporation (KGC)	0.1	0.0044	0.979	1,2,6,8,9,10,11,12,13,14,15,16,17,18,19,20
[AUSTRALIA] Newcrest Mining Limited (NCM)	0.1	0.0284	0.8375	1,2,6,8,9,10,11,12,14,15,16,17,18,19,20
[CHINA] Zijin Mining Group Co Ltd Class A (601899)	-	–	(Negative)	–
[CANADA] Endeavour Mining Corp (EDV)	0	0.0292	0.7208	1,2,5,6,8,9,10,11,12,13,14,15,16,17,18,19,20
[AUSTRALIA] Northern Star Resources Ltd (NST)	0	0.0302	0.8646	1,2,6,8,9,10,11,12,13,14,15,16,17,18,19,20
Silver Futures				
[USA] Silver Futures (SI=F)	0.1	0.0052	0.9664	1,2,6,8,9,10,12,13,14,15,16,17,18,19,20
[CHINA] Silver Futures (SAGc1)	0.2	0.0076	0.9295	1,2,8,9,10,12,14,15,16,17,18,20
[INDIA] Silver Futures (MSVc1)	0.6	0.0064	0.9699	1,6,9,10,12,14,15,16,17,18,19,20

TABLE 12.1 *(Continued)*

Asset Name	Alpha	MSE	R^2	Feature Selected*
Silver ETF				
[USA] iShares Silver Trust (SLV) – [Commodities]	0.1	0.006	0.9602	1,2,6,8,9,10,12,13,14,16,17,18,19,20
[USA] Global X Silver Miners ETF (SIL) – [Equity]	0.1	0.008	0.9386	1,2,6,8,9,10,12,14,15,16,17,18,19,20
[USA] Aberdeen Standard Physical Silver Shares ETF (SIVR)	0.1	0.0061	0.9669	1,2,6,8,9,10,12,13,14,15,16,17,18,19,20
– [Commodities]	1	0.0119	0.9091	1,2,6,8,9,10,11,12,13,14,15,16,17,18,19,20
[USA] ETFMG Prime Junior Silver Miners ETF (SILJ) – [Equity]	0.1	0.0064	0.969	1,2,6,8,9,12,14,15,16,17,18,19,20
[USA] iShares MSCI Global Silver and Metals Miners ETF (SLVP)	1	0.0073	0.9663	1,2,8,9,10,12,13,14,15,16,17,19,20
– Equity]				
[AUSTRALIA] ETFS Physical Silver ETC (ETPMAG) – [Commodities]				
Silver Equity				
[UK] Fresnillo plc (FRES)	0.2	0.0365	0.7601	1,2,6,8,11,14,15,16,17,18,19
[POLAND] KGHM Polska Miedz S.A. (KGH)	0.1	0.0114	0.9195	1,2,6,9,10,11,12,14,15,16,17,18,19,20
[UK] Glencore plc. (GLEN)	0.7	0.0111	0.9380	1,2,6,8,9,10,12,13,14,15,16,17,18,19,20
[INDIA] Hindustan Zinc Limited (HZNC)	1	0.0229	0.8253	1,2,6,8,9,10,11,12,13,14,15,16,17,18,19,20
[UK] Polymetal International plc (POLYP)	0.1	0.0066	0.9778	1,2,6,8,9,10,12,13,14,15,16,17,18,19
[CANADA] Pan American Silver Corp. (PAAS)	0.9	0.0104	0.926	1,2,6,8,9,10,13,14,15,16,17,18,19,20
[USA] Southern Copper Corporation (SCCO)	–	–	(< 0.7)	–
[MEXICO] Industrias Peñoles, S.A.B. de C.V. (PEOLES)	0.9	0.0245	0.8926	2,6,9,10,11,12,13,14,15,16,17,18,19,20
[AUSTRALIA] South32 Limited (S32)	0.9	0.0178	0.9057	1,2,6,8,10,11,12,13,14,15,16,17,18,19,20
[JAPAN] Sumitomo Corp. (8053)	0.7	0.0196	0.8451	1,2,6,8,10,11,13,14,16,17,18,19,20
[USA] Compañía de Minas Buenaventura S.A.A. (BVN)	1	0.0202	0.7637	1,2,6,8,9,10,11,14,15,16,17,18,19,20
[USA] Hecla Mining Company (HL)	0.8	0.0154	0.8082	1,2,6,8,9,10,11,12,13,14,15,16,17,18,19,20
[USA] First Majestic Silver Corp. (AG)	–	–	(Negative)	–
[USA] BHP Group (BHP)	0.2	0.0071	0.96	1,2,6,8,9,10,11,12,14,15,16,17,18,19,20
[UK] Hochschild Mining plc (HOCM)	–	–	(< 0.7)	–
[SWEDEN] Boliden AB (publ) (BOL)	0.4	0.0139	0.7957	1,2,6,8,9,10,12,13,14,15,16,17,18,19,20
[USA] Teck Resources Limited (TECK)	1	0.0202	0.871	1,2,6,8,9,10,12,13,15,16,17,18,20

TABLE 12.1 *(Continued)*

Asset Name	Alpha	MSE	R^2	Feature Selected*
Platinum Futures				
[USA] Platinum Futures (PL = F)	–	–	(< 0.7)	–
[JAPAN] Platinum Futures (JPLc1)	–	–	(< 0.7)	–
Platinum ETF				
[USA] Aberdeen Standard Physical Platinum Shares ETF (PPLT)	–	–	(< 0.7)	–
– [Commodities]	0.1	0.017	0.8358	1,2,6,8,9,10,11,12,13,14,15,16,17,18,19,20
[SOUTH AFRICA] NewGold Platinum ETF (NGPLTJ) – [Commodities]				
Platinum Equity				
[SOUTH AFRICA] Anglo American Platinum Limited (AMSJ)	–	–	(< 0.7)	–
[SOUTH AFRICA] Impala Platinum Holdings Limited (IMPJ)	–	–	(< 0.7)	–
[USA] Sibanye Stillwater Limited (SBSW)	–	–	(Negative)	–
[USA] Vale S.A. (VALE)	0.7	0.008	0.9362	1,2,6,8,9,10,11,12,13,15,16,17,18,19,20
[CANADA] Platinum Group Metals (PTM)	–	–	(Negative)	–
Palladium Futures				
[USA] Palladium Futures (PA=F)	0.1	0.0126	0.9369	1,2,6,8,9,10,11,12,14,15,16,17,18,19
[JAPAN] Palladium Futures (JPAc1)	0.1	0.0162	0.9192	2,6,9,10,14,15,16,17,18,19,20
Palladium ETF				
[USA] Aberdeen Standard Physical Palladium Shares ETF (PALL)	0.1	0.0145	0.9206	1,2,6,8,9,10,11,12,14,15,16,17,18,19
– [Commodities]	0.6	0.0161	0.9428	1,2,6,8,9,10,11,12,14,16,17,18,19,20
[SOUTH AFRICA] NewGold Palladium ETF (NGPLDJ) – [Commodities]				
Palladium Equity				
[CANADA] Ivanhoe Mines Ltd. (IVN)	–	–	(< 0.7)	–
[CANADA] New Age Metals (NAM)	–	–	(< 0.7)	–

*1: Supply; 2: Demand; 3: Supply (silver/palladium); 4: Demand (silver/palladium); 5: Gold reserve; 6: Market; 7: Market (silver/palladium); 8: Dow jones precious metal index; 9: Dow jones precious metal commodity index; 10: Stock index; 11: OPEC; 12: WTI; 13: Brent; 14: Total reserves; 15: Exchange rate; 16: Real GDP growth; 17: Inflation; 18: Interest rate; 19: Unemployment rate; and 20: Bond rate.

MAKIMA an effective solution. Gold market is tested against 17 factors, whereas white metals (silver, platinum, and palladium) with 16 factors. Some of the assets (NEM, AMSJ, SBSW, and PTM) are mining companies producing more than one metal, suggesting that more variables might affect their prices. The inputs unique to each particular metal (supply, demand, and primary production market) are incorporated into their dataset. Simulations were conducted over the entire range of α with a step size 0.1 in an OFAT analysis. *Table 12.1* also presents the results from best-performing configurations through the MSE and regression coefficient (R^2).

Results from Table 12.1 demonstrate the effectiveness of tuning parameter (α) within the implemented EN algorithm, where 33 out of 58 assets performed satisfactorily through LASSO-ridge combinations. Seven of the remaining assets demonstrated high performance with LASSO ($\alpha = 1$), indicating that the selected feature dataset presented an approximate linear approximation of the targets. However, two assets (EDV and NST) required the ridge approximation ($\alpha = 0$), implying that the data correlations might present high variance. Moreover, EDV represented a relatively poor fit ($R^2 < 0.75$) despite low errors, which might indicate poor regressive results over the prediction due to high nonlinearities. The remaining 16 assets demonstrated relatively poor fit ($R^2 < 0.7$) for the feature selection results, with six targets producing negative regression coefficient values. Therefore, their open, high, low, and volume values for futures prediction, as well as, open, high, low, close, and volume values within ETF and equity datasets are utilized. These negative R^2 values arise when no linearities can be determined between the input-output data [47]. A possible explanation could indicate the asset's continuous nonlinearities within the data, requiring prediction algorithms with high-degree computing capabilities. Another justification for these results could be related to the much-reviewed haven characteristics of the precious metal markets. To confirm haven behavior, the prediction accuracies of these assets could be investigated using the proposed NARX-RNN model. Overall, the performance of feature selection could be further improved by analyzing the sensitivity of shrinkage (λ) towards tuning parameters or employing nonlinear regression models such as random forests, extreme gradient boost, and support vector machines [22–24].

12.3 PREDICTION USING DEEP LEARNING

The refined dataset obtained after feature selection is the basis for deploying predictive models to estimate future prices. The accuracy of these predictions varies greatly between several statistical models employed in the literature

[20, 23, 24]. ANNs are highly prevalent nonlinear regression tools presenting crucial applications such as pattern recognition, cybersecurity, and stock price forecasting [48–50]. An ANN computes information through a hidden layer containing neurons assigned for each input (x). Neurons typically employ a nonlinear transfer function (g), which transforms the input value into a signal response (V) [51]. These input signals are assigned a weight ($0 < w < 1$), representing their strength with the predicted output (y). A bias (b) term is added to scale the prediction curve, with *equations 6* and *7* exhibiting the complete algorithm [52].

$$y_i = \Sigma_{(j=1)}^{k} w_j V_j \pm b \tag{6}$$

Where,

$$V_j = g\left(x_j\right) \tag{7}$$

The ANN weights (w) in *equation 6* are similar to correlations (β) obtained from the feature selection, as both concepts are regression-based. Regression quality significantly improves by incorporating multiple hidden layers, creating a DLNN capable of outperforming conventional regressive models [25, 26]. DLNNs can resolve highly nonlinear dynamics and represent important models to build reliable AI-based prediction applications.

12.3.1 NONLINEAR AUTOREGRESSIVE WITH EXOGENOUS INPUT

Historical data utilized for feature selection represents a time series, that is often involved in financial analysis. Time-varying data requires computations of a continuous series where the model's current state is affected by its previous values. NARX model provides relatively higher memory than other RNNs, such as long short-term memory. This property proves advantageous as NARX-RNN could provide high-accuracy forecasts over an extended range. The overall system predicts the output $y(t)$ at any time step as a function of previous inputs $(u(t-i))$ and previous output predictions $(y(t-i))$, as demonstrated in *equation 8*.

$$y(t) = f\left(u(t-1), u(t-2) \ldots .u(t-d), y(t-1), y(t-2) \ldots .y(t-d)\right) \tag{8}$$

The d in *equation 8* refers to delays, which indicate the property of NARX-RNN. Delays are time steps from input and output series stored within network memory as an initial condition. The incorporation of delays can improve performance, although an excessive number of delays might produce errors due to large memory requirements. A generic single hidden layer NARX-RNN structure can be represented in *figure 12.1* trained on historical input and output data to project future values. The network trains in an open structure, receiving input-output values and computing correlations from the data. The output signal is replaced with a feedback loop during testing, resulting in a closed structure. A feedback signal allows the network to track its output predictions for accurate time series modeling [53].

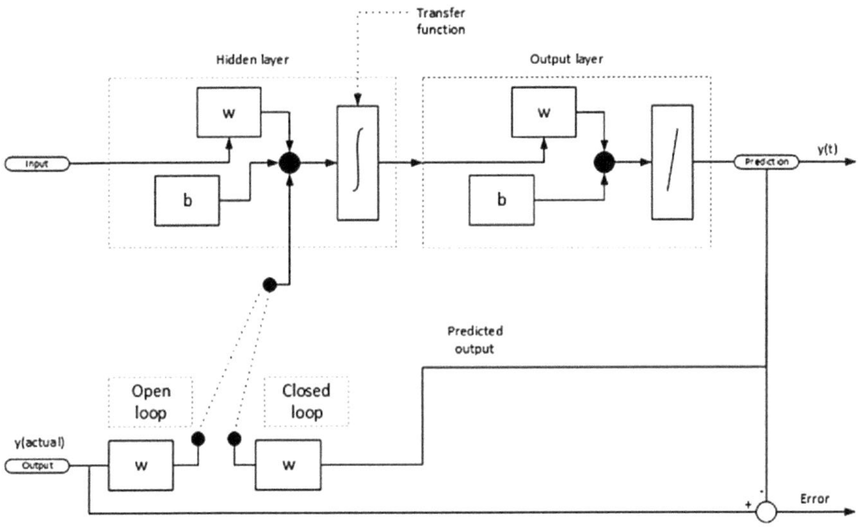

FIGURE 12.1 NARX-RNN with a single hidden layer.

12.3.1.1 *THE TRAINING ALGORITHM*

Training is the most crucial part of prediction using RNNs, directly influencing forecast accuracy. While the process is affected by several parameters (neurons, epochs, transfer function, and others), the training algorithm holds significant importance as it updates the network weight over each iteration. These weights (w) directly compute the network output and the neuron response as previously demonstrated in *equation 6*. Several approaches are available in the literature based on the network type; however, RNNs commonly utilize the Gradient Descent (GD) training algorithms. GD possesses the parameter LR (η) for controlling the sensitivity of predictions with fluctuating values observed in dynamic data. The tracked error gradient (∇w) and overall NARX cost function (C) from *equation 8*, along with η values, compute the change in weights (Δw) as illustrated in *equation 9* [54] (Liška, Kruszewski, and Baroni 2018).

$$\Delta w = \eta \nabla_w C \tag{9}$$

Updated weights alter future time-step prediction and stabilize network learning over highly nonlinear dynamics. However, the error gradient (∇_w) eventually drops to 0, leading to a halt in training, even though the desired accuracy or fit might not be achieved. This issue is common among RNNs employing GD algorithm, referred to as the vanishing gradient [55, 56]. Resolving this issue requires updating LR in response to error gradients, which are possible through the Adaptive GD (AGD) training procedure [57]. Values of η are stepped inversely in response to an error threshold (E_{min}), below which the LR drops by a specified range (η_{min}). This behavior avoids overfitting by controlling the training performance as described in *equation 10* [58].

$$if\ E < E_{\min}$$

$$\Delta w = (\eta - \eta_{\min})\nabla_w C \tag{10}$$

The step response (η_{min}) is usually minor compared to the initial LR since it is a sensitive parameter, and large fluctuations may destabilize the network. Therefore, exploring the value of initial LR as a potential critical learning parameter in the AGD algorithm is necessary to achieve viable training.

12.3.1.2 PERFORMANCE OPTIMIZATION

In addition to training algorithms, the predictive performance of NARX-RNN relies on several other learning and structural parameters. Values of these parameters occur over a wide range, making it challenging to define a standard network structure. For the current analysis, the selection of several configuration parameters is described in *Table 12.2*. These values are employed based on the complexity of selected data and commonly observed values within the literature for market predictions.

TABLE 12.2 NARX-RNN Configuration

Parameter Name	Value/Range
Hidden layers	4
Hidden layer neurons	5
Epochs	3,000
Transfer function (g)	Tangent-sigmoid [–1,1]
Initial LR (η)	0.01–0.05
LR step range (η_{min})	0.05η (5%)

Hidden layers and neurons add complexity to the model, enabling the network to model nonlinearities. However, numerous hidden layers can overfit the network, which in turn generates high errors. Thus, selecting a NARX-RNN structure with four hidden layers containing five neurons each for the current analysis is sufficient (Uzair and Jamil 2020). Epoch is completed when the entire training dataset is processed through the network. Repetition of epochs can reduce the error gradient over multiple iterations, and a value of 3000 is configured for the proposed NARX-RNN (Maknickienė, Rutkauskas, and Maknickas 2011; Moghar and Hamiche 2020). Input data is regularized for regression applications to scale the prediction curve within a specified range for prediction. In the current analysis, the inputs are normalized using min-max scaling to adopt a working prediction range of [-1,1]. Furthermore, employing a tangent-sigmoid transfer function with the same operation range as min-max can avoid conversion data loss for predictive iteration in NARX-RNN (Dorofki et al. 2012; Koyuncu 2018). The network predictions are highly sensitive to LR, and significant changes can compromise its training. Hence, the step range for the AGD algorithm is selected as 5% to avoid unstable responses (Lu, Zhang, and Renais 2016). Moreover, the initial LR values are tested between 0.01 to 0.05 with a step size of 0.01 in another OFAT optimization approach to select the best-performing configuration.

12.3.2 PRECIOUS METAL MARKET PREDICTIONS

NARX-RNN configuration described in the previous section utilizes the dataset obtained after feature selection. The five-year historical values operate as training data to predict the selected assets three months ahead. *Table 12.3* demonstrates the highest-performing results for each asset through the computed errors and R^2 values. The entire prediction dataset defines error estimations through average values and maximum deviations. These errors indicate the correlations for average values and volatility, which are beneficial for developing accurate portfolio strategies. A sum of averages and deviations provides the maximum expected error over the three-month predictions, with a 10% total threshold for selecting portfolio assets. Poor regression fit can imply incorrect correlations, affecting the overall accuracy of volatility forecasts. Thus, R^2 is assigned a threshold value (> 0.85) to ensure favorable portfolio performance.

TABLE 12.3 Market Prediction Results

ASSET NAME	Data Point	Prediction Point	Optimum Learning Rate	Percent Error	Percent Deviations	R^2
Gold Futures						
[USA] Gold Futures (GC = F)	1256	64	0.01	1.58077	2.94268	0.96503
[CHINA] Gold Futures (SHAUc1)	1215	64	0.01	1.97258	3.5431	0.97433
[INDIA] Gold Futures (MGPLc1)	1284	66	0.03	1.17925	2.0574	0.98056
Gold ETF						
[USA] SPDR Gold Shares (GLD) – [Commodities]	1258	64	0.03	1.91837	3.60646	0.95846
[USA] iShares Gold Trust (IAU) – [Commodities]	1258	64	0.02	1.75523	2.9513	0.85464
[INDIA] Nippon India ETF Hang Seng BeES (HNGS) – [Equity]	1233	63	0.04	2.91581	4.79455	0.6566
[CHINA] Huaan Gold ETF Fund (518880) – [Commodities]	1214	64	0.03	1.13527	2.31048	0.97164
Gold Equity						
[USA] Newmont Corporation (NEM)	1258	64	0.02	17.45754	6.83355	0.9592
[USA] Barrick Gold (GOLD)	1258	64	0.02	9.6034	14.8112	0.9594
[RUSSIA] Polyus PAO (PLZL)	1258	66	0.03	2.50533	10.99011	0.97966
[USA] AngloGold Ashanti Ltd. (AU)	1258	64	0.02	31.12731	30.00587	0.73248
[USA] Gold Fields Limited (GFI)	1258	64	0.03	6.32044	14.23559	0.97405
[USA] KIndiaoss Gold Corporation (KGC)	1258	64	0.01	17.71013	10.21015	0.9612
[AUSTRALIA] Newcrest Mining Limited (NCM)	1266	66	0.02	8.55817	5.13207	0.91353
[CHINA] Zijin Mining Group Co Ltd Class A (601899)	1214	64	0.01	5.80329	8.17037	0.88142
[CANADA] Endeavour Mining Corp (EDV)	1254	63	0.02	2.28287	4.78137	0.89197
[AUSTRALIA] Northern Star Resources Ltd (NST)	1266	66	0.02	7.77604	16.64081	0.95213
Silver Futures						
[USA] Silver Futures (SI=F)	1256	64	0.01	9.12349	8.55356	0.62901
[CHINA] Silver Futures (SAGc1)	1216	64	0.03	5.28353	11.51234	0.93453
[INDIA] Silver Futures (MSVc1)	1284	66	0.02	6.22973	11.40514	0.95697

TABLE 12.3 *(Continued)*

ASSET NAME	Data Point	Prediction Point	Optimum Learning Rate	Percent Error	Percent Deviations	R^2
Silver ETF						
[USA] iShares Silver Trust (SLV) – [Commodities]	1258	64	0.01	2.69038	7.97013	0.95271
[USA] Global X Silver Miners ETF (SIL) – [Equity]	1258	64	0.02	10.75021	17.88206	0.92868
[USA] Aberdeen Standard Physical Silver Shares ETF (SIVR) – [Commodities]	1258	64	0.05	9.33822	13.39734	0.95422
[USA] ETFMG Prime Junior Silver Miners ETF (SILJ) – [Equity]	1258	64	0.04	17.25954	18.94755	0.92839
[USA] iShares MSCI Global Silver and Metals Miners ETF (SLVP) – Equity]	1258	64	0.04	9.60219	15.85931	0.9112
[AUSTRALIA] ETFS Physical Silver ETC (ETPMAG) – [Commodities]	1258	64	0.01	6.87803	7.23158	0.96425
Silver Equity						
[UK] Fresnillo plc (FRES)	1264	65	0.05	4.60552	9.10728	0.9604
[POLAND] KGHM Polska Miedz S.A. (KGH)	1295	66	0.02	10.10743	13.59574	0.90842
[UK] Glencore plc. (GLEN)	1264	64	0.01	3.39619	4.26683	0.46499
[INDIA] Hindustan Zinc Limited (HZNC)	1233	63	0.05	2.41217	4.67717	0.93383
[UK] Polymetal International plc (POLYP)	1264	64	0.02	7.14606	12.45827	0.97867
[CANADA] Pan American Silver Corp. (PAAS)	1254	63	0.02	22.83195	12.74573	0.9557
[USA] Southern Copper Corporation (SCCO)	1258	64	0.04	20.49849	12.49682	0.89119
[MEXICO] Industrias Peñoles, S.A.B. de C.V. (PEOLES)	1256	65	0.04	8.13871	7.26915	0.94702
[AUSTRALIA] South32 Limited (S32)	1266	66	0.03	5.56331	13.66317	0.89958
[JAPAN] Sumitomo Corp. (8053)	1241	61	0.04	4.28001	4.90035	0.86918
[USA] Compañía de Minas Buenaventura S.A.A. (BVN)	1258	64	0.03	17.23609	17.95915	0.90212
[USA] Hecla Mining Company (HL)	1258	64	0.04	35.80251	17.37275	0.96001
[USA] First Majestic Silver Corp. (AG)	1258	64	0.01	5.53011	11.63013	0.41677
[USA] BHP Group (BHP)	1258	64	0.03	13.69849	26.53682	0.97336
[UK] Hochschild Mining plc (HOCM)	1264	65	0.01	15.30487	17.33074	0.36682
[SWEDEN] Boliden AB (publ) (BOL)	1257	66	0.05	6.54296	13.93246	0.90926
[USA] Teck Resources Limited (TECK)	1258	64	0.02	5.86224	10.89744	0.93184

TABLE 12.3 *(Continued)*

ASSET NAME	Data Point	Prediction Point	Optimum Learning Rate	Percent Error	Percent Deviations	R^2
Platinum Futures						
[USA] Platinum Futures (PL=F)	1256	64	0.01	6.64783	9.69287	0.29223
[JAPAN] Platinum Futures (JPLc1)	1224	61	0.01	3.64917	7.21382	0.28603
Platinum ETF						
[USA] Aberdeen Standard Physical Platinum Shares ETF (PPLT) – [Commodities]	1258	64	0.04	4.99346	7.85814	0.28818
[SOUTH AFRICA] NewGold Platinum ETF (NGPLTJ) – [Commodities]	1261	64	0.02	6.59118	9.24757	0.88814
Platinum Equity						
[SOUTH AFRICA] Anglo American Platinum Limited (AMSJ)	1261	64	0.03	15.57416	31.7657	0.81749
[SOUTH AFRICA] Impala Platinum Holdings Limited (IMPJ)	1261	64	0.01	16.06298	37.20022	0.90941
[USA] Sibanye Stillwater Limited (SBSW)	1258	64	0.05	10.84148	8.7049	0.67708
[USA] Vale S.A. (VALE)	1258	64	0.01	9.25927	23.12464	0.95643
[CANADA] Platinum Group Metals (PTM)	1254	63	0.05	8.79855	20.66376	0.8941
Palladium Futures						
[USA] Palladium Futures (PA=F)	1256	64	0.05	12.92939	24.48149	0.98329
[JAPAN] Palladium Futures (JPAc1)	1221	61	0.01	12.38696	8.43693	0.98252
Palladium ETF						
[USA] Aberdeen Standard Physical Palladium Shares ETF (PALL) – [Commodities]	1258	64	0.02	7.88966	12.70769	0.98079
[SOUTH AFRICA] NewGold Palladium ETF (NGPLDJ) – [Commodities]	1261	64	0.05	11.10424	13.76721	0.97899
Palladium Equity						
[CANADA] Ivanhoe Mines Ltd. (IVN)	1254	63	0.02	8.62895	7.92219	0.72913
[CANADA] New Age Metals (NAM)	1254	63	0.04	9.18657	18.3482	0.21969

As observed in *Table 12.3*, majority of the assets (49 out of 58) produced significant errors (> 10% total) or unsatisfactory regression fit (R2 < 0.85) and could not be included in portfolio analysis. These results can be justified due to the possibility of highly dynamic characteristics superseding the potential of selected NARX-RNN configurations.

Prediction performance could be improved by optimizing other key training parameters to explore multi-variate effects on model accuracy. Optimizing several parameters requires multi-objective modeling, analyzed using advanced statistical optimization techniques such as Response Surface Methodology (RSM), capable of capturing complex input-output correlations. RSM models incorporate a higher degree of complexity, which could be investigated through a deeper technical analysis of these markets. The remaining nine assets produced acceptable results, and their prediction responses are portrayed in *Figure 12.2* for comparison.

NARX-RNN performed well for five assets (USA gold futures, GLD, IAU, 518880, and 8053), signifying that the network modeled the price values and market volatility. On the other hand, accurate calculation of market variance is not achieved within three assets (India gold futures, EDV, and HZNC), as they demonstrate flat responses. Furthermore, China gold futures produced high errors in the beginning, and the response approaches its actual values towards the end of forecasting period. Inconsistencies in predictive performance could be related to the accuracy of feature selection under the defined threshold (R2 > 0.7). EDV and HZNC demonstrate moderate regression fit (R2 < 0.85) using the EN algorithm, which might indicate the inclusion of a few non-correlated inputs. These inputs could map false correlations, resulting in reduced estimation accuracy. Thus, improving the efficiency of feature selection could directly affect the performance of NARX-RNN. Adopting an effective asset allocation strategy requires an evaluation of the prediction errors impact towards portfolio risk-return levels.

12.4 PORTFOLIO OPTIMIZATION

The selected well-performing assets during prediction can be further analyzed to implement diversification techniques. The diversification approach requires an in-depth assessment analysis of risk-return to determine worthy assets and construct an optimal portfolio (Beasley 2013; Doering et al. 2019). Optimization algorithm targets the maximum returns at a specified risk level or the lowest risk to yield a specific return. MV and CVaR are well-known strategies for efficient asset allocation within a certain period (Tian et al. 2010; Doering et al. 2019).

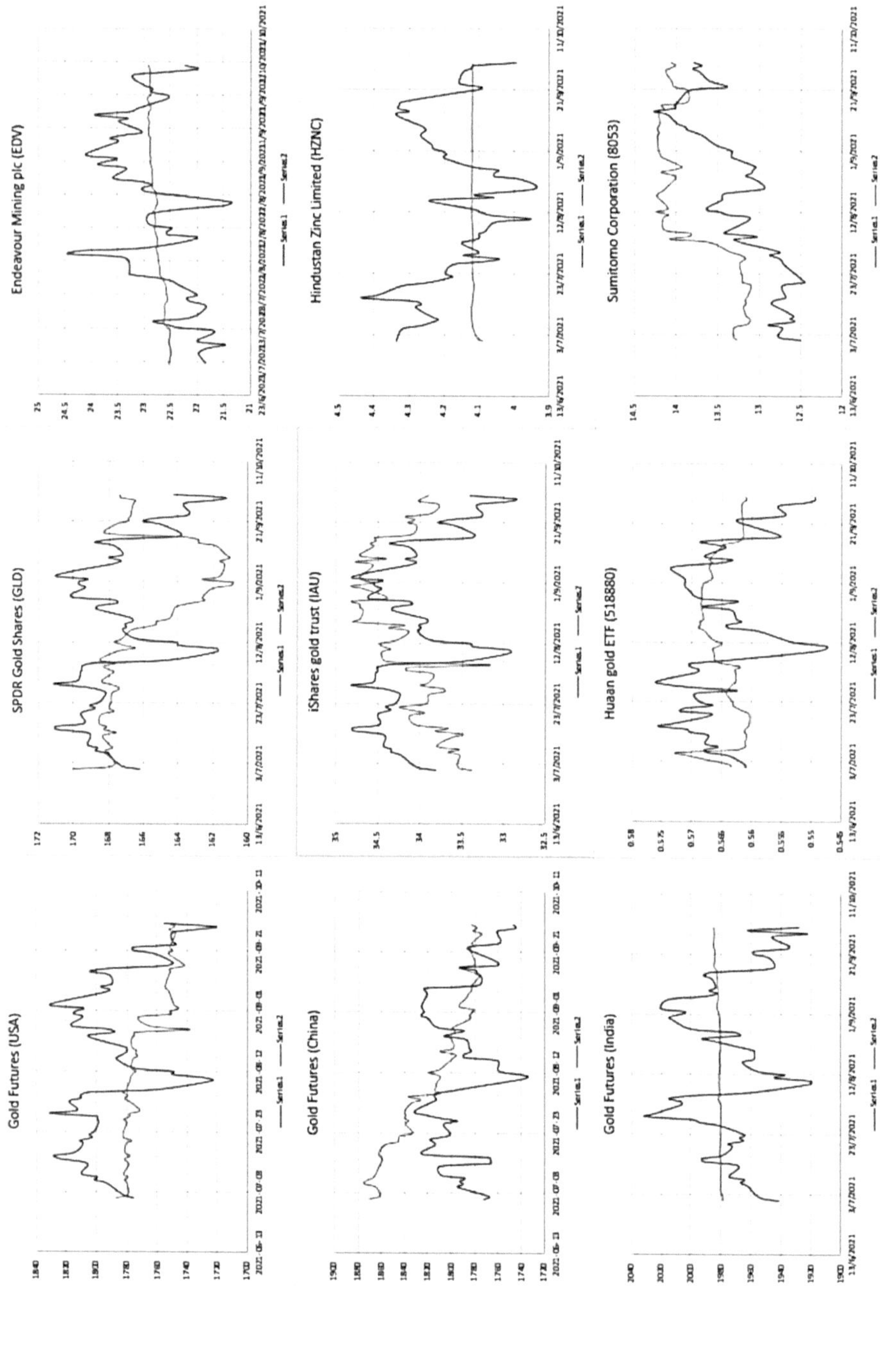

FIGURE 12.2 Predicted (red) and actual (blue) responses for selected assets.

12.4.1 MEAN-VARIANCE PORTFOLIO

MV asset allocation strategy computes the portfolio through the mean of estimated returns and standard deviations as a risk measure. *Equations 11 and 12* describe the algorithm calculations for both variables, targeting maximum mean and minimum variance [68].

$$Mean = w'^{T} \mu \tag{11}$$

$$Variance = w'^{T} \in w' \tag{12}$$

Where, μ is the estimated return; and $\in$ describes the covariance (volatility).

Note that the term 'w' in *equations 11 and 12* above denotes the weight value describing a portion of total investment dedicated to a particular security. The MV algorithm assumes that the data provided is normally distributed, which is not applicable in most dynamic time series [69]. Non-Gaussian data produces incorrect risk-return values caused by skewness from normal conditions [70]. The calculated MV risk indicates the average percentage change in estimated returns.

12.4.2 CONDITIONAL-VALUE-AT-RISK

Risk in an MV portfolio measures the average standard deviation in data, which is dubious for volatile assets. Such approximations in MV produce incorrect asset allocation by incorporating high-risk assets with an unstable response [71]. Realistic markets present risk through probable investment losses over time [72]. Probabilities of expected changes in the market are stated to a certain threshold β, altering the portfolio risk. Estimating the maximum percentage loss in the capital is achievable within a specific confidence interval (α). Therefore, CVaR considers losses above the defined confidence intervals, providing a worst-case investment scenario by measuring the tail risk [73]. Mean of portfolio returns is computed by employing the same correlations as MV (*equation 11*), and losses resulting from each possible portfolio (*f (x, y)*) display unexpected scenarios (y) above the threshold value. *Equation 13* computes the function describing losses in CVaR as F (x, β) [74].

$$F(x,\beta) = \beta + (1-a)^{(-1)} \textstyle\sum_{j=1}^{k} \pi_j . [f(x,y_j) - \beta]^{+} \tag{13}$$

Where; π_j is the probability of a loss scenario $f(x, y)$, and $[n]^{+} = max\ [n,0]$.

Therefore, this research aims to examine MV and CVaR risk-return values, portfolio weights, and degree of diversification to obtain the most suitable approach.

12.4.3 PORTFOLIO RESULTS

We analyze risk-return levels from efficient MV and CVaR portfolios utilizing the nine assets from the predictive analysis. The error threshold (< 10%) for prediction served as a basis to define the confidence interval describing expected losses in CVaR. Results from predicted portfolios are compared with actual values to determine the impact of NARX-RNN performance on generated returns. MV and CVaR strategies compute scenarios implementing varying investment weights (w') assigned to each asset. These scenarios are represented on a graph called a 'frontier plot' graph depicting portfolio returns as a risk function.

Since both strategies compute returns through *equation 11*, the same frontier plot can be converted to describe both portfolios for comparison. In the current analysis, we convert both estimations to CVaR standards. Therefore, the frontier plots in *Figures 12.3(a)* and *12.3(b)* highlight computed MV and CVaR efficient portfolios.

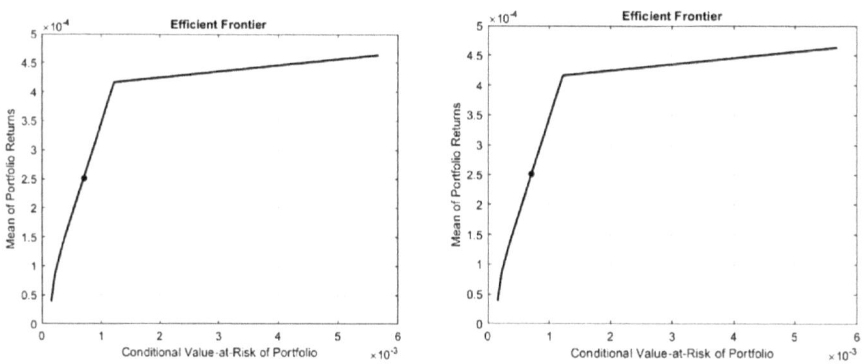

FIGURE 12.3 Predicted efficient portfolios for (a) MV; and (b) CvaR.

Both predicted portfolios demonstrate similar risk-return ratios, implying that the data distribution is approximately normal. In such cases, CVaR strategies often incorporate unnecessary risk estimations, leading to lower returns and increased risk values. The computed optimal portfolio (red point on the frontier plot) is a function of target returns, defined through the mean of maximum possible returns over selected scenarios. It is observed that the actual optimum portfolio within the scenarios can generate 1.7 times higher returns (0.00042) compared to the selected targets (0.00025). However, the current analysis observes risk-return levels through mean targets, providing conservative risk estimates. Variations between predicted and actual data can alter the optimal portfolio weights and the level of diversification. Hence, we plot efficient frontiers describing optimal portfolios using actual market data during the defined prediction period (*Figures 12.4(a)* and *12.4(b)*).

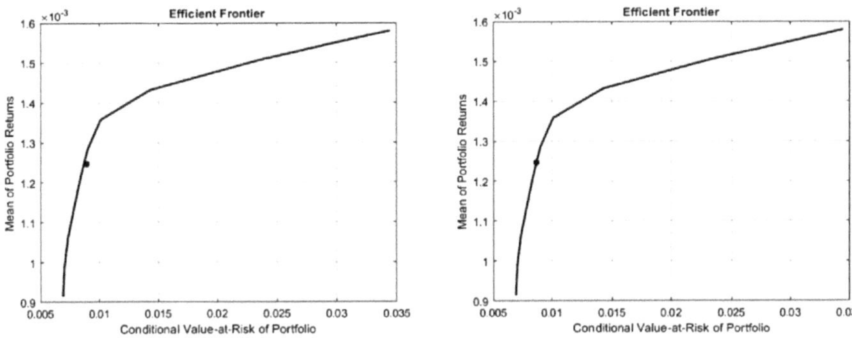

FIGURE 12.4 Actual efficient portfolios using (a) MV; and (b) CVaR.

The actual data observed similar outcomes using both strategies, with risk-return values significantly higher than predicted data. Actual scenario target returns (0.00125) were roughly five times higher than the predicted value. The risk estimations also observed a 10-fold increase (0.008–0.009), resulting in an undervalued risk-return ratio (2.83 for predicted). The actual value of this ratio (7.04) is approximately 2.5 times higher, indicating that investments are severely risky. Risk-return ratio values greater than 1 imply high-risk conditions, requiring further assessment regarding the computational inaccuracies in portfolio optimization. Optimal portfolio weights computed from both strategies are available in Table 12.4, representing the asset allocation utilized for predicted and actual data. The differences in weight distributions assist in justifying the observed miscomputations, leading to undervalued risk-return levels.

Among the speculated haven assets from feature selection (*Section 12.2.1.3*), only one asset (IAU) is present within the portfolio dataset. However, this asset experienced a plunge during the selected three-month period, which could potentially generate investment losses and thus, excluded from both portfolio strategies. The majority of the actual portfolio investments (48%

TABLE 12.4 Optimum Weight Distributions

Asset Name	Predicted Portfolio Weights		Actual Portfolio Weights	
	Optimum MV Weights	**Optimum CVaR Weights**	**Optimum MV Weights**	**Optimum CVaR Weights**
[USA] Gold Futures (GC=F)	–	–	–	–
[CHINA] Gold Futures (SHAUc1)	–	–	0.48	0.434
[INDIA] Gold Futures (MGPLc1)	0.458	0.463	0.136	0.118
[USA] SPDR Gold Shares (GLD) – [Commodities]	0.045	0.045	–	–
[USA] iShares Gold Trust (IAU) – [Commodities]	–	–	–	–
[CHINA] Huaan Gold ETF Fund (518880) – [Commodities]	–	–	–	–
[CANADA] Endeavour Mining Corp (EDV)	0.491	0.492	0.069	0.09
[INDIA] Hindustan Zinc Limited (HZNC)	–	–	0.04	0.075
[JAPAN] Sumitomo Corp. (8053)	0.007	–	0.275	0.284

in MV and 43% in CVaR) are dedicated to China gold futures due to stable average values over the prediction period. The predicted portfolios utilized India gold futures to protect investments, dedicating almost half (around 46%) of the total investments. This selection can be justified based on the flat prediction response (*Figure 12.2*), which allows the portfolio to recognize India's gold futures as a stable investment despite the high variance in actual data. EDV observes similar inaccuracies in market volatility, which led to its incorporation as a return generator in predicted portfolios. A significant portion (approximately 49%) of investment was allotted to EDV to maximize the returns, even though the actual asset response is unstable. The market data suggests that Sumimoto (8053) possesses a higher return-generation ability than EDV since it presents increasing price and low variance. Therefore, nearly one-third of the investment is assigned to this asset within actual portfolios to generate stable returns with minimum possible risk. Correlations relating to data variance are critical market risk indicators, and predictive performance (average errors and deviations) must be improved. Optimal computed weights are utilized within real market data to determine the outcomes of predictive strategies. *Figure 12.5(a) and 12.5(b)* exhibit frontier plots describing results where distance from efficient line interprets the deviations from actual optimal investments.

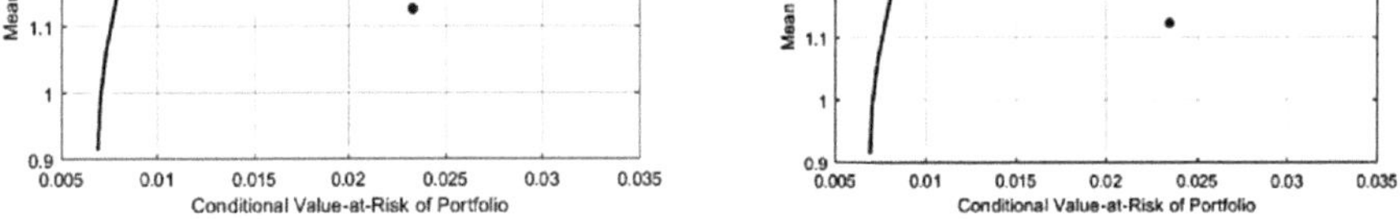

FIGURE 12.5 Simulated scenarios based on predicted (a) MV; and (b) CVaR portfolio.

The figures above clearly demonstrate the effect of risky assets (India gold futures, GLD, and EDV) incorporated within predicted portfolios. Although the outcome accomplished 90% of the actual target returns (0.00125) sounds profitable, portfolio risk was increased by a factor of 2.7 (0.0233), suggesting the possibility of losses over prolonged investment periods. These results imply the importance of variance as a measure of prediction accuracy, in addition to the average errors. Periodic deviations in time-series data serve as the basis for asset selection in diversification strategies. Achieving an accurate model of such nonlinear dynamics is crucial towards obtaining positive returns with minimal risk. Therefore, this study justifies the importance of performance optimization in predictive models, which is observed through NARX. NARX-RNNs present substantial modeling capabilities with the possibility of enhancement through successful training to predict lucrative investment markets such as precious metals.

12.5 CONCLUSION

This chapter portrays a comprehensive analysis of global precious metal markets as an investment. The significance of these metals is justified through their haven behavior amid financial crises, making them superior protective assets. We assessed the investment potential of 58 assets over three months, from July to September 2021. The literature review identified several variables affecting market prices, representing critical correlations required for forecasting. Feature selection was conducted to test these correlations, utilizing five years of historical price data from June 2016 to June 2021. EN algorithm was implemented to extract the necessary features with high accuracy, as it combines the modeling properties of LASSO and ridge. Then, OFAT analysis was conducted to test the dataset under step changes introduced within the tuning parameter. Results for 17 assets indicate that it detects no observable correlations, which was speculated as nonlinear dynamics or possible haven characteristics.

Reduced input from feature selection was utilized within the NARX-RNN predictive model to generate market forecasts and create an effective short-term portfolio. The model was trained over the five-year historical period to simulate multi-step predictions. Values of several fixed structural parameters were employed from other studies, along with an AGD training algorithm to avoid vanishing gradient. Additionally, OFAT optimization techniques were adopted to test the initial LR values within a specified range (0.01 - 0.05) and select the best-performing configuration. Only nine assets could achieve the required accuracy threshold for errors (< 10%) and regression coefficient ($R^2 > 0.85$). Predicted series responses for these assets were further analyzed to evaluate network performance. Flat responses were observed for several assets, indicating the NARX-RNN's insufficiency in modeling the nonlinear behavior of these markets. The impact of network inaccuracies on diversification approaches was tested by constructing portfolios based on predicted responses. Optimal investment allocation was computed through MV and CVaR strategies, comparing risk-return levels generated between predicted and actual data. Predicted portfolios included several high-variance assets due to inaccuracies in predicting market dynamics. Volatility forecasts are an essential aspect of prediction performance besides average errors, which require robust model training for achieving high accuracy. A multi-objective RSM approach is recommended to optimize the combination of several training parameters. Including these statistical models adds further complexity to the analysis, requiring increased computation time.

In conclusion, market data analysis requires a high degree of nonlinear modeling using statistical predictive tools. Reliable predictions are crucial in developing efficient portfolios to achieve high returns with minimum possible risk. Furthermore, implementing DLNN models requires careful configuration and efficient training to achieve the desired accuracy. While comparing different deep learning models provides a generic interpretation of the system, performance optimization is necessary to develop practical financial applications in the future. This research provides investors with reliable predictions for appropriate investment decisions and knowledge of international financial exposure.

KEYWORDS

- **international financial exposure**
- **market data analytics**
- **nonlinear modeling**
- **practical financial applications**
- **statistical models**
- **training parameters**
- **volatility**

REFERENCES

1. Mazur, M., Dang, M., & Vega, M. (2021). COVID-19 and the March 2020 stock market crash. Evidence from S&P1500. *Finance Research Letters, 38*, 101690.
2. Mishra, P. K., & Mishra, S. K. (2021). COVID-19 pandemic and stock market reaction: empirical insights from 15 Asian countries. *Transnational Corporations Review, 13*(2), 139–155.

3. Maram Al, Boucherbi, & Qasim, A. (2022). Modern financial investment tools, future contracts as a model. *Eurasian Journal of History, Geography and Economics, 9*, 1–11. https://geniusjournals.org/index.php/ejhge/article/view/1647
4. Hamad, H. A., Qader, K. S., Gardi, B., Abdalla, P., Hamza, Dr, & Anwar, G. (2021). The essential variables to consider before investing in financial markets during COVID-19. *International Journal of Electrical, Electronics and Computers* 6 (5): 34 - 45 https://doi.org/https://dx.doi.org/10.22161/eec.65.5.
5. Low, R. K. Y., Yao, Y., & Faff, R. (2016). Diamonds vs. precious metals: What shines brightest in your investment portfolio? *International Review of Financial Analysis, 43*, 1–14.
6. Klein, T. (2017). Dynamic correlation of precious metals and flight-to-quality in developed markets. *Finance Research Letters, 23*, 283–290.
7. Li, S., & Lucey, B. M. (2017). Reassessing the role of precious metals as safe havens–What colour is your haven and why? *Journal of Commodity Markets, 7*, 1–14. DOI: 10.1016/j.jcomm.2017.05.003
8. Rehman, M. U., & Vo, X. V. (2021). Energy commodities, precious metals and industrial metal markets: A nexus across different investment horizons and market conditions. *Resources Policy, 70*, 101843.
9. Sensoy, A. (2013). Dynamic relationship between precious metals. *Resources Policy, 38*(4), 504–511. DOI: 10.1016/j.resourpol.2013.08.004
10. Sverdrup, H., Koca, D., & Ragnarsdottir, K. V. (2014). Investigating the sustainability of the global silver supply, reserves, stocks in society and market price using different approaches. *Resources, Conservation and Recycling, 83*, 121–140. DOI: 10.1016/j.resconrec.2013.12.008
11. Oktay, B., Öztunç, H., & Serin, Z. V. (2016). Determinants of gold reserves: an empirical analysis for G-7 countries. *Procedia Economics and Finance, 38*, 8–16.
12. Hammoudeh, S., Malik, F., & McAleer, M. (2011). Risk management of precious metals. *The Quarterly Review of Economics and Finance, 51*(4), 435–441.
13. Zhu, X., Chen, J., & Zhong, M. (2015). Dynamic interacting relationships among international oil prices, macroeconomic variables and precious metal prices. *Transactions of Nonferrous Metals Society of China, 25*(2), 669–676.
14. Eryiğit, M. (2017). Short-term and long-term relationships between gold prices and precious metal (palladium, silver and platinum) and energy (crude oil and gasoline) prices. *Economic research-Ekonomska istraživanja, 30*(1), 499–510.
15. Wang, X., Liu, H., Huang, S., & Lucey, B. (2019). Identifying the multiscale financial contagion in precious metal markets. *International Review of Financial Analysis, 63*, 209–219.
16. Alkhazali, O. M., & Zoubi, T. A. (2020). Gold and portfolio diversification: A stochastic dominance analysis of the Dow Jones Islamic indices. *Pacific-Basin Finance Journal, 60*, 101264. https://doi.org/10.1016/j.pacfin.2020.101264
17. Ali, F., Jiang, Y., & Sensoy, A. (2021). Downside risk in Dow Jones Islamic equity indices: Precious metals and portfolio diversification before and after the COVID-19 bear market. *Research in International Business and Finance, 58*, 101502. https://doi.org/10.1016/j.ribaf.2021.101502
18. Nti, I. K., Adekoya, A. F., & Weyori, B. A. (2020). A systematic review of fundamental and technical analysis of stock market predictions. *Artificial Intelligence Review, 53*(4), 3007–3057.

19. Obthong, M., Tantisantiwong, N., Jeamwatthanachai, W., & Wills, G. (2020). A survey on machine learning for stock price prediction: algorithms and techniques. *International Conference on Finance, Economics, Management and IT Business, 2*(1), 63–71. https://doi.org/10.5220/0009340700630071.
20. Vijh, M., Chandola, D., Tikkiwal, V. A., & Kumar, A. (2020). Stock closing price prediction using machine learning techniques. *Procedia Computer Science, 167*, 599–606.
21. Farooq, A., & Chawla, P. (2021). Review of Data Science and AI in Finance. In *2021 International Conference on Computing Sciences (ICCS)*.
22. Wanjawa, B. W., & Muchemi, L. (2015). ANN Model to Predict Stock Prices at Stock Exchange Markets. *ArXiv abs/1502.06434, 1*, 1–23. https://doi.org/https://doi.org/10.48550/arXiv.1502.06434.
23. Xiao, C., Xia, W., & Jiang, J. (2020). Stock price forecast based on combined model of ARI-MA-LS-SVM. *Neural Computing and Applications, 32*(10), 5379–5388. DOI: 10.1007/s00521-019-04698-5
24. Yun, K. K., Yoon, S. W., & Won, D. (2021). Prediction of stock price direction using a hybrid GA-XGBoost algorithm with a three-stage feature engineering process. *Expert Systems with Applications, 186*, 115716. https://doi.org/10.1016/j.eswa.2021.115716
25. Nikou, M., Mansourfar, G., & Bagherzadeh, J. (2019). Stock price prediction using DEEP learning algorithm and its comparison with machine learning algorithms. *Intelligent Systems in Accounting, Finance and Management, 26*(4), 164–174. DOI: 10.1002/isaf.1459
26. Mehtab, S., & Sen, J. (2020). A Time Series Analysis-Based Stock Price Prediction Using Machine Learning and Deep Learning Models. *ArXiv 4*(2), 272–335. https://doi.org/https://doi.org/10.48550/arXiv.2004.11697.
27. Yu, Y., Si, X., Hu, C., & Zhang, J. (2019). A review of recurrent neural networks: LSTM cells and network architectures. *Neural Computation, 31*(7), 1235–1270.
28. Zhao, J., Zeng, D., Liang, S., Kang, H., & Liu, Q. (2021). Prediction model for stock price trend based on recurrent neural network. *Journal of Ambient Intelligence and Humanized Computing, 12*(1), 745–753.
29. Miky, Y., Kaloop, M. R., Elnabwy, M. T., Baik, A., & Alshouny, A. (2021). A Recurrent-Cascade-Neural network-nonlinear autoregressive networks with exogenous inputs (NARX) approach for long-term time-series prediction of wave height based on wave characteristics measurements. *Ocean Engineering, 240*, 109958.
30. Kuranga, C., & Pillay, N. (2022). A comparative study of nonlinear regression and autoregressive techniques in hybrid with particle swarm optimization for time-series forecasting. *Expert Systems with Applications, 190*, 116163.
31. Mensi, W., Nekhili, R., Vo, X. V., & Kang, S. H. (2021). Quantile dependencies between precious and industrial metals futures and portfolio management. *Resources Policy, 73*, 102230.
32. Oloko, T. F. (2018). Portfolio diversification between developed and developing stock markets: The case of US and UK investors in Nigeria. *Research in International Business and Finance, 45*, 219–232. DOI: 10.1016/j.ribaf.2017.07.153
33. Thomas, N. M., Kashiramka, S., Yadav, S. S., & Paul, J. (2022). Role of emerging markets vis-à-vis frontier markets in improving portfolio diversification benefits. *International Review of Economics & Finance, 78*, 95–121. DOI: 10.1016/j.iref.2021.11.012

34. Lili, L., & Chengmei, D. (2013). Research of the Influence of Macro-Economic Factors on the Price of Gold. *Procedia Computer Science, 17*, 737–743. DOI: 10.1016/j.procs.2013.05.095
35. Apergis, N., Christou, C., & Payne, J. E. (2014). Precious metal markets, stock markets and the macroeconomic environment: a FAVAR model approach. *Applied Financial Economics, 24*(10), 691–703.
36. Balcilar, M., & Ozdemir, Z. A. (2019). The volatility effect on precious metals price returns in a stochastic volatility in mean model with time-varying parameters. *Physica A: Statistical Mechanics and its Applications, 534*, 122329. https://doi.org/10.1016/j.physa.2019.122329
37. Hammoudeh, S., Santos, P. A., & Al-Hassan, A. (2013). Downside risk management and VaR-based optimal portfolios for precious metals, oil and stocks. *The North American Journal of Economics and Finance, 25*, 318–334. https://doi.org/10.1016/j.najef.2012.06.012; https://www.sciencedirect.com/science/article/pii/S1062940812000630
38. Ghasemi, P., Aslani, M., Rollins, D. K., Williams, R. C., & Schaefer, V. R. (2018). Modeling rutting susceptibility of asphalt pavement using principal component pseudo inputs in regression and neural networks. *International Journal of Pavement Research and Technology, 11*(7), 679–690.
39. Barbedo, J. G. A. (2018). Impact of dataset size and variety on the effectiveness of deep learning and transfer learning for plant disease classification. *Computers and Electronics in Agriculture, 153*, 46–53. https://doi.org/10.1016/j.compag.2018.08.013
40. Bun, M. J. G., & Harrison, T. D. (2019). OLS and IV estimation of regression models including endogenous interaction terms. *Econometric Reviews, 38*(7), 814–827. https://doi.org/10.1080/07474938.2018.1427486
41. Cocchi, M., Biancolillo, A., & Marini, F. (2018). Chemometric methods for classification and feature selection. In *Comprehensive analytical chemistry* (pp. 265–299). Elsevier.
42. Çiftsüren, M. N., & Akkol, S. (2018). Prediction of internal egg quality characteristics and variable selection using regularization methods: ridge, LASSO and elastic net. *Arch. Anim. Breed., 61*(3), 279–284. https://doi.org/10.5194/aab-61-279-2018.
43. Weaving, D., Jones, B., Ireton, M., Whitehead, S., Till, K., & Beggs, C. B. (2019). Overcoming the problem of multicollinearity in sports performance data: A novel application of partial least squares correlation analysis. *PLoS One, 14*(2), e0211776.
44. Aheto, J. M. K., Duah, H. O., Agbadi, P., & Nakua, E. K. (2021). A predictive model, and predictors of under-five child malaria prevalence in Ghana: How do LASSO, Ridge and Elastic net regression approaches compare? *Preventive Medicine Reports, 23*, 101475. https://doi.org/10.1016/j.pmedr.2021.101475
45. Ren, K., Moudud, A., Nielsen, P., Gussmann, M., & Rönnegård, L. (2022). Interpolation Methods to Improve Data Quality of Indoor Positioning Data for Dairy Cattle. *Frontiers in Animal Science, 3*, 1–11. https://doi.org/10.3389/fanim.2022.896666.
46. Panda, J., & Meher, S. (2022). Efficient 2D image Upscaling using Iterative Optimized Sharpening filtering. *Displays, 74*, 102196. DOI: 10.1016/j.displa.2022.102196
47. de Heus, P. (2012). R squared effect-size measures and overlap between direct and indirect effect in mediation analysis. *Behavior Research Methods, 44*(1), 213–221. https://doi.org/10.3758/s13428-011-0141-5

48. Manzi, D., Brentan, B., Meirelles, G., Izquierdo, J., & Luvizotto, E. (2019). Pattern Recognition and Clustering of Transient Pressure Signals for Burst Location. *Water, 11*(11), 2279. DOI: 10.3390/w11112279
49. Davis, A., Gill, S., Wong, R., & Tayeb, S. (2020). Feature Selection for Deep Neural Networks in Cyber Security Applications. In *2020 IEEE International IOT, Electronics and Mechatronics Conference (IEMTRONICS)* (pp. 9–12).
50. Hernández-Casas, S., Beltrán-Morales, L. F., Vargas-López, V. G., Vergara-Solana, F., & Seijo, J. C. (2022). Price Forecast for Mexican Red Spiny Lobster (Panulirus spp.) Using Artificial Neural Networks (ANNs). *Applied Sciences, 12*(12), 6044.
51. Yonaba, H., Anctil, F., & Fortin, V. (2010). Comparing sigmoid transfer functions for neural network multistep ahead streamflow forecasting. *Journal of Hydrologic Engineering, 15*(4), 275–283.
52. Yegnanarayana, B. (2009). *Artificial neural networks*. PHI Learning Pvt. Ltd.
53. Abbas, F., Feng, D., Habib, S., Rahman, U., Rasool, A., & Yan, Z. (2018). Short Term Residential Load Forecasting: An Improved Optimal Nonlinear Auto Regressive (NARX) Method with Exponential Weight Decay Function. *Electronics, 7*(12), 432. https://www.mdpi.com/2079-9292/7/12/432
54. Liška, A., Kruszewski, G., & Baroni, M. (2018). Memorize or generalize? searching for a compositional rnn in a haystack. arXiv arXiv:1802.06467, *2*, 1–9. https://doi.org/https://doi.org/10.48550/arXiv.1802.06467.
55. Le, P., & Zuidema, W. (2016). Quantifying the vanishing gradient and long distance dependency problem in recursive neural networks and recursive LSTMs. *arXiv* arXiv:1603.00423, *1*, 87–93. https://doi.org/10.48550/arXiv.1603.00423.
56. Ribeiro, A. H., Tiels, K., Aguirre, L. A., & Schön, T. (2020). Beyond exploding and vanishing gradients: analysing RNN training using attractors and smoothness. *International Conference on Artificial Intelligence and Statistics, 108*(3), 2370–2380. https://doi.org/https://doi.org/10.48550/arXiv.1906.08482.
57. Takase, T., Oyama, S., & Kurihara, M. (2018). Effective neural network training with adaptive learning rate based on training loss. *Neural Networks, 101*, 68–78.
58. Xie, C., Koyejo, O., Gupta, I., & Lin, H. (2019). Local adaalter: Communication-efficient stochastic gradient descent with adaptive learning rates. *arXiv* arXiv:1911.09030, *2*, 1–16. https://doi.org/https://doi.org/10.48550/arXiv.1911.09030.
59. Uzair, M., & Jamil, N. (2020). Effects of hidden layers on the efficiency of neural networks. *2020 IEEE 23rd International Multitopic Conference (INMIC)*.
60. Maknickienė, N., Rutkauskas, A. V., & Maknickas, A. (2011). Investigation of financial market prediction by recurrent neural network. *Innovative Technologies for Science, Business and Education, 2*(11), 3–8.
61. Moghar, A., & Hamiche, M. (2020). Stock market prediction using LSTM recurrent neural network. *Procedia Computer Science, 170*, 1168–1173.
62. Dorofki, M., Elshafie, A. H., Jaafar, O., Karim, O. A., & Mastura, S. (2012). Comparison of artificial neural network transfer functions abilities to simulate extreme runoff data. *International Proceedings of Chemical, Biological and Environmental Engineering, 33*, 39–44.
63. Koyuncu, I. (2018). Implementation of high speed tangent sigmoid transfer function approximations for artificial neural network applications on FPGA. *Advances in Electrical and Computer Engineering, 18*(3), 79–86.

64. Lu, L., Zhang, X., & Renais, S. (2016). On training the recurrent neural network encoder-decoder for large vocabulary end-to-end speech recognition. *2016 IEEE International Conference on Acoustics, Speech and Signal Processing (ICASSP), 1*(1), 5060–5064. https://doi.org/10.1109/ICASSP.2016.7472641.
65. Beasley, J. E. (2013). Portfolio optimisation: models and solution approaches. In *Theory Driven by Influential Applications* (pp. 201–221). Informs.
66. Doering, J., Kizys, R., Juan, A. A., Fito, A., & Polat, O. (2019). Metaheuristics for rich portfolio optimisation and risk management: Current state and future trends. *Operations Research Perspectives, 6*, 100121.
67. Tian, R., Cox, S. H., Lin, Y., & Zuluaga, L. F. (2010). Portfolio risk management with CVaR-like constraints. *North American Actuarial Journal, 14*(1), 86–106.
68. Lai, T. L., Xing, H., & Chen, Z. (2011). Mean–variance portfolio optimization when means and covariances are unknown. *The Annals of Applied Statistics, 5*(2A), 798–823. DOI: 10.1214/10-AOAS422
69. Hjalmarsson, E., & Manchev, P. (2012). Characteristic-based mean-variance portfolio choice. *Journal of Banking & Finance, 36*(5), 1392–1401.
70. Al Janabi, M. A. (2021). Is optimum always optimal? A revisit of the mean-variance method under nonlinear measures of dependence and non-normal liquidity constraints. *Journal of Forecasting, 40*(3), 387–415.
71. Sawik, B. (2016). Triple-objective models for portfolio optimisation with symmetric and percentile risk measures. *International Journal of Logistics Systems and Management, 25*(1), 96–107.
72. Li, W. C., Wu, Y., & Ojiako, U. (2014). Using portfolio optimisation models to enhance decision making and prediction. *Journal of Modelling in Management, 9*(1), 36–57. https://doi.org/10.1108/JM2-11-2011-0057.
73. Bedoui, R., Noiali, S., & Hamdi, H. (2020). Hedge funds portfolio optimisation using a vine copula-GARCH-EVT-CVaR model. *International Journal of Entrepreneurship and Small Business, 39*(1–2), 121–148.
74. Ayodeji, O. A., & Ingram, L. (2015). Efficient portfolio optimisation using the conditional value at risk approach. *Journal of Organisational Studies and Innovation, 2*(2), 39–65.

CHAPTER 13

Leveraging Banking Customer Experience Through Artificial Intelligence: An Application of Structural Equation Modelling

ANKITA CHATURVEDI,[1] SHAIFALI MATHUR,[1] and ASHISH PORWAL[2]

[1]*IIS (Deemed to be University), Jaipur, Rajasthan, India*

[2]*Assistant Professor, Finance and Accounting, Institute of Law, Nirma University, Ahmedabad, Gujarat, India*

ABSTRACT

Drawing on literature from Artificial Intelligence in the banking sector, the present study examined AI Awareness, AI Application, and Customer Experience as second-order factors and investigated whether AI Application moderates the relationship between AI Awareness and Customer Experience. Confirmatory factor analysis (CFA) and structural equation modeling (SEM) were used to test a model using a sample of 300 commercial bank customers in India. Results supported the three-dimensional second-order factor of AI Awareness and AI Application, and the four-dimensional second-order factor of Customer Experience. The results also indicated (a) a significant but very low impact of AI Awareness on Customer Experience, and (b) a positive significant effect of AI Awareness and AI Application on Customer Experience, with AI Application being a strong mediating variable. The main theoretical contribution relates to the inclusion of the three dimensions of AI Awareness and Application, and the four dimensions of Customer

Experience in a single model. Findings are discussed with respect to their theoretical and practical applicability.

13.1 INTRODUCTION

Artificial intelligence means human-like intellectual machines, particularly smart computer programs [1]. This definition can be explained as follows: The humanoid capabilities of a computer, like cognitive skills, grievance handling, and specifications, and the use of high-level logical and rational capabilities, are defined as artificial intelligence. Artificial intelligence is a simulation that helps humans work smarter. AI can solve problems and make decisions in the same way that humans do. It is now widely used in many industries to perform routine tasks, including banking [2]. The banking sector is utilizing artificial intelligence in a very groundbreaking manner, saving both time and money. Banks are using algorithms to improve customer service and increase sales, thereby increasing their revenues. Banks are using algorithms to offer certain products and to perform certain operations, which help to improve customer service and generate better sales revenue in order to generate higher profits [3]. The banking industry has been revamping its entire system into a technological system since two decades ago. A huge number of clients in the banking industry are also adopting advanced banking technology procedures to carry out their banking functions. A study reveals that by indulging mobile technology in the banking sector, there is a substantial surge in customers in the Middle East from 20% to 25% [4].

AI applications used in banks include machine learning, which helps to reduce errors in banking operations by predicting the repayment behavior of prospective customers, customer management services, KYC, passbook update kiosks, credit details, Frequently Asked Questions (FAQ) blog, Financial Assistance Services to the customers, cybersecurity, risk management, fraud management, sales, Internal Audit, Financial Assistance, Assets, Loan Management, and Customer Management, etc. [5]. Cloud computing, Machine Learning models and the simultaneous dispensation of a massive volume of information have paved the way for Artificial Intelligence solutions. Natural Language Processing, a branch of AI, can assist banks in automating tasks such as the congregation of clients' information and parsing documents. Machine learning algorithms can aid with financial predictions and cross-selling by reducing risk [6]. The banking industry is under pressure to provide 24-hour services, but profit margins are shrinking and customer satisfaction is declining. Robotic Process Automation is the modern-day equivalent of technology outsourcing. RPA is quick and inexpensive and facilitates generating a superior return on investment (ROI) for banks.

Bankers will not be replaced by artificial intelligence. It will improve how banks operate by assisting them in becoming more agile, making better decisions, and, ultimately, remaining competitive. Artificial intelligence (AI) is having a significant impact on customers' lives, and its impact on and applicability for individuals and businesses is growing. This study aims to examine the awareness of banking customers towards Artificial Intelligence, the level of application of artificial intelligence by the banks in carrying out their daily operations, and also how the awareness level and level of application of AI in banks leverage the customer's experience.

Artificial Intelligence can be applied to the banking industry in four ways: analytics; bots; robotic process automation (RPA); report generation and risk mitigation as well. The present study has taken Analytics, Chatbot, RPA, and Risk mitigation aspects of Artificial intelligence used in banking operations [7] (Figure 13.1).

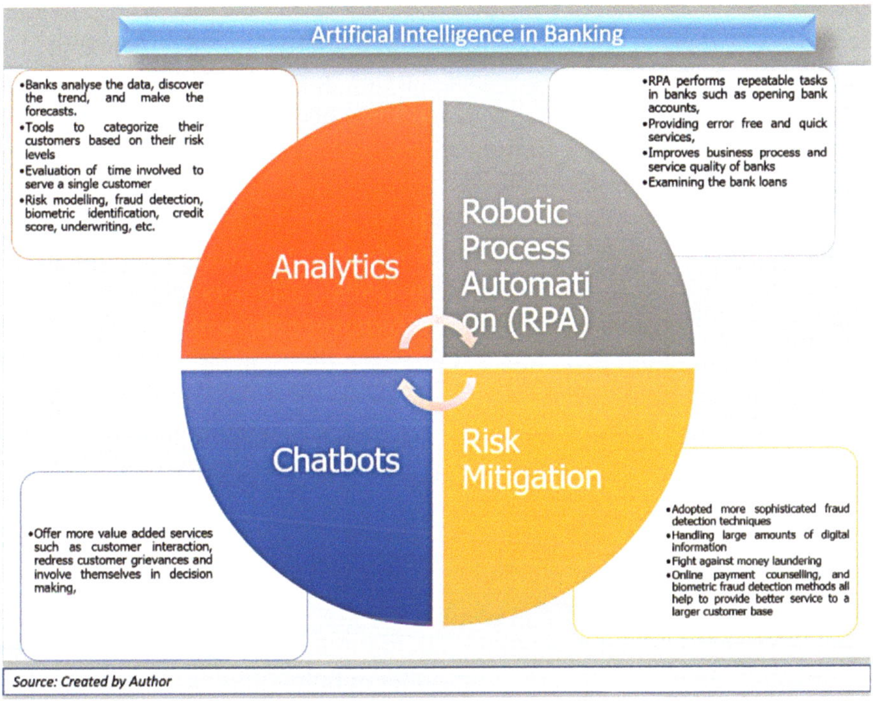

FIGURE 13.1 Artificial intelligence in banking.

13.2 ANALYTICS

Banking analytics is the application of artificial intelligence and machine learning to manage customer data to facilitate decision-making. Banks analyze the data, discover trends, and make forecasts. Banks can make error-free decisions, thereby improving their efficiency by utilizing data analytics tools and processes [7]. Financial institutions use banking analytics tools to categorize their customers based on their risk levels. Another application of banking analytics in banks is the evaluation of the time involved to serve a single customer from the start of a transaction until its completion. Machine learning accelerates various algorithms used in banks such as risk modeling, fraud detection, biometric identification, credit score, underwriting, etc.

13.3 ROBOTIC PROCESS AUTOMATION

Robotic research in banks focuses on finding technical solutions to meet the demanding customer market. RPA performs definable and repeatable tasks in banks such as opening bank accounts, which in turn results in providing error-free and quick services, speeding up repetitive routine operations, and improving the business process and service quality of banks [7]. Through RPA, bankers can offer more value-added services such as customer interaction, addressing customer grievances, and involving themselves in decision-making. This will enable banks to provide their customers with the best possible experience. Employees' ability to focus on more customer-facing roles is likely to improve customer satisfaction, acquisition, and retention. Chatbots are needed by banks to reach potential customers for digital account opening, in problem-solving, customer turnover rates will naturally reduce, and customer experience towards banks will improve. Simple banking queries can be resolved quickly with automation. Banking chatbots can easily automate questions about opening a savings or current account, credit card plans, various loan information, and even checking account balances [8].

13.4 RISK MITIGATION

There are innovative and efficient methods for detecting fraud in this age of digital technology. There is a need to adopt more sophisticated fraud detection techniques by banks due to the volume of information available through electronic documents, contracts, emails, SMS, and bank transactions. On account of handling large amounts of digital information and the ease with which language and information can be evaluated, artificial intelligence and machine learning are perfect for fraud recognition. In the fight against money laundering, an artificial intelligence program may do in seconds what would normally take hours or days. Banks may also benefit from AI's ability to quickly extract actionable information from massive data sets. Artificial intelligence bots, online payment counselors, and biometric fraud detection methods all help to provide better service to a larger customer base.

Artificial intelligence (AI) technologies are having an increasing impact on the lives of customers, from instant translation to conversational interfaces. Banks are now unlocking new value through improved efficiency, expanded market access, and increased customer lifetime value by reimagining customer engagement. Customers have grown accustomed to the service standards set by consumer internet companies, and they now expect the same level of reliability, convenience, security, and personalization from their banks. Customer satisfaction is enhanced when businesses are fulfilling their expectations in terms of delivering quality service [9]. By utilizing AI, banks are reducing credit risk, improving payment security, automating compliance-associated operations, saving time as well as costs, and boosting overall business performance, thereby offering quality services to their customers and improving their experiences with the banks.

13.5 REVIEW OF LITERATURE

13.5.1 AI AWARENESS AND ITS APPLICATIONS IN BANKS

Unni & Bh [10] conducted a study whose primary goal was to comprehend how artificial intelligence is affecting contemporary banks. This study focuses on how AI is viewed in the banking sector, how it has significantly changed banks, and how it affects human resources. Being aware that humans have a flawed inclination but that the world is changing and that creativity requires a lack of knowledge, automation is necessary. With the use of leading-edge technology, a lot of the effort and craftsmanship ever completed by people have been enhanced [10].

Blockchain technology is present in the valuation of accounting assets; despite the opponents' confidence, the data in the database is reliable and true. Trading is permitted only with the approval of every member. It can be decrypted into a secure, transparent across groups, and stress-free to-use design with the help of web accounting. The necessity for data validation and protection arises as a result of technological innovation. By offering a trustworthy distributed ledger, it links marketplaces, dealers, customers, and banks by resolving the issue of defining different ledgers and issuing them independently. Even while we typically only think about blockchain in terms of digital money, it has a variety of conversion technology-related applications in accounting and audit [11].

Inefficient technological processes in Indian commercial banks are being reduced through the use of artificial intelligence (AI) in chatbots, virtual assistants, and ATMs. The influence of artificial intelligence (AI) on 47 Indian commercial banks under examination has decreased technical inefficiency, which is mostly caused by internal causes or decision-making, to 11%. The decision supports accelerating the adoption of artificial intelligence (AI), as well as increasing asset levels and lowering non-performing debt, particularly for public sector banks [12].

El-Gohary et al. [13] in their study look at how the use of artificial intelligence in the banking industry has impacted customer satisfaction in general. It focuses on how the growth of digital banking has been impacted by consumer personal digital transformation and in what way this has additionally impacted customer outlooks and experiences. The situation evaluates in what way banks employ chatbots and other AI cybernetic agents to change how customers utilize their financial services. Last but not least, this study looks into the reach of neobanks in the banking industry. As per the report, customers nowadays have higher hopes for their banks because of digital advancements. Clients are not interacting with virtual agents at the desired rate, despite the fact that banks are revolutionizing their customer service offerings with them [13].

The main goal of this systematic literature review (SLR) was to locate, evaluate, and synthesize the available data regarding the advantages and disadvantages of using artificial intelligence (AI) in the banking industry. The SLR makes it clear that AI offers the industry a number of opportunities. Banking regulators are encouraging the adoption of AI through law and collaboration, and there are numerous fin-tech start-ups that provide banking AI solutions. Personalized services, smart wallets, problem-solving and decision-making, customer satisfaction and loyalty, process automation (especially focusing on repetitive tasks), transactional security and cybersecurity advancements, and promotion of digital financial inclusion are additional opportunities. However, the major players in the banking sector must develop effective plans to address current and future AI concerns. The following issues were listed as the top AI challenges that need to be addressed: job loss and user acceptance issues, privacy violations, the loss of creativity and adaptability, stringent operational and implementation requirements, the digital divide, the availability of abundant high-quality data, alignment of the AI-business strategy, and the loss of the emotional "human touch" [14]. In the research, the authors reveal the overall shape of AI adoption in banks. Based on evidence from 17 banks functioning in the Afyonkarahisar jurisdiction of Turkey, it is determined that AI technologies are useful in almost every area of the banking sector. Furthermore, the usage of AI is assessed as a potential that offers ease of use and lessens costs [15].

The study focuses on Nordea, a sizable banking organization that operates predominantly in the Nordic region, and the governance of robotic process automation (RPA). Numerous software robots have been implemented by Nordea for a variety of business operations, including transaction processing, internal and external reporting, and managing queries about the General Data Protection Regulation (GDPR). Three people, Group Head of Robotics Agnieszka Belowska Gosawska, Head of Robotic Process Automation Operations Piotr Stolarczyk, and Acting Head of Robotics Execution Jaroslaw Motylewski, meet to discuss the condition of robotic process automation implementation at Nordea. In connection with any deployment of robotic process automation at a rather substantial scale within a company, a number of governance-related concerns and decision points are outlined in the presentation. The main concerns concern the governance of robotic process automation, IT infrastructure, and software development and maintenance. After working through the case, students ought to be able to: (1) explain archetypal and hybrid governance approaches for robotic process automation; and (2) weigh the benefits and drawbacks of each for a reliable foundation and efficient software development and maintenance [16].

The use of Artificial Intelligence and associated technologies in the Indian banking and financial sector has been studied in Ref. [17]. The use of AI-driven technologies must be improved, particularly in banks' internal and back-end activities. These comprise risk evaluation, fraud detection, KYC, and other processes. 51% of banks and other financial institutions worldwide still manually oversee KYC and AML procedures. The application of AI in the KYC process considerably cuts down on time, expense, and human mistakes.

A speculative study demonstrated how commercial banks can use AI technology to merge financial activities. It has been discovered that banks may use AI to lower the risk of credit, improve secure payment, automate compliance-related tasks, and grow their overall operations. This article addresses how AI abilities might increase customer acceptability by guaranteeing transparency, privacy, and adequate documentation. Finally, it suggests a behavioral finance research methodology [18].

Banks have been pursuing digital transformation as a result of technological improvement. The situation turns out to be essential for banks to quicken back-end activities and procedures in order to effect this transformation. Being customer-centric and developing improved service methods are equally crucial. Big Data Analytics and artificial intelligence have made it possible for data-driven solutions to provide superior customer service. This has facilitated the customization of many features, increasing client involvement. The empirical study shows that BDA and AI technology are used in various banking activities by both the international and Indonesian banking sectors [19].

The experimental study emphasizes on the system, information, and service aspects of the front-end customer experience provided by chatbots. To determine if perceived risk moderates the connection between the three eminent characteristics and client experience, a hypothesis test is conducted. The research enables banks to build a relationship with customers by providing chatbots that meet their needs. The process of gathering the data involves a survey [20].

13.5.2 CUSTOMER EXPERIENCE

The increasing use of robotic process automation (RPA) technology in the Czech financial sector between 2015 and 2020 is examined in this article. Future technological spillovers are anticipated thanks to the advancements made and lessons learned during the "hype-and-fear" period. The most likely candidates for the inventory and financial business process integration, installed Enterprise Resource Planning, and Customer Relationship Management systems if ICT skills are the cause of performance discrepancies. The RPA should not be viewed as simple automation but rather as a complicated tool with many benefits that prioritizes the interests of internal and external stakeholders [21].

The study focuses on the usage of artificial intelligence (AI) in Chennai's banking and financial services to monitor both bank applications of AI techniques and client or consumer responses. According to the study's findings, private banks and other financial institutions employ a variety of AI services to their client's advantage in order to make them happy with their services while also making financial services more efficient because some customers aren't happy with banking services. The outcome also indicated that by providing creative training to advance workplace AI practices, clients should expect stronger dedication from representatives to banking and financial services [22].

The executive management of KAS Bank examined numerous business and client trends and their impact on future banking during an annual board meeting in 2016. Based on the conversation, they realized they needed to enhance internal business operations in order to raise client satisfaction levels. They discussed employing automation in the conference as a means of achieving their objective because KAS Bank has always welcomed technological advancements since its founding in 1806. They were considering where to begin, whether operations could be automated, whether or not they had the internal resources to be effective, and how this new duty would affect their staff. This case study details the actual circumstances surrounding KAS Bank's implementation of robotic process automation tools. Three stages make up the structure that is used: the development stage, the implementation stage, and the operational stage. There are two components to this instructional case. The first section introduces KAS Bank and robotic process automation, and the second section talks about the three stages and associated difficulties [23].

The research examined how artificial intelligence (AI) has affected the growth of the banking industry. Banks use AI to assess customers' financial position, offer digital help and financial advice, and more. The study also offers examples of marketing for AI products and some concepts for innovative AI-based banking services. Despite the quick adoption of AI across several industries, this technology's effectiveness is largely dependent on how people feel about and are loyal to it. According to our research, businesses and consumers in Russia are favorable toward AI. The AI implementation in the work of Sberbank professionals is viewed favorably by them; they see these solutions as aids in carrying out mundane tasks and are not scared of being fired. In their daily lives and at business, they employ AI solutions. The concerns that are starting to surface are related to potential technological issues, unauthorized data transmission, a lack of privacy, and unanticipated effects of AI implementation. However, analysts are generally aware that this technology will play a role in the financial sector's future. Employees of Sberbank claim that customers frequently show some amount of mistrust toward AI, which may be due to a lack of understanding of how this technology functions and how it may affect people's way of life. In the meantime, both sides' AI resistance weakens over time. As a result, governments and financial intermediaries may establish the necessary conditions for the development of banking based on contemporary technologies [24].

In their research on the experience of users with AI-driven chatbots, researchers found that chatbots had a big impact on customer happiness. The SBI's virtual assistant, SIA, has reportedly cut the cost of support services by 52%, according to a case study. However, data security and privacy are important and have a big impact on customer happiness [25]. The banking sector is currently using additional AI-related technical applications in customer care and cost-tailored client service. Yet, data safety and privacy are important and have a big impact on how satisfied customers are [25].

Another article illustrates how AI is being used to automate banking processes and improve client engagement. The findings show a clever framework for banking and financial organizations that could enhance their operations. For international banks, a theoretical analysis is done in the research [26].

A study on Consumer Awareness and usage of E-Banking through Mobile at State Bank of India finds out the awareness level and most preferred e-banking services among the customers of State Bank of India Ltd. The study reveals that most of the respondents are aware of mobile banking applications and they avail of these services as it saves time there is less interaction with banking officials, and transactions are completed in a short span of time [27].

Customer service issues and website issues are the main causes of customers' unhappiness with Internet banking services, according to a study [28]. The experience of using Internet banking services has been greatly improved by banks.

According to studies, e-banking improves customer service, which helps businesses keep their clients. Recent technological advancements have created an environment that allows Virtual Agents to interact with customers, answer their concerns, make recommendations, and give guidance whenever they are needed. This has essentially led to a total revolution in the customer experience [29].

As technology grows and progresses, banking consumers' requirements and hopes for amenities are rising. These days, the customer desires to function and conduct banking business without physically going to the bank, at any time without being constrained by bank working hours, and to complete all of his or her transactions (purchases, bills, and stocks) quickly and at a reasonable cost [30].

According to the above literature review, there are numerous studies on AI technologies and the banking sector with the advent of new AI trends. However, no studies have been done on the relationship of AI awareness, AI application, and customer experience of banking customers. Therefore, the study focuses on AI technology and banking customer experience on the usage of AI applications in banking activities and services.

13.6 RESEARCH METHODOLOGY

The research attempts to find out the awareness level of AI and its application among banking customers and their impact on customer experience towards AI-based banking operations. The research is empirical in nature. The target population is tech-savvy banking customers and the sample frame comprises the customers of Indian commercial banks. The study sample consists of 300 respondents availing banking services and products both online and by visiting the banks. The sample was selected using a convenient sampling technique.

A questionnaire based on prior literature was created to collect data to study these variables. The questionnaire was divided into four sections: The first section consists of the demographic profile of the respondents, the second section consists of questions to explore the awareness level of AI among banking customers, the third section includes questions to find out the level of application of AI in banks, and the fourth section consists of questions related to customers' experience of AI application-based banking operations. The second, third, and fourth sections of the questionnaire contained a series of questions designed to assess respondents' awareness, AI application, and customer experience of AI application using Likert scale questions. A five-point scale ranging from "1-strongly disagree" to "5-strongly agree" has been used to evaluate the statements. In AI Awareness (main construct), there are 13 statements divided into sub-constructs: Analytics (4), RPA and Chatbots (5), and Risk Mitigation (4). There are 10 statements in AI Application (main construct) divided into sub-constructs: Analytics (3), RPA and Chatbots (4), and Risk Mitigation (3). And there are 16 statements in Customer Experience (main construct) divided into sub-constructs: Timely Response (3), Convenience & Accessibility (5), Security & Risk Mitigation (5), and Technical Empowerment (3) (Table 13.1).

TABLE 13.1 Respondents' Demographic Profile

Variables	Categories	Frequency and Percentage
Gender	Male	185 (61.67%)
	Female	115(38.33%)
Age	18–30	57(19%)
	31–45	107 (35.67%)
	46–50	96 (32.00%)
	More than 60	40(13.33%)
Educational qualification	Undergraduate	42 (14%)
	Graduate	96(32.00%)
	Postgraduate	115 (38.33%)
	Professional	47(15.67%)
Occupation	Service	82 (27.33%)
	Professional	26(8.67%)
	Student	162(54.00%)
	Homemaker	30 (10%)

13.7 MODELING PROCESS

The structural model and the measurement model are the two parts of structural equation modeling (SEM). Using Amos (V. 23), the maximum likelihood estimation approach was utilized to assess the overall fit of the measurement and structural models. The initial fit index was the chi-square. The study includes the goodness of fit index (GFI), comparative fit index (CFI), normed fit index (NFI), incremental fit index (IFI), parsimonious goodness of fit index (PGFI), and parsimonious normed fit index (PNFI) as well as the root mean square error of approximation (RMSEA). The acceptable range for CMIN/DF is ≤ 5 [23], GFI is ≥ 0.9 [35], CFI is close to 1, IFI is close to 1, NFI is < 0.9 [36], PGFI > 0.5, and PNFI > 0.50 have values between 0 and 1, RMSEA values ranging from 0.01 to 0.08, suggesting a strong model fit.

The phenomenon of Banking Customer Experience through Artificial Intelligence has its roots in Awareness of Artificial Intelligence and the Application of Artificial Intelligence. Also, there are many studies related to Awareness and Application of Analytics, RPA & Chatbots, and Risk Mitigation that enhance customer experience. Concerning these attributes, a conceptual model was framed. This conceptual model, as shown in Figure 13.2, describes causal linkages between the measurements and explains how the variables are operationalized through their indicators. First, the overall measurement model for Awareness of AI, Application of AI, and Customer Experience was tested one by one. The fit indices were then used to evaluate the overall fit. Second, the whole measuring approach was examined, which included AI awareness, AI application, and Customer Experience. As a consequence, seven statements were removed. After respecifying the measurement model, the total fit was assessed using the fit indices. The derived composite reliability and variance were utilized to further assess the entire measurement model's reliability and validity.

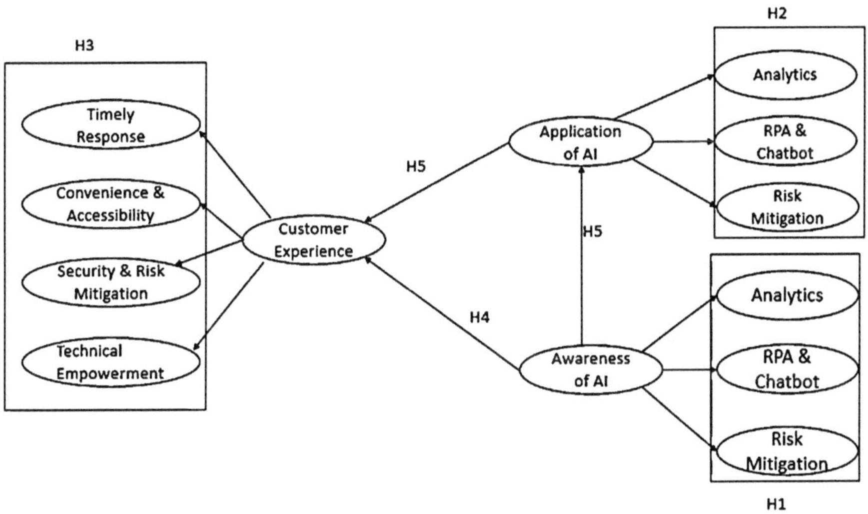

FIGURE 13.2 Proposed model.

The following hypotheses were framed based on the theorized model, acting as a foundation for further study. These are given below:

- **Hypothesis 1:** Awareness of artificial intelligence is a second-order factor comprised of the sub-dimensions of analytics, RPA & chatbot, and risk mitigation.
- **Hypothesis 2:** The application of artificial intelligence is a second-order factor comprised of the sub-dimensions of Analytics, RPA & Chatbot, and Risk Mitigation.
- **Hypothesis 3:** Customer experience is a second-order factor comprised of the sub-dimensions of timely response, convenience & accessibility, security & risk mitigation, and technical empowerment.

- **Hypothesis 4:** Awareness of artificial intelligence has a significant effect on customer experience.
- **Hypothesis 5:** The application of artificial intelligence moderates the relationship between awareness of artificial intelligence and customer experience.

13.8 DATA ANALYSIS AND DISCUSSION

13.8.1 NORMALITY ASSUMPTION

Skewness and kurtosis (descriptive statistics) were calculated for all variables to ensure data normality. According to Kim [31] and West et al. [37], a significant deviation from normality is indicated by an absolute value of skewness (proper) and kurtosis (proper) larger than 2 and 7, respectively [31]. The data was found to be normal and is suitable for further investigation using SEM because the absolute values of all variables were within acceptable ranges (absolute skewness values of 2 and absolute kurtosis values of 7).

13.8.2 CONFIRMATORY FACTOR ANALYSIS

The first stage involved putting the second-order factor model for AI Awareness, AI Application, and Customer Experience to the test. The second-order factor model was examined to see if the three sub-dimensions (Analytics, Chatbots, and RPA, Risk Mitigation) may be seen as relevant indicators of AI Awareness. The model fit indices for the AI awareness components were good (Table 13.2): CMIN/DF = 3.423; GFI = 0.904; CFI = 0.973; PGFI = 0.530; PNFI = 0.625; IFI = 0.975; NFI = 0.838; and RMSEA = 0.037. This suggests that the model matches the data rather well. In conclusion, the findings suggest that AI awareness is represented as an overarching notion (i.e., second-order factor) comprised of Analytics, Chatbots, and RPA, and Risk Mitigation (first-order factors). The second-order factor model was examined to see if the three sub-dimensions (Analytics, Chatbots, RPA, and Risk Mitigation) may be seen as relevant indications of AI applications. CMIN/DF = 3.124; GFI = 0.983; CFI = 0.935; PGFI = 0.541; PNFI = 0.647; IFI = 0.936; NFI = 0.910; and RMSEA = 0.063 were the model fit indices for the Application components (Table 13.2). This suggests that the model matches the data rather well. In conclusion, the results show that AI application is represented as an overarching notion (i.e., second-order factor) that includes Analytics, Chatbots, RPA, and Risk Mitigation (first-order factors). The second-order factor model was examined to see if the four sub-dimensions (Timely Response, Convenience & Accessibility, Security & Risk Mitigation, and Technical Empowerment) are adequate indicators of Customer Experience. The Customer Experience measuring model exhibited strong model fit indices (Table 13.2): CMIN/DF = 3.029; GFI = 0.950; CFI = 0.904; PGFI = 0.615; PNFI = 0.705; IFI = 0.975; NFI = 0.945; and RMSEA = 0.054. This suggests that the model matches the data rather well. In summary, the findings show that the application is represented as an overarching concept (i.e., second-order factor) that includes Timely Response, Convenience & Accessibility, Security & Risk Mitigation, and Technical Empowerment (first-order factors).

TABLE 13.2 As a Second-Order Factor, Overall Measurement Model Indices for AI Awareness, AI Applicability, and Customer Experience

	CMIN/DF	GFI	CFI	PGFI	PNFI	IFI	NFI	RMSEA
AI awareness	3.423	0.904	0.973	0.530	0.625	0.975	0.938	0.037
AI application	3.124	0.983	0.935	0.541	0.647	0.936	0.910	0.063
Customer experience	3.029	0.950	0.904	0.615	0.705	0.975	0.945	0.054

13.8.3 CONVERGENT AND DISCRIMINANT VALIDITY

The evidence for convergent and discriminant validity is shown in Table 13.3. The composite reliability, average variance extracted, maximum variance shared, and average variance shared values are displayed. The composite dependability values for each design were revealed to be greater than Malhotra and Dash's recommended cut-off point of 0.7 [32]. As a result, it assures the scale's dependability. The values of AVE and CR are utilized to confirm the convergent validity of notions. The amount to which the scale correlates favorably with other measures of the same construct is measured by convergent validity [32]. Furthermore, the value of AVE should be 0.5, as proposed by the researcher [32], and the CR of each construct should be bigger than its AVE. All of these requirements are now satisfied.

Discriminant validity, on the other hand, demonstrates that the produced scale's determined constructs are not conceptually connected with each other and are considerably distinct from each other [33]. It entails establishing a lack of link between several constructs [32, 34]. Furthermore, in order to measure discriminant validity, the value of MSV must be less than the value of AVE, and the value of ASV must be less than the value of AVE (Figure 13.3).

TABLE 13.3 Reliability and Validity Analysis of Measurement Scale

Latent Variables	Composite Reliability (CR)	Average Variance Extracted (AVE)	Maximum Shared Variance (MSV)	Average Shared Variance (ASV)
Awareness of artificial intelligence	0.93	0.83	0.81	0.82
Analytics	0.76	0.52	0.51	0.49
Robotic process automation and Chatbot	0.70	0.62	0.57	0.59
Risk mitigation	0.82	0.69	0.62	0.64
Application of AI	0.98	0.94	0.90	0.93
Analytics	0.85	0.65	0.57	0.61
Robotic process automation and Chatbot	0.85	0.65	0.53	0.62
Risk mitigation	0.80	0.67	0.65	0.65
Customer experiences	0.97	0.88	0.85	0.82
Timely response	0.94	0.85	0.79	0.83
Convenience and accessibility	0.91	0.68	0.59	0.67
Security and risk mitigation	0.87	0.67	0.62	0.65
Technical empowerment	0.92	0.70	0.66	0.69

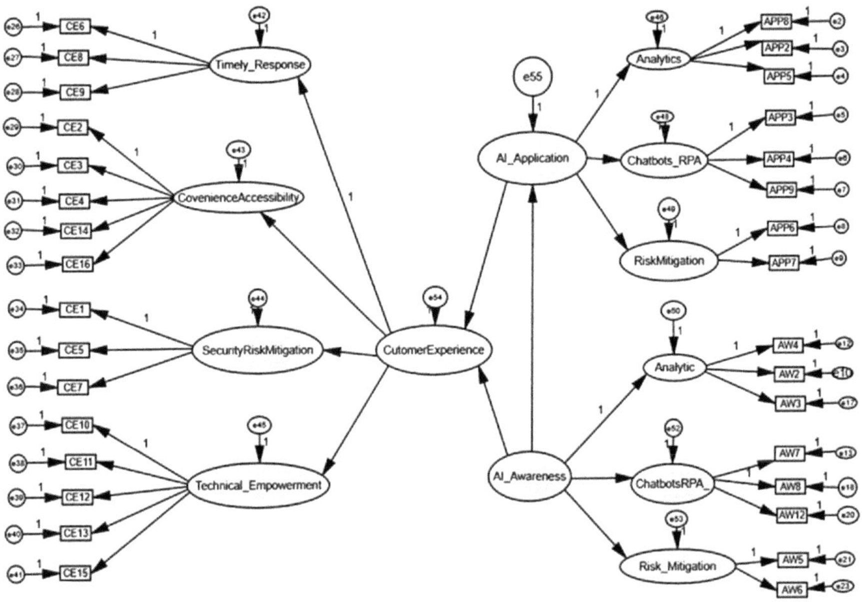

FIGURE 13.3 Structural model.

Seven statements were removed during the initial testing of the overall measuring model. Table 13.4 shows the model fit indices for the final overall measurement model, which indicated that it was acceptable: GFI = 0.949, CFI = 0.923, PGFI = 0.554, PNFI = 0.623, IFI = 0.922, NFI = 0.958, and RMSEA = 0.047 (Table 13.5).

TABLE 13.4 Structural Equation Model Indices

Model	CMIN/DF	GFI	CFI	PGFI	PNFI	IFI	NFI	RMSEA
SEM	3.104	0.949	0.923	0.554	0.623	0.922	0.958	0.047

- Hypothesis 1 tested the Awareness of Artificial Intelligence as a second-order factor comprised of the sub-dimensions of Analytics, Robotic Process Automation, Chatbot, and Risk Mitigation. Findings show the significant effect of Awareness of AI (main construct) on sub-constructs: Analytics (β= 0.82), Chatbots & RPA (β= 0.96), and Risk Mitigation (β= 0.93). The results depict all $0 < \beta < 1$ and $p < 0.001$.
- Hypothesis 2 tested the Application of Artificial Intelligence as a second-order factor comprised of the sub-dimensions of Analytics,

TABLE 13.5 The Regression Path Coefficient and its Significance

Hypothesis	Construct	Path	Construct	Estimates	S.E.	C.R.	P	Decision
H1	Analytics	←	AI awareness	Reference point				
	RPA Chatbots	←	AI awareness	0.686	0.072	9.532	***	Accepted
	Risk mitigation	←	AI awareness	0.720	0.076	9.443	***	Accepted
H2	Analytics	←	AI application	Reference point				
	RPA Chatbots	←	AI application	1.903	0.487	3.904	***	Accepted
	Risk mitigation	←	AI application	1.896	0.485	3.912	***	Accepted
H3	Timely response	←	Customer experience	Reference point				
	Convenience and accessibility	←	Customer experience	1.065	0.060	17.825	***	Accepted
	Security and risk mitigation	←	Customer experience	1.002	0.065	15.498	***	Accepted
	Technical empowerment	←	Customer experience	0.891	0.070	12.802	***	Accepted
H4	Customer experience	←	AI awareness	0.851	0.102	2.228	0.016	Accepted
H5 a	AI application	←	AI awareness	0.651	0.096	8.831	***	Accepted
H5 b	Customer experience	←	AI application	0.228	0.101	6.464	***	Accepted

Robotic Process Automation, Chatbot, and Risk Mitigation. Results show the significant effect of the Application of AI (main construct) on sub-constructs: Analytics (β= 0.92), Chatbots & RPA (β= 0.99), and Risk Mitigation (β= 0.99). The results depict all $0 < \beta < 1$ and $p < 0.001$.

- Hypothesis 3 tested the Customer Experience as a second-order factor comprised of the sub-dimensions of Timely Response, Convenience & Accessibility, Security & Risk Mitigation, and Technical Empowerment. The findings show a significant effect of Customer experience (main construct) on sub-constructs: Timely Response (β= 0.96), Convenience & Accessibility (0.94), Security & Risk Mitigation (0.89), Technical Empowerment (β= 0.97) as results depict all $0 < \beta < 1$ and $p < 0.001$. Hypothesis 4 tested the Awareness of Artificial Intelligence has a significant effect on Customer Experience. Results show a very low β= 0.21, but a significant effect as $p < 0.05$. Hypothesis 5 tested: Application of Artificial Intelligence moderates the relationship between Awareness of Artificial Intelligence and Customer Experience. It is observed that the Application of AI acts as a strong mediator variable between Awareness of AI and Customer Experience (Awareness of AI to Application of AI β= 0.80, Application of AI to Customer Experience β= 0.65).

13.9 CONCLUSION

AI technologies have the potential to transform both the physical and digital experiences of banking customers. It is now essential for banks to offer artificial intelligence-enabled banking services to their customers to empower them with technical knowledge, save their time and transaction costs, provide security, reduce the risk of cyber fraud, and make banking convenient for their customers by providing prompt services and timely responses. AI is a powerful tool for companies to meet or exceed consumer expectations. AI also enables banks to manage huge volumes of data at record speed to derive valuable insights from it. The current study evaluated whether AI Awareness, AI Application, and Customer Experience as second-order factors modify the association between AI Awareness and Customer Experience. The findings validated the three-dimensional second-order factors of AI Awareness, AI Application, and Customer Experience, as well as the four-dimensional second-order factor of Customer Experience. Furthermore, it was discovered that (a) AI Awareness has a considerable yet very modest influence on

Customer Experience. (b) a considerable beneficial influence of AI Awareness and AI Application on Customer Experience, with AI Application serving as a powerful mediating variable. The key theoretical contribution relates to the inclusion of the three dimensions of AI Awareness and Application and four dimensions of Customer Experience in a single model.

The study suggests that banks use different strategies to incorporate Artificial Intelligence into their processes. AI application is found to be the strong mediating variable between AI awareness and customer experience. As a result, it suggests that artificial intelligence-enabled banking services are important for supporting consumers with their financial demands and even dealing with banking concerns. Banks can continue to enhance their banking apps and strive to provide more services to their customers through their banking applications in order to fulfill all of the expectations that consumers have through their banking applications and, as a consequence, improve banking client relationships.

There are some limitations to this study. The study is limited to AI awareness, AI application of Artificial Intelligence, and its impact on customer experience. More variables like policy violation and the digital divide can be considered in further studies. Moreover, the sample size of 300 from commercial banks may be small when compared to the total population of banking customers in India. A sector-wise comparative study can be done to assess the banking customers' experiences with artificial intelligence, which can suggest banks' areas of implementation of artificial intelligence-enabled banking operations.

KEYWORDS

- **analytics**
- **artificial intelligence**
- **awareness**
- **banking customers**
- **banks application**
- **chatbot**
- **customer experience**
- **risk mitigation**
- **robotic process automation**

REFERENCES

1. Budiman, R. (2013). Utilizing Skype for providing learning support for Indonesian distance learning students: A lesson learnt. *Procedia – Social and Behavioral Sciences, 83*, 5–10. https://doi.org/10.1016/j.sbspro.2013.06.002.
2. Meena, P., Chaturvedi, A., & Gupta, S. (2022). Impact of Artificial Intelligence on Development and Growth of Entrepreneurship. In P. Meena, A. Chaturvedi, & S. Gupta (Eds.), *Impact of Artificial Intelligence on Organizational Transformation* (pp. 131–146). John Wiley and Sons Inc and Scrivener Publishing LLC.
3. Kaur, N., Sahdev, S., Sharma, M., & Siddiqui, L. (2020). Banking 4.0: The influence of artificial intelligence on the banking industry & how AI is changing the face of modern-day banks. *International Journal of Management (IJM), 11*(6), 577–585. https://doi.org/10.34218/IJM.11.6.2020.049.
4. Joseph, M., Sekhon, Y., Stone, G., & Tinson, J. (2005). An exploratory study on the use of banking technology in the UK. *International Journal of Bank Marketing, 23*(5), 397–413. https://doi.org/10.1108/02652320510612474.
5. Parsons, G., Gotlieb, C. C., & Denny, M. (1993). Productivity and Computers in Canadian Banking. *Journal of Productivity Analysis, 4*, 95–113. https://econpapers.repec.org/article/kapjproda/v_3a4_3ay_3a1993_3ai_3a1_3ap_3a95-113.htm.
6. Bhattacharya, C., & Sinha, M. (2022). The role of artificial intelligence in banking for leveraging customer experience. *Australasian Accounting Business & Finance Journal, 16*(5), 89–105.
7. Adegoroye, O. F. (2019). Effect of Artificial Intelligence on Customer Satisfaction in Deposit Money Banking in Akure, Ondo State. A Project Research Submitted To The Department Of Project Management Technology, School of Management Technology. [PDF document]. Retrieved from EFFECT_OF_ARTIFICIAL_INTELLIGENCE_ON_CUS.pdf.
8. Eura, K. O. (2020). A Study of the Impact of the Adoption of Robotic Process Automation (RPA) on Work Productivity in the Retail Banking Industry [Master's thesis, KDI School of Public Policy and Management]. https://archives.kdischool.ac.kr/bitstream/11125/41439/1/A%20Study%20of%20the%20impact%20of%20the%20adoption%20of%20Robotic%20Process%20Automation%20%28RPA%29%20on%20work%20productivity%20in%20the%20retail%20banking%20industry.pdf.
9. Eren, B. A. (2021). Determinants of customer satisfaction in chatbot use: Evidence from a banking application in Turkey. *International Journal of Bank Marketing, 39*(2), 294–311. https://doi.org/10.1108/IJBM-02-2020-0056.
10. Unni, M. V, Bh, R., Kuncha, R. K., Antony, P., & Vinod, P. (2022). Unleashing the efficacy of AI for smart banking: A demographic survey of Indian private banks. *Annals of Forest Research, 65*(1), 2868–2883. Retrieved from: https://www.e-afr.org/.
11. Porwal, A., Chaturvedi, A., & Gupta, S. (2022). Artificial Intelligence with Special Reference to Blockchain Technology: A Future of Accounting. In P. Meena, A. Chaturvedi, & S. Gupta (Eds.), *Impact of Artificial Intelligence on Organizational Transformation* (pp. 289–303). John Wiley and Sons Inc and Scrivener Publishing LLC.
12. Mor, S., & Gupta, G. (2021). Artificial intelligence and technical efficiency: The case of Indian commercial banks. *Strategic Change, 30*(3), 235–245. https://doi.org/10.1002/jsc.2406.

13. El-Gohary, H., Thayaseelan, A., Babatunde, S., & El-Gohary, S. (2021). An exploratory study on the effect of artificial intelligence-enabled technology on customer experiences in the banking sector. *Journal of Technological Advancements, 1*(1), 1–17. https://doi.org/10.4018/jta.20210101.oa1.
14. Ghandour, A. (2021). Opportunities and challenges of artificial intelligence in banking: Systematic literature review. *TEM Journal, 10*(4), 1581–1587. https://doi.org/10.18421/TEM104-12.
15. Öztürk, R., & Kula, V. (2021). A general profile of artificial intelligence adoption in banking sector. *Journal of Corporate Governance, Insurance and Risk Management, 8*(2), 146–157. https://doi.org/10.51410/jcgirm.8.2.10.
16. Kedziora, D., & Penttinen, E. (2020). Governance models for robotic process automation: The case of Nordea Bank. *Journal of Information Technology Teaching Cases, 11*(1), 20–29. https://doi.org/10.1177/2043886920937022.
17. Malali, A. B., & Gopalakrishnan, S. (2020). Application of artificial intelligence and its powered technologies in the Indian banking and financial industry: An overview. *IOSR Journal Of Humanities And Social Science (IOSR-JHSS), 25*(6), 55–60. https://doi.org/10.9790/0837-2504065560.
18. Königstorfer, F., & Thalmann, S. (2019). Applications of artificial intelligence in commercial banks – A research agenda for behavioral finance. *Journal of Behavioral and Experimental Finance, 27*, 100352. https://doi.org/10.1016/j.jbef.2020.100352.
19. Indriasari, E., Gaol, F. L., & Matsuo, T. (2019). Digital banking transformation: Application of artificial intelligence and big data analytics for leveraging customer experience in the Indonesia banking sector. In *8th International Congress on Advanced Applied Informatics (IIAI-AAI)*. https://doi.org/10.1109/IIAI-AAI.2019.00175.
20. Trivedi, J. (2019). Examining the customer experience of using banking chatbots and its impact on brand love: The moderating role of perceived risk. *Journal of Internet Commerce*. https://doi.org/10.1080/15332861.2019.1567188 (accessed on 27 May 2024).
21. Zelenka, M., & Vokoun, M. (2021). Information and communication technology capabilities and business performance: The case of differences in the Czech financial sector and lessons from robotic process automation between 2015 and 2020. *Review of Innovation and Competitiveness, 7*(1), 99–116.
22. Geetha, A. (2021). A study on artificial intelligence (AI) in banking and financial services. *International Journal of Creative Research Thoughts, 9*(9), 110–114.
23. Oshri, I., & Plugge, A. (2022). Introducing RPA and automation in the financial sector: Lessons from KAS Bank. *Journal of Information Technology Teaching Cases, 12*(1), 88–95. https://doi.org/10.1177/2043886921994828.
24. Ryzhkova, M., Soboleva, E., Sazonova, A., & Chikov, M. (2020). Consumers' perception of artificial intelligence in banking sector. *SHS Web of Conferences, 80*, 01019. https://doi.org/10.1051/shsconf/20208001019.
25. Cheng, Y., & Jiang, H. (2020). How do AI-driven chatbots impact user experience? Examining gratifications, perceived privacy risk, satisfaction, loyalty, and continued use. *Journal of Broadcasting & Electronic Media, 64*(4), 592–614. https://doi.org/10.1080/08838151.2020.1834296.
26. Agarwal, P. (2019). Redefining banking and financial industry through the application of computational intelligence. *Advances in Science and Engineering Technology*

International Conferences (ASET). https://doi.org/10.1109/ICASET.2019.8714305 (accessed on 27 May 2024).

27. Shekhawat, S., & Mathur, S. (2021). A study on consumer awareness and usage of E-Banking through mobile at State Bank of India. *Research Methodology in Commerce and Management*, 103–109. Inspira Publication. Retrieved from: https://www.researchgate.net/publication/353644639_A_Study_on_Consumer_Awareness_and_usage_of_E-Banking_through_Mobile_at_State_Bank_of_India.
28. George, A., & Kumar, G. S. G. (2015). Validation of a scale for measuring problems in internet banking and their effect on customer satisfaction. *Vision, 19*(4), 312–323. https://doi.org/10.1177/0972262915610856.
29. Joseph, M., Sekhon, Y., Stone, G., & Tinson, J. (2005). An exploratory study on the use of banking technology in the UK. *International Journal of Bank Marketing, 23*(5), 397–413. https://doi:10.1108/02652320510612474.
30. Khalfan, A. M., & Alshawaf, A. (2004). Adoption and implementation problems of e-banking: A study of the managerial perspective of the banking industry in Oman. *Journal of Global Information Technology Management, 7*(1), 47–64.
31. Kim, H.-Y. (2013). Statistical notes for clinical researchers: Assessing normal distribution (2) using skewness and kurtosis [Online]. http://synapse.koreamed.org/Synapse/Data/PDFData/2185RDE/rde-38-52.pdf (accessed on 27 May 2024).
32. Malhotra, N. K., & Dash, S. (2010). *Marketing Research: An Applied Orientation* (6th ed.). Pearson Education, India.
33. Casalo, L. V., Flavian, C., & Guinaliu, M. (2008). The role of satisfaction and website usability in developing customer loyalty and positive word of mouth in the e-banking services. *The International Journal of Bank Marketing, 26*(6), 399–417.
34. Hair, J. F., Black, W. C., Babin, B. J., & Anderson, R. E. (2013). *Multivariate Data Analysis* (7th ed.). Pearson Education, UK.
35. Hu, L., & Bentler, P. M. (1998). Fit Indices in Covariance Structure Modeling: Sensitivity to Underparameterized Model Misspecification. *Psychological Methods, 3*, 424–453. http://dx.doi.org/10.1037/1082-989X.3.4.424.
36. Bentler, M., & Bonett, G. (1980). Significance Tests and Goodness of Fit in the Analysis of Covariance Structures. *Psychological Bulletin, 88,* 588–606. https://doi.org/10.1037/0033-2909.88.3.588.
37. West, S. G., Finch, J. F., & Curran, P. J. (1995). Structural equation models with nonnormal variables: problems and remedies. In R. H. Hoyle (Ed.). *Structural Equation Modeling: Concepts, Issues and Applications*. Newbery Park, CA: SAGE.

CHAPTER 14

Recommender Systems Using AI and ML: Future of Sales and Marketing

KSH. KRISHNA B. SINGHA and MUKTA SHARMA

Associate Professor, Trinity Institute of Professional Studies, Delhi, India

ABSTRACT

Organizations have an abundance of data, and it is essential for the organizations to filter, predict, and analyze the data for their business growth. The technological advancement in today's time is well displayed by computers in terms of processing a huge amount of data and analyzing it in real-time. In the business world, artificial intelligence (AI) is receiving more and more attention, and this is the underlying cause. By employing Artificial Intelligence and its subfield, Machine Learning (ML) technologies, many business organizations are adopting tools to grow their businesses. One such technology is a recommender system; a software tool used by e-commerce sites to advertise and increase sales of things by suggesting relevant items that customers have explored. These systems learn from the customer; in the process, they collect information about them, their browsing behavior, purchase history, demographic details, and so on. Based on the huge amount of information, recommender systems, in a way, present customized websites to the users showing only the items the user would prefer to see and purchase. This chapter discusses the various functions, and present-day recommender systems employed in different e-commerce applications, as well as the different techniques adopted by them and their pros & cons. This content also covers some of the concerns and challenges faced while developing recommender systems, such as the analysis and processing of huge data, quality of data involved in the processing, unpredictable nature of user behavior, capability to recommend unseen items, and so on.

Artificial Intelligence and Machine Learning for Business. Namita Mishra, A. V. Senthil Kumar (Eds.)

Later, the chapter sheds light on various real-time examples and cases where the recommender system has helped companies grow their business.

14.1 INTRODUCTION

In the modern era, artificial intelligence (AI) is a buzzword in every field; whether it is business, sports, governance, health, service, or the tourism industry, our day-to-day walk of life, and so on. The adoption of AI has become a vital part of organizations in almost all sectors. It is enabling them to rethink business strategies in terms of recognizing relevant business opportunities and thereby creating a competitive edge among the players in the field. AI was originally a discipline in computer science. It is concerned with the subject matter of making systems intelligent by using different tools and technologies and implementing appropriate algorithms. Although AI first originated as a discipline in the 1950s, its first commercial use didn't materialize until the 1980s, when the expert system paradigm achieved success [23]. Making systems train and learn from historical data is the focus of the AI branch of machine learning (ML) [24].

This present study is organized as follows: section one gives a brief introduction of the chapter; Section two gives a detailed description of recommender systems, their purpose, and various functions of the system; the third section is about the different techniques adopted by these systems; section four is about the roles played by artificial intelligence and machine learning in the implementation and fulfilling the objectives of modern-day recommender systems in e-commerce applications; section five is all about the many challenges in achieving the goal while implementing the system, followed by section six which is about the various examples of recommender systems adopted by many reputed business brands and platforms. Section seven, the last section, is a case study of a world-famous business name, which emphasizes how a brand goes up the ladder of success by boosting sales through the use of recommender systems in its application.

14.2 RECOMMENDER SYSTEMS

In the context of online stores, recommender systems recommend items that may best cater to the needs of a particular customer. E-commerce sites use these systems to suggest items to their customers. It is true that the business strategies adopted by e-commerce applications are far different from those of the physical world. This is because the business in the latter case is limited to very few. It would be impossible to think of a popular store branch in one's locality that caters to all one's needs and another that caters to all their needs. In his book Mass Customization published in 1993, Joe Pine advanced the idea that businesses needed to transition from the old world of mass itemization, where "standardized items, homogeneous markets, and long item life and development cycles were the rule," to the new world, where "variety and customization supplant standardized items." Businesses used to mass produce goods for a single market and audience in the previous techniques of shopping. Pine agrees that producing just one item is no longer sufficient in this situation. Companies must be able to create a minimum of different products that cater to various consumer wants. To make the customers choose among the many available items on the e-commerce platform, information is also increased. And so, information overload develops as a result of the increased amount of information that consumers must go through before they can decide which items best suit their needs. When Jeff Bezos, CEO of Amazon.com, said, "If I have 2 million consumers on the Web, I should have 2 million stores on the Web," he was referring to the idea of mass customization. One of the primary methods for attaining mass customization on e-commerce platforms is the use of recommender systems.

Today, as the internet is reaching every nook and corner of the world and the paradigm is shifting for people accomplishing their daily and routine tasks from paying utility bills to shopping online, and so on, the virtual world has come a long way. However, for the producers, this new paradigm shift has made them an incumbent to customize items and services as per customers' needs while providing more options than were possible before. To stay in the market and be a lead player among the many competitors in the field, it's crucial that the producers need to build up their loyal customer base. For a company, the movement towards attaining a good and loyal customer base in the virtual world has also become rather more challenging as the site's competitor is just a click away from a potential customer. Recommender systems are powerful tools employed in many e-commerce sites to convert random browsers to buyers. These systems help sites recommend personalized items to their visitors. However, the appropriate information is reaching the visitor based on the anticipated needs instead of seeking the information. Recommender systems exploit the mass data collected through the visiting history and the activities performed by the respective visitors. Based on the huge data, these systems customize and recommend personalized items to the visitor. In fact, recommender systems enable the creation of a customized store, personally designed for each consumer. Of course, in the virtual world, all that changes are the selection of items shown to the consumer, not the underlying physical store.

The more a user makes use of a website's recommendation system and imparts his preferences to it, the more attached he grows to it. Pine et al. elaborated in his work [19] the need for mass customization in order to cater to the different needs of every customer and also the situations and conditions where mass customization won't work.

14.2.1 PURPOSES OF RECOMMENDER SYSTEM

Increased sales are the primary reason recommender systems are used in e-commerce applications. Additionally, they aid in the growth of more varied product sales, user happiness, and user loyalty along the road. The recommender system establishes itself for a better grasp of what the user wants, which makes all of these things possible. A recommender system must either analyze the previous preferences of users who share their interests or take advantage of the descriptive information about the things in order to provide a list of recommended items for the visitor and/or forecast how much they would enjoy a certain item.

14.2.2 FUNCTIONS OF RECOMMENDER SYSTEMS

1. **Finding Some Good Items:** The primary recommendation job that many commercial systems focus on is to suggest to a user a list of items in a ranked order coupled with estimates of how much the user will enjoy each item.
2. **Finding all Good Items:** Provide every product that can satisfy a customer's needs. In these conditions, it is insufficient to just find some high-quality items. This is especially true when there aren't many items around or when the system is crucial to running things, like in financial or medical applications. In addition to the benefit of carefully weighing all the options, the user may benefit from the system's ranking of these items or from any additional justifications the system generates in these situations.
3. **Contextual Annotation:** Given a context already in place and a list of objects, highlight some of them based on the user's long-term preferences. A TV recommender system, for instance, might mark which TV shows in the computerized program guide are worthwhile.

4. **Recommend a Sequence:** The objective is to offer a succession of items that are desirable when taken all at once, rather than focusing on the formulation of a single proposal.
5. **Suggest a Bundle:** Provide a group of complementary products. An itinerary for a trip, for instance, might list a variety of locations to see, places to stay, and other activities, all of which are located in a single region.
6. **Just Browsing:** Without immediately planning to make a purchase, the consumer browses the catalog. The recommender's role is to guide the user toward items that are more likely to be relevant to that user's interests during that particular browsing session.
7. **Find a Credible Recommender:** Some people test out recommender systems to evaluate how effective they are since they don't trust them. Consequently, a particular system could additionally include certain features in addition to those that are just necessary for getting suggestions so that users can test how the system behaves.
8. **Improve the Profile:** This has to do with the user's capacity to tell the recommender system what he or she loves and doesn't like. To give individualized advice, this basic work is essential. The algorithm can only offer suggestions that would be given to an "average" user if it has special knowledge about the active user.
9. **Express Self:** The suggestions may mean absolutely nothing to certain users. They value the freedom to voice their thoughts and values, as well as the ability to participate in their evaluations, more. Nevertheless, the user's enjoyment of that action may function as leverage, causing them to continue using the application.
10. **Aid Others:** Some people are content to share information with others, such as their ratings of products, because they believe it will benefit the community. This might be a key driver for information entry into a recommender system that is not frequently utilized. When using a car recommender system, for instance, a user who has already purchased a new automobile is aware that the rating entered into the system is probably more helpful to other users than to themselves the following time a new car purchase is taken into consideration.

11. **Influence Other Users:** There are people who actively try to persuade other users to buy specific things using web-based recommendation systems. In actuality, malevolent users are also there who may take advantage of the system to either reward or punish particular goods.

14.3 TYPES OF RECOMMENDER SYSTEMS

Every business has the sole objective of increasing its sales of items. E-commerce applications present item information online to visitors, thereby increasing online data. This often leads to the problem of information overload, resulting in a frustrating experience for users. Recommender systems determine the interests of users and help them search and find their desired items. Determining the interests of users involves the implementation of different mining algorithms on huge data. Depending on the data on which user recommendations are made, recommender systems can be categorized into two main types:

- Personalized; and
- Non-personalized.

Personalized recommender systems work on user-specific data collected based on the user's profile, browsing history, previous purchase information, feedback given by the user, and more. The recommendations made by these systems are customized and tailored according to the interests of the user. Two major techniques employed in Personalized recommender systems are Content-based filtering and Collaborative filtering. Some e-commerce applications adopt Hybrid filtering to combine the advantages of both approaches. Collaborative filtering is further subdivided into three subtypes: model-based, memory-based, and a hybrid of the former two types. Memory-based recommender systems can be either item-based or user-based.

On the other hand, non-personalized recommendation types work based on the concept of popularity or ratings given to the items. The different recommendation techniques are described in subsections.

14.3.1 COLLABORATIVE FILTERING

This approach has been the most popular and widely implemented among the available techniques used by e-commerce sites. The working of this filtering technique is focused on the customer and their choice of items. Collaborative filtering's major goal is to acquire data on the attitudes and behaviors of the previous user so that they may be compared to those of the new user and determine whether they are similar or not [31]. Customers of similar characteristics, like their purchasing habits/patterns, browsing history, opinion on items, interaction with the online platform, profile, age, etc., are grouped. The vast amounts of information gathered about the customers are processed, so it is necessary to use machine learning algorithms like Bayesian Networks, K-nearest neighbors, Clustering, and Matrix factorization to understand how the customers perceive various products and to present them with alternatives that other users who share their preferences have already purchased. This strategy is based on the idea that customers with similar past choices will likely have similar future preferences as well [2]. When there is low data dependency, implementation of the collaborative filtering technique is easy. This technique also provides accurate suggestions for recommendations [14]. The main advantage of the collaborative filtering technique has been its ability to provide serendipitous recommendations.

A collaborative filtering system's essential participant is the active user who wants a rating prediction or ranking of items. This recommender produces suggestions based on the preferences of suitable users by using prior preferences as a cue to develop correlation across users.

This method typically consists of a list of m users $U = u_1, u_2, \ldots, u_m$ and 'n' items $P = p_1, p_2, \ldots, p_n$. The system builds an m x n user-item matrix that holds user ratings for items, with each entry ri, j denoting the rating provided by user ui for item pj. This filtering algorithm predicts a rating for q or suggests a referral when a recommendation for the user on the target item q is required.

Collaborative filtering is further branched into three subcategories: model-based, memory-based, and hybrid-based collaborative filtering.

14.3.1.1 MODEL-BASED

This approach uses machine learning algorithms and data mining techniques to build an offline model of the system. Building and training these models allow the estimation of predictions for online Collaborative Filtering tasks. Some of these algorithms are Bayesian models, clustering models, decision trees, and singular value decomposition models [27].

The matrix is filled using a model-based approach by anticipating the products that the client has not yet seen. Using data mining techniques, it is possible to forecast the ratings of the unrated items [18]. Here, instead of using a dataset each time, the data gathered from the repository is used to create a model for recommendation [16]. The two aspects that are enhanced by using this method are speed and scalability. Additionally, it raises the algorithm's prediction accuracy value [29].

14.3.1.2 MEMORY-BASED

Similarity between individuals or things is calculated for recommendations in memory-based techniques. Users who share similar preferences will be more similar [18]. This method looks for users who share the target user's preferences and dislikes before recommending new things to the target user. It is a simple and efficient approach to use [16]. Users who share similar preferences are grouped [29].

User-based, item-based, or mixed memory-based approaches are all possible. The user-item matrix as a whole is used by the memory-based collaborative filtering algorithms to detect comparable things. After identifying the closest neighbors, previous evaluations of these bodies are used to provide recommendations [6]. The ratings of comparable things to item q are used in the item-based approach, whereas the past preferences of nearest neighbors to the user are used in user-based collaborative filtering [1].

The two types of memory-based filtering approaches are item-based and user-based. The user-based filtering strategy assesses user similarity based on the ratings each user has given a specific item [2]. In contrast, an item-based approach calculates item similarity to provide predictions. The item-based technique consists of two phases; the first examines the degree of similarity between two items using similarity measures. The ratings for unidentified items are predicted in the following phase using similarity values.

14.3.1.3 ADVANTAGES OF COLLABORATIVE FILTERING

Being the oldest yet popular recommendation system approach, the collaborative filtering technique has the following advantages over the other approaches:

1. **Excellent Accuracy:** Many engines are now built to monitor additional context-related factors in order to broaden the scope of parameters taken into account and more accurately gauge user similarities. Collaborative filtering, often referred to as context-aware

collaborative filtering, combines user data with contextual information such as location, time, device, etc., to precisely describe the context in which a customer operates and deliver more useful ideas.

2. **Easy Implementation:** Collaborative filtering techniques are easier to implement.
3. **Coincidence-based Recommendations:** These algorithms can foretell consumers' interest in a product they weren't even aware existed by noting that it has attracted the attention of other customers with comparable interests.
4. **No Accurate Description:** Recommendation engines can function fairly well without understanding the nature of each item by focusing more on the relationships between items than the item itself. This suggests that platforms implementing such systems won't need to accurately describe each item to make the system function properly and increase sales for e-commerce platforms like Amazon.
5. It is simple to add new data in an incremental manner.

14.3.1.4 DISADVANTAGES OF COLLABORATIVE FILTERING

1. **Data Sparsity:** A lot of products are sold on e-commerce websites. However, not every user rates every item. Because so few products in the database are rated, the recommendation might not be entirely appropriate.
2. **Synonymy:** The problem of synonymy arises when the same item is referred to by different names. A recommender system views these items as separate items since it is challenging to identify the underlying relationship.
3. **Shilling Attack:** Also known as a "profile injection attack," this tactic involves creating fictitious profiles to sway the behavior of the recommendation process [10]. Some consumers would leave positive feedback for their products and negative feedback for their competitors' products [16].
4. **Cold Start:** When a new user signs in and there are no previous records of the user, a cold start difficulty arises [8]. In this scenario, a vast amount of data is needed to offer appropriate recommendations [29].

14.3.2 CONTENT-BASED FILTERING

Compared to collaborative filtering, this method is newer and easier to use to increase suggestion accuracy. Content-based filtering recommender systems, sometimes referred to as cognitive filtering, are based on two factors: the user's preferences and their profile. The system collects information about the interests of the user when the system starts. This information may include age, gender, region, browsing data, etc. The things that the user prefers are those that they have already bought, loved, and rated and that also match their characteristics. Content-based filtering works well and makes good recommendations when the attributes are presented to the system in a clear and proper way. Therefore, this technique has everything to do with the user profile and the description of items that the user is related to. Once the attributes of the item are compared with the user preferences, item filtering is done to segregate items to be recommended to the active user from the ones that are not of interest to the user. When there aren't many things and we don't know as much about the user yet, this algorithm usually performs pretty well.

14.3.2.1 ADVANTAGES OF CONTENT-BASED FILTERING

- The recommendations are done exclusively for the active user based on the user profile and its item preferences; hence, there is a maximum possibility of resulting in better personalized recommendations.
- This technique may give recommendations for items that might not have been used earlier by anyone, which may be favorable for the active user.
- By suggesting products that are relevant to those the active user has already purchased, these systems may be subtly biased in favor of the user.

14.3.2.2 DISADVANTAGES OF CONTENT-BASED FILTERING

The content-based filtering technique also suffers from some disadvantages; they are:

- Identifying attributes for some items is difficult.
- This technique may suffer from an overspecialization problem as it can recommend items only from the same category or type.
- In Content-Based Filtering, user feedback is not gathered because users don't submit ratings for the items, hence it is impossible to determine whether the suggestions are accurate or not.

- This approach is computationally expensive when there are many items (which is the typical scenario), and the suggestions start to deteriorate.

14.3.3 HYBRID FILTERING

Hybrid recommender systems combine several recommender systems to create a more reliable recommending model to achieve the best of both worlds. The shortcomings of the many constituent strategies of one method can be lessened by the advantages of another system, and therefore a better system can be built by integrating the features of multiple recommender systems. For instance, by incorporating collaborative filtering techniques, where the model fails when new things don't yet have ratings, the accurate and successful suggestion is made possible when feature information about the item is accessible.

There are certainly issues that are concerns in hybrid recommending techniques which can be put down through the following points:

- The key features from different techniques need to be selected and combined to accomplish the business solution.
- To decide upon the number of systems to be combined and the outcomes from the combination for good suggestions.

14.3.4 NON-PERSONALIZED OR POPULARITY RECOMMENDERS

This filtering technique is probably the easiest approach to generate a recommendation for items for active users. It simply recommends the most popular items based on ratings, most ordered, most watched, most positive feedback, and so on. In the case of Netflix, it might be the most watched movies; in the case of Amazon, the most popular products, and so forth. With this method, there are also a number of options: the recommender can propose the most popular videos or vlogs on YouTube right now, which are the items that have become trending; alternatively, there might be recommendations for every category that a user might frequently search for.

The simplicity of this method, which implies less computing processing, is an advantage. Additionally, it's quite simple to maintain the technique current. The lack of personalization and poor recommendation accuracy are drawbacks of this strategy, which results in lower profitability for the business owner.

14.3.5 MISCELLANEOUS TYPES

In addition to the above-mentioned techniques, there are the following techniques of recommender systems:

1. **Demographic:** Based on the user's demographic profile, this type of technology makes product recommendations [5]. Based on the idea that different recommendations ought to be produced for various demographic niches. Many websites use straightforward personalization techniques that are based on demographics. For instance, website content may be altered based on user language or location. Or, based on the user's age, suggestions could be tailored. Although these strategies are fairly common in marketing literature, proper recommendation system research on demographic systems has not been explored all that much.
2. **Knowledge-based:** These systems make product recommendations based on detailed domain expertise about how individual product characteristics satisfy consumers' wants and preferences and, ultimately, how the item is valuable for the user. In these systems, a similarity function determines how closely the user's wants (issue description) and the recommendations match (solutions to the problem). The utility of the advice for the user can be easily inferred from the similarity score in this case. Knowledge-based systems often perform better than other systems at first, but if they lack learning components, they may be outperformed by other, less sophisticated techniques that may make use of the logs of human-computer interaction, such as collaborative filtering.
3. **Constraint-based:** Another kind of knowledge-based recommender system is one with constraints. Both systems gather user needs, automatically suggest fixes for inconsistent requirements in cases where no solutions could be discovered, and then explain recommendations. The method used to calculate the answers is where the main difference is found between the two techniques. While constraint-based recommenders primarily use preexisting knowledge bases that include explicit rules on how to match customer needs with item attributes, case-based recommenders base their recommendations on similarity metrics.

14.4 ROLE OF AI AND ML FOR RECOMMENDER SYSTEMS

Due to information saturation, it is getting tougher for regular computer users to find relevant, interesting, and valuable content as internet usage spreads and user engagement soars along with data storage capacity. A recommender system's operation is based on the vast amounts of data that have been acquired over time. Predicting the items the active user might like to purchase is an intelligent decision-making process to be done in a split second. This way the system assists its users in many decision-making processes by suggesting and giving recommendations. Different Artificial Intelligence (AI) and Machine Learning (ML) techniques are used to provide users with individualized and tailored recommendations. The accuracy of the data and the machine learning technique used determine how well a recommender system performs.

14.5 CHALLENGES

Present-day approaches for recommender systems are not devoid of challenges as the task of a recommender system should be multifaceted. Recommendation of items should not only be limited to the related calculated items; they should also be able to discover new items. Out of the many challenges, some prominent ones faced by recommender systems are as follows:

1. **Lack of Data:** A good recommender system needs user and item data, which it must collect and evaluate for the recommendation algorithm to operate. A recommender system has a better likelihood of providing the active user with useful recommendations the more item and user data it has to work with. The companies with the most consumer user data, like Google, Amazon, Netflix, etc., are those most associated with having outstanding suggestions.

2. **Changing Data:** According to Paul Edmunds, CEO-intelligent recommendations, systems are typically "inclined towards the old and have trouble revealing new." It is accurate since trends are always evolving and following them is challenging, if not impossible.

3. **Changes in User Preferences:** User preference changes are a significant problem. For instance, a user may be shopping for a costly watch one second and then crockery the next.

4. **Response Time Optimization:** The amount of time required to get the items is incredibly important for producing recommendations.

5. **Sparsity of data or Plummeting Data:** Stores have a large inventory, but not every item will receive a lot of customer ratings. Only a few individuals genuinely rate various items. Due to this sparsity, training these models computationally becomes ineffective.
6. **Shilling Attacks:** Dealing with those who are trying to manipulate the item recommendation algorithms is a tough nut to crack.

14.6 EXAMPLES OF RECOMMENDER SYSTEMS

Some examples of Recommender system techniques used in different domains are as below [27]:

1. **Book Recommendation Agents:** LIBRA is one of them; it is a hybrid-based feature-augmentation kind. By utilizing the ratings on a scale of 1 to 10 and the Bayesian learning algorithm, it learns the user's profile and forecasts the titles.

   BookCrossing is another option for book recommendations. It is a collaborative recommender system that gives users book recommendations. The topic diversification algorithm and offline data are used to anticipate the data.

   Another site that employs collaborative filtering is Library Thing, which also solicits user feedback in the form of ratings.

2. **Movie Suggestions:** A system of recommendations for movie fans is called Love Film. The system creates recommendations based on the user's preferences by combining ratings with collaborative filtering.

   A project of GroupLens Research, MovieLens is a collaborative filtering recommender system that matches user choices with other users' preferences in order to recommend movies. Collaborative filtering is the basis for Netflix's movie suggestions.

3. **Music Suggestions:**
   - One of the web-based music recommender system is Last.fm. It uses collaborative filtering using implicit feedback and social circles data to determine music recommendations.
   - A music recommendation system called Pandora makes music recommendations to users depending on their interests. From the Music Genome Project, it has emerged.

- Ringo is a collaborative filtering-based online music recommendation service that creates tailored recommendations.

14.7 CASE STUDY OF RECOMMENDER SYSTEMS

Amazon was launched on July 5, 1994, by Jeff Bezos; one of the biggest global e-commerce platforms [25]. His vision was to grow fast and become an e-commerce leader while venturing online in 1995. He launched an e-commerce website exclusively meant for selling books. In 1998 it acquired a movie database and started selling movies and music online. Also, in the same year, Amazon acquired German and British online book retailers to launch its worldwide business in 1998. In 1999, the company was selling electronics, video games, software, toys, home appliances, and much more. By the year 2000, Amazon had become a popular household name. Amazon featured a smile on its logo with a curved arrow from A to Z, demonstrating that the company carries products from A to Z. Amazon started Prime in 2005 and launched a membership-based service. In 2007, Amazon introduced Kindle to provide a platform for avid readers to easily access, download, and read their favorite e-books [3, 31, 33]. The company's mantra since inception was to "get big fast." The company is working hard and has also moved into cloud computing with Amazon AWS, Amazon Video, App Store, Locker, Amazon Echo, Alexa, and many more.

Amazon.com is one of the best-selling e-commerce sites, but according to Jeff Bezos, Amazon is a technological/technical company. Amazon's first recommendation engine using collaborative filtering was considered revolutionary 22 years ago, as it recommends popular items to users.

Amazon introduced its first collaborative filtering recommendation engine in 1998 [4, 12, 13]. Making assumptions about a specific customer's interests based on the preferences of other customers is referred to as "collaborative filtering." For instance, a user who purchased a video camera would be suggested a tripod, memory card, lenses, camera bag, etc., which have been purchased by other users who also have a video camera. "Frequently Bought Together" is a good and elementary feature that is still available on Amazon, where customers get suggestions on selected/purchased products/items.

Later, the algorithm combined collaborative filtering with heuristics with the thought of actually giving personal recommendations and suggesting to the consumer different tailored product recommendations rather than just suggesting popular or most frequently purchased items with the item selected/purchased by the user. The recommendation system would look at the visitor's recent purchase history and provide a list of pertinent products for each transaction using item-to-item collaborative filtering (Recommended for You). Candidates for the visitor's recommendation were items that frequently featured on all the lists (User's Browsing History), and their weight depended on how closely they connected to the visitor's prior purchases [11]. If clients who purchase one product are more likely than not to also purchase another, the two products are connected. The concept of relatedness is still based on prior customer transactions. However, the Amazon Personalization team discovered through empirical research that item-level analysis of purchase histories produced superior suggestions than customer-level analysis.

In 2012, to further improve the recommendation system, the Matrix completion problem was proposed. Consider a grid where the columns represent Prime Video movies and the rows represent Prime Video subscribers. If a customer has watched a certain movie, the corresponding cell in the grid contains a one; otherwise, it is blank or zero. As part of the matrix completion process, the grid needs to be populated with the probabilities that each consumer will view each movie. Matrix factorization was the popular method at the time for creating customized recommendations, but the outcomes were not very encouraging [14]. Matrix factorization finds very small matrices that, when multiplied together, would resemble a much larger matrix. Therefore, in 2014, Amazon delved deeper into Machine Learning and proposed a model based on Neural Networks. Matrix completion methods commonly employ an autoencoder, a type of neural network. Only the input data is taught to the autoencoder's output. In a deep neural network, layers are constructed from millions or even thousands of simple processing nodes. The output of the top layer shows the result of the computation. Data is fed into the nodes in the bottom layer, which process it and send the updated data up to the next layer, and so on. A large number of sample inputs and outputs must be available for the network to be trained. To reduce the average discrepancy between the output of the top layer and the desired outputs during training, the network's settings are continuously adjusted.

The company now uses AI to improve customer experience and operational efficiency, which is increasingly important. Amazon has an edge over competitors due to its early deployment of automation and artificial intelligence. Today's trillion-dollar company, Amazon, has altered its business model over time to include AI in every facet of operations. Amazon is a master at exploiting customer-centric innovation to drive its growth. Amazon strives to enhance the buying experience for users and helps in upselling and cross-selling products. Amazon uses tailored product recommendations as a marketing tool to help it continue to grow its market share and keep its consumers happy by correctly predicting their demands.

14.8 CONCLUSION

This book chapter presents a brief introduction to how effective and impactful technology can be. The recommender system is helping organizations not only grow their revenue and profitability but also build loyal customers and increase the lifetime value of the organization. A detailed description of many techniques adopted in present-day recommender systems, along with their advantages and disadvantages, is also discussed. The challenges faced by these recommendation techniques are highlighted here. Many popular examples are cited for better understanding. A case study on one of the pioneers and key leaders of e-commerce is also discussed for better clarity.

This chapter will benefit readers with basic but fundamental knowledge about recommender systems and the different techniques employed by these systems. Readers will also become acquainted with how recommender systems can boost sales of e-commerce applications. This chapter will provide a base for readers to further enhance their research work in this direction to meet the challenges mentioned herein.

KEYWORDS

- **artificial intelligence**
- **business tools**
- **collaborative filtering**
- **content-based filtering**
- **e-commerce**
- **machine learning**
- **recommendation systems**

REFERENCES

1. Aggarwal, C. C., & Aggarwal, C. C. (2016). An introduction to recommender systems. In: *Recommender Systems.* Springer, Cham. https://doi.org/10.1007/978-3-319-29659-3_1.
2. Ambulgekar, H. P., Pathak, M. K., & Kokare, M. B. (2019). A survey on collaborative filtering: Tasks, approaches and applications. In *Proceedings of International Ethical Hacking Conference 2018: eHaCON 2018, Kolkata, India* (pp. 289–300). Springer Singapore.
3. Armstrong, C. (n.d.). The history of Amazon.com. *Techwalla.* Retrieved January 30, 2023, from https://www.techwalla.com/articles/the-history-of-amazoncom (accessed on 27 May 2024).
4. Bhattarai, D. (2021). 5 Companies Making the Most of Recommendation Systems. *Leapfrog.* Retrieved from: https://www.lftechnology.com/blog/5-companies-making-the-most-of-recommendation-systems/ (accessed on 27 May 2024).
5. Bobadilla, J., Ortega, F., Hernando, A., & Gutiérrez, A. (2013). Recommender systems survey. *Knowledge-Based Systems, 46*, 109–132.
6. Breese, J. S., Heckerman, D., & Kadie, C. (2013). Empirical analysis of predictive algorithms for collaborative filtering. *arXiv preprint arXiv:1301.7363.* https://doi.org/10.48550/arXiv.1301.7363.
7. Chen, L., De Gemmis, M., Felfernig, A., Lops, P., Ricci, F., & Semeraro, G. (2013). Human decision making and recommender systems. *ACM Transactions on Interactive Intelligent Systems (TiiS), 3*(3), 1–7.
8. Ghodsad, P. R., & Chatur, P. N. (2018). Handling user cold-start problem for group recommender system using social behaviour wise group detection method. In *2018 International Conference on Research in Intelligent and Computing in Engineering (RICE)* (pp. 1–5). IEEE.
9. Guo, G., Zhang, J., Thalmann, D., & Yorke-Smith, N. (2014). Leveraging prior ratings for recommender systems in e-commerce. *Electronic Commerce Research and Applications, 13*(6), 440–455.
10. Guo, L., Liang, J., Zhu, Y., Luo, Y., Sun, L., & Zheng, X. (2019). Collaborative filtering recommendation based on trust and emotion. *Journal of Intelligent Information Systems, 53*, 113–135.
11. Hardesty, L. (2019). The history of Amazon's recommendation algorithm. Amazon Science. https://www.amazon.science/the-history-of-amazons-recommendation-algorithm, dated 22nd November 2022, (accessed on 30th Jan 2023).
12. Harigan, P. J. (2022). How Amazon Uses AI to Dominate Ecommerce: Top 5 Use Cases. https://www.godatafeed.com/blog/how-amazon-uses-ai-to-dominate-ecommerce, dated 17th November, 2022, (accessed on 30th January 2023).
13. Jarrell, M. (n.d.). How Amazon Uses AI in eCommerce – Two Use-Cases. Emerj. The AI Research and Advisory Company. Retrieved from: How Amazon Uses AI in eCommerce – Two Use-Cases | Emerj Artificial Intelligence Research. https://emerj.com/ai-sector-overviews/artificial-intelligence-at-amazon/ dated 30th August 2021, (accessed on 30th January 2023).
14. Jenny Freshwater keynote. (2019). *re:MARS 2019: Jenny Freshwater keynote presentation.* Amazon Science. https://www.amazon.science/re-mars-2019-jenny-freshwater-director-forecasting-presentation, dated-26th November 2019 (accessed 30th January 2023).

15. Li, J., Zhang, K., Yang, X., Wei, P., Wang, J., Mitra, K., & Ranjan, R. (2019). Category preferred canopy–K-means based collaborative filtering algorithm. *Future Generation Computer Systems, 93*, 1046–1054.
16. Mustafa, N., Ibrahim, A. O., Ahmed, A., & Abdullah, A. (2017). Collaborative filtering: Techniques and applications. In *2017 International Conference on Communication, Control, Computing and Electronics Engineering (ICCCCEE)* (pp. 1–6). IEEE.
17. N.A. (n.d.). Introduction to recommender systems. Things Solver. Retrieved from: Introduction to recommender systems – Things Solver. (thingsolver.com), 24th January 2024.
18. Patel, A., Thakkar, A., Bhatt, N., & Prajapati, P. (2019). Survey and evolution study focusing comparative analysis and future research direction in the field of recommendation system specific to collaborative filtering approach. In *Information and Communication Technology for Intelligent Systems: Proceedings of ICTIS 2018, Volume 1* (pp. 155–163). Springer Singapore.
19. Pine, B. J., Victor, B., & Boynton, A. C. (1993). Making mass customization work. *Harvard Business Review, 71*(5), 108–11.
20. Ricci, F., Rokach, L., & Shapira, B. (2015). Recommender systems: introduction and challenges. *Recommender Systems Handbook,* 1–34. Springer, Boston, MA. https://doi.org/10.1007/978-1-4899-7637-6_1.
21. Schafer, J. B., Konstan, J. A., & Riedl, J. (2001). E-commerce recommendation applications. *Data Mining and Knowledge Discovery, 5*, 115–153.
22. Schafer, J. B., Konstan, J., & Riedl, J. (1999). Recommender systems in e-commerce. In *Proceedings of the 1st ACM Conference on Electronic Commerce* (pp. 158–166).
23. Sestino, A., & De Mauro, A. (2022). Leveraging artificial intelligence in business: Implications, applications and methods. *Technology Analysis & Strategic Management, 34*(1), 16–29.
24. Sharma, M., Goel, A. K., & Singhal, P. (2023). Explainable AI Driven Applications for Patient Care and Treatment. In M. Mehta, V. Palade, & I. Chatterjee (Eds.), *Explainable AI: Foundations, Methodologies and Applications* (Intelligent Systems Reference Library, Vol. 232). Springer, Cham. https://doi.org/10.1007/978-3-031-12807-3_7
25. Sharma, M., Sharma, V., & Kapoor, R. (2022). Study of E-Commerce and Impact of Machine Learning in E-Commerce. https://doi.org/10.4018/978-1-6684-4969-1.ch001 (accessed on 27 May 2024).
26. Sivapalan, S., Sadeghian, A., Rahnama, H., & Madni, A. M. (2014). Recommender systems in e-commerce. In *2014 World Automation Congress (WAC)* (pp. 179–184). IEEE.
27. Sridevi, M., Rao, R. R., & Rao, M. V. (2016). A survey on recommender system. *International Journal of Computer Science and Information Security, 14*(5), 265.
28. Su, X., & Khoshgoftaar, T. M. (2009). A survey of collaborative filtering techniques. *Advances in Artificial Intelligence,* Wiley Online Library, *2009*(1), 421–425.
29. Thorat, P. B., Goudar, R. M., & Barve, S. (2015). Survey on collaborative filtering, content-based filtering and hybrid recommendation system. *International Journal of Computer Applications, 110*(4), 31–36.
30. Vlachos, M., Vassiliadis, V. G., Heckel, R., & Labbi, A. (2016). Toward interpretable predictive models in B2B recommender systems. *IBM Journal of Research and Development, 60*(5/6), 11–1.

31. Walch, K. (n.d.). The Twenty Year History of AI at Amazon. *Forbes*. Retrieved from: https://www.forbes.com/sites/cognitiveworld/2019/07/19/the-twenty-year-history-of-ai-at-amazon/?sh=7f438b9568d0 (accessed on 27 May 2024).
32. Yanxiang, L., Deke, G., Fei, C., & Honghui, C. (2013). User-based clustering with top-n recommendation on cold-start problem. In *2013 Third International Conference on Intelligent System Design and Engineering Applications* (pp. 1585–1589). IEEE.
33. Yasar, K. (n.d.). What is Amazon? *TechTarget*. TechTarget. https://www.techtarget.com/whatis/definition/Amazon (accessed 30th January 2023).

CHAPTER 15

Trends and Future of AI in Sales and Marketing

MEENAKSHI SHARMA,[1] HINIKA SHAIL,[1] A. V. SENTHIL KUMAR,[2] and PRAMOD PAINULY[1]

[1]*UPES, Dehradun, Uttarakhand, India*

[2]*Director & Professor, Hindustan College of Arts and Science, Coimbatore, Tamil Nadu, India*

ABSTRACT

Artificial intelligence (AI) in recent years has developed the ability for machines to learn based on the data obtained, the potential to create previously unexciting information, the processing of various data types like numerical data, artificial intelligence processes texts, images, and sounds, and the advantages and benefits of the marketing as the main beneficiary of information technology. Businesses using AI in the marketing sector have expanded significantly over the past few years. This study is an attempt to study the current and future trends of AI in the Field of Sales and Marketing. Modern marketing experts are aware of the need to have a thorough understanding of their target market. Using a variety of data sources, today's AI systems enable marketers and organizations to provide rich consumer insights that may strengthen customer relationships, foster genuine interaction, and increase conversion rates. The study opens horizons for researchers to explore and do further research in this arena. Marketers will be able to automate some cognitive processes with AI-powered solutions. Additionally, they will be able to recognize present trends and forecast them for the future, which will help secure the success of their marketing operations.

Artificial Intelligence and Machine Learning for Business. Namita Mishra, A. V. Senthil Kumar (Eds.)

15.1 INTRODUCTION

In the last two decades, a lot has changed in terms of adopting customer-focused marketing tactics and bringing in technologies, moving from traditional marketing to the current era of digital marketing. The process by which industries look to market has also been sped by technical developments made possible by AI.

Engineers, IT professionals, and analysts have previously been interested in AI, but it is now expanding beyond its conventional [1]. Because AI is dependent on data analysis in nearly all its applications, the ever-increasing amount of consumer data available online, in big data platforms, or on mobile devices makes it a crucial ally of marketing [1]. From traditional marketing to the current age of digital marketing, a lot has changed in the last two decades in terms of adopting customer-focused marketing strategies and bringing in technologies. In addition, technological advancements with the help of AI have further accelerated the process of how industries are looking to market.

Artificial intelligence (AI) seems likely to have an impact on marketing tactics, as well as business structures, sales procedures, and customer service alternatives. Businesses using AI in the marketing sector have expanded significantly over the past few years and are anticipated to reach $48.8 billion by 2030. Furthermore, sales leaders anticipate that their adoption of AI will expand more quickly than that of any other technology, according to a Salesforce State of Sales survey. Salesforce also discovered that teams with high performance are 4.9X more likely to be employing AI than teams with low performance [2]. Consumer behavior is changing due to technological advancements, which are also influencing corporate strategy, particularly in marketing. As a result, AI in marketing has permeated the realm of competition. The potential of artificial intelligence in the sphere of sales and marketing must therefore be emphasized. The role of AI in sales and marketing, present trends, advantages, drawbacks, and future applications are just a few of the sections that make up this chapter.

15.2 OVERVIEW OF ARTIFICIAL INTELLIGENCE

Information technology is the ancestor of artificial intelligence [1]. It frequently appears in the same sentence as ideas like automation or robotization. Additionally, it frequently gets mixed up with algorithm applications or machine learning. The Oxford Dictionary defines artificial intelligence (AI) as "the theory and development of computer systems able to do tasks typically requiring human intelligence, such as visual perception, speech recognition, decision-making, and language translation."

AI has advanced beyond the level of following a set of predefined rules thanks to machine learning (ML). As a result, the employment of algorithms in AI has evolved because of ML. By creating connections between various data points, ML has made it possible for computers to learn on their own based on the information that is already accessible.

As it is built on learning algorithms that do not require manual management, deep learning (DL) is a more advanced form of machine learning. By utilizing massive data and computational resources (such as server farms, CPUs, and cloud computing), DL enables the instantaneous decoding and provision of the outcome for a new piece of information.

One of the uses of ML and DL for speech recognition is natural language processing (NLP). Large amounts of data (text samples) that serve as sources of the context, the vocabulary, the grammar, and the semantic meaning have been available thanks to years of research in this field.

The development of AI in the fields of voice, text, and picture recognition, decision-making, and autonomous robotics and vehicles has been made possible by advancements made in those technologies. Each of these areas has a use in the real world. For example, mobile phones provide voice recognition (e.g., Siri, Google Assistant). Text recognition tools are used as virtual assistants that offer quick responses (e.g., Deakin University and IBM Watson).

By comparing the user's face with a picture, the system can authorize payments using image recognition (e.g., food chain KFC). The IBM Elements decision-making system is specifically designed for educators to help them assess students and provide personalized development paths for each student. Lastly, autonomous robots and vehicles are utilized to manage inventory in warehouses (e.g., in Amazon's Kiva system).

15.3 CURRENT TRENDS IN AI IN THE FIELD OF SALES AND MARKETING

The dynamics of the corporate world have changed because of technological advancements, which have also sped up globalization and heightened rivalry on a worldwide scale. The businesses' entry point into and penetration of new markets was this occurrence. The contemporary, highly competitive, global company climate constantly calls for innovation; the body of existing knowledge is becoming less and less useful; as a result, process improvement is thriving and new models for marketing activities are being sought.

Artificial intelligence (AI) in recent years has developed the ability for machines to learn based on the data obtained, the potential to create previously unexciting information, the processing of various data types like numerical data, artificial intelligence processes texts, images, and sounds, and the advantages and benefits of the marketing as the main beneficiary of information technology developments. They support marketing professionals with a variety of tasks, including lead generation, social media management, market analysis, and customer experience customization.

Some current trends that AI is using in marketing and sales are as follows [3]:

1. **Automated Digital Communication:** Voice assistants have been introduced by most technology-based businesses in recent years across a variety of platforms, including websites, mobile apps, and customer care portals. Chatbots and AI assistants engage customers without the need for human interaction by recognizing your desire to connect and tracking your online and device activity.

   By providing prompt advice, the AI assistants assist the user in finding exactly what they are seeking and stop them from leaving the website. Drift and Convers Ica are two platforms that are now being utilized for customer engagements, both of which leverage AI to help with real conversions.

2. **Voice and Visual Search:** A user's search experience, which is frequently undervalued, can have a favorable or bad impact on a business and its website, depending on whether they are able to do so or not. In both voice and visual formats, cognitive search—also known as AI-powered search—plays a significant part in this.

   The goal is to swiftly return pertinent contextual results even if a user types a query incorrectly or incorrectly. On their applications and websites, brands have begun to include voice and picture search capabilities.

   Image recognition technology is widely used by well-known internet businesses like Google, Pinterest, eBay, and others to identify items.

3. **Predictive Analytics and Forecasting:** Another crucial area where artificial intelligence will have an impact on the future of the marketing sector is predictive analytics. By empowering marketers to study and predict future consumer behavior, businesses can create efficient solutions, products, and strategies that work to their advantage.

   For instance, integrating AI into an online course can assist the company in better understanding student behavior and using that knowledge to enhance student engagement. Discovering data insights and predictions, as well as combining all the data to enhance processes and produce effective results, will be the key uses of AI in predictive analytics.

   Some of the AI tools in predictive analytics are Crayon for tracking and data analysis, Google Cloud AI for data labeling, data science, and predictions, and Pattern89 for predictive AI marketing on Google Ads, Facebook, etc.

4. **Personalized Dynamic Advertising:** The marketing sector has been completely taken over by digital advertising, and AI has so far had a significant impact. Marketers are focusing their efforts on fewer, more specialized groups rather than a larger audience, and these groups will continue to grow as a result of AI-powered marketing procedures.

   Because AI marketing divides consumers into several groups based on their online activities and behavior, brands can only focus on those who are appropriate for their business. Additionally, brands gain more revenue and quality leads, while also increasing the effectiveness of their advertising initiatives.

   Leading companies like Meta, Google, LinkedIn, and Apple are already developing hyper-targeted adverts, and as the volume of data increases, so does the potency of their AI algorithms.

5. **AI-Powered Content Marketing:** Users are receiving more recommendations for the same type of content because AI algorithms being more adept at identifying the type of content they are consuming. One of the prevalent examples that adheres to this essential idea is social media.

AI is increasingly employed not only for content delivery but also for content production. Bramework, AI content for blog creation, Cortex for digital content optimization on social media platforms, and Atomic Reach for content editing are a few examples of AI tools used in content marketing.

15.4 IMPACT OF AI ON MARKETING

In their 2019 study "Marketing and Artificial Intelligence," Jarek and Mazurek separate the effects of AI on marketing operations from three angles: 1) The effects of AI on marketing, 2) How AI affects consumers, and 3) How AI affects marketing management. First, research results show how AI has an impact on the marketing mix. The dual impact on marketing was emphasized, with "new solutions affecting the entirety of sought marketing efforts" and "beneficiary of changes in the consumer." Second, the study identifies new consumer experiences through mass-scale hyper-personalization and a new dimension of consumer-brand interaction as benefits of AI for consumers. Thirdly, and finally, the research emphasizes the impact of AI on removing time-consuming and arduous tasks, creative and strategic activities, design innovations, developing staff competencies, and creating a new ecosystem.

CRM, or customer relationship management, is a crucial component of marketing that AI may enhance. Based on the findings of data mining and profiling, deep learning techniques can optimize the work assignment and schedule of service providers for better service. Furthermore, by integrating corporate cognitive computing into their offerings, enterprises can automate the more time-consuming and complex operations to save time and boost productivity. AI is frequently used in advertising and marketing to learn more about consumers, target them more precisely, and tailor the messaging to them.

The current crop of AI marketing tools is focused on assisting the transition to a more digital environment, including CRM, layer connections, customization, automation, and augmentation of marketing operations and profiling. Tools for deep learning and labeling allow for precise and effective customer and environmental profiling. Independent machines and robots might be considered future developments in the field of artificial intelligence (AI), particularly in marketing activities like intense customer connection, networking with diverse players, customizations, and personalization.

Applications of AI are used in every aspect of marketing (marketing mix and marketing communication). As technology advances, machines will become increasingly autonomous. This implies that there will be more information available and more efficient and quick ways to engage with clients. The adoption of AI enhances marketing managers' efficiency, performance, and overall marketing strategy.

15.5 ROLE OF AI IN SALES

Artificial intelligence and sales enable profit-driven firms to digest mountains of eye-opening data more quickly and use that data to learn more about client behavior and purchasing patterns [4]. Additionally, it means reduced reliance on human staff, which can be challenging to keep in a tight labor market.

In sales, AI plays the role of using data analysis algorithms to undertake cognitive tasks that take too long or require too much data for individuals to manage independently. It makes sense to hand off part of the analytical thinking to software because computers are experts at identifying patterns concealed in massive amounts of data.

Using artificial intelligence, your preferred voice assistant, such as Alexa or Siri, can comprehend what you say just like a human would, and then react appropriately. By assuming your interests, just like a fellow product or movie enthusiast might, Amazon and Netflix's AI recommendation engines provide you with things and movies you might enjoy.

Large datasets are analyzed by these technologies. However, they do more than merely compute numbers. To glean insights from data, they employ cutting-edge computational methods and powerful computing capacity. Then, forecasts, advice, and choices can be made using these revelations. The most astounding sales capabilities are powered by "machine learning," a sort of AI.

Machine learning is a subset of AI that finds patterns in massive data sets. These patterns are used by the algorithm to anticipate outcomes. Then, over time, it makes these predictions better by using more and more data. Machine learning-based technology improves over time, frequently without human intervention.

Your accounting software is an example of a typical non-AI system that depends on human inputs to function [5]. People have hard-coded rules in the system. Then, it precisely follows those guidelines to assist you in filing your taxes. The system can only be made better by human programmers. However, machine learning software can get better on its own. This enhancement results from a machine analyzing fresh data and its performance. For instance, there is a marketing AI solution that can create your email subject lines. Machine learning for the tool is trained by humans using examples of marketing material from various companies. The tool then creates its email subject lines, though.

15.6 BENEFITS OF AI IN MARKETING AND SALES

While AI will continue to create a huge impact in the world of technology, here are some known benefits of AI marketing and sales [3]:

- Using past data to analyze user behavior and make predictions for marketing campaigns.
- Using sentiment analysis to observe a brand's image and user needs.
- Uncovering trends using big data analysis to optimize strategies and ad campaigns.
- Automating repetitive mechanical tasks such as scheduling emails, meetings, and social media postings.
- Improving the user experience on the website and other marketing platforms.

Moreover, Sales are facilitated by AI without the need for a human salesman to be replaced. It improves the sales team's overall effectiveness by delivering curated data and mechanization tools [9].

Some more benefits of AI in sales and marketing:

1. **Building Better Customer Retention Strategies:** AI will assist businesses in retaining consumers by identifying the customers who are most likely to leave at any given time. It can foretell a customer's propensity to leave before they express their dissatisfaction, enabling you to act before it's too late.

   AI and machine learning enable the mass production of customized offers, promotions, and experiences. Personalization occurs when Netflix uses data to analyze your interests and provide highly tailored content recommendations. The usage of AI to tailor the consumer experience will increase as more businesses use it.

2. **Greater Personalization:** The Netflix recommendation engine has been previously mentioned. Personalization is crucial in this situation and marketing in general. Consider whether Netflix would still

be there today if its recommendation engine were inaccurate. Only AI has the speed and ability to gather detailed data necessary to produce recommendations and content that are specific to each user navigating a website or app.

3. **Access to Real-Time Analytics and Insights:** Access to real-time statistics and insights is one of the most beneficial features of artificial intelligence for marketing. AI gives marketers the ability to mine customer data in real time and identify trends that might not be obvious otherwise. These enable you to see daily interactions between your content and your audience. AI may provide useful insights into how customers are interacting with your business, how they progress through your sales funnel, and what influences their purchasing decisions by processing a wealth of customer data from numerous sources. This enables you to decide on promotions, content, and goods that are most likely to appeal to buyers.

4. **Increases Leads:** It utilizes the chance to meet with all the information. To establish and sustain a business relationship, it also needs time to review leads and follow up with them. The algorithms take over these duties and provide speedy results when you utilize AI for sales. Because AI enables them to pursue specific and targeted leads, leads grow as a result.

   In a McKinsey study that was published in the Harvard Business Review, sales teams that have adopted AI have seen an increase in leads and engagements of about 50%. The time-consuming tasks of connecting with leads, confirming them, following up with them, and maintaining the connection in those organizations have reportedly been replaced by AI, claims the study.

5. **Improves Forecasting Accuracy:** The challenge of forecasting quarterly sales figures is one that sales managers routinely encounter. It has an impact on hiring, payroll, and all elements of performance.

   Additionally, a single inaccurate estimate could damage a company's reputation. AI helps sales managers predict revenue for the upcoming quarter more precisely. This makes it possible for the sales staff to better plan for upcoming problems.

6. **Builds Customer Involvement:** Consumer dedication and loyalty are the foundation of a successful company. The foundation of client interactions is built on these two qualities. In the lack of backup

information, sales professionals find it challenging to maintain customers' interest.

One application of artificial intelligence in sales is chatbots. The chatbots that you would encounter on a company's website should be familiar to you. AI at work, guiding a potential customer to the sales funnel.

15.7 LIMITATIONS OF AI IN SALES AND MARKETING

Artificial intelligence can have a transformative effect on marketing, making campaigns more personalized, productive, and predictive [6]. But the technology comes with very real disadvantages and limitations such as:

1. **Lack of Common Sense:** Emotional intelligence can be applied to text analysis, voice analysis, picture identification (e.g., recognizing happiness in a face or identifying indications of deception in facial expressions), and voice analysis (e.g., detecting dissatisfaction in an online review). We are a long way from a day when AI will be able to feel emotions, even though it can be taught to recognize and even simulate them.

   An AI program may discover on its own that there are statistical correlations between the terms "king" and "crown," and it may be able to exploit these correlations to auto-generate sentences that appear to make sense to a human, but which the AI program is unaware of the true meaning of. In a similar vein, an autonomous vehicle may be programmed to avoid pedestrians at all costs, but it wouldn't recognize the inherent worth of human life.

2. **Objective Functions:** An objective function defines the collection of rewards (or penalties) that the AI system will attempt to maximize (or minimize) over time in reinforcement learning.

   In marketing, researchers and managers frequently develop goals that take into account utility maximization, product cannibalization, profit and market share maximization, and product cannibalization. The definition of a holistic objective function has paramount significance because an AI algorithm is not constrained by common sense and is not constrained by a preset set of features or model specifications to operate from.

Applications of AI do not even have the issue of poorly stated objective functions. For instance, in response to the sponsor organization's first request, Natter created a decision-support system for pricing and promotion that aimed to maximize profit. "Emotional discussions with merchandising managers" arose when it became clear that the approach frequently increased earnings at the expense of sales quantities.

3. **Safe and Realistic Learning Environment:** Another barrier to the quick adoption of reinforcement learning in marketing is our inability to precisely describe and quantify a broad range of firm's objectives. Through hundreds, if not millions, of trials and errors while balancing exploration and exploitation, an AI agent will learn to map the function f (S, A) R. A computer simulation can nevertheless offer a suitable learning environment if the world is more complicated and realistic but still abides by a limited number of clearly established regulations.

   It is alluring to think that artificial intelligence has diminished our need to comprehend the connections between inputs and outputs. With neither prior knowledge nor in-depth knowledge of the phenomenon being studied, a deep learning model can approximate any causal link given a sizable enough dataset and a potent enough deep learning algorithm.

   To put it another way, applications of AI, particularly those involving reinforcement learning, may help rather than hinder the need for comprehensive consumer behavior theory.

4. **Biased Artificial Intelligence:** Even in the case of unsupervised learning, there is a risk of biased predictions. The likelihood of a disgruntled customer leaving the company increases further if management decides to cut its losses and direct marketing investments and loyalty program efforts toward more promising customers in response to a model that predicts the customer will likely leave the company after a service incident.

   Endogeneity problems in marketing environments are certain to arise in the form of data, predictions, decisions, and data. It is an established phenomenon that is not unique to the application of AI. But for two reasons, AI-based solutions are probably going to make this issue worse. First, AI-based predictive models, more notably deep-learning neural networks, have demonstrated their greater capacity to uncover hidden patterns in data, increasing the likelihood that biases and endogeneities would be detected by the model. Second, because of these models' high level of complexity, many managers have already made the decision to take their projections at face value, turning them into "black boxes."

5. **Explainable Artificial Intelligence:** The topic of explainable and interpretable AI is expanding within the AI community in terms of both scope and strategic significance, notably in the social sciences. It refers to AI methodologies and processes where the outcomes (such as forecasts, classifications, and action suggestions) can be understood by professionals on the human side. It entails clarifying (1) the system's purpose, (2) the data sources employed, and (3) how the inputs correspond to the model's outputs. The idea of "intellectual debt" and explainable AI are intertwined concepts.

15.8 FUTURE TRENDS AND SCOPES OF AI IN SALES AND MARKETING

Artificial intelligence is fast revolutionizing the marketing business, not just in terms of product advancements but also in terms of trends across many marketing sectors. The capability of machine learning opens new avenues for experimentation and advancement in the field of marketing. But that's not the case.

The information analysis, data collection, and understanding of the niche-specific requirements from social interactions, campaigns, and engagements will be considerably aided by these AI marketing trends. As time goes by, marketing AI will become more effective and reliable at curating precise personalization and forecasts, something that was previously out of reach for enterprises.

Additionally, machine learning (ML) and artificial intelligence (AI) have the potential to completely change the way that businesses conduct sales because they give businesses the ability to create adaptive, strategic sales processes that can be customized to improve each customer's purchasing experience.

Even at this early stage of development, AI has already demonstrated its value in assisting businesses in increasing productivity and profitability. However, just a small fraction of businesses possess AI solutions, and even fewer employ them on a daily basis. AI is expected to contribute $15.7 trillion to the global economy by 2030, thanks to its enormous potential.

15.8.1 SCOPES OF AI IN SALES AND MARKETING

1. **Helps in managing customer relationships by forecasting and data analytics:** In the modern business world, customer journeys are complicated. Throughout the shopping procedure, noises are continuously around them [7].

   With artificial intelligence, users' experiences could be tailored through predictive or anticipatory marketing. Artificial intelligence makes very certain predictions and recognizes the data pattern. Enterprises can share customized services, offers, and other facilities by leveraging customer data analytics.

   Additionally, businesses can use AI to pinpoint the ideal client, increasing their marketing efficiency in a cutthroat industry. They can recognize the upmarket activities and strengthen account-based strategies.

2. **AI provides optimized customer engagement processes:** The correct offer, as well as the right product and the right information, can all be delivered to the right prospect at the right time thanks to AI-optimized customer engagement processes. AI makes use of and manages the complicated calculations involved in permutation optimization.

   - By comprehending user behavior, businesses may make precise product recommendations.
   - A user can quickly get all the information via an AI-based chatbot, depending on their needs.

3. **Reducing the gap between sales and marketing:** Since sales and marketing work toward the same objective of business growth, but employ different strategies to get there, these differences can result in disputes and wasted effort.

   AI promotes marketing and sales cooperation by determining the appropriate buyer persona. Marketing can easily create personalized collateral that draws in and engages clients who truly fit the persona with the correct buyer persona in place. This encourages businesses to concentrate more on innovative business practices and decision-making areas.

4. **AI with its automation feature explores new opportunities:** Process optimization is one of a company's most important characteristics. Process improvement is carried out to improve responsiveness, which would improve market circumstances and demand.

   AI solutions in marketing assist in automating manual tasks including conducting research, establishing process-based processes, having discussions, and updating CRM. AI will handle the laborious work, freeing up marketing to concentrate on other crucial duties.

   Automation and data analytics enable businesses to increase customer satisfaction by providing accurate and individualized services and goods.

5. **AI enhances customer experiences:** The marketing industry is moving toward a more personalized and customer-focused approach. A key strategy for the company or its product is customer interaction. However, integrating customer experience is efficient with AI due to its real-time adaptation.

   By allowing customers to switch between channels, powerful AI software enables marketing by raising knowledge of the context and results of customer contact.

15.9 CONCLUSION

One of the business operations sectors where artificial intelligence (AI) is commonly expected to create significant change is marketing and sales [8–17]. According to a McKinsey study, marketing is the one corporate function that will have the biggest financial impact, along with sales. In other words, if you're a marketer and you're not using AI, you're missing out on what may be the most transformative technology's advantages.

As we previously discussed, artificial intelligence (AI) will have a big impact on the sales process. It will also alter the job of customer support as many tasks currently performed by people will be handled by AI voice. The client will be given even more power by AI than they already have. Customers will be able to progress through the purchasing process much further before they need to connect with a human when AI is completely integrated with websites. There won't be any human interaction for a lot of transactions. Additionally, AI will improve the predictability of inside sales by enabling the salesperson to handle more difficult deals in a timely manner. The salesperson will now be able to conduct sales planning sessions using AI rather than having to engage their sales manager.

Modern marketing experts are aware of the need to have a thorough understanding of their target market. Using a variety of data sources, today's AI systems enable marketers and organizations to provide rich consumer insights that may strengthen customer relationships, foster genuine interaction, and increase conversion rates.

AI may give advertisers more insight into the wants, habits, and journeys of their customers. Even forecasting various actions and buying motivations may benefit from it.

It is crucial for a company to help people who are already specialists in their industry to upskill and comprehend the significance of the technology as it continues to establish a data- and AI-literate culture. Marketing staff will be able to automate some cognitive processes with AI-powered solutions. Additionally, they will be able to recognize present trends and forecast them for the future, which will help secure the success of their marketing operations.

KEYWORDS

- **artificial intelligence**
- **automation**
- **conversion rates**
- **customer relationships**
- **data analytics**
- **marketing operations**

REFERENCES

1. Jarek, K., & Mazurek, G. (2019). Marketing and Artificial Intelligence. *Central European Business Review, 8*(2), 46–55. doi:10.18267/j.cebr.213
2. Peyravi, B., Nekrošienė, J., & Lobanova, L. (2020). Revolutionised technologies for marketing: theoretical review with focus on artificial intelligence. *Business: Theory and Practice, 21*(2), 827–834. https://doi.org/10.3846/btp.2020.12313

3. Newstex Trade & Industry Blogs. (2022). What is AI in Marketing: Growing Trends in Coming Years. Retrieved from https://adrants.com/2022/09/what-is-ai-in-marketing-growing-trends.php (accessed on 27 May 2024).
4. Zendesk. (2021). The Role of AI and Machine Learning in Sales in 2022. Retrieved from https://www.zendesk.com/in/sell/features/ai-for-sales/ (accessed on 27 May 2024).
5. Kaput, M. (2022). AI for Sales: What You Need to Know. *Marketing AI Institute*. Retrieved from https://www.marketingaiinstitute.com/blog/ai-in-sales (accessed on 27 May 2024).
6. De Bruyn, A. (2020). Artificial Intelligence and Marketing: Pitfalls and Opportunities. *ScienceDirect*. Retrieved from https://www.sciencedirect.com/science/article/abs/pii/S1094996820300888 (accessed on 27 May 2024).
7. Loveonn. (2020). The scope of Artificial Intelligence in Marketing. Retrieved from https://www.loveonn.com/single-post/2020/07/30/the-scope-of-artificial-intelligence-in-marketing (accessed on 27 May 2024).
8. Marr, B. (2022). Artificial Intelligence And The Future Of Marketing. *Forbes*. Retrieved from https://www.forbes.com/sites/bernardmarr/2022/09/09/artificial-intelligence-and-the-future-of-marketing/?sh=412dd9c3697f (accessed on 27 May 2024).
9. Helfrich, T. (2021). Why Artificial Intelligence Can't be Trusted. The AI Journal. Retrieved from https://aijourn.com/why-artificial-intelligence-cant-be-trusted/.
10. Kopalle, P. K., Gangwar, M., Kaplan, A., Ramachandran, D., Reinartz, W., & Rindfleisch, A. (2022). Examining artificial intelligence (AI) technologies in marketing via a global lens: Current trends and future research opportunities. *International Journal of Research in Marketing, 39*(2), 522–540.
11. Koldyshev, M. V. (2020). Future marketing in B2B segment: Integrating artificial intelligence into sales management. *International Journal of Innovative Technologies in Economy*, 4(31). https://doi.org/10.31435/rsglobal_ijite/30092020/7149 (accessed on 27 May 2024).
12. Davenport, T., Guha, A., Grewal, D., Bressgott, T. (2020). How artificial intelligence will change the future of marketing. *Journal of the Academy of Marketing Science, 48*, 24–42. https://doi.org/10.1007/s11747-019-00696-0
13. Yang, Y., & Siau, K. L. (2018). A Qualitative Research on Marketing and Sales in the Artificial Intelligence Age. In *MWAIS 2018 Proceedings* (p. 41). Retrieved from http://aisel.aisnet.org/mwais2018/41 (accessed on 27 May 2024).
14. Peyravi, B., Nekrošienė, J., & Lobanova, L. (2020). Revolutionised Technologies for Marketing: Theoretical Review with Focus On Artificial Intelligence. *Verslas: Teorija ir praktika / Business: Theory and Practice. 21*(2), 827–834. ISSN: 1648-0627/. eISSN: 1822-42022020. https://doi.org/10.3846/btp.2020.12313.
15. Davenport, T., Guha, A., Grewal, D., & Bressgott, T. (2019). How artificial intelligence will change the future of marketing. Retrieved from How artificial intelligence will change the future of marketing. SpringerLink. *J. Acad. Mark. Sci. 48*, 24–42 https://doi.org/10.1007/s11747-019-00696-0D.
16. Siau, K. (2018). A Qualitative Research on Marketing and Sales in the Artificial Intelligence Age. Retrieved from https://www.researchgate.net/publication/325934359_A_Qualitative_Research_on_Marketing_and_Sales_in_the_Artificial_Intelligence (accessed on 27 May 2024).
17. Salesforce. (2021). The Role of AI in Marketing. Retrieved from https://www.salesforce.com/ap/resources/guides/role-of-ai-in-marketing/ (accessed on 27 May 2024).

CHAPTER 16

Predicting People's Personalities From Their CVs, Using Machine Learning and Deep Learning

UMRAH DAR[1] and MAHUYA DEB[2]

[1]*Department of Advanced Computing, St. Joseph's University, Bangalore, Karnataka, India*

[2]*Assistant Professor, Department of Commerce, Gauhati University, Assam, India*

ABSTRACT

Advanced research over the recent years has established that the personality of an individual plays a pivotal role in all domains of their life, guiding their daily life processes as well as critical decision-making. The significance of personality, particularly in the employment domain, has been attaining traction with companies trying to recruit people with one-of-a-kind personalities for improved work performance and added profits. For accurate personality recognition, researchers are trying to develop and experiment with computational methods that might effectively predict people's personalities. Several machine learning tools have been used for this purpose with analysis being carried out on the digital footprints of different users, including their smartphone, social media, and email data. Analysis of the CV data of various employment-seeking individuals using machine learning models has provided suggestive results. However, there is still scope for advancement as some stark limitations are present in the studies, such as personality recognition being treated as a binary problem resulting in highly polarized outcomes and inaccurate descriptions of the models' performance. This study

Artificial Intelligence and Machine Learning for Business. Namita Mishra, A. V. Senthil Kumar (Eds.)

makes use of various machine learning models such as Logistic Regression, SVMs, kNN, and Naive Bayes, and explores the possibility of diving into deep learning for personality recognition from CV data to obtain improved accuracies. The deep learning models used in this study handily outperform the machine learning models, although the need for larger amounts of data is highlighted significantly.

16.1 INTRODUCTION

Personality is defined as "the various aspects of a person's character that combine to make them different from other people" [1]. Personality encompasses moods, stances, and convictions, and is plainly expressed in people's interactions with other people. Several behavioral attributes, which might be inherent to an individual or acquired, are included in their personality. These attributes differentiate individuals from one another, and they can be observed in how people interact with their environment and social groups [2]. Various studies and research point to how the personality of an individual plays a significant role in their daily life processes [3] and their critical decision-making [4]. Results have shown how various personality attributes of individuals can suggestively impact their day-to-day emotional processes, such as average level, variability, subjective evaluation of everyday experiences, and reactivity. It has also been observed that various personality traits have a significant impact on people's decision-making abilities. Higher extroversion has been linked with a lower rational decision-making style while a higher level of agreeableness and conscientiousness is correlated with a higher rational decision-making style. It has also been observed that individuals who are more extroverted and open to experience have a higher intuitive style. Studies have also argued about the close relationship between personality traits and individuals' decision-making styles and how an individual's emotional intelligence is a mediating factor between personality attributes and decision-making styles. Several researchers also emphasize the effects of the personality of an individual on their job prospects and performance. Arguments for how organizations can make use of one-of-a-kind personalities for an added effectual work performance to increase their profits have also been made. Studies also indicate that although the use of individuals with specific personality traits can prove beneficial to an employer, this area of research is developing as a novel, complex, and important field to scientists as well as companies [5].

Over the recent years, various empirical studies have tried to analyze the relationship between the personality of an individual and how it might potentially affect their chances of employment. These studies have sought to analyze an individual's personality traits and how they might play a significant role in determining whether a person possessing specific personality traits is fit for a particular employment role or not. Some of these studies have made use of machine learning to analyze people's personalities, while deep learning models have been left relatively untouched for the said analyses. While the use of machine learning has provided significant accuracy in determining the personality of individuals from their CV data, better results and accuracy can still be achieved by exploring various Deep Learning models. By comparing the relative accuracies of the previously used machine learning models in various studies, the best one can be identified.

This study aims to carry out a comparison between the performance of various machine learning models in the prediction of personalities from people's CVs and explore the possibility of using deep learning models to potentially achieve better prediction results and higher accuracy.

16.2 RELATED WORK

Multiple studies focusing on the analysis of personality traits and their effects on individuals have been performed. One such study attempted to deduce the personality of different users from the content present in their emails. This deduction was sought to be valuable in several applications such as personalized advertising, improved customization, and recommendations. Because of the sensitive nature of the information contained in people's emails, a privacy-preserving approach was put forward for the collection of this email and personality data. The Big Five Personality Model was used to frame the personality prediction, and the predictors were trained on the extracted features from the emails. The prediction performance of three generative models was reported, all containing different assumptions. The results obtained showed personality prediction to be achievable, and the email feature set used proved to predict personality with valid accuracies [6]. In another study, the Big Five Model of personality was used to predict people's personalities from their Facebook data. The implementation of some deep learning architectures was used in the study and they were compared with other machine learning models used in similar studies through the accuracy results obtained. An average accuracy of 74.17% was achieved, which outmatched similar research performed previously [7]. Another study probed the predictability of personality attributes of different Facebook users, determined from the several characteristics and measures of the Big 5 model. The "My Personality Project" dataset was used to inspect the occurrence of structures of social media and linguistic features in relevance to personality interactions. Four machine learning algorithms were analyzed and compared, and a correlation analysis was performed between each of the feature groups and personality traits. The various prediction accuracy results obtained pointed out that the XGBoost classifier outperforms the average baseline for all the feature groups, even if they're tested for the same dataset, achieving the highest prediction accuracy of 74.2%. The extraversion trait was able to achieve the best prediction performance with the use of individual social network analysis features set, with a prediction accuracy of 78.6% [8].

One study tried to address the problem of elevated labeling costs and privacy issues by using a large-scale dataset derived from Reddit, a very important source that is usually overlooked for personality prediction. The Myers-Briggs Type Indicator (MBTI) was used to label the dataset and included a vast set of features for more than nine thousand users. A preliminary feature analysis was performed, which exposed the marked dissimilarities between the MBTI dimensions and poles. The dataset was additionally used to train and test the standard personality prediction models, through which macro F1 scores ranging from 67% to 82% were obtained on individual dimensions. For one-off accurate type prediction, an 82% accuracy was achieved. These results attained are significant and analogous to the credibility of other structured tests [9]. Another study tries to address what is presently known about human and computer-based personality assessments, how accurate these assessments are, and how this area of research is progressing. The trends in present findings are evaluated, an overview of the methodological approaches is provided, and for future research, some recommendations are suggested. It is argued that the analysis of digital footprints with computer-based algorithms can potentially curtail the requirement for personality questionnaires, thus enabling assessments to be carried out with real-time behavioral data. This also sets into place a possibility of biased assessments by computer algorithms if all researchers use digital footprints to predict self-report data. Although there are some approaches available to bypass this problem, they are still very rare. As a result, using aggregate target and informant reports for the stipulation of more precise and realistic personality assessments is suggested as a future endeavor. It is also suggested that if new and improved methodologies are adopted by researchers for personality prediction, they could potentially serve a myriad of disciplines: criminal investigations, enlistments, health, etc. [10].

One study aimed to review several machine learning algorithms that have been extensively exploited for automated personality prediction. The study placed an added emphasis on deep learning methods. A synopsis was provided of the most preferred methodologies for automated personality prediction, commonly used computational datasets, their various industrial applications, and the most popularized machine learning models for personality prediction with significant emphasis on multimodal approaches. This survey explicitly focused on computational methods for personality prediction and not on psychological studies. From the results obtained, the CVPR First Impressions dataset [16] was found to be the most widely used multimodal dataset for personality prediction. Although there are many datasets available for the Big Five personality measure, other personality measures like MBTI, PEN, etc., were found to severely lack resources. The MBTI personality measure was found to be the most extensively used throughout the world. The MBTI traits were found to be more difficult and elaborate to predict than the Big Five traits; however, deep learning models were observed to achieve improved accuracy in this area as well. Using deep learning techniques in addition to multimodal fusion features, advanced personality prediction has been achieved. Bimodal fusion techniques were found to be very popular, and trimodal fusion for personality prediction was found to be an active research area for further exploration. With increased improvement in accuracies for personality predictions, the possibility of integrating automated personality prediction with human-machine interactions (voice assistants, cars, etc.) was found. Deep neural networks demonstrated the best performance in most modalities for personality prediction [17]. Another study tried to overcome the challenge of low accuracy for personality recognition because of the small sample size and an imbalanced sample distribution by analyzing the impact of imbalanced data distribution and positive and negative sample overlap on the machine learning classification algorithm. The classification model under consideration is based on the data resampling technique, which can enhance classification accuracy. A personality prediction method is proposed based on particle swarm optimization (PSO) and synthetic minority oversampling technique+Tomek Link (SMOTETomek) resampling (PSO-SMOTETomek). In addition to the effectual SMOTETomek resampling of data samples, it can implement PSO feature optimization for each set of feature combinations. A simulation is applied to validate the results obtained from the analysis, and the PSO-SMOTETomek appears to be effective for a small dataset. The accuracy of personality recognition also increases by about 10%. These results are significantly improved from results obtained in similar analyses. The average accuracies come out to be 75.34% and 78.78% for the plain text dataset and the non-plain text dataset, respectively. For the short text dataset and the long text dataset, the average accuracies obtained are 75.34% and 64.25%, respectively. The experimental results point out that a better classification effect is achieved by short text than by long text. It is also observed that for plain text data, a high personality discrimination accuracy may be present but related external data are absent. The presented model effectively aids the strategy and execution of a personality recognition system, and the said model substantially outperforms the prevalent models [12].

In a different study, sensor, and log data collected from the smartphones of several users were used to evaluate the extent to which the individuals' Big Five personality traits could be predicted depending on six different classes of behavioral information. A machine learning methodology was adopted to predict the personality of individuals at broad domain (r_{median}=0.37) and narrow facet levels (r_{median}=0.40). This was done by the behavioral information gathered from 624 volunteers over a period of 30 consecutive days (which amounted to 25,347,089 logging episodes). The cross-validated results show definite patterns in behaviors in areas of 1) communication and social behavior, 2) music consumption, 3) app usage, 4) mobility, 5) overall phone activity, and 6) day-and-night-time activity, which are all characteristically predictive of the Big Five personality traits. The accuracy results obtained appear to be similar to those of other predictions for digital footprints from several social media platforms. This substantiates the potential of obtaining data about people's private attributes from behavioral patterns, passively gathered from their smartphones. Altogether, the results demonstrate the benefits (research purposes) as well as the risks (privacy issues) associated with the large-scale collection and modeling of behavioral information gathered from smartphones [13].

A recent study predicts the personalities of individuals by extracting their digital content into features and mapping them onto a personality model. This study highlights the limitations of the existing algorithms used for this purpose, such as RNNs and LSTMs. Because of the sequential inputs, these algorithms take considerable time to train the model and they also suffer from the inability to capture the actual (semantic) meaning of words, resulting in a slight loss of context. To overcome these drawbacks, a new prediction method is proposed, which uses a multi-model deep learning architecture in combination with several pre-trained language models like BERT, RoBERTa, and XLNet as feature extraction methods based on various social media platforms. To make a decision, the system uses model averaging for predictions. The proposed model makes use of several social media data sources such as Facebook and Twitter, as opposed to previous works that use a single social media data with open and closed vocabulary extraction methods. A predictive model is produced for each trait with the use of a bidirectional context feature in combination with extraction methodology. This model gives promising results with a maximum accuracy of 86.2% and 0.912 F1 measure score for the Facebook dataset, and for the Twitter dataset, an accuracy of 88.5% with 0.882 F1 measure score [14]. Similarly, in another study, various machine learning methodologies are examined with the use of Natural Language Processing (NLP) techniques for the prediction of personalities from people's CVs. The Big Five Personality model is used to analyze which personality an individual fits in. The data for analysis is obtained from various websites hosting CV data as well as personal communications with potential employment seekers. To achieve the objective of predicting individuals' personalities based on their scores for various personality traits such as openness, extraversion, neuroticism, etc., an approach to parse the whole CV data and look for keywords relevant to the Big Five Test is adopted. After the data is incorporated into the models, Random Forest provides the best accuracy of about 0.71, followed by Bayes, kNN, SVM, and Logistic Regression. Random Forest is also observed to have the least mean squared error [15].

Although these studies have acquired important results, there are some glaring shortcomings such as the reduction of different personalities into a binary problem, good and bad, which can be very polarizing and not show how well a model or methodology performs while trying to predict what type of personality type an individual can be grouped into. Similarly, the effect of gender and age on the personality of individuals has also been neglected. Such shortcomings can be rectified, whilst also trying to improve upon the previous prediction accuracies.

16.3 METHODOLOGY

The goal of our paper is to use machine learning and deep learning to predict the personality of people based on their scores of openness, extroversion, agreeableness, neuroticism, and conscientiousness, the five main components of personality according to the OCEAN personality model.

A dataset of over 700 CVs was processed to derive the scores for each of the personality traits of each person. The relevant information such as skills, gender, and experience was extracted using a Python library used to parse résumés called pyresparser. The parsed data was then analyzed using a Python library used for Natural Language Processing (NLP) tasks, known as Natural Language Toolkit (NLTK), and a score on a scale of 1–10 was awarded to each trait for each CV based on the occurrence of OCEAN keywords and properties (Table 16.1).

TABLE 16.1 Keywords and Properties Associated with OCEAN Personality Traits

Openness	Extroversion	Agreeableness	Neuroticism	Conscientiousness
Imagination	Sociableness	Altruism	Awkwardness	Persistence
Insightfulness	Assertiveness	Trust	Pessimism	Ambition
Varied interests	Merriness	Modesty	Moodiness	Thoroughness
Originality	Outgoing nature	Humility	Jealousy	Self-discipline
Daringness	Energy	Patience	Oversensitivity	Consistency
Preference for variety	Social confidence	Moderation	Fear	Predictability
Cleverness	Ability to be articulate	Consideration	Nervousness	Control
Creativity	Fun-loving nature	Amiability	Anxiety	Reliability
Curiosity	Tendency for affection	Kindness	Timidness	Resourcefulness
Perceptiveness	Friendliness	Loyalty	Wariness	Hard work
Intellect	Talkativeness	Sensitivity	Self-criticism	Planning
Complexity/depth	–	Helpfulness	Insecurity	Perseverance

These scores were then used to categorize each person as having one of the five personalities according to the OCEAN model: serious, dependable, lively, extraverted, or responsible.

This final parsed dataset was split into two parts, one for training the machine learning and deep learning models (80%) and the rest for validating the results and checking the performance of the models.

Although a plethora of models are available that can be used for prediction purposes, we chose the following few for our study:

16.4 LOGISTIC REGRESSION

A statistical model is mainly used for classification and prediction problems. Given an independent dataset of variables, it estimates the probability of an event occurring. Since the result obtained is always in the form of a probability, the dependent variable ranges from 0–1. Logistic regression applies a logit transformation on the odds. The following formulas are used to represent the logistic function:

$$Logit(pi) = 1/(1 + exp(-pi))$$

$$ln(pi/(1 - pi)) = Beta\_0 + Beta\_1 * X\_1 + \ldots + B\_k * K\_k$$

Here, logit(pi) represents the dependent or the response variable, and x represents the independent or the predictor variable. Maximum Likelihood Estimation (MLE) is used to estimate the beta parameter or coefficient. Various estimates of beta are tested through multiple iterations to obtain an optimized fit of log odds. The log-likelihood function is produced through all the iterations and to obtain the best parameter estimate, logistic regression aims to maximize this function. When the best coefficient is found, the conditional probabilities are calculated for all the observations and they are logged and summed together to obtain a predicted probability value. In the case of binary classification, probabilities that are less than 0.5 will be predicted as 0 while probabilities greater than 0 will be predicted as 1. After the model is obtained, the goodness of fit can be used to evaluate how well the model predicts the dependent variable.

1. **Support Vector Machines (SVM):** It is a very popular supervised learning algorithm that finds use in classification and regression problems. The SVM algorithm aims to produce the best line or decision boundary to separate an n-dimensional space into various classes so that a new sample point can easily be placed in the correct class in the future. The decision boundary is also known as a hyperplane. SVM creates hyperplanes by making use of extreme points or vectors. These extreme points are the support vectors and the algorithm derives its name from them. There are two types of SVMs: Linear SVM and Non-linear SVM. For data that is linearly separable, i.e., data that can be segregated into two classes by a straight line, the classifier used is the Linear SVM classifier. Non-linear SVM is used for data that cannot be classified using a straight line. SVM works by maximizing the margin, i.e., the distance between the hyperplane and the vectors.

2. **Naïve Bayes:** It is a supervised learning algorithm that makes use of the Bayes Theorem to solve classification problems. It is extensively used in text classification problems that consist of a high-dimensional dataset for training. It is one of the easiest and most efficient algorithms to implement for constructing fast machine-learning models to make rapid predictions. Naïve Bayes makes predictions based on the probabilities of objects, making it a probabilistic classifier. Some

areas where this algorithm finds constant applications are spam filtration, sentiment analysis, and article classification.

3. **KNN:** It is a basic machine learning algorithm for supervised learning. KNN works by assuming similarity between new data and the already available data and places a new data point in a category that is most similar to the already available categories. It keeps a record of all the available data and when a new data point appears, it classifies it based on similarity. This algorithm finds use in classification as well as regression problems. Because KNN is a non-parametric algorithm, no assumptions for the underlying data are made. KNN does not learn immediately from the training data but instead stores the data and takes actions when the classification is performed; it is therefore also called a lazy learner algorithm.
4. **Long-Short Term Memory (LSTM):** It is a type of recurrent neural network, designed by Hochreiter & Schmidhuber. It overcomes the limitation of long-term dependencies of an RNN because of which it is unable to predict the word stored in its long-term memory and is only able to provide more precise predictions for recent data. An RNN performs very poorly as the gap length increases. LSTM can retain information for a longer period. LSTM finds use in processing, classifying, and predicting based on time-series data. LSTM is a chain-like structure comprising four neural networks and several memory blocks, known as cells. Information in an LSTM is stored by cells and memory manipulations are performed by gates. LSTM finds applications in language modeling, image captioning, machine translation, handwriting generation, etc.
5. **Stacked LSTM:** An extension of the standard LSTM model consists of several hidden LSTM layers with multiple memory cells present in each layer. A deeper model is obtained by stacking various LSTM layers together, thus being described as a deep learning technique. Stacked LSTMs were introduced by Graves et al. as an application for speech recognition. Stacked LSTMs are now proving to be a consistent technique for complex sequence prediction problems. The structure of a stacked LSTM comprises multiple LSTM layers, with an LSTM layer above providing the output as a sequence rather than a single value to the LSTM layer present below. Since LSTMs work on sequence data, the addition of more layers results in added

levels of abstraction of input observations over some time. A stacked LSTM possesses greater model complexity.

The methodology followed in the study has also been described in the flow diagram in Figure 16.1.

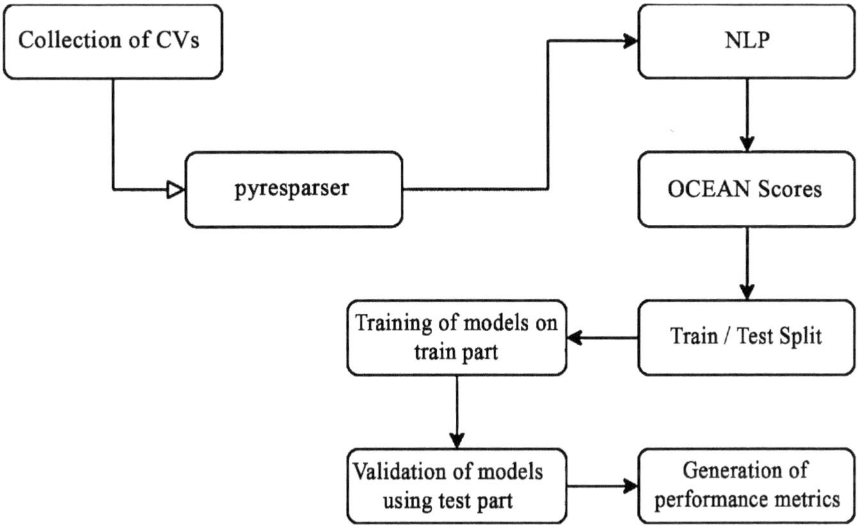

FIGURE 16.1 Methodology followed in the study.

16.5 RESULTS

The performance of the different machine learning and deep learning models was analyzed using a basic metric of accuracy as well as using confusion matrices, which provide a much more comprehensive look into the performance of the models.

The Naïve Bayes model was the best performer amongst the machine learning models with an accuracy of 64% using the Gaussian algorithm provided within the model, followed by SVM and kNN, which both acquired an accuracy of 62%, although SVM produced a higher number of false positives. However, the results acquired using logistic regression showed a drastic drop in accuracy to only a measly 42%, making the results quite unusable. This drop was further exaggerated upon using resolvers other than lbfgs, such as liblinear and newton-cg. The results of each of the models are described in Table 16.2 and their confusion matrices are in Table 16.3.

TABLE 16.2 Accuracy of Different Machine Learning Models in Predicting Personalities

Model	Accuracy
Naïve-Bayes model	64%
SVM	62%
kNN	62%
Logistic regression	42%

TABLE 16.3 Confusion Matrices for the Different Machine Learning Models Used

Model	Confusion Matrix
Naïve-Bayes model	[63 11 40 28]
SVM	[62 42 12 26]
kNN	[66 33 21 22]
Logistic regression	[43 46 36 17]

The deep learning models, on the other hand, completely outperformed the machine learning models, with the LSTM model achieving an accuracy of 73% using the Adam optimizer, ReLU activation algorithm, and a total of 42 epochs. This accuracy was further improved by stacking the LSTM models eight layers deep, reaching a value of 81%. The accuracy did not show any significant increase with further layer stacking, so we decided to stop at eight layers. Table 16.4 displays the accuracies of the LSTM and Stacked LSTM models, while Table 16.5 provides details of their confusion matrices.

TABLE 16.4 Accuracy Achieved Using Deep Learning Models

Model	Accuracy
LSTM	73%
Stacked LSTM	81%

TABLE 16.5 Confusion Matrices for the Deep Learning Models Used

Model	Confusion Matrix
LSTM	[74 16 22 30]
Stacked LSTM	[79 13 14 36]

16.6 CONCLUSION

In this paper, we have successfully analyzed the relative performance of different machine learning and deep learning models in predicting the personality of individuals based on their CVs. The results indicate a clear edge in favor of deep learning models. The processes and models used can prove beneficial to employers, allowing them to target their hiring process towards individuals that better fit the personalities they require.

However, the attained accuracy is still below par for results expected from deep learning models. This is mainly due to the unavailability of a large amount of data, something that is considered a requisite for training deep learning models well. As such, future work can focus on combining data from different sources such as social media, recordings showing the behavior of individuals, and CVs. More advanced deep learning models such as recurrent neural networks (RNNs) and convolutional neural networks (CNNs) can potentially provide a higher degree of accuracy, given a large amount of data is used to train them.

KEYWORDS

- **Adam optimizer**
- **convolutional neural networks**
- **deep learning models**
- **machine learning models**
- **recurrent neural networks**
- **social media**

REFERENCES

1. Oxford Learner's Dictionary. (n.d.). Retrieved from https://www.oxfordlearnersdictionaries.com/definition/english/personality (accessed on 27 May 2024).
2. Britannica Encyclopaedia. (n.d.). Retrieved from https://www.britannica.com/topic/personality (accessed on 27 May 2024).
3. Komulainen, E., Quilty, L. C., Tiihonen, J., Hakkanen-Nyholm, H., Keatley, D., & Lagerspetz, K. M. J. (2014). The effect of personality on daily life emotional processes. *PloS one, 9*(10), e110907.
4. El Othman, R., Haddad, C., Hallit, S., Obeid, S., & Kazour, F. (2020). Personality traits, emotional intelligence and decision-making styles in Lebanese universities medical students. *BMC psychology, 8*(1), 1–14.
5. Simmank, D. (2013). *Personality and Job Performance – Models and impact of individual attributes*. Munich: GRIN Verlag. Retrieved from https://www.grin.com/document/211759 (accessed on 27 May 2024).
6. Shen, J., Brdiczka, O., & Liu, J. (2013). Understanding email writers: Personality prediction from email messages. In *International Conference on User Modeling, Adaptation, and Personalization*. Springer, Berlin, Heidelberg.

7. Tandera, T., et al. (2017). Personality prediction system from Facebook users. *Procedia Computer Science, 116*, 604–611.
8. Tadesse, M. M., Lin, H., Xu, B., & Yang, L. (2018). Personality predictions based on user behavior on the Facebook social media platform. *IEEE Access, 6*, 61959–61969.
9. Gjurković, M., & Šnajder, J. (2018). Reddit: A gold mine for personality prediction. In *Proceedings of the Second Workshop on Computational Modeling of People's Opinions, Personality, and Emotions in Social Media* (pp. 87–97).
10. Hinds, J., & Joinson, A. (2019). Human and computer personality prediction from digital footprints. *Current Directions in Psychological Science, 28*(2), 204–211.
11. Mehta, Y., Majumder, N., Gelbukn, A., & Cambria, E. (2020). Recent trends in deep learning-based personality detection. *Artificial Intelligence Review, 53*(4), 2313–2339.
12. Wang, Z., Wu, C., Zheng, K., Niu, X., & Wang, X. (2019). SMOTETomek-based resampling for personality recognition. *IEEE Access, 7*, 129678–129689.
13. Stachl, C., Au, Q., Schoedel, R., & Buhner, M. (2020). Predicting personality from patterns of behavior collected with smartphones. *Proceedings of the National Academy of Sciences, 117*(30), 17680–17687.
14. Christian, H., Suhartono, D., Chowanda, A., & Zamli, K. Z. (2021). Text based personality prediction from multiple social media data sources using pre-trained language model and model averaging. *Journal of Big Data, 8*(1), 1–20.
15. Kulkarni, A., Shankarwar, T., & Thorat, S. (2021). Personality Prediction Via CV Analysis using Machine Learning. *International Journal of Engineering Research & Technology (IJERT), 10*(9), 2278–0181.
16. McCurrie, M., Beletti, F., Parzianello, L., Westendorp, A., Anthony, S., & Scheirer, W. J. (2017, May). Predicting first impressions with deep learning. In *2017 12th IEEE International Conference on Automatic Face & Gesture Recognition (FG 2017)* (pp. 518–525). IEEE.
17. Mehta, Y., Majumder, N., Gelbukh, A., & Cambria, E. (2020). Recent trends in deep learning based personality detection. *Artificial Intelligence Review*, *53*(4), 2313–2339.

Index

N

O

S